W9-CIH-862

MAKING THE MANAGERIAL PRESIDENCY

Peri E. Arnold

MAKING THE
MANAGERIAL PRESIDENCY

Comprehensive
Reorganization Planning
1905-1980

PRINCETON UNIVERSITY PRESS

Copyright © 1986 by Princeton University Press
Published by Princeton University Press,
41 William Street, Princeton, New Jersey 08540
In the United Kingdom:
Princeton University Press, Guildford, Surrey

Library of Congress Cataloging in Publication Data
will be found on the last printed page of this book
ISBN 0-691-07704-5

Publication of this book has been aided by the
Whitney Darrow Publication Fund of Princeton University Press

This book has been composed in Linotron Sabon

Clothbound editions of Princeton University Press books are printed
on acid-free paper, and binding materials are chosen for strength
and durability. Paperbacks, although satisfactory for personal
collections, are not usually suitable for library rebinding

Printed in the United States of America by
Princeton University Press
Princeton, New Jersey

For Joseph Arnold and
in memory of Eve Arnold

TABLE OF CONTENTS

LIST OF TABLES

PREFACE

The past century has seen the growth of a vast administrative apparatus within an 18th-century, pre-bureaucratic American regime. American government became bureaucratic while still conforming to the arrangements of a pre-bureaucratic regime. The accommodation between the administrative state and the traditional regime is one of the grand themes that must be pursued as we search for an understanding of American political development. My purpose in this book is to conduct an inquiry which goes to the heart of that accommodation. In the pages that follow I shall examine the nearly century-long project of large-scale, official, administrative reorganization as it portrayed, justified, and attempted to implement a new, managerial role for the American presidency. Generically, this book stands amidst work which explores the nexus between politics and administration. But, contrary to the characteristic focus of that genre of work on the way political life shapes administration, my focus is on influence flowing in the other direction, from administration to politics. I seek to understand how new administrative realities shaped the way the presidential role was reformulated and exercised in this century.

The plan for this book took shape from an unexpected discovery I made while studying the first Hoover commission.[1] In researching the commission's success as an efficiency-centered approach to administrative reform, I discovered a feature of the Hoover commission which raised more fundamental concerns. I learned that the Hoover commission's internal considerations had more to do with the mission of justifying an expansive conception of the presidency than with administrative reform in itself.

Scholars who have written about executive reorganization have noted its particular ties to the presidency. For example, Harold Seidman writes that "the lasting contributions of the first Hoover commission, the President's Committee on Administrative Management, and the earlier Taft Commission on Economy and Efficiency are to

---

[1] This research was reported in P. E. Arnold, "The First Hoover Commission and the Managerial Presidency," *Journal of Politics* 38 (February 1976), 46-70. Chapter Five below offers an expanded version of the analysis contained in that article.

be found in their recommendations to strengthen the office of the presidency. . . ."[2] But beyond the observation that comprehensive reorganization planning has been instrumental in the development of the institutionalized presidency, scholarship has shed little light on the relationship between reorganization planning and the evolution of the presidency. Yet comprehensive reorganization planning is ubiquitous within the 20th-century presidency. Since Theodore Roosevelt, American presidents have assumed responsibility for administrative efficiency in the executive branch. In the 20th century the presidency became managerial; indicative of this, eleven of the century's fifteen presidents have been involved in peace-time comprehensive reorganization.[3] In sharp contrast, the managerial dimension of the presidency has little foundation or precedent in either 19th-century practice (after the first third of the century) or in the Constitution.

Why did presidency-enhancing recommendations evolve within reorganization planning? What role did presidents play in the creation of comprehensive reorganization planning, and toward what end did they act? What relationship, if any, exists between the reform agenda that developed within successive episodes of reorganization planning and the evolution of the presidency in this century? Ultimately, why did reorganization planning become ubiquitous in the modern presidency? These questions, which go to the heart of the nature, role, and importance of comprehensive reorganization planning, cannot be addressed without close examination of all the evidence left behind by reorganization planning—recommendations and reports, archival records, and the memories of participants. This book dissects every instance of comprehensive reorganization planning in the federal government in this century, using archival records, interviews, and the public record.[4] In the two cases where archival records are still in-

---

[2] Harold Seidman, *Politics, Position, and Power* (3rd ed., New York: Oxford University Press, 1980), p. 38.

[3] The following represents leading examples of the literature on comprehensive executive reorganization: Herbert Emmerich, *Federal Organization and Administrative Management* (University, Alabama: University of Alabama Press, 1971); Barry D. Karl, *Executive Reorganization and Reform in the New Deal* (Cambridge, Mass.: Harvard University Press, 1963); Harvey C. Mansfield, Sr., "Federal Executive Reorganization: Thirty Years' Experience," *Public Administration Review* 29 (July/August 1969), 332-345, and by the same author, "Reorganizing the Executive Branch: The Limits of Institutionalization," *Law and Contemporary Problems* 35 (Summer 1970), 461-495; Richard Polenberg, *Reorganizing Roosevelt's Government* (Cambridge, Mass.: Harvard University Press, 1966); and Harold Seidman, *Politics, Position, and Power*.

[4] For reasons that are made clear in Chapter Two, the first reorganization planning episode of the century, the Keep Commission, is given only brief treatment. In that

accessible to scholars, those within the Nixon and Carter administrations, I have had to make interviews and the public record suffice.

In what follows I address two different, but I hope overlapping, kinds of readers. One kind of reader will come to this with an interest in American political development; I aim to show that reader a relationship between past efforts at administrative reform and the evolution of the presidency in this century. Another kind of reader will come to this book for narrower purposes—to learn of the efficacy of past experiences with comprehensive reorganization planning. I aim to show this reader that reorganization planning must be assessed within a context larger than its own past assumptions and its own built-in views of the executive branch. By analyzing the experience of reorganization planning within the larger context of its consequences for the presidency and the American regime, I hope to offer a more complete and hence more useful understanding of reorganization planning's accomplishments and limits than has been heretofore available.

My decision that reorganization planning was worth studying had its seed in conversations with the late Herbert Storing. In a way, this book constitutes a full development and exposition of my side of our argument. I regret that the discussion cannot continue. Herbert Storing's death was a tragedy for our discipline as well as for his family, friends, and students.

Without the Ford Foundation's generous support this book could not have been researched. Earlier, the American Council of Learned Societies supported a pilot project from which the project's plan developed. This book's completion was substantially aided by Notre Dame's College of Arts and Letters; I am indebted to my former acting dean, Robert Burns. My college also provides its members with remarkable secretarial and word-processing facilities, and I have been reliant on the skills of Cheryl Reed for more drafts than I care to remember.

All of us who conduct research in archives would be lost without competent guides to those mazes of records. I have been helped by the archivists of the Hoover Presidential Library, West Branch, Iowa; the Franklin D. Roosevelt Library, Hyde Park, New York; the Harry S Truman Library, Independence, Missouri; the Dwight Eisenhower

chapter I stress its importance as an initiative while suggesting that it represented a style or approach more characteristic of 19th-century congressional reform efforts than it did the subsequent reform effort of the Taft administration. On the Keep Commission, see Oscar Kraines, "The President Versus Congress: The Keep Commission, 1905-1909," *Western Political Quarterly* 23 (March 1970), 5-54.

Library, Abilene, Kansas; and the Lyndon B. Johnson Library, Austin, Texas. I also received aid from the staffs of the Ohio Historical Society, Columbus, Ohio; the Michigan Historical Collections, Ann Arbor, Michigan; and the National Archives, Washaington, D.C. Some of my interview subjects requested anonymity, and I think it best honors their request to cite none of them here. Those who spoke to me on the record are cited in footnotes. However, as a group, I want to thank those who shared their experiences and insights with me; they were generous with their time and information and, more than any other source I used, they helped me to learn the language and customs of administrative reform.

Three graduate students in the Department of Government at Notre Dame served as research assistants for this project: Richard Kinney, Susan Roberts McCarthy, and Penny Weiss. I am grateful to fellow researchers who have commented upon earlier forms of some of the analyses that appear below and to those who have shared with me their insights and results of their own research. I am also grateful to several friends at Notre Dame in disciplines other than politics who have enriched my intellectual life. For all these gifts, I wish to thank James Bellis, Michael Brown, John Dempsey, Steven Erie, James Garnett, Stanley Hauerwas, Hugh Heclo, John J. Kennedy, Oscar Kraines, Ronald Moe, William Pemberton, Irwin Press, Harold Seidman, Jeffrey Tulis, and Dwight Waldo.

Princeton University Press commissioned Larry Berman, Fred Greenstein, and Harvey Mansfield, Sr. to read this book in manuscript form. Their criticism helped me to strengthen it. I especially want to express my indebtedness to Harvey Mansfield for his acute and extremely detailed comments. I am also indebted to Sandy Thatcher of Princeton University Press for his early interest in this project, for his editorial judgment, and for his support. Miriam Brokaw's skills smoothed the way from manuscript to this book.

Authorship involves more than libraries, universities, and colleagues; books are written within families. My own family grew as this book took form. My wife, Beverly Kessler Arnold, had Emma, our first child, as I began this project, and Rachel, our second child, was born thirty months later. At times during this book's making I wished that I might now be able to write that conventional salutation to my family for their silence in the presence of authorship. I had no such luck, and consequently I have more for which to be grateful. My family has taught me that there are matters of such importance that they cannot be set aside until later.

MAKING THE MANAGERIAL PRESIDENCY

Chapter One

ADMINISTRATION, REORGANIZATION, AND THE AMERICAN REGIME

Experience tends universally to show that the
purely bureaucratic type of administrative
organization—that is, the monocratic variety of
bureaucracy—is . . . capable of attaining the
highest degree of efficiency and is in this sense
formally the most rational known means of
carrying out imperative control over human
beings.[1]

Max Weber

Should a president reorganize the executive branch? Custom would
seem to dictate yes; eleven of the fourteen presidents elected in this
century have either initiated comprehensive reorganization planning
or supported implementation of the recommendations of a preceding
planning endeavor. Efficiency was the manifest purpose of the eleven
official, national episodes of comprehensive reorganization planning
in this century.[2] Reorganization has become a commonplace tool of
the presidency, and one might infer that reorganization has been successful at its manifest purpose of increasing government's efficiency.

But behind reorganization planning's facade of increasing administrative efficiency is a more complex story in which reorganization's
effects are more profound but less predictable than they first appear.
Within the development of reorganization planning as a presidential
tool during this century is embedded a change in the definition of
efficiency that guided reorganization planning, a change in the conception of the proper locus of administrative authority in the American
regime, and a changed conception of the role of the presidency in
administration. Thus reorganization's story is a crucial chapter in the

[1] Max Weber, *The Theory of Social and Economic Organization*, translated by
H. M. Henderson and T. Parsons (New York: Free Press, 1947), p. 337.

[2] Overviews of the history of comprehensive reorganization planning can be had in
Herbert Emmerich, *Federal Organization and Administrative Management* (University,
Alabama: University of Alabama Press, 1971); and Harvey Mansfield, Sr., "Reorgan-
izing the Executive Branch: The Limits of Institutionalization," *Law and Contemporary
Problems* 35 (Summer 1970), 461-495.

story of the evolution of the modern presidency. Before one can commend reorganization to a president, one must comprehend it in this larger context.

This book examines reorganization planning's uses and its relationship to the presidency in the 20th century. It aims to understand reorganization's effects by understanding its past. The study focuses first on the emergence of reorganization planning as a presidential concern early in the 20th century, reversing 19th-century congressional dominance of large-scale administrative reform. Next it turns to the successive phases of presidential uses of reorganization planning, first to develop mechanisms for asserting presidential direction over administration and, second, to develop tactics for attempting to make those mechanisms fulfill their ends, all under the rationale of increasing efficiency.

Underlying the development of 20th-century reorganization planning is a conception of a managerial presidency. Portraying and justifying a new managerial role for the presidency, comprehensive reorganization planning (and the administrative theory which sustained it) specified the organizational conditions for this new executive role. Dissecting successive episodes of reorganization planning, the book examines the evolution of the concept of the managerial presidency through to its routine acceptance in the 1950's and 1960's. But as the presidencies of these years suggest, and as the 1970's make clearer, the managerial presidency is a doctrine which imposes increasingly large burdens on the president. Its success in broadening the expanse of presidential authority caused presidents to act upon assumptions and responsibilities that were finally unfulfillable.

If reorganization planning's conception of an efficient, executive-centered governmental system is unsustainable, reorganization planning's ubiquity is far more of a puzzle than were it possible to explain its recurrence through its ability to increase efficiency in government. So, besides attempting to understand reorganization planning's development and uses in this century, this book must in the end also address its persistence. The last chapter will return to this and associated questions in light of the universe of 20th-century efforts at comprehensive reorganization planning.

But before we turn to the beginnings of comprehensive executive reorganization, two preliminary issues demand attention. First, it is necessary to consider the uncertain role of administration in the American Constitution, creating an ambiguity about the place of administration in the regime. Second, it is necessary to understand the attack on American government launched by the earliest American theorists of administration. This attack lays the groundwork for virtually all 20th-century administrative reform.

ADMINISTRATION IN THE CONSTITUTION

The 20th century's challenge to American public administration was twofold. First, the disorganized elements of the growing administrative state had to be transformed into a bureaucratized administrative apparatus. Second, the traditional design of American national government was at odds with the requirements of large-scale, "monocratic," bureaucratization and had to be overcome to confront the first challenge. On the one hand, bureaucracy necessitates centralized authority.[3] But the American regime was an antique system of dispersed authority. As Stephen Skowronek observes: "The challenge of constructing a new governmental order informed every stage of the process of administrative modernization."[4] More than any other change in the American government, what administrative modernization required was an executive at the top. The bureaucratic state required coherence, centralized authority, speed, and expertise; these were executive and not legislative qualities. But how could the regime be reoriented around the president?

The Constitution gives no systematic treatment to public administration, but scattered through it are provisions that bear upon administration. The first sentence of Article II states: "The Executive power shall be vested in a President of the United States of America." But is the vesting clause a grant of power? Traditionally this sentence is taken as indicating the subject-matter of Article II. Edward Corwin doubted that it could be interpreted as anything else.[5] The extra-constitutional dimension of the role of modern administration in America is hinted at in the evolution of interpretation of the vesting clause. Corwin's posthumous collaborators who revise his two major works on constitutional interpretation conclude that the weight of modern opinion is now on the side of the vesting clause as a grant of power.[6] In the

[3] Max Weber, *The Theory of Social and Economic Organization*, p. 328. See H. H. Gerth and C. Wright Mills (eds.), *From Max Weber* (New York: Oxford University Press, 1946), Chap. 8.

[4] Stephen Skowronek, *Building a New American State: The Expansion of National Administrative Capacities, 1877-1920* (Cambridge, England: Cambridge University Press, 1982), p. 210.

[5] Edward S. Corwin, *The President: Office and Powers* (4th rev. ed., New York: New York University Press, 1957), p. 12.

[6] See Edward S. Corwin, *The Constitution and What It Means Today*, revised by Harold W. Chase and Craig Ducat (Princeton: Princeton University Press, 1974), p.

face of an already expanded presidency, the vesting clause is taken to justify a *fait accompli*.

Does the Constitution make the president chief administrator when in Article II, sec. 3 it states that: ". . . he shall take care that the laws be faithfully executed . . ."? Is execution a synonym for administration? Corwin interpreted this clause to mean that: ". . . the President has the right to take any necessary measures which are not forbidden by statute to protect against impending danger those great interests which are entrusted by the Constitution to the National Government."[7] The powers of the "take care" clause are powers to see that the laws are enforced and obeyed and not powers over the organizational byways through which policy is administered. C. Herman Pritchett says of this clause that while broad it: ". . . also served the limiting function of emphasizing the American notion of the executive as subordinate to the law, in contrast with the wide prerogative powers of the English executive."[8]

"Executive" as a term within American constitutional parlance, broadly understood, cannot be taken to signal the presence of settled administrative authority in the presidency. We use that term in several ways—giving it different meanings within each usage and rendering it ambiguous. "Executive" can refer to an activity whereby a given end is effected. The word can also denote a place (the executive branch) where such activity is conducted. Furthermore, "executive" can also suggest a directing authority over the means of execution (its common usage in the private sector).

Several other provisions of Article II carry administrative weight. The president is granted the authority to appoint high officials, with the advice and consent of the Senate. But the Constitution is parsimonious with the appointment power. In addition to a required Senate concurrence on the appointment of high officials, it specifies that Congress: "May . . . vest the appointment of . . . inferior officers . . . in the President alone . . . or in the heads of departments." It is Congress which shall determine whether to centralize or disperse the lines of authority over minor appointments.

The only authority the Constitution gives to the president explicitly regarding his appointees is to allow him to call upon the heads of departments for their opinions "in writing . . . upon any subject re-

---

111; and Jack Peltason, *Corwin and Peltason's Understanding the Constitution* (7th ed., Hillsdale, Ill.: Dryden, 1976), p. 83.

[7] Edward S. Corwin, *The Constitution*, p. 149.

[8] C. Herman Pritchett, *The American Constitution* (New York: McGraw-Hill, 1959), pp. 309-310.

lating to the duties of their respective offices. . . ." This is the only point in the document in which reference is made to administrative organization; it also implies a limited authority of the president over heads of these departments. In 1789 Congress gave the president what the Constitution itself did not specify, the removal power over department heads he appoints.[9]

The president's powers over administration are weakened even further when one notices the Congress' powers. The formal mandate of agencies, their organization, their funding and subsequent discretion in spending, the specification of the number of positions they might fill, the qualifications attached to those positions, and the precise definition of the actual jurisdiction of that agency all rest upon congressional will. If anything, it is Congress and not the presidency that is the institution intended by the Constitution to exert predominant responsibility over administration. But, in fact, the story is more complex than that either-or choice.

The treatment of administration in the Constitution reflects a consideration of government in a pre-bureaucratic context. Quite the contrary to thinking that administration is not important, the Founders sought a government capable of effective administration.[10] As Hamilton put it in No. 70 of the *Federalist*: "A feeble Executive implies a feeble execution of the government. A feeble execution is but another phrase for a bad execution; and a government ill-executed, whatever it may be in theory, must be, in practice, a bad government."[11] But administration was simple in the Founding era. The issue of the role of administration in the Constitution takes on a different flavor when it is realized that in 1808 the *total* number of executive branch employees in Washington was 126![12] With such scale, control of higher

[9] On this congressional debate and the succeeding removal controversy, see Louis Fisher, *The Constitution Between Friends* (New York: St. Martins, 1978), pp. 50-81. Also see Corwin, *The President: Office and Powers*, pp. 85-93; Leonard White, *The Federalists* (New York: Macmillan, 1948), pp. 20-25. For the most detailed account of the debate in the first Congress on presidential removal power, see Charles Thach, *The Creation of the Presidency* (Baltimore: Johns Hopkins University Press, 1922), Chap. 6. A warning on the very good treatment by Thach: he is too ready to interpret the constitutional convention's intentions through the decision of the first Congress on removal power. Leonard White, perhaps guided by Thach, might be also criticized for this too facile explanatory device.

[10] See Thach, *The Creation of the Presidency*, pp. 13-24.

[11] Alexander Hamilton, John Jay, James Madison, *The Federalist* (New York: Modern Library, 1937), p. 455.

[12] Pre-Census Bureau figures for federal employment are gathered in Noble E. Cunningham, Jr., *The Process of Government Under Jefferson* (Princeton: Princeton University Press, 1978), pp. 325-326.

administration did not mean the manipulation of mechanisms; it meant face-to-face communication between superior and subordinate.

A second factor that clarifies the Constitution's lack of sustained treatment of administration is that the Founders, once in power, behaved with certainty about administration.[13] The presidents of the Founding generation, Washington, Adams, Jefferson, and Madison along with some of their immediate successors, behaved toward administration as if they were responsible for it.[14] They brought energy to administration that was missing in the Constitution itself. Andrew Jackson was the last of that era of presidents who assumed for themselves a power over administration that was not specified by the Constitution. Jackson fought a Senate that rejected his assumption that the Secretary of the Treasury was the president's subordinate, to be chosen and removed at his wishes.[15] A more momentous example of Jackson's interest in administration was his reform activity in several key agencies of government, in particular the Post Office and the Land Office. Under Jackson, what had been loose, personalized working situations were tightened and routinized.[16]

Jackson ended an era. The rest of the 19th century saw a presidential retreat from administration, with the Congress victorious over the executive branch. The context within which the presidents of the first era of the republic asserted primacy over administration changed radically. Three intertwined changes distinguished the later 19th century from that earlier period: they are the increased diversity of the economic and political interests within society, the expansion of political patronage as an instrument of party, and the increasing absolute size of the federal administrative system.

Growth and increasing complexity within American society multi-

[13] My point parallels one Herbert Storing has made about the difference between the narrow conception of statesmanship the Founders built into the Constitution and the broad, more traditional conception of statesmanship that guided them in the politics of the early republic. Herbert Storing, "American Statesmanship: Old and New," in Robert A. Goldwin (ed.), *Bureaucrats, Policy Analysts, Statesman: Who Leads?* (Washington: American Enterprise Institute, 1980), pp. 98-99.

[14] On the administrative roles of the presidents prior to Jackson, see Leonard White, *The Federalists* and *The Jeffersonians* (New York: Macmillan, 1951). There is a superb study of Jefferson's administrative role in Noble E. Cunningham, *The Process of Government Under Jefferson.*

[15] This conception of officials as independent from the president in fulfilling their statutory duty was supported by the Supreme Court in Kendall v. Stokes, 12 Pet. 524 (1838). On Jackson era administration see Leonard White, *The Jacksonians* (New York: Macmillan, 1954).

[16] Matthew Crenson, *The Federal Machine* (Baltimore: Johns Hopkins University Press, 1975), pp. 2-6, 104-157.

plied the stakes involved in government's activities. The simpler notions of geographical representation or presidential evocation of a common interest that would have seemed self-evidently true in the republic's first era withered in the face of growing complexity. Multiplying interests fragmented government and exerted pressure upon it for expanded recognition.[17]

An increasing federal work force during the 19th century gave patronage-hungry parties and their congressional minions good reason to claim first authority over administration.[18] At the same time, presidents were less able to assert personal authority over the public service because command over an expanded public service required more elaborate arrangements than face-to-face contact. Whereas the total federal work force in 1816 had been 4,837, with just 535 employees located in Washington, in 1841 the total force was 18,038 and 1,014 of them worked in the capital city. Thirty years later, in 1871, there were 51,020 federal civilian employees; now Washington was the work site for 6,222 public servants, and that number would double in the next decade.[19] President Rutherford B. Hayes described to his diary the logic through which the patronage system leveraged the Senate into the center of political power in Washington. Hayes wrote that it was the Constitution's intention that the president appoint officials and that the Senate confirm them. The reality, rather, was what Hayes called "the Senators' doctrine." He understood the senators to be saying: "We will appoint the officers and our officers shall rule the party, and our party shall rule the country."[20]

While society and government changed rapidly, the presidency remained the same. Amid a growing executive branch and a Congress becoming more capable of specialized work through committees, the president still limped along with staff support comprising a handful

[17] See William E. Nelson, *The Roots of American Bureaucracy, 1830-1900* (Cambridge, Mass: Harvard University Press, 1982), Chaps. 1 and 2; V. O. Key, *Politics, Parties, and Pressure Groups* (5th ed., New York: Knopf, 1964), pp. 128-130.

[18] For an analysis of the premises underlying the party system of the middle and late 19th century, see James Ceaser, *Presidential Selection* (Princeton: Princeton University Press, 1979), Chap. 3. On the transformation of this system during and after the critical election of 1896, see Walter Dean Burnham, *Critical Elections: The Mainsprings of American Politics* (New York: Norton, 1970), Chap. 4. For a detailed examination of the 19th-century political party style as played out in one region, see Richard Jensen, *The Winning of the Midwest* (Chicago: University of Chicago Press, 1971).

[19] U.S. Bureau of the Census, *Statistical History of the United States* (New York: Basic Books, 1976), p. 1,102.

[20] T. Harry Williams (ed.), *The Diary of Rutherford B. Hayes* (New York: McKay, 1964), p. 137.

of clerks and a secretary or two. As Leonard White said of these presidents, their minds were "directed primarily to Congress, not to the executive departments."[21]

The American regime's shifting locus of administrative authority from the presidency early in the 19th century to the Congress later in the century indicates a lacuna in the Constitution. There is no well-demarcated place for administrative authority within the American plan of government. In the 19th century the actual locus of primary authority over administration depended not on the Constitution but rather on extra-constitutional factors—character and circumstance. Presidents of the first four decades of the republic impressed onto the office their own strong understandings of executive authority. Later presidents had weaker conceptions of the executive role and found that the administrative system had grown beyond the ability of a president to dominate it through personalist methods.

The separation of powers is not a scheme that one would take as an optimal model for creating an efficient, modern state. As Mr. Justice Brandeis wrote: "The separation of powers was adopted . . . not to promote efficiency but to preclude the exercise of arbitrary power."[22] The Founders' understanding of separation of powers might support efficiency in the administration of small-scale government. But the Constitution had not been written to cope with large-scale administration. In the face of the growth of the administrative state, Brandeis was correct; the Founders' choice for a method of ensuring safety in government had made efficient administration harder to achieve.[23]

---

[21] Leonard White, *The Republican Era* (New York: Macmillan, 1958), p. 392.

[22] Myers *v.* U.S. 272 U.S. 52 (1926).

[23] Coherent organization is proposed as a precondition to efficiency throughout the public administration literature. Herbert Simon undermined an earlier view of the relationship of efficiency and structure but replaced this with another conception, viewing decisions as structured or preformed by organization. See Herbert Simon, *Administrative Behavior* (2nd Ed., New York: Free Press, 1957), Chap. 11. Also note that the generalized posited relationship between administrative structure and efficiency fits very different administrative doctrines. For example, whether one looks at an administrative system as a series of interrelated units assigned functions or whether one looks at that same system as a managerial problem in linear, process terms, coordinating and controlling the provision of resources and the end product of work, the premise remains that administration's format is causally related to the achievement of efficiency. See Peter Self, *Administrative Theories and Politics* (Toronto: University of Toronto Press, 1973), pp. 77-85. While structure and efficiency relationships are hypothesized throughout the administrative literature, it is important to also note that: ". . . no explicit theory of organization structure . . . can explain, let alone predict, the relationship between structural inputs and outcomes such as performance, productivity, and satisfaction." Gene W. Dalton, Louis B. Baines, and Abraham Zaleznik, *The Distribution of Authority in Formal Organizations* (Cambridge, Mass.: MIT Press, 1973), p. 2.

The last two-thirds of the 19th century presents an extended case in point of the consequences of the Constitution's dispersion of power. The shift of authority over administration from the president to Congress dispersed authority in Congress, particularly within the Senate, where the patronage interests of the political parties were most pointedly expressed. The effect of this development was to explode outward the lines of administrative responsibility, linking agencies to congressional committees and interested politicians instead of subordinating them to ordered, central lines of responsibility within the executive branch.[24] The disorganized, disordered administration in 19th-century Washington—what Woodrow Wilson saw as the "sinecurism, and corruption ever and again discovered in the bureaux at Washington"— violated the notion that administration should exhibit ordered, hierarchical organization.[25]

The problem of administrative disarray was addressed by a group of reformer-intellectuals who were beginning the enterprise of building an American discipline of public administration. Amid the progressive critique of American government in the late 19th century, these reformers reasoned toward an administrative solution to a constitutional problem. In general, the progressive reformers did not attack the separation of powers but only its consequences.[26] Ingeniously, the leading administrative theorists saw that the great problem of congressional domination of the system of the separation of powers might be addressed through a series of relatively small-scale reforms, producing the reestablishment of presidential authority over administration.

THE ADMINISTRATIVE REFORM OF THE SEPARATION OF POWERS

As American national administration was sinking to its nadir, other sectors demonstrated that models of good administration were present in America. The first example lay in the rise of the integrated business firm after the mid-19th century. The second example emerged in the

[24] The shattering of unified authority in the period affected Congress itself, with the House Appropriations Committee's power reduced and distributed to other committees after 1879. Leonard White, *The Republican Era*, pp. 64-66. See *Origins and Development of Congress* (Washington: Congressional Quarterly, Inc., 1976), p. 103; George B. Galloway, *History of the House of Representatives* (New York: Crowell, 1969), pp. 174-178.

[25] Woodrow Wilson, "The Study of Administration," *Political Science Quarterly* 66 (December 1941, reprint of original of 1887), 485-486. Wilson had described the disaggregated character of congressional government—its government by committees— in his *Congressional Government* (Boston: Houghton Mifflin, 1885).

[26] M.J.C. Vile, *Constitutionalism and the Separation of Powers* (Oxford: Clarendon Press, 1967), pp. 266-267.

early 1870's with the reform of city government. For the critic of American national administration in the late 19th and early 20th century, the business firm and the reformed city provided models of good administration. An interesting feature shared by both models is that within neither did separation of powers hold an inviolate status. It was not simply a loose figure of speech that led the early administrative reformers to bemoan the degree to which the presidency fell short of constituting a general managership for national administration.[27] For them and their contemporaries that metaphor was redolent with a recent example of successful, large-scale administration.

Stepping Stones to Reform

The rise of the large-scale firm teaches lessons about the relationship of size to coordination and subordination. The American economy of the pre-Civil War era was still one of modest, mono-functional firms. But the tendency in key areas of the economy was toward rapid growth in scale. This was evident first in the railroads as they developed organizations to manage expanding regional and then near-continent sized operations. Later, industrial firms incorporated more and more of the stages of production and distribution. Consequently the industrial revolution in America became a managerial revolution as the organizations created by industrialism required innovations in management to cope with increased scale and organizational complexity.[28]

If the rise of the large firm exemplified new modes of large-scale management, the reform of city government exemplified that the balance between the branches of government within the separation-of-power system could be restruck. The target of municipal reform was the legislative branch of city government and its ties with political machines and private interests. The aim of the municipal reformers was to make the executive responsible for city government, with the city council serving a distant role of discussion and oversight. The reformers' success was marked by adoption of the strong mayor form of government and the spread of the idea of a politically neutral city

[27] In a text on American politics, Frederick Cleveland, a leading student of administration, wrote: "The modern democratic institution finds its prototype in the modern institution developed for efficiency in private undertakings." Frederick Cleveland, *Organized Democracy* (New York: Longmans, Green, & Co., 1913), p. 452.

[28] Alfred D. Chandler, Jr., *The Visible Hand: The Managerial Revolution in America* (Cambridge, Mass: The Belknap Press, 1977), esp. Chaps. 9, 10, 11. Also see Herman Daems, "The Rise of the Modern Industrial Enterprise," in Chandler and Daems (eds.) *Managerial Hierarchies* (Cambridge: Harvard University Press), pp. 203-223.

manager. Thus the municipal reform movement suggested the utility for good administration of both a strengthened executive and an apolitical conception of administration.[29]

Restriking the Balance Within the Separation of Powers

One strain of government's reformers went beyond attributing government's foibles to bad men, political parties, and too little participation by the right people. They thought that an essential element of government's failings was the absence of a science of administration to direct citizen, scholar, and practitioner toward principles of correct practices. Writing in 1887, Woodrow Wilson noted the growing demand for government's services at the same time that government was incapable of effective action:

> This is why there should be a science of administration which shall seek to straighten the paths of government, to make its business less unbusiness-like, to stengthen and purify its organization, and to crown its duties with dutifulness. This is why there is such a science.[30]

Wilson had argued for a discipline of public administration that would not only study government but also reform it. Following Wilson, Frank Goodnow elaborated Wilson's principle upon which a study of administration would rest. Goodnow also identified two aspects to government, the expression of its will and the execution of that will— politics and administration.[31] A separation of politics and administration became a foundation principle of American public administration, even if the nature of that separation was not fully clear.[32]

A second foundation element that Wilson and Goodnow contributed to the study of public administration was a negative perspective on the practice of separation of powers in the United States. Like their peers among late-19th-century political reformers, Wilson and Goodnow saw congressional dominance of government's activities as proof

[29] Martin Schiesl, *The Politics of Efficiency* (Berkeley: University of California Press, 1977), Chaps. 3, 4, and 6.

[30] Woodrow Wilson, "The Study of Administration," p. 485.

[31] Frank Goodnow, *Politics and Administration* (New York: Macmillan, 1900), p. 22.

[32] On the ambiguities of the separation-of-powers concept of orthodox public administration see Dwight Waldo, *The Administrative State* (New York: Ronald Press, 1948), pp. 106-111; and Gerald Caiden, "The Search for an Apolitical Science of American Public Administration, 1886-1946" (University of Southern California, School of Public Administration Working Papers, 1978).

of a constitutional malfunction. As it developed as a body of thought in the early 20th century, public administration took the problem of the separation of powers as a focal point. Virtually every major writer in the field addressed it.[33] The problem of the separation of powers might be constitutional in origin, but reform intellectuals within public administration in the 20th century saw that there could be a narrow and apolitical administrative solution to a fundamental constitutional problem. Justification of the managerial unity required for efficiency might overcome defense of the dispersion of authority among the parts of the national government. Arguing that the Constitution's flaw was its creation of a politics of dispersed authority, key administrative reformers saw a possibility of what might be called managerial de-politicization of administratively relevant issues. Theorist reformers as different as Frederick Cleveland and William F. Willoughby exemplify this logic.

Frederick Cleveland was a leading figure of the generation of students of public administration after Frank Goodnow. Trained in public finance, he held faculty positions at the University of Pennsylvania and New York University and was a prominent activist in municipal reform. In 1910 Cleveland joined President Taft to plan administrative reforms for government. His major scholarly work in public administration began after his work for Taft.

To Cleveland, the flaw of the American regime was that the Constitution did not clearly incorporate the logical distinctions necessary for any democratic system. He proposed that: "In a democracy the *determining* and the *doing* functions are divided—the first being used to control the second."[34] What Cleveland argued was that policy choosing and policy implementing were inherently different and necessarily separate but that the latter must be linked to the former *after the fact*. That is, the representative body must have the means for clearly identifying the locus of responsibility for implementation and overseeing the accuracy with which administration fulfills the legislature's will.[35] Cleveland's analysis of this problem is novel; admitting that the American regime's failure to place administrative responsibility in the president lies in the Constitution, he goes on to ignore

[33] For an overview on the place of separation of powers on the reform agenda in American politics, see M.J.C. Vile, *Constitutionalism*, Chap. 10.

[34] Frederick Cleveland and Arthur E. Buck, *The Budget and Responsible Government* (New York: Macmillan, 1920), p. 388 (emphasis in original). Also see Cleveland, *Organized Democracy*, p. 454.

[35] See Cleveland and Buck, *The Budget*, pp. 454-456.

the Constitution *per se*, suggesting a kind of a higher law resolution of the issue.

Cleveland begins by specifying prerequisites for a democratic regime. Where the Constitution does not support these, it must be interpreted so as to make it consistent with democracy's needs. In Cleveland's view, modern society requires executive government, and the fate of democracy rests on its ability to produce effective presidential government. He asked whether legislators would continue to work their will over administration through its labyrinth committees and without responsibility or, "whether . . . rules will be so changed that the popularly elected executive will be made responsible and accountable to the electorate. . . ."[36]

William F. Willoughby, like Frederick Cleveland, moved between action and the academy. After receiving a Ph.D. in politics from Johns Hopkins, Willoughby entered public service, working for the Department of Labor, the colonial government at Puerto Rico, and then the Census Bureau in Washington. With Frederick Cleveland he then served President Taft's reform program. In 1912 he joined Princeton's faculty, entering the distinguished company who have held the McCormick Professorship of Jurisprudence. Before the First World War Willoughby left Princeton to direct the recently established Institute for Government Research in Washington, a predecessor of the Brookings Institution. While at Princeton and at the Institute, Willoughby was prolific, producing work that helped define the scope and contents of a discipline of public administration.

W. F. Willoughby began his thinking about administration in the American regime at a polar opposite point from where Frederick Cleveland had begun. Cleveland had argued that one had to read the Constitution as amenable to a coherent administrative system responsible to the president. Willoughby saw the Constitution as decisively placing administrative authority in Congress. In his 1927 *Principles of Public Administration*, he wrote:

> The administrative function, that is, the function of direction, supervision, and control of the administrative activities of the government, resides in the legislative branch. . . . Congress is the source of all administrative authority.[37]

But instead of reaching an opposite conclusion to Cleveland's, Willoughby concluded that the functional demands of modern adminis-

[36] *Ibid.*, p. 395.

[37] William F. Willoughby, *Principles of Public Administration* (Washington: Brookings Institution, 1927), p. 11.

tration required coherent administrative organization placed in the president. It is not uncommon for modern writers to attribute the Brookings Institution's attack on the Brownlow Report in 1937 to the lingering influence there of Willoughby's view of congressional administrative authority.[38] True as this may be, it is also ironic in that the controversy undermined ends that Willoughby cherished.

Willoughby's evaluation of the consequences of congressional administrative authority can be seen in his comparison of the British and American regimes in *The Government of Modern States*.[39] There he observed the paradox of the British system's being one of unitary responsibility held by a single institution, parliament, while it was also a system of sharply divided powers in functional terms. Administration was wholly separated from parliamentary participation; the legislature's role was one of after-the-fact control through the practices of cabinet and ministerial responsibility. In contrast, the American system is one of apparent separated powers that are in fact blended together by checks and balances, with the result that the powers are unified in functional terms and controlled by Congress.[40] To Willoughby these differences were not simply arbitrary matters of tradition:

> The evils resulting from the Congress intervening in executive and administrative matters are constantly in evidence. . . . The damage done by the attempt of Congress to control matters of administration affects . . . almost every branch and phase of administration.[41]

Willoughby's argument about administration in the American regime was to the end of articulating an equivalent to the British system's allowance of functional independence for administration. Thus he stressed that Congress' proper role regarding the administrative agencies was through control by information rather than through command. The legislature made laws setting the goals of administrative action, and its interest should be in an after-the-fact surveillance of the agencies' accomplishments of those goals. This is what Willoughby meant by desirable control. A legislature could attempt to control administration by specifying in advance the details of its implementing activities. Or, it could survey the performance of administration after the fact. Willoughby notes: "As between these two systems there can

[38] For example, Don K. Price, "The Institutional Presidency and the Unwritten Constitution" (a paper presented to the White Burkett Miller Center of Public Affairs of the University of Virginia, March 1980), p. 18.

[39] Willoughby, *Government of the Modern State* (New York: Century Co., 1919).

[40] *Ibid.*, pp. 227-267.

[41] *Ibid.*, p. 267.

be little question that the latter is the superior. Unfortunately, the former is the method commonly employed by our legislative bodies."[42]

The result of legislative detailing of administration was for Willoughby indisputably negative. The system, he wrote, "under which the legislature seeks to control the details of administrative organization . . . directly . . . instead of indirectly through the chief executive . . . is radically wrong."[43] The test of its being wrong was that it produced bad administration. With this conclusion, Willoughby joined company with Cleveland. But where Cleveland argued for a conception of the chief executive as the primary source of administrative authority, Willoughby argued for broad congressional delegation to the chief executive as the basis for assembling a hierarchical, coherent, and presumably efficient administrative system within the executive branch. Willoughby wrote that this transformation must come about through three "distinct, though closely related, forms."[44] One, in creating legislation Congress must confer administrative power directly upon the president rather than lodging it in the operating agencies. Two, a budget system must place the authority for detailing the administrative agencies' future expenditures in the president's hands. Three, the organization of the executive branch must be reorganized to properly integrate its diverse activities and place them in logical relationship to each other and to centralized authority.[45]

As Cleveland's and Willoughby's writings illustrate, the new field of public administration's major theorists saw administrative pathology caused by the structure of the American regime. Yet these students of administration were not outwardly dedicated to reforming the Constitution. They proposed mere administrative changes, rationalized by principles of efficiency and the value of good order. Were they offering to do anything but tinker with the administrative machine, even though the barriers to competent administration lay deep within the regime? It was precisely the moderate, instrumental, and apolitical character of public administration's conception of reform that was its strength. To address the Constitution's failures head-on would have left public administration's intellectuals as mere external critics of government. But an apolitical-technical model of good administration deflected politically based conflict over presidency-strengthening reforms, and it justified a role for scholars of public administration within government as neutral experts with skills to make government work better.

[42] Willoughby, *Principles of Public Administration*, p. 34.
[43] *Ibid.*, p. 39.
[44] *Ibid.*
[45] *Ibid.*, pp. 9-51.

But there was something of the Trojan Horse about public admin-istration's ideas of efficient organization. Frederick Cleveland said of the administrative reform agenda within the national government that it was the instrument for creating presidential leadership; he made it absolutely clear that he expected great ends to follow upon mechanical reforms. He wrote:

> It was in the quest for a means of developing responsible government . . . through leadership that could interpret and at the same time was accountable to the people, that those who sought popular sup-port [for governmental reform] turned to administration reorgani-zation and budget making.[46]

Managerial depoliticization would be the instrument for revitalizing government and recreating the possibility of political leadership.

The Managerial Presidency and Executive Reorganization

Leading public administration theorists proclaimed that reconstitution of national administration required an enhanced presidency. However, a reconception of the presidency was an oblique element within ad-ministrative theory. Within Cleveland's or Willoughby's framework, for example, the main focus was on administration and not the pres-idency. Instead of being a headlong attack on the status of the pres-idency, orthodox public administration theorists began by inquiring after the requirements for making administration effective.

Who Shall Direct Bureaucracy?

In the last third of the 19th century, congressional leaders assumed that only the legislature could impose changes on administrative prac-tices. But Congress was too unfocused for the task of administrative reform; there are always more pressing issues for the members, and Congress' interests in administration are necessarily episodic, depend-ing on the agency under scrutiny, its specific task, and the constitu-encies affected by that task. Addressing the mismatch between what he called "dilettante" politicians and professional administration, Max Weber said: "Under normal conditions, the power position of a fully developed bureaucracy is always overtowering."[47]

However, bureaucracy's political power impedes its own instru-

---

[46] Cleveland and Buck, *The Budget*, p. 102.
[47] Hans Gerth and C. Wright Mills (eds.), *From Max Weber*, p. 232.

mental rationality. Rational bureaucracy must maintain some means for adjustment to changing circumstances.[48] Its "power position" cannot be allowed to make it autonomous from authority, for that autonomy would reduce its malleability—its rationality. If bureaucracy's rationality lies in its superior ability to translate externally given mandates into concrete results, then its capacity to be changed to fit a changing context is a prerequisite for its continuing rationality. Charles Perrow speaks to this characteristic of bureaucracy when he says of bureaucratic organizations that they are "tools for shaping the world. . . ."[49] But how shall the tool be shaped to the task? The managerial presidency was a solution to bureaucracy's guidance problem. If the "dilettante" politicians of Congress could not do the job, then the president would have to be transformed into a manager. Make the presidency responsible for administration, and the incumbent president will have a political incentive for rising to that task. Give that president the specialized staff support and bureaucratic tools to supervise and guide administration, and he will act managerially.

In the 19th century, congressional select committees attempted to reform the executive branch.[50] These reform efforts produced an enormous mass of data and made some contributions to the progress of personnel classification and the development of government accounting, but congressional administrative reforms concerned the details of administrative activities and failed to address overall questions of organization, budget, and direction. Furthermore, congressional reform efforts had demonstrated another failing of Congress as an administrative reformer. The legislature could not consistently concern itself with guiding administration. Administration under a congressional domain would operate with little guidance from day to day, only to be overwhelmed sporadically by detailed attention. With Congress responsible for the state of administration, there was no locus of responsibility which could be continually attentive to administration's operations.

President Theodore Roosevelt stepped into the vacuum left by Con-

[48] Gerald Caiden, *Administrative Reform* (Chicago: Aldine Publishing Co., 1969), pp. 65-68.

[49] Charles Perrow, *Complex Organizations* (2nd ed., Glenview, Illinois: Scott, Foresman, 1979), p. 13.

[50] On the late-19th-century congressional efforts at administrative reform, see Oscar Kraines, *Congress Against Big Government* (New York: Bookman's Associates, 1958) and Leonard White, *The Republican Era*, pp. 84-92. Also see U.S. Congress, Senate, Select Committee to Inquire into the Methods of the Executive Departments, *Report*, 50th Cong., 1st Sess., March 8, 1888.

gress' failure as an administrative reformer. He created a committee of public officials to investigate and make recommendations for the improvement of administration in the executive branch. As the next chapter will show, Roosevelt's administrative reorganization effort had little effect on the executive branch; its signal contribution was its own existence. Roosevelt's action assumed that the president ought to be responsible for the condition of administration and that he could plan and effect administrative reforms. The governmental context of national administration was turning upside down from its 19th-century condition.

As the context of public administration turned upside down, so did the notion of efficiency by which the administrative system would be evaluated. Efficiency took on different meanings for congressional reformers of administration and for presidency-oriented reformers. In the 19th century the congressional conception had dominated, but in the 20th century the conception of efficiency held by the latter would become the measure of good administration. For the congressional critic of administration, efficiency was synonymous with economy. Thus for an agency to be efficient was for it to reduce its spending. But, the early 20th-century administrative theorists who had the most impact on comprehensive executive reorganization planning understood efficiency as different from and more important than economy. Efficiency for them was a measure of the quality of work of the administrative system. They judged efficiency in terms of the social good attained from given resources. They also viewed efficiency as an organizational concept. Thus efficiency, in terms of a capacity to fulfill the ends of a policy through good administration, could be achieved through an organization which abides by the principles of good administration. The congressional reformers had wanted to end waste (and their successors in Congress during this century often speak in similar terms), but the presidency-oriented reformers would seek more positive ends through the concept of efficiency.

Continuity Within Change

In the 20th century the doctrine of the relationship between good administration and the presidency took three different prescriptive foci. Initially, the conception of administration that guided reorganization planning fixed on structure and fiscal control as the crucial characteristics through which administration could be reformed and brought under presidential direction. Next, reorganization planning's main focus shifted to the top of the organizational system, assuming that increased attention to top-level resources for management would provide the critical mass of administrative capacity so that the president could succeed at directing the administrative system. Finally, there was a prime focus on the intellectual tools of policy analysis as a means for extending the president's reach over organizations and their activities.[51] Superficially, each of these foci might be seen as separate in the history of comprehensive reorganization planning. But that view would misjudge the developmental character of the administrative reform agenda. Examined closely, successive foci of reorganization planning are evolutionary. So, for example, the prescription of departmental reorganization by purpose or function remained a powerful norm within all three phases of reorganization planning.

Thus, the history of comprehensive reorganization planning exhibits a consistent problem addressed through different potential managerial solutions. Whether seen through the perspectives of the need for a national budget, the need for increased presidential staff, or the need for increased policy analytic capacity, it was the managerial presidency that comprehensive reorganization planning consistently aimed at justifying, constructing, and strengthening. What Frederick Mosher says about successive reorganizations in single organizations is applicable to the history of successive reorganization planning episodes within the federal government:

> A reorganization effort and, in fact, a successful reorganization effort, can best be perceived not as a single episode with a beginning and end but as a step or a stage in the development, transition, or decline of an organization.[52]

The next chapter turns to the beginning of comprehensive reorganization planning by the executive and the first step in the making of the managerial presidency.

[51] For a similar but distinct and, I think, too exclusive set of doctrinal categories for the history of administrative reform of the executive, see Hugh Heclo's description of Micheal McGeary's work for the National Academy of Public Administration. Hugh Heclo, "Introduction, in Heclo and Lester Salamon (eds.), *The Illusion of Presidential Government* (Boulder: Westview Press, 1981), pp. 12-13.

[52] Frederick Mosher, *Governmental Reorganization* (Indianapolis: Bobbs-Merrill, 1967), p. 502.

Chapter Two

EXECUTIVE REORGANIZATION AND THE BEGINNINGS OF THE MANAGERIAL PRESIDENCY: 1905-1913

"... anything which undermines executive
authority in this country seriously threatens our
national integrity and balance."[1]
Herbert Croly

Although a managerial conception of the presidency would develop other friends and justifications, the progressive movement between 1900 and the First World War was crucial in its creation.[2] As Herbert Croly exemplified, the progressives were enamoured of executive authority and its possibilities for action.[3] They were also distrustful of the separation of powers dimension of the American regime, and it was an article of faith among them that a strong president was necessary for good government. In this belief they shared a concern of the Founders that the legislature more than the executive menaced stable, competent government.[4] As Herbert Croly wrote: "... when Congress attempts to dominate the executive, its objects are generally bad and its methods furtive and dangerous."[5]

The progressives' discernment of the presidency's importance was a symptom of change within the American regime. Big government

[1] Herbert Croly, *The Promise of American Life* (New York: Macmillan, 1909), p. 69.

[2] On the political ideas of the Progressive Era see Richard Hofstadter, *The Age of Reform* (New York: Alfred Knopf, 1950), Chaps. 4-7; Eric Goldman, *Rendezvous With Destiny* (New York: Vintage, 1956), and for an examination of progressivism as a perspective upon society that went far beyond politics and harkened back to earlier ideals, see Robert Crunden, *Ministers of Reform* (New York: Basic Books, 1982).

[3] On Croly's thought, see Eric F. Goldman, *Rendezvous With Destiny* pp. 146-161.

[4] Speaking on July 17, 1787 in the Constitutional Convention, James Madison said that he "was not apprehensive of being thought to favor any steps towards monarchy. The real object with him was to prevent its introduction. Experience has proved a tendency ... to throw all power into the Legislative vortex. ...." From "Madison's Notes of Debates" in Winton Solberg (ed.), *The Federal Convention* (Indianapolis: Bobbs-Merrill, 1958) p. 228.

[5] Herbert Croly, *The Promise of American Life*, p. 69.

was coming to America. In 1909, the federal civilian work force numbered 372,379 employees, and it had grown by a third since the turn of the century.[6] In 1887 Woodrow Wilson had written that ". . . the functions of government are every day becoming more complex and difficult."[7] Growth was not simply a matter of numbers; government's work had become more technical, with the national government stepping into the economy through the Sherman Anti-trust Act, the Interstate Commerce Commission, and the Pure Food and Drug Act, to cite but several examples.

Speaking for a large part of his intellectual generation, Herbert Croly thought that administration failed because Americans overly restrained the president. Croly argued that the principle of executive authority ought to be that the president "shall have full power to do either well or ill" and bear full responsibility for the outcome, whichever it is.[8]

THE PROLOGEMENA TO THE REORGANIZATION MOVEMENT

Theodore Roosevelt seemed the embodiment of a Crolyian ideal; his pose of robust manliness, his interest in reform, his sympathy for large-scale organization, and his taste for exuberant leadership, marked him as the natural leader for an era of progressive reform.

But Roosevelt's performance never matched his promise. As Croly observed, his reforms did "not go very far in purpose or achievement."[9] In regard to administrative reform, his possibilities were particularly promising because he was arguably the best-prepared administrator to enter the presidency up to that time. He had been a U.S. Civil Service Commissioner, the head of the New York Police Commission, Assistant Secretary of the Navy, and then Governor of the State of New York. Additionally, Roosevelt gained his administrative experience in the last two decades of the 19th century amid an American organizational revolution.[10]

Yet Roosevelt was an imperfect student of the managerial changes of his era. The lessons that he did absorb concerned micro-level admin-

---

[6] U.S. Bureau of the Census, *The Statistical History of the United States* (New York: Basic Books, 1976), p. 1,102.

[7] Woodrow Wilson, "The Study of Administration," *Political Science Quarterly* 56 (December 1941), 481-506 (reprinted from original 1887 publication). Also see William E. Nelson, *The Roots of American Bureaucracy, 1830-1900* (Cambridge, Mass.: Harvard University Press, 1982), Chaps. 4 and 5.

[8] Herbert Croly, *The Promise of American Life*, p. 338.

[9] *Ibid.*, p. 167.

[10] See Alfred D. Chandler, Jr., *The Visible Hand: The Managerial Revolution in American Business* (Cambridge, Mass.: Belknap-Harvard, 1977), Chaps. 3-5, 9, 10.

istration, techniques for controlling expenditure and organizing work, but he failed to evidence any strong conceptions of macro-level administration. The lessons Roosevelt learned as an administrator were probably pre-selected by his cast of mind. He was not a theoretical man, and he seemed most comfortable with details. As a reformer he believed in change by increments, and as an administrator he believed in administration by experts.[11]

Roosevelt's administrative reforms in the presidency had more to do with his view of his office than they had to do with his understanding of administration. He created a new relationship between the presidency and administration, but his compass was his idea of presidential "stewardship" rather than a theory of administration. In his view:

> The executive power was limited only by specific restrictions and prohibitions appearing in the Constitution or imposed by the Congress under its Constitutional powers. . . . I declined to adopt the view that what was . . . necessary for the nation could not be done by the President unless he could find some specific authorization to do it.[12]

Administration was an area of government where Roosevelt thought action was necessary, and he acted. The result was a precedent of real importance; the chief executive himself took responsibility for the order and efficiency of the agencies of the executive branch. However, as bold as was his action, his choice of instrument was weak.

On June 1, 1905, Roosevelt created a commission of officials to recommend administrative improvements.[13] It had five members: Charles Keep, Assistant Secretary of the Treasury; James R. Garfield, Commissioner of the Bureau of Corporations; Frank Hitchcock, First Assistant Postmaster General; Lawrence Murray, Assistant Secretary of the Department of Commerce and Labor; and Gifford Pinchot, Chief of the Forest Service. Keep was designated chairman by Roosevelt.[14]

---

[11] John M. Blum, *The Republican Roosevelt* (Cambridge, Mass.: Harvard University Press, 1954), pp. 5, 19, 73.

[12] Theodore Roosevelt, *Autobiography* (New York: Macmillan, 1913), p. 338.

[13] This was but a specific instance of Roosevelt's assumption that he could rely on individuals as "unpaid volunteers" for short periods without having them become "officers" who would have to occupy positions created by Congress. During his term in office, Congress hotly contested this assumption. Edward S. Corwin, *The President: Office and Powers* (4th rev. ed., New York: New York University Press, 1957), p. 71.

[14] Oscar Kraines, "The President Versus Congress: The Keep Commission, 1905-1909," *Western Political Quarterly* XXIII, No. 1 (March 1970), 5-54.

The commission went beyond the specific practices of individual agencies. It looked into the government's salary policy and into centralizing some purchasing.[15] But Roosevelt's directions to the Keep Commission did not touch upon the presidential administrative role. He was concerned with the assessment of the methods of the executive branch and not with the authority relations within it. As Roosevelt wrote to his commission: "The existence of any method, standard, custom or practice is no reason for its continuance when a better is offered."[16] Because of its mandate and its composition, the Keep Commission's approach was identical to those of earlier congressional committees which studied administrative reforms. It had entered a new era with only one foot; while its initiation was presidential, its orientation reflected an older, non-executive-centered tradition of reform. But from the Congress' perspective, even that degree of change went too far.

For the president to assume responsibility for the executive branch's efficacy was a blow against Congress' dominance of administration. Realizing Congress' hostility on this matter, Roosevelt told the commission that he would value their recommendations "in proportion as they do not call for legislation."[17] Congress struck back, granting the commission only a $5,000 appropriation in response to a presidential request that $25,000 be given for outside experts. Later Congress attempted to foreclose the possibility of similar commissions with the Tawney amendment to the 1909 supplemental appropriations act, prohibiting the expenditure of public funds to support presidentially created commissions unless appropriated for that express purpose.[18]

Yet there was nothing threatening to Congress in the Keep Commission's recommendations. They were aimed at very specific administrative processes and entailed no major changes. The commission issued reports on eleven different areas, ranging from records management to the economies of window envelopes for mailing. The only recommendations which rose above this kind of mundane specificity were those for a central purchasing agency and a central statistical agency. But clearly, in these latter two recommendations, the com-

[15] Leonard White, *The Republican Era* (New York: Macmillan, 1958), p. 92.
[16] *Ibid.*
[17] Quoted in Kraines, p. 35.
[18] 32 Stat. L. 1027 (1909). That the thrust of this amendment was against the President's capacity as a manager was made clear by one congressional opponent who argued that the amendment would "hamper the Executive in the management of the Government." U.S. Congress, *Congressional Record*, 60th Cong., 2d Sess., 1909, vol. 43, part 4, 3,120.

mission sought to achieve economies of scale rather than to increase presidential control.[19]

The Keep Commission marks the cusp between traditional, congressional approaches to administrative reform and modern, presidential approaches. It is the starting point of presidentially dominated executive reorganization but itself contributed little to the ability of presidents to act managerially. In contrast, its successor at comprehensive executive reorganization would contribute greatly to that end, becoming the first instance of modern reorganization planning.

THE PRESIDENT'S COMMISSION AND THE CONCEPT OF THE MANAGERIAL PRESIDENCY

Although they were soon to part ways, William Howard Taft entered the presidency as Theodore Roosevelt's chosen successor, committed to his mentor's policies, such as administrative reform.[20] There was, as well, a more pressing reason for Taft to pursue reform. The national government ran deficits in four of the six years between 1904 and 1909; these included 1908 and 1909.[21] There was a huge increase in the fiscal scale of government during the preceding decades. Between 1878 and 1908, the expenditures of government increased almost 400 percent while the population grew by only 84 percent.[22] In about the same period, the civilian employment of the federal government increased by 300 percent.[23] This growth was symptomatic of the trans-

[19] The Keep Commission's reports were not printed for general public distribution. Thus its recommendations are not readily obtainable in their original form. But details on these recommendations can be found in Gustavus Weber, *Organized Efforts for the Improvement of Methods of Administration in the United States* (New York: Appleton, 1919), pp. 74-83.

[20] On the Taft administration, see Donald F. Anderson, *William Howard Taft* (Ithaca, New York: Cornell University Press, 1973); Judith Anderson, *William Howard Taft* (New York: Norton, 1981), and Paolo E. Coletta, *The Presidency of William Howard Taft* (Lawrence: University Press of Kansas, 1973). These treatments are far better on Taft's personality, politics, and policies than they are on the administration of government during his presidency. In this, these histories share a weakness common to historical treatments of the presidents prior to Franklin Roosevelt.

[21] The budget deficits and surpluses during the period cited were: 1904, $-42,573,000$; 1905, $-21,004,000$; 1906, $+24,782,000$; 1907, $+86,732,000$; 1908, $-57,334,000$; 1909, $-89,423,000$. U.S. Bureau of the Census, *The Statistical History of the United States*, p. 1,104.

[22] Figure cited by Henry Jones Ford, *The Cost of Our National Government* (New York: Columbia University Press, 1910), p. 2.

[23] U.S. Bureau of the Census, *The Statistical History of the United States*, pp. 1,102-1,103.

formation of a decentralized, agricultural republic into an expansive, industrial republic.

Writing in 1909, Henry Jones Ford observed that government's inability to control expenditure against revenues was evidence "that in some way constitutional government has become seriously deranged."[24] The traditional system of legislative dominance of governmental finance had failed.[25] But what would replace it? Theodore Roosevelt had made no contribution to untangling this knot. It is likely that Roosevelt had the deficit problem in mind as he urged the Keep Commission to find ways to effect savings in administration. But this did not differ from Congress' penurious view of administration—efficiency as economy.

The real problem was of a different order. Expanded government posed a new structural problem in the control of its fiscal processes. Modern government and the American economy were both too big and too integrated, one into the other, to depend upon the static routines of the 19th century, when small government and tariff income guaranteed surplus revenues. William Howard Taft understood that the real issue was that of choosing among ends given limited means. In his inaugural address, he said:

> The obligation on the part of those responsible for the expenditures made to carry on the Government, to be as economical as possible, and to make the burden of taxation as light as possible, is plain. . . . But when the desire to win the popular approval leads to the cutting off of expenditures really needed to make the Government effective and to enable it to accomplish its proper objects, the result is as much to be condemned as the waste of government funds in unnecessary expenditures.[26]

The Inception of Taft's Reorganization Study

In 1909 there was no mechanism for choosing among limited resources. Who would balance priorities, and through what means? To address this problem Taft created a successor to the Keep Commission, but he did more than recreate that earlier effort.

Unlike Roosevelt, Taft could not establish a study committee by

[24] Henry Jones Ford, *Cost of Our National Government*, p. 4.

[25] On the appropriations system of the last half of the 19th century, see Leonard White, *The Republican Era*, pp. 46-67.

[26] *Inaugural Addresses of the President of the United States* (Washington: United States Government Printing Office, 1965), p. 189.

presidential directive; the Tawney amendment foreclosed that option. In addition, the issues Taft wished to deal with entailed Congress' role in the revenues and appropriations processes. So for reasons of law and good sense, Taft sought congressional sanction for an administrative reform effort.

Members of Congress were as troubled by deficits as was the President. In March 1909, James A. Tawney (Rep., N.Y.), chairman of the House Committee on Appropriations, said of the just-passed appropriations bill: "In no period except in time of war have the expenditures of our National Government increased so rapidly. . . . This fact may well cause our people . . . to consider the necessity of checking this growing tendency towards excess."[27] A month later Nelson W. Aldrich (Rep., R.I.), chairman of the Senate Finance Committee, stated: "The rapidity with which our national expenditures have increased within the last three years is a source of anxiety if not of alarm. . . . I am myself satisfied that the appropriations made last year could have been reduced at least $50,000,000 without impairing the efficiency of the public service."[28] Yet these legislators were responsible for the process they bemoaned.

At this time no system existed whereby the estimate of spending needs were balanced against the government's expected revenues. Within Congress, appropriations were still primarily in the hands of the authorizing committees which had created the agencies and programs that they were now considering for funding. The Treasury Department compiled the so-called book of estimates that passed agency requests on to Congress, but presidents did not routinely effect changes in those estimates.[29] Even when presidents attempted to achieve some changes in them, more fundamental problems emerged; there was no systemic means for ordering and analyzing the estimates that were put before the Congress and no limit on the ability of agencies to go around the president to congressional committees.

That Congress was groping toward some resolution to this dilemma is suggested by a provision of the 1909 civil appropriations act; it specified that in future years the Secretary of the Treasury should compare expected revenues against the estimates for appropriation submitted by the agencies. Should it appear that there would be a short-fall in revenues:

[27] Quoted in Henry Jones Ford, *Cost of Our National Government*, p. 3.
[28] *Ibid.*
[29] See Louis Fisher, *Presidential Spending Power* (Princeton: Princeton University Press, 1975), pp. 9-35.

The Secretary of the Treasury shall transmit the estimates to Congress as heretofore required by law and at once transmit a detailed statement of all the said estimates to the President, to the end that he may in giving Congress information on the State of the Union . . . advise the Congress how in his judgment the estimated appropriation could with least injury . . . be reduced. . . .[30]

Yet while Congress turned toward the presidency for resolution of the fiscal dilemma, it signaled its ambivalence about increased presidential authority by adding the Tawney Amendment to the same act, placing it just two sections below the provision just described; Congress gave authority to the presidency but only out of dire necessity and, even then, meagerly.

Administrative reform appealed to Congress as another means out of its fiscal dilemma, and in early 1910 it entertained various proposals for a new reform study. Two views were evident in Congress' approach to administrative reform. First, it was assumed that expenditures could be reduced substantially by eliminating waste in administration. Second, it was assumed that administrative reform planning could be handled by the president, given proper congressional authorization. But while this seems to be a striking turn-around in Congress' view of administration, it amounted to nothing more than an extension of the legislature's 19th-century view of its dominance over administration. The president could play an essentially ministerial role. Reforms would aim at eliminating waste and simplifying procedure, and it was safe to let these matters rest in presidential hands.

President Taft, however, was unwilling to be Congress' instrument, even as he sought to take advantage of congressional favor for a new administrative reform study. He proposed that, instead of creating a new commission, Congress appropriate $100,000 and give him the discretion to determine the best means for organizing a reform study. Part of Taft's rationale for this presidential discretion was the new duty imposed upon him by section 7 of the 1909 civil appropriations act, quoted above. The study would prepare Taft to make judgments about which expenditures could be reduced with least harm to government's services.[31] Congress gave the President both the money and the discretion that he desired. In appropriating the funds, Congress stated that it was to be used to employ "accountants and experts from official and private life . . . with a view of inaugurating new or changing

---

[30] 35 Stat. L 1027, sec. 7 (1909).

[31] Memorandum, Young to Norton, May 17, 1910, series 6, file 215, reel 374, William Howard Taft Papers (microfilm edition).

old methods of transacting . . . business so as to attain greater efficiency and economy. . . ."[32] This language suggests that the appropriated funds would be used for a study that would look very much like that of the Keep Commission, but nothing in the language of the appropriation act required that outcome.

Selecting a Means to Reform

President Taft began by broaching the broadest question: How should a far-reaching study of administration be organized? The President entrusted the search for an answer to his secretary, Charles D. Norton. Norton, a former Chicago insurance executive, had previously been an assistant secretary of Treasury, responsible for administrative reforms in that department.[33] Norton spent the summer of 1910 consulting with "efficiency experts."[34] One of the most interesting and apparently influential of these discussions was with William S. Rossiter, formerly chief clerk at the Census Bureau, whom Theodore Roosevelt used as a trouble-shooter at the Government Printing Office.[35] Rossiter stressed the necessity of independence for the projected study, urging that it not use government officials. As for areas of attention, he recommended that a new study concern itself with centralization of authority in the executive branch, this being, in his view, the major prerequisite for improved economy and efficiency in government.[36]

Among the experts whom Charles Norton consulted were representatives of the New York Bureau of Municipal Research, the country's leading private organization in the research and advocacy of governmental reform.[37] In a first meeting, Drs. William Allen and

[32] 36 Stat. L. 703.

[33] *The National Cyclopedia of American Biography* (New York: James T. White, 1929), vol. 6, pp. 489-490.

[34] Letter, Norton to Hine, August 2, 1910, President's Commission on Economy and Efficiency, 080.2, RG 51, National Archives, Washington, D.C. Hine's acceptance of the commission is given through a letter, Hine to Norton, August 2, 1910, series 6, file 215, reel 375, Taft Papers. Hine was a transportation expert who had served as superintendent of several railroads after having been inspector of safety appliances for the Interstate Commerce Commission. In 1907 he had been a consultant to the Department of Interior on improving "business methods." *The National Cyclopedia of American Biography*, vol. 38, p. 587.

[35] *The National Cyclopedia of American Biography*, vol. 23, p. 333.

[36] Letter, Rossiter to Norton, August 19, 1910, President's Commission on Economy and Efficiency, 080.8, RG 51, National Archives, Washington, D.C.

[37] Letter, Allen to Norton, August 12, 1910, series 6, file 215, reel 374, Taft Papers. For a discussion of the founding of the New York Bureau of Municipal Research, see Jane Dahlberg, *The New York Bureau of Municipal Research* (New York: New York

Frederick Cleveland, two of the officers of the bureau, discussed the general problem of reform with President Taft but hesitated to make any recommendations without time for reflection. At a second meeting, Frederick Cleveland presented a set of tentative ideas for approaching the study. The nature of Cleveland's presentation can be inferred from the overall character of the Bureau of Municipal Research. It was founded in 1907 in New York by a small group of urban reformers of scholarly inclinations who sought to combine research and advocacy. The bureau was a product of thirty years of municipal reform and reflected the existence of a body of expert, technical information which was germane to improving government's performance. The bureau differed from competing "efficiency experts" in its methods but even more so in its conception of efficiency itself.

The term "efficiency" can mean different things.[38] By efficiency one can refer to the attainment of a goal with the least cost. Or, one can mean the efficiency of a mechanical process, the maintenance of optimal performance from a machine with the least expenditure of energy. Under certain conditions, the second definition of efficiency can contradict the first. If that energy source which optimizes machine performance with the least expenditure of energy is priced at a higher rate than alternative energy sources which would fuel the machine at sub-optimal performance, the engineer's inefficiency may be the economist's efficiency. A parallel potential tension with economic efficiency lies in what can be called social efficiency. A narrow view of economic efficiency might lead one to think in terms of the desirability of reducing the expenditures of public organizations while retaining as much of that organization's performance as possible. In contrast, one could argue that the influence of that organization on society is so salutary that a true appreciation for its efficiency would lead to added expenditures. The Bureau of Municipal Research sprang from that part of the progressive movement which valued government's work by standards more akin to social efficiency than economic efficiency.[39]

On September 15, 1910, the President and Norton considered op-

---

University Press, 1966), pp. 1-23. On the municipal reform movement out of which the bureau grew, see Martin J. Schiesl, *The Politics of Efficiency* (Berkeley: University of California Press, 1977).

[38] For a discussion of varying conceptions of efficiency in the context of the progressive reformers, see Samuel Haber, *Efficiency and Uplift* (Chicago: University of Chicago Press, 1964), pp. ix-x.

[39] On the notion of efficiency in the municipal reform movement and on the rise of a broader, more social notion of that term, see Martin Schiesl, *Politics of Efficiency*, pp. 101-110.

tions uncovered by the summer's inquiry. Echoing William Rossiter's advice, Norton urged against using officials of the executive branch, and he advised the President to keep the study "within his own hands" and refuse to "permit the Executive to be blocked ... by the Cabinet."[40] They agreed that the best way to assure presidential control of the investigation was to base it at the White House and make its director a presidential aide. And they concluded that the director ought to be Frederick Cleveland. After some discussion, which included an agreement that Cleveland could remain an officer of the Bureau of Municipal Research, Cleveland accepted the assignment.[41]

The process through which President Taft launched his efficiency study suggests that he was looking beyond a conventional approach to administrative reform. First, he eschewed the easy precedent of the Keep Commission. Next, after surveying the available pool of prominent efficiency experts, he chose an individual to lead his study who differed from them in his conception of efficiency, his greater concern for overall management, and his experience with the political ramifications of administrative reform. The September 15 meeting of Taft and Norton provides evidence also that they were considering administrative reform in a political context. Discussing the possibility of Congress' refusing further funds, should the legislators become unhappy with Taft's study, Norton observed that such congressional opposition might provide an occasion for Taft to become efficiency's champion. Norton had discussed this possibility with Julius Rosenwald, a Chicago financier, and Rosenwald offered to head a public campaign to raise funds for the study, should Congress cut off appropriations.[42]

The President's Inquiry

Taft's study of the national administration system began with the title of the President's Inquiry in Re-Efficiency and Economy. Frederick Cleveland took as his early tasks the development of an information-gathering system and the establishment of cooperative relations with the agencies. By information gathering, Cleveland intended more than the random collection of facts that had characterized earlier reform efforts. In the style of the Bureau of Municipal Research, he believed that information must be organized systematically with an eye toward

[40] Minute of meeting, September 15, 1910, series 6, file 215, reel 375, Taft Papers.
[41] Letter, Norton to Cleveland, September 27, 1910, *ibid*.
[42] Minute of meeting, September 15, 1910, *ibid*.

the structure of the organization which that information describes.[43] Meaningful reform could only follow upon a systematic knowledge of existing executive branch organization.[44]

There were two obvious directions the study could take. Certain pressing subjects could be selected for investigation, leaving most areas untouched. Or, government could be considered, in the language later adopted by the study, "as a unit, as one great problem," with an eye to determining "the fundamental principles that should prevail in its organization. . . ."[45] In an early report to Taft, Cleveland wrote: "One of the reasons why more notable results have not been obtained from previous investigations is due to the fact that these investigations have not concerned themselves with the problem of Government as a whole."[46] Cleveland won Taft to his view, as evidenced by the President's later congressional message reporting the progress of the reorganization study. Taft said: "This vast organization has never been studied in detail as one piece of administrative mechanism. Never have the foundations been laid for a thorough consideration of the relation of all its parts."[47]

An overall picture of the executive branch was to be the framework for data collection. From a modern perspective, it is difficult to appreciate how innovative was Cleveland's model of the organization of the executive branch. No longer were these agencies to be understood as single units tied to Congress by an umbilical cord of statute and appropriation. Rather, they would be seen as part of a whole that had hierarchy and ordered authority—a bureaucracy. When seen through this new conception, the traditional picture of the dominant tie of agency to legislature is an intrusive element—a pathology.

A practical problem Cleveland faced was winning the cooperation of agencies. At a cabinet meeting in late September 1910, President Taft ordered each department secretary to appoint a "committee on

---

[43] On the methods of the Bureau of Municipal Research, see Jane Dahlberg, *The New York Bureau*, pp. 39-43.

[44] But perhaps as a ploy to ward off agency opposition, Cleveland referred to his information-gathering activity as a replication of the data collection of the congressional Cockrell Committee in 1889. Minute of meeting between Cleveland and agency representatives, October 7, 1910, series 6, file 215, reel 375, Taft Papers.

[45] President's Commission on Economy and Efficiency, *Circular No. 30* (Washington: Government Printing Office, 1913), p. 31.

[46] Frederick Cleveland, "Report on the Organization of the Government," p. 3, President's Commission on Economy and Efficiency, 210.1, RG 51, National Archives.

[47] U.S. Congress, *Congressional Record*, 62nd Cong., 2d sess., 1912, vol. 48, part 1, 1,026.

business methods" to report to Cleveland.[48] But the White House was careful to maintain an unobtrusive profile for the inquiry. So when Cleveland planned a subsequent meeting with departmental representatives, Charles Norton asked that he say nothing controversial; the meeting, Norton suggested, should be informational.[49]

Norton's caution was sensible; for the first time a president was conducting an extensive reorganization planning effort that was totally White House centered. There was no active role for cabinet members, career officials, or members of Congress. Its potential opponents were legion. In a preliminary way, the study, understood both as a staff and as a process, became a foray into the managerial presidency; staff expertise in the White House was developed to provide direction over a process of centralizing change in the executive branch.[50]

The first phase of President Taft's study spanned the period from October 1910 through March 1911. As Frederick Cleveland fashioned an overall picture of the administrative system, he began to identify priorities for further study. His concerns spanned both substance and process in government, and he understood government's ends to be inextricably related to process. Exemplifying this connection of ends and means (or politics and administration), Cleveland sought to identify those substantive policy areas "in which the people of the United States are deeply interested" and "which the National Government would seem especially well qualified to handle. . . ."[51] These were, according to Cleveland, public health, education, child care, and business conditions. As an overall goal, he suggested an expansion of government's informational, statistical, and coordinating services in regard to existing programs in these areas.[52]

---

[48] Memorandum on cabinet meeting, October 8, 1910, series 6, file 215, reel 375, Taft Papers.

[49] Letter, Norton to Latta, October 7, 1910, *ibid.*

[50] Cleveland's staff role and the position of the President's Commission in relation to President Taft constitute early cases of a functional expansion of the presidency toward greater managerial competence. It should be kept in mind that at the time Cleveland was appointed, the President's office included only eight positions above the seventy or so file clerks, telephone clerks, messengers, etc., that staffed his office and the executive mansion. These eight were President Taft's secretary, his military aide, executive clerk, chief clerk, appointment secretary, accounting and disbursing clerk, social clerk, and Mrs. Taft's secretary. In organization charts prepared in the White House during the Taft administration, Cleveland's position is the only role functionally specific to an aspect of governance; he was also the highest paid member of the President's staff. Organization chart, President's Commission on Economy and Efficiency, 420.2, RG 51, National Archives.

[51] Letter, Cleveland to Norton, November 10, 1910, series 6, file 215, reel 375, Taft Papers.

[52] *Ibid.*

Cleveland built a staff of five acountants, a law clerk, and four stenographers. His instruments for data gathering were questionnaires sent to the agencies which elicited information about their powers, duties, business methods, such as record-keeping practices, methods of correspondence processing and transactions of funds, and the methods by which estimates of appropriation needs were prepared.[53] It was not the character of this data but what Cleveland did with it that distinguished the President's Inquiry from preceding reform efforts. It was the search for an organizing principle that led it in a new direction. That interest was demonstrated in the view that the whole of the administrative system had to be conceived within the reform study and in the notion that administrative reform must begin with a conception of the substance of government's activities.

The President at the Center

Cleveland's search for an integrating approach led to his realization that the real problem of governmental administration was not its practices but its fragmented authority. This can be seen in his contrast of Frederick Taylor's system of "scientific management" applied in the factory to his own approach in the federal government.[54] Frederick Cleveland had spent a day with Taylor, considering the possible contributions the "Taylor system" could make to his own work. Cleveland saw that Taylor's method was inapplicable but also saw a similarity between his approach and Taylor's. The "Taylor system" assumed the existence of hierarchical relations in the factory, and Cleveland was attempting to institute them in the executive branch. As Cleveland wrote about Taylor after visiting him; he "has worked in institutions which have the means for getting information from the shop to the head of the corporation, whereas in the Government, whatever methods may be developed in the shop, there is no present means whereby this information can get to the President or to the head of a Department in a regular and systematic manner."[55]

The study, consequently, would focus on the lack of central authority in the executive branch. Given Cleveland's background in municipal reform, it was natural for him to see a centralization of the process by which spending estimates were devised as the most practical means for increasing the coherence of the administration system. Since

[53] Ibid.

[54] On "the Taylor system" see Frederick Taylor, *The Principle of Scientific Management* (New York: Harper, 1911). On Taylor himself, see Sudhir Kakar, *Frederick Taylor: A Study in Personality and Innovation* (Cambridge, Mass.: MIT Press, 1970).

[55] Memorandum, January 16, 1911, series 6, file 215, reel 375, Taft Papers.

the 1880's the municipal reformers had used centralized fiscal processes to transfer power from city councils to executives, creating the strong mayor form of city government.[56]

That reform in fiscal practices was linked to a changed balance of authority between the branches was evident in Charles Norton's testimony to the House Appropriations Committee about the progress of the President's Inquiry. Norton explained to the committee that reform in the way the appropriation estimates were drawn together was the central goal of the Inquiry. As part of this explanation, he described the Inquiry's development of an organization for the estimates based upon "a new classification of objects of governmental expenditure."[57] Norton lauded this development as promising clearer information for the department heads and the president.[58]

Members of the Appropriations Committee failed to raise the issue of increased presidential authority over administration. Rather, they wondered whether the investigation conducted by Cleveland would "demonstrate the wisdom of the proposition of concentrating jurisdiction over all appropriations in one committee."[59] But, while still unclear to the congressmen, two different and conflicting perceptions of administration are evident in these hearings.

The first view of administration observable therein was congressional; in regard to the estimates, it had it that the full authority over them lay in Congress and that the prime purpose of authority over administration was economy. Members of the Appropriations Committee railed at Norton about agency waste. They shared the succinct administrative doctrine stated by Senator Hernando De Soto Money (Dem., Miss.) in the discussion over the original appropriation for President Taft's study: "Efficiency means economy. . . ."[60]

In contrast, the other view of administration present in the hearings was Norton's cautious statement of Frederick Cleveland's administrative doctrine. For Cleveland, good administration was something quite different from what it was for Senator Money and his colleagues. It was defined in terms of executive capacity rather than operating

[56] See Martin Schiesl, *Politics of Efficiency*, Chap. 3. Also see Dwight Waldo, *The Administrative State* (New York: Ronald Press, 1948), pp. 28-38.

[57] Transcript of Charles Norton's testimony of February 6, 1911 to the House Committee on Appropriations concerning the progress of the President's Inquiry in Re-Economy and Efficiency, pp. 4 and 7, President's Commission on Economy and Efficiency, 080.2, RG 51, National Archives.

[58] *Ibid.*, pp. 5 and 8.

[59] *Ibid.*, p. 6.

[60] U.S. Congress, *Congressional Record*, 61st Cong., 2d sess., 1910, vol. 45, part 2, 1,261.

economies. In Cleveland's view, good administration entailed the capacity of a president to guide it; the mechanism for this guidance would be fiscal control—budgeting. Also, Cleveland's understanding of efficiency had little to do with economy; government was most efficient when it served the welfare of society.

Early in the Inquiry, Cleveland had primed Charles Norton on his conception of administrative efficiency. Among his efforts in this regard were memoranda addressing the subject of the Inquiry's agenda written by some of Cleveland's associates. One of these, authored by William Allen of the Bureau of Municipal Research, suggested that it was meaningless to be concerned about the health of government's administration without reference to society's health. According to Allen, government:

> should not only make its business management a model of efficiency . . . but should . . . conduct that national business in such a spirit and such universal understanding and appreciation that not one of the social, educational or political lessons derived from its experience shall be lost . . . by either a majority or any considerable minority of its citizens. No obligation of nationalism can be so binding upon the national government as to interpret . . . truly the best intelligence . . . of our people. . . . Hence the importance of such governmental activities—such educational and standard setting agencies—as the government of the District of Columbia, the United States Bureau of Standards, the national inspection of foods and the national bureau of education.[61]

THE PRESIDENT'S COMMISSION ON ECONOMY AND EFFICIENCY

In early March 1911 Frederick Cleveland recommended to President Taft that the reorganization study be expanded to a commission format. The election of 1910 weakened Taft's congressional support, and a study associated with some eminent experts serving as commissioners might have a better chance with Congress.[62] Cleveland proposed a five-member commission that would include an engineer, a lawyer,

[61] W. H. Allen, "The National Government's Part in Studying and Solving Social and Industrial Problems," series 6, file 215, reel 375, Taft Papers.

[62] The congressional election of 1910 produced a Democratic majority in the House of Representatives and greatly weakened the Republican hold on the Senate. The 62nd Congress, which opened in January 1911, had 228 Democrats in the House as against 161 Republicans. In the 61st Congress, the Republicans had held 219 seats. In the Senate of the 62nd Congress, the Republicans declined to 51 seats from the 61 they had held in the 61st Congress.

two individuals experienced in administration and/or accounting, and an individual who could serve as a secretary.[63] Taft approved, stipulating that the expanded format would not diminish the study's immediate responsibility to him.[64] He also appointed Cleveland the commission's chairman, indicating that it would be titled the Commission on Economy and Efficiency. Taft also designated William F. Willoughby and Merritt O. Chance as members. Willoughby was assistant director of the Bureau of the Census, had done research on local administration in Puerto Rico, held a Ph.D., and had taught politics at Johns Hopkins. Chance was auditor of the Post Office. Taft asked Cleveland to nominate three others: a lawyer, an engineer, and an administrator or accountant. Cleveland designated for membership Frank J. Goodnow, Walter Warwick, and Harvey S. Chase. Goodnow was a professor of administrative law at Columbia. Warwick was auditor of the Panama Canal Commission, and Chase was both an engineer and a distinguished public accountant with experience in municipal budget reform. In creating the commission, Cleveland aimed to bring together a group that would be acceptable to both parties.[65]

The Commission at Work

The new commissioners were shaped by the same intellectual forces that had formed Frederick Cleveland—the municipal reform movement and the beginnings of public administration as a field of study. Three other members in addition to Cleveland were veterans of municipal reform. Harvey Chase had worked with the National Municipal League on improved accounting practices for cities. Frank Goodnow had drafted model ordinances for the City Club of New York, and had worked with the National Civic Federation in studying municipally owned utilities. Lastly, William Willoughby had been an investigator of urban social conditions for the Bureau of Labor. In regard to the influence of the nascent field of public administration, Cleveland, Goodnow, and Willoughby held Ph.D.'s in politics and had taught at the university level. Goodnow, of course, had already made a major contribution with his book *Administration and Politics*.[66] Thus the majority of the President's Commission had worked for strong ex-

[63] Memorandum, Cleveland to Norton, March 6, 1911, *Ibid.*

[64] Letter, Taft to Norton, March 8, 1911, *ibid.*

[65] Letter of F. A. Cleveland, quoted in Walter O. Jacobsen, "A Study of President Taft's Commission on Economy and Efficiency and a Comparative Evaluation With Three Other Commissions" (unpublished masters thesis, Columbia University, 1941), p. 37.

[66] Frank Goodnow, *Administration and Politics* (New York: Macmillan, 1900).

ecutive government in the cities, and by the first decade of the new century they had concluded that their doctrine of executive authority was applicable to the national government.

The commission's initial plans for its work represented a major enlargement over the President's Inquiry. A system of coordinated subcommittees was planned, each subcommittee to focus on one detailed issue, using the data base developed in the initial stage of the work. There was also to be a committee of arbitration to negotiate differences between the commission and the agencies and a committee of consulting experts to serve as an external board of advisers.[67] Much of this was still-born because of congressional refusal to fully fund the continuing work. Yet, the actual productivity of the commission was spectacular. It undertook 110 separate studies ranging from the administration of the Patent Office through the handling of correspondence.[68]

President Taft maintained a close relationship to the commission. As a consequence of the commission's status as a presidential satellite, it was alienated from both the executive branch bureaus and, even more so, the Congress. In demanding cooperation from the agencies, the commission was tightening the very loose ties that had connected them to the chief executive. Furthermore, in assuming that the whole of the administration was its responsibility, the commission necessarily offended congressional sensibilities about its prerogatives over administration.

Despite President Taft's request that the departments cooperate with the commission, Cleveland ran into tenacious opposition in parts of the executive branch. This was articulated by an outside critic of the commission, Stephen Gilman, a professor of business at the University of Wisconsin. Having watched the impact of the study on agencies to which he was well connected, Gilman wrote to President Taft complaining that the study was generating hostility in the departments. He wrote: "De-Centralization is the cure. There should be continuous work . . . back in the Department discussing the problems in the atmosphere of the departments where the tradition of the departments may be appreciated."[69]

The most uncooperative department was Treasury; it is historically

---

[67] "Chart Showing the Organization and Work of the President's Commission," series 6, file 215, reel 375, Taft Papers.

[68] F. A. Cleveland's testimony; U.S. Congress, House, Committee on Appropriations, *Hearings*, 62nd Cong. 2d sess., 1913, p. 4.

[69] Letter, Gilman to Charles D. Hilles (who had replaced Norton as Taft's secretary), April 21, 1911, series 6, file 215, reel 375, Taft Papers.

linked to Congress through the constitutional authority over taxing and appropriations, and it is one of the most prestigious departments of government, boasting a constituency among America's elite.[70] That the commission's intrusion into Treasury seemed to violate that status was the theme of a complaint from a banker with the Guaranty Trust Company of New York; he urged that the commission should busy itself with other agencies "and permit the Treasury Department to continue their [sic] own house cleaning without interruption."[71] Ultimately, the President had to intervene in this department to force its cooperation with the commission. For example, on the matter of the department's failure to respond to a questionnaire which requested certain information by October 1, 1911, Charles Norton wrote to Secretary of the Treasury Franklin MacVeagh, inquiring about the oversight. On January 18, 1912, President Taft wrote to the Secretary on the same subject.[72] MacVeagh responded on January 25, submitting two of the three requested categories of information.[73] Later, Taft chided Secretary MacVeagh on his lack of cooperation with the commission, and the Secretary responded, in an injured tone, that he and his subordinates would never be disloyal to the President. He avowed: "I know of no basis whatever for the suspicion that has evidently been expressed to you by Mr. Cleveland or some of his associates." But he added: "To be entirely frank, I never have entertained a high opinion of the services of the Cleveland Commission."[74]

Just as the commission's study threatened agency autonomy, so it threatened Congress' authority over administration. The centralizing spirit of the enterprise, its promise to the President "to provide for *complete, accurate,* and *prompt* information about each subject of administrative concern, [emphasis in original]," augured a new and potentially dominant authority over the executive branch.[75] However, the agencies and Congress did not take this threat lightly, and Frederick

---

[70] However, the problems went beyond the Treasury Department. As late as December 1911, Cleveland had to seek the President's aid in securing cooperation from several departments concerning the commission's request for various information. Minutes, President's Commission on Economy and Efficiency, December 18, 1911, 017.12, RG 51, National Archives.

[71] Letter, Patterson to Andrews, April 10, 1911, series 6, file 215, reel 375, Taft Papers.

[72] Letter, Taft to MacVeagh, January 18, 1912, *ibid.*

[73] Letter, Cleveland to Taft, January 25, 1912, *ibid.*

[74] Letter, MacVeagh to Taft, Oct. 24, 1912, series 6, file 3,868, reel 441, Taft Papers.

[75] "Report to the President," December 18, 1912, President's Commission on Economy and Efficiency, 080.2, RG 51, National Archives.

Cleveland saw his work hampered by a tacit lobby against the commission formed by its opponents in the executive branch and legislature.[76]

The commission's most vulnerable flank was its failure to produce great reductions of expenditures. Critics zeroed-in on that weakness, as exemplified by Representative Mondell (Rep., Wyo.): ". . . my experience has been, with most of these economy commissions, that they generally end up with some recommendation for changes with a considerable increase of expense."[77] The most direct way for Congress to express its dissatisfaction was through appropriations. After the $100,000 it granted for the efficiency study in 1910, Congress granted only one more of President Taft's appropriation requests for it, in 1911 adding $75,000. But in 1912 Congress refused a presidential request of $250,000 and again appropriated $75,000, adding a punitive stipulation prohibiting more than three salaries to be paid from the appropriation.[78] Consequently, Taft directed that after August 14, 1912, the commission's membership would be reduced to Cleveland, Walter Warwick, and Merrit Chance.[79] Harvey Chase, who had already become inactive due to illness, had no more contact with the study, but Frank Goodnow and William Willoughby maintained close contact with the work after leaving the payroll.

Could Cleveland and his fellow commissioners have avoided the deterioration of relations with Congress? It seems unlikely; at an operating level Taft had instructed his Commission not to confer with legislators. . . . He had insisted: "The function of the Commission is to assist the President. . . ."[80] But even if that practice had changed, the fact remains that the commission broached issues that were fundamentally threatening to congressional habit and authority. And in doing so, it was not even able to use the justification of economizing.

Even as the commission's work disappointed expectations of major savings, leaving it (and the President) politically vulnerable, it took a direction toward a different solution to government's fiscal problem than attempted savings through micro-administrative reforms. Cleve-

---

[76] Draft letter, Cleveland to Taft, May 21, 1912, *ibid.*

[77] U.S. Congress, *Congressional Record*, 62nd Cong., 2d sess., 1912, vol. 48, part 10, 10,402.

[78] Correspondence, Cleveland to Taft, July 13, 1912; Cleveland to Hilles, July 13, 1912; Taft to Senator Warren, July 16, 1912; Warren to Taft, July 17, 1912, series 6, file 216, reel 375, Taft Papers.

[79] Letter, Taft to Cleveland, August 10, 1912, President's Commission on Economy and Efficiency, 080.2, RG 51, National Archives.

[80] Letter, Taft to Cleveland, August 17, 1911, *ibid.*

land and his associates taught the President that macro-level administrative reforms were more likely than micro-reforms to provide tools for coping with the problems of the executive branch.

The Commission's Recommendations

The recommendations of the commission were made through presidential messages to Congress, commission reports to Congress, and through thirty-five circulars published by the commission.[81] These recommendations were of two sorts: one of administrative details, micro-administration; and one of overall centralizing reforms for the executive branch, macro-administration.

In the first category, recommendations dealt with three problems; those of personnel, financial procedure, and business practice. In personnel, the commission's most important recommendations were for an expansion of the classified services to include all non-policy-making positions, the creation of efficiency records for each employee on a standardized basis, a superannuation program for career public servants, and a more orderly classification system for employees. None of these was immediately implemented, but the landmark Classification Act of 1923 was influenced by these recommendations.[82] Under the rubric of financial procedures, the commission studied the accounting procedures of agencies, recommending greater standardization of practice and of reporting documents throughout the government. It also established a classification system for the objects of expenditure in government. The only part of these recommendations to be adopted were some of those concerning improvement of accounting systems. Finally, in the area of business practices, the commission made recommendations concerning the handling of correspondence, the use of window envelopes, duplication through the photostatic process, and the centralization of the public distribution of government publications. The recommendations for window envelopes and photostatic duplication were widely and rapidly adopted, with the claim of substantial economies. In the only congressional action of adoption of the commission's recommendations the Appropriation Act of 1912 specified that the distribution of all government publications was to be centralized at the Government Printing Office.

In the category of macro-administration, the commission urged that the executive branch should be unified and, once unified, controlled.

---

[81] A complete bibliography of the commission's reports and circulars can be found in Gustavus Weber, *Organized Efforts*, pp. 94-103.

[82] 42 Stat. 1488.

It rejected the contemporary, atomized administrative universe dominated by congressional authority. The commission's ideal was an executive branch under the authority of the chief executive. It offered two coordinate means to achieve this end; the first was organizational and the second was fiscal.

The commission's first means for unifying administration is an early formulation of a key principle of administrative orthodoxy: agencies should be organized by purpose. The justification for this principle was that:

> Only by grouping services according to their character can substantial progress be made in eliminating duplication of work and plant and proper working relations be established between services engaged in similar activities. Until the head of a department is called upon to deal exclusively with matters falling in but one or a very few distinct fields, effective supervision and control is impossible.[83]

This principle originated in the commission's modeling "in full detail how the government was organized for the performance of its work"[84] Federal organization was without order, and arrangement by purpose seemed to give it the order it lacked. In this abstraction of administration the commission broke with its predecessors by making administrative reform a theoretical matter, implicitly tying together the reform enterprise and academic public administration.

The commission broached the problem of organization through several projects. The most important of these considered the groupings of agencies and purposes. The commission recommended the abolition of several agencies, the Revenue Cutter Service of the Treasury, the Returns Office of the Interior, and the elimination of the Life Saving Service of Treasury through consolidation with the Bureau of Lighthouses in Commerce and Labor. It also recommended the consolidation of the six auditors' offices in the Treasury Department, and it recommended a non-cabinet-level health administration that would include the Public Health and Marine Hospital Service from Treasury and other agencies such as the Bureau of Chemistry in Agriculture and the Bureau of the Census in Commerce and Labor.[85]

---

[83] "Report on the Organization of the U.S. Government," President's Commission on Economy and Efficiency, 080.2, RG 51, National Archives. President Taft presented an abridged version of this commission report as a presidential message to Congress on January 17, 1912. U.S. Congress, *Congressional Record*, 62nd Cong., 2d sess., 1912, vol. 48, part 1, 1,026-1,032.

[84] Gustavus Weber, *Organized Efforts*, p. 91.

[85] These recommendations were contained in two reports of President Taft to Con-

The recommendations for macro-administrative change required legislative approval. None received serious congressional attention. Furthermore, the funds of the commission ran out before it was able to carry out its full ambitions. For example, the commission had intended to compile its studies of the War Department into a recommendation for a unified Defense Department, but time and events overtook it.[86]

The logic behind the commission's concern with organization unified by purpose ran beyond an interest in order for its own sake; the notion that the executive branch agencies ought to be organized by purpose and hierarchically arranged rested on the view that the chief executive is the locus of authority over administration. Thus the organizational recommendations assumed the necessity for enhancing the president's capacity to manage the administrative system. And the tool for directly enhancing the president as manager was the creation of an executive budget. As President Taft told Congress in 1912: "The United States is the only great Nation whose Government is operated without a budget."[87] Frederick Cleveland attacked the existing system of estimates as "destructive of . . . efficiency and improperly intruding upon the chief executive's discretion with which he stands responsible for the conduct of business in the executive branch."[88]

The commission's ultimate criticism of the existing appropriations process was that it made no "provision for considering . . . expenditures from the viewpoint of the policy to be adopted with respect either to work done, organization provided, character of expenditures made, or method of financing."[89] For the president to have authority to control the estimates of the agencies would alleviate this problem, provided he had the means to gather and analyze relevant information.

---

gress. All but the recommendation for a unified health service were presented in a report to Congress on April 4, 1912 (62nd Cong., 2d. sess., House Doc. No. 670). The recommendation for a unified health service was presented in a report to Congress dated January 8, 1912 (62nd Cong., 3d. sess., House Doc. No. 1252).

[86] William F. Willoughby, "One War and Navy Department," *New Republic* (May 7, 1916), 89-91.

[87] U.S. Congress, *Congressional Record*, 62nd Cong., 2d sess., 1912, vol. 48, part 1, 1030. For background on presidential roles in estimates prior to the Budget and Accounting Act of 1921, see Louis Fisher, *Presidential Spending Power*, Chap. 1.

[88] Frederick Cleveland, "What Is Involved in the Making of a National Budget," paper read to the annual meeting of the Efficiency Society, New York, June 28, 1913, p. 10, President's Commission on Economy and Efficiency, 080.2, RG 51, National Archives.

[89] President's Commission on Economy and Efficiency, "Tentative Outline of Need for a National Budget," September 13, 1911, series 6, file 215, reel 375, Taft Papers.

But what of Congress? Would that reform give the president a part of what had traditionally been Congress' power over the appropriations process? The commission's answer was that as well as transforming the president's capacity to lead, the budget would transform Congress' capacity to make policy choices and hold agencies responsible for their execution. The commission proposed that the budget "is the only effective means whereby the Executive may get before the country a comprehensive program with respect to which the legislator must assume responsibility either for action or inaction."[90]

President Taft embraced the budget recommendation presented to him on September 13, 1911.[91] He directed the commission to create the format for a budget system which could be used parallel to the current estimates so as to demonstrate the superiority of the new method. On July 10, 1912, he ordered the heads of departments and agencies to place their estimates for the next fiscal year into the format drafted by the commission. It required that agencies show their expenditures for the fiscal year ending June 30, 1911, their appropriations for fiscal year 1912, and their requested appropriation for fiscal year 1913, also using the commission's new classification categories.[92]

Upon learning of the President's budget experiment, Congress acted to crush the threat to its authority. On August 23, 1912, through an amendment to the Sundry Civil Appropriations Act, the Congress ordered that "the . . . estimates of appropriations . . . shall be prepared and submitted to Congress, by those charged with the duty . . . only in the form and at the time now required by law, and in no other form. . . ."[93] This created a quandary for the agency heads; should they follow the President's directive or the new law? Inquiries rushed into the White House, many of them evincing hostility to the new budget format. Samuel Adams, acting Secretary of Interior, wondered whether he should continue to follow the President's directive, observing that "a continuance of the work will involve this Department in a considerable expense and will delay other important matters."[94] Taft answered, "I desire the work continued which I have already

[90] Draft report, "The Practical Aspects of a National Budget," n.d., President's Commission on Economy and Efficiency, 311, RG 51, National Archives.

[91] President's Commission on Economy and Efficiency, "Tentative Outline of the Need for a National Budget," September 13, 1911, series 6, file 215, reel 375, Taft Papers.

[92] President's Commission on Economy and Efficiency, *Report to the President*, Circular No. 30 (Washington: Government Printing Office, 1913), pp. 12-13.

[93] Sundry Civil Appropriations Act of 1912, sec. 9.

[94] Letter, Adams to Taft, August 27, 1912, series 6, file 3868, reel 447, Taft Papers.

directed. It will not be submitted to Congress by you in the form of a budget but by me in the form of a message."[95]

President Taft was set on a crash course with Congress over budget authority, but he needed justification for that course. Frederick Cleveland drafted a statement which Taft made public in the form of an open letter to Secretary of the Treasury MacVeagh. He argued that presidential authority to order the agencies to prepare a budget was implicit within the powers of the office; legislation was unnecessary. It is particularly interesting that the letter did not rest its argument on the explicit constitutional power of the presidency. Rather, it argued from a functional view of the office; if the presidency was to perform the functions thrust upon it by an expanding economy and society, it must have the required powers. If the Constitution was viable, then it must adapt in the wake of change.[96] Taft's letter to MacVeagh stated:

> If Congress is permitted to assume exclusive jurisdiction over what the President may seek to learn about the business transactions by the departments . . . if heads of departments are to be considered purely as the ministerial agents of Congress in the preparation and submission of estimates, then as far as the business of Government is concerned, the President . . . is short of most important executive power and duty.
>
> If the President is to assume . . . any responsibility for either the manner in which business of the Government is transacted . . . it is evident that he cannot be limited by Congress to such information as that branch may think sufficient for his purposes. In my opinion, it is entirely competent for the President to submit a budget, and Congress cannot . . . prevent it. . . . And this power I propose to exercise.[97]

In accepting the commission's recommendation for an executive budget, Taft accepted much of the expansive vision of the executive office which underlay its work. Even in the face of the charge that the executive budget threatened the balance of functions and authority between the president and Congress, Taft held his ground. The meaning of the commission's recommendations and Taft's embrace of them was evident to contemporary observers. Writing in 1914, Ernst Freund, the era's leading authority on administrative law, observed that the basic "problem of American public law is to assert against unrestrained

[95] Letter, Taft to Adams, September 1, 1912, *ibid.*

[96] Memorandum and accompanying draft statement, Cleveland to Taft, September 5, 1912, *ibid.*

[97] Letter, Taft to MacVeagh, September 18, 1912, *ibid.*

legislative discretion the legitimate claims of principle. One way would be the according of a larger and perhaps a controlling influence to . . . executive power. This has been the burden of recommendations of President Taft's Commission. . . ."[98]

Underlying its preference for a presidential as against a congressional view of administration, the commission had operated upon a different conception of administrative efficiency than was held by most legislators. Reflecting the congressional view, Representative John Fitzgerald (Rep., N.Y.) maintained that any new agency created to collect and analyze information regarding estimates be attached to Congress because there it would be encouraged to get into the bureaus after waste "like a ferret in a rat hole."[99] The commission's concept of efficiency was more expansive and "social" in that it posited efficiency as a principle to be assessed in terms of government's delivery of services and the public's benefit from government expenditures. While the commission by no means rejected economy, it made it a subservient value to efficiency. For example Cleveland wrote:

> The demand for efficiency must go farther than to require that the government shall get a dollar for every dollar spent; it must constitute a demand that the government is doing the thing most needed, is conserving those ends and purposes which cannot be adequately reached through private undertakings.[100]

Cleveland viewed the capacity to assess the social efficiency of expenditures as executive; thus, to be efficient government must maintain a strong executive managerial capacity. The federal government was inefficient not because this or that agency wasted money but because it lacked the executive capacity to assess its expenditures and their consequences.

The commission addressed executive weakness at three levels. First, it taught that efficiency is logically prior to economy. It asserted that

[98] Ernst Freund, "The Substitution of Rule for Discretion in Public Law," *International Journal of Ethics* 25 (October 1914), 102. Freund made a similar point earlier in a letter to Frederick Cleveland, when he observed that in the area of appropriations and spending, "the only really democratic principles at stake have been legality and economy of expenditures. Neither is in the slightest degree promoted by legislative initiative while their greatest safeguard lies in the concentration of responsibility." Freund to Cleveland, n.d., President's Commission on Economy and Efficiency, 311, RG 51, National Archives.

[99] U.S. Congress, House Appropriations Committee, *Hearings*, 62nd Cong., 2nd sess., 1913, p. 38.

[100] Frederick Cleveland, "The Need for Coordinating Municipal, State and National Activities, *Annals* 61 (May 1912), 27.

an organization that cannot articulate goals and their means, and coordinate their achievement, cannot control expenditure. Second, the commission posited efficiency as an executive value. In this, its assumption of a broad, active concept of efficiency led directly to a "modern" position on presidential power over administration. Third, with an active conception of efficiency as its conceptual base, the commission sketched a formula for the managerial presidency. It recommended the reform of the executive branch on the basis of organization by purpose. It recommended that the president be given the central control and planning functions through an executive budget, recommending also that a bureau of administrative control be created to support the president in his new managerial responsibilities.[101]

THE FATE OF THE COMMISSION'S RECOMMENDATIONS

The recommendations for large organizational changes and the empowering of a president through an executive budget posed a direct threat to the role of congressional committees and their chairmen. It should come as no surprise that Congress gave little heed to these recommendations. Inattention was the legislature's best defense. To actually open full consideration of the recommendations would have invited substantive discussion on the merits of the reforms; this was dangerous because there were friends of the recommendations in the Congress. These friends were not so much allies of the commission as practical politicians who saw the necessity for reforms that would decrease traditional legislative powers while sharpening the capacities of government as a whole. One of those was Representative Swagar Sherley (Dem., Ky.) who told his colleagues:

> We dislike to give up power. A Committee having charge of a bill does not want any supervision over it. Yet I appeal to this House that we ought to rise above the question of our own particular power as members or chairmen . . . and bring about a system whereby there can be presented in the House at the beginning of the session a real budget.[102]

[101] The recommendation for a new presidential staff agency was sent to Congress by Taft along with the message that accompanied the new format budget that the commission had prepared at his request. Message of President, February 26, 1913 (62nd Cong., 3d sess., Senate Doc. No. 113).

[102] U.S. Congress, *Congressional Record*, 62nd Cong., 2d Sess., 1912, vol. 48, part 2, 1706. Frederick Cleveland attributed the failure of the commission's recommendations to gain a serious hearing in Congress to the House Committee on Appropriations' defense of its growing power over the estimates and its consequent prestige in the House

The commission's recommendations came at an inauspicious time. Speaker Joe Cannon was defeated by disgruntled reformers, and Taft was not an ally of Cannon's critics. Furthermore, the weakening of the speaker devolved power into the committees of the House, and the members were not likely to suddenly surrender authority they had just won. Finally, Taft lost the three-way 1912 election fight among Woodrow Wilson, Theodore Roosevelt, and himself, and the Democratic Party won both houses of Congess.

Yet President Taft made a strong plea for the commission's continuance. Its last appropriation ran through June 1913. Taft pleaded for its continuance by Congress, but without success. Leading progressives were disappointed about the commission's impending death. There was a flurry of discussion of the possibility of a public crusade to convert it into a privately funded reform effort.[103] But nothing came of it. Throughout its life the commission had shunned a large public role in favor of a direct, confidential relationship with President Taft. Thus it was less visible than would be ideal for a reform effort seeking to become independent on the basis of private sector support.

The last attempt to save the commission came about a month after President Wilson's inauguration. Wilson met with Henry Bruere, one of the directors of the New York Bureau of Municipal Research; John Purroy Mitchel, a leading New York City progressive Democrat; and Louis D. Brandeis, who was soon to be appointed by Wilson to the Supreme Court. Wilson could not be convinced to save the commission, explaining that he had major issues on his agenda and that, while he was interested in its work, it had no place in his administration.[104]

That the commission's life ended with none of its major recommendations implemented ought not be taken as a measure of failure. In hindsight the commission was strikingly successful, even if that success was longer in coming than any of its members would have preferred. Its work formed the template of modern comprehensive reorganization planning. Its twin goals of organizational rationaliza-

---

as well as its power over administration. Cleveland to Charles McCarthy, March 17, 1913, President's Commission on Economy and Efficiency, 080.8, RG 51, National Archives.

[103] Cleveland informed ex-President Taft of these efforts. Letter, Cleveland to Taft, June 28, 1913, President's Commission on Economy and Efficiency, 080.2, RG 51, National Archives.

[104] This attempt to revive the commission was described by Frederick Cleveland in an interview with Walter O. Jacobson on February 22, 1939, and reported in Jacobson, "A Study of President Taft's Commission on Economy and Efficiency," pp. 69-70. Cleveland also expressed the nub of Wilson's objection in Letter, Cleveland to C. A. Royce, May 31, 1913, *ibid.*

tion and the expansion of the president's capacity for management dominated the reorganization agenda until mid-century.

In the shorter run, an indication of the commission's influence can be seen in the spate of similar enterprises created in the states. In 1915 alone, thirteen state-level reorganization planning commissions reported recommendations.[105] Another short-run signal of its impact was Congress' attempt to maintain some of the commission's work. In 1912 the Civil Service Commission was directed by Congress to take over the commission's research into classification within the federal service. In the next year the Civil Service Commission created a Division of Efficiency to conduct the work, employing Herbert D. Brown to head it; Brown had been a commission staff member in charge of research into personnel classification. In 1916 Congress chose to broaden the division's mission and reconstituted it as an independent agency, the Bureau of Efficiency. Clearly Congress wanted to institutionalize an investigative capacity, but it was more comfortable with that operation tucked safely under legislative supervision. Thus the annual appropriation to the bureau allocated funds directly for specific studies.

Another aspect of the commission's success was its influence on the intellectual development of public administration as a field of inquiry. When the commission began its work there was very little that could be identified as an American literature of public administration. What intellectual guidance there was came largely from the experience of the municipal reform movement or the earlier developing field of scientific management.

The first phase of public administration jelled in the work of the President's Commission. Out of its eclectic background it pulled together a theoretically informed investigation of administration, issuing recommendations which reflected theoretical perspectives on efficiency, organizational coherence, and executive primacy. Furthermore, two of the commission's members, Cleveland and Willoughby, went on to become major figures shaping the study of public administration for the generation prior to the New Deal.[106]

Most important, the commission left behind an insistent argument

---

[105] "Efficiency and Economy in State Government," *American Political Science Review* 8 (February 1914), 63-64; John A. Sapp, "Legislative Notes and Reviews," *American Political Science Review* 10 (February 1916), 96-97.

[106] For examples of the influential, post-commission scholarship of Cleveland and Willoughby, see Cleveland and A. E. Buck, *The Budget and Responsible Government* (New York: Macmillan, 1920); W. F. Willoughby, *Principles of Public Administration* (Washington: The Brookings Institution, 1927).

for presidential priority regarding administration and the executive branch. Under different political conditions, the incumbent president could have benefited more from the recommendations. But Taft benefited in some concrete ways. First, he had in it staff support that improved his reach over several areas of administration, most particularly that of agency estimates about which Congress had recently allowed him to make recommendations. Taft's activity in this area was enhanced by the commission's service as an information gathering and processing mechanism.[107] Second, the President obtained political benefit from the commission in that its mandate was high on the progressive agenda, and Taft needed whatever credit he could get from his party's reform wing.

But it is the presidency more than Taft which profited from the commission's work. The commission's agenda for reform was a blueprint for a 20th-century presidency that was as new as the problem of regular governmental deficits and as old as Alexander Hamilton's ideal of the presidency. With the wartime emergency, Woodrow Wilson would be granted temporary powers that fit him to the model of the President's Commission, although he had not been interested in continuing its work. In the dozen years after Wilson left the presidency, the commission's model of executive management guided new efforts at reorganization and became, as well, the basis for a sophisticated, self-conscious literature of public administration. So the commission's importance is best seen from the vantage point of reorganization in the 1920's and early 1930's.

---

[107] This role for the commission can be seen, for example, in its preparation of a work sheet onto which appropriation bills could be described, giving President Taft accessible, easy information about the characteristics of these bills. Memorandum for President, "For Message Relative to Appropriation Bills," n.d., series 6, file 215, reel 376, Taft Papers.

Chapter Three

REORGANIZING FOR NORMALCY: PRESIDENTIAL REORGANIZATION REDUX

When Hamilton laid out the scheme of
executive departments he placed the different
functions of administration . . . into groups of the
same general purpose under single headed
responsibility. But ever since that time we have
been busy dividing responsibility by scattering
services directed to substantially the same major
purpose over many different executive
departments . . . without any thought of a sound
basis of organization. . . .[1]

Herbert Hoover

Nineteen-twenty was an election year about which opposition politicians dream. Incumbent Democrats had to defend Wilson's peace
treaty, expanded government, and record deficits. The Republicans
only had to pledge the opposite, and Senator Warren Harding of Ohio
won by promising "a return to normalcy." The presidency that Harding won over the Democratic nominee, James M. Cox (also of Ohio),
had changed during the previous two decades.[2] Roosevelt, Taft, and
Wilson had extended its prominence and authority. Roosevelt had
enlarged the presidency's economic concerns and sharpened its place
at the focal point of public attention. Taft left the precedent of activism
in government's fiscal operation. Wilson became the first president to
conduct social and industrial mobilization for war.[3] Wilson's war ex-

---

[1] Secretary of Commerce Herbert Hoover speaking before the Thirteenth Annual
Meeting of the Chamber of Commerce of the United States. Quoted in Leonard White,
Introduction to the Study of Public Administration (New York: Macmillan, 1926),
p. 66.

[2] Harding polled 16,143,407 popular votes (about 60 percent) to Cox's 9,130,328
(about 34 percent). Eugene Debs's candidacy accounted for over 5 percent of the vote.

[3] Although Wilson placed substantive policy considerations ahead of his interest in
government organization during his presidency, in wartime he was forced to give major
attention to organizational arrangements. To give the President maximum discretion in
this area, Congress passed the Overman Act (40 Stat. 556) of 1918. During the duration
of the war it gave the President authority to effect any reorganization necessary for the
war's conduct, with the qualification that such changes would revert back to the status
quo ante six months after the war's end.

perience affirmed a lesson present in an inchoate form in earlier administrations: as the burden of government grew, the presidency would
strengthen.

Harding would need strength to return to "normalcy," if by that
he meant antebellum public service employment levels and spending
totals. Between 1916 and 1920 the debt of the federal government
had risen from $1,225,146,000 to $24,299,321,000; the total number
of civilian employees in federal service had more than doubled, from
399,382 to 845,500. Federal outlays over these four years had accel-
erated greatly, 1916's outlay of $712,967,000 rising to 1920's
$6,357,677,000 (down from a high in 1919 of $18,492,665,000).[4]

REORGANIZATION'S FIRST SUCCESS: THE BUDGET

The weight of wartime deficits accomplished what William Howard
Taft and Frederick Cleveland could not; in early 1921 Congress passed
into law the Budget and Accounting Act, endowing the president with
budget authority.[5] The distinguished practitioner-scholar Herbert Emmerich judged the act to be "the greatest landmark of our administrative history except for the Constitution itself."[6] Consistent with the
recommendation of Taft's commission, the act established a Bureau
of the Budget to support presidential use of his new budget authority.
However, while the new bureau was understood to be the president's,
it was placed in the Treasury Department. Actually, the bureau's location was a compromise between a House version of the bill which
attached the bureau directly to the president and a Senate version
which placed it in Treasury, responsible to the secretary. In the compromise, the Bureau of the Budget was placed in Treasury, but the act
made explicit its direct relationship to the president.[7]

A second major component of the Budget and Accounting Act was
the General Accounting Office, headed by a comptroller general (serv-

[4] U.S. Bureau of the Census, *The Statistical History of the United States* (New York:
Basic Books, 1976), pp. 1,102-1,117.

[5] In 1920 Congress had passed and sent to President Wilson a quite similar bill, but
Wilson had vetoed it. His objection was that the bill specified that the Comptroller-
General could be removed from office short of his fixed term by concurrent resolution,
a legislative action not requiring presidential signature. In Wilson's view this was an
unconstitutional violation of the President's removal power. The bill that was passed
and signed into law in 1921 required a joint resolution for removal of the Comptroller-
General; this instrument requires a presidential signature. See Louis Fisher, *Presidential
Spending Power* (Princeton: Princeton University Press, 1975), pp. 31-35.

[6] Herbert Emmerich, *Federal Organization and Administrative Management* (University, Alabama: University of Alabama Press, 1971), pp. 40-41.

[7] In particular, see 42 Stat. 18 (1921), sections 207-210, 213, 215, and 216.

ing a fixed tenure of fifteen years in office). It was to be an auditing arm of Congress, asserting congressional responsibility over the expenditure of appropriated funds by administrative agencies. Through this auditing instrument the Congress was able to assert its place in government's fiscal operations.

The new budget authority did not go as far as it might have in disciplining government's fiscal life through presidential authority; Congress could disregard the president's budget figures. But the law promised to impose some discipline on appropriations, and the disciplining hand was the president's. Contemporary observers saw the new authority as a great increment to presidential power. Writing in the *Constitutional Review*, Henry Campbell Black stated: "It cannot be denied that the . . . executive budget does enormously increase the control of the executive over the entire government, because it makes the executive, and not the legislature, the policy-determining organ."[8] Donald Wilhelm made a similar comment when he wrote that the new law restores "the President to power over the tremendous . . . activities carried on under him, and looks to affording relief to Congress as an administrative factor."[9]

Increased control over administration was the Bureau of the Budget's ambition from its inception. Charles Dawes, a Chicago banker and supply officer for the American army during the war, was chosen by President Harding as the first budget director. From the beginning Dawes understood the bureau's potential as an executive weapon. Despite the fact that the new law was not to take effect until fiscal year 1923, the Harding administration quickly devised a budget for fiscal year 1922. This was done without formal authority and rested on President Harding's orders, implemented through the new bureau.[10] The lesson Dawes drew from this experience was that of his bureau's importance as an extension of the president's will:

> As long as the President is not indifferent to his business duty, Budget law or no Budget law, the system will work. The minute the impres-

[8] Henry Campbell Black, "A National Budget System," *The Constitutional Review*, vol. 4, no. 1 (January 1920), 43.

[9] Donald Wilhelm, "Executive Reforms at Washington," *World's Work*, 43 (November 1921), 633.

[10] President Harding used the new authority and the bureau with effectiveness. He ordered the new director to reduce by 10 percent all the agency estimates projected for fiscal 1922. The centralized character of the budget system made such control possible with follow-up guaranteed through the Bureau of the Budget. For a look at the early use of the new presidential authority, see Charles Dawes, *The First Year of the Budget of the United States* (New York: Harper and Brothers, 1923).

sion is created among the business organization of the government that his eye and the eyes of his agents are not watchful, Budget law or no Budget law, the system will fail.[11]

Dawes's organization of the budget bureau aimed at making it a centralizing, presidential staff. In particular, he meant the bureau to counteract the autonomy of the agencies. Each of the budget officers would be responsible for specific agencies; as Dawes described their responsibility: ". . . they will bring to the heads of the departments and the chiefs of bureaus . . . a better realization of how the plan of their particular department can be made to better accord with the plan which the President has established. . . ."[12] Thus the budget bureau would provide steady direction over administration, even while presidential attention shifted from one priority to another.

Yet there remained a role for the budget bureau in the plans of the President's Commission on Economy and Efficiency which was not consistently fulfilled by that agency under President Harding.[13] Frederick Cleveland and his colleagues had hoped that it would enrich the agencies' substantive work. Such a centralized staff could provide a neutral assessment of administrative work. From this perspective Dawes's budget bureau failed. He developed an organization which penetrated into the administrative system sufficiently to affect agency behavior, but his interest was limited to economizing—reducing expenditures. From the perspective of the more ambitious administrative reformers, Dawes had built the right kind of instrument but was using it for too limited ends. It was as if the end product of large-scale administrative reforms, shifting substantial authority to the president, was simply the transference of Congress' niggardly view of administration to the president.[14]

[11] *Ibid.*, pp. ix-x.

[12] *Ibid.*, p. 115.

[13] The Bureau of the Budget did attempt to use its budgetary authority as an instrument to allow it to coordinate the activities of conflicting agencies. By direction of President Coolidge, the bureau's chief coordinator struggled to rationalize overlapping responsibilities between the departments of Commerce and Agriculture in early 1925, to no avail. The departments and their cabinet-level secretaries were too strong to tolerate the attempted imposition of the bureau into their functional turf. Letter, H. C. Smither (the chief coordinator) to Herbert Hoover, March 14, 1925, Cotton: Advisory Board, Official File, Commerce Papers, Herbert Hoover Presidential Library, West Branch, Iowa: and Letter, Smither to Hoover, May 20, 1925, Committees: Commerce and Agriculture, *ibid.*

[14] Frederick Cleveland was highly critical of the uses to which Harding and Dawes put the Bureau of the Budget. See his observations in Frederick Cleveland, "The National Budget," *The Survey*, 15 (August 1922), 604-605.

The Reorganization Vogue

Public administration as a field of study flourished in the years preceding 1920. Students of administration shifted from the local level of government to large-scale problems of the state and national governments, following the lead of the President's Commission on Economy and Efficiency. A notable instance of this development, creating the infrastructure for a discipline, was the establishment, in 1916, of the Institute for Government Research in Washington, with William F. Willoughby as its first director; this was one of the forerunners of the Brookings Institution. Also seeking a larger-scale focus, in 1921 the New York Bureau of Municipal Research renamed itself the National Institute of Public Administration.

A favored enterprise for students of administration was the development of plans for government reorganization. In 1921 a business-sponsored organization, the National Budget Committee, published a plan for federal reorganization that sparked substantial notice, with Columbia University's Academy of Political Science devoting a conference to it. Frederick Cleveland used that occasion to forward his own plan for federal reorganization. At about the same time William Willoughby published his detailed proposals for federal reorganization.[15] As if to stay in fashion, business-sponsored, civic-improvement organizations of the major cities formed study groups on government reorganization. The Federal Reorganization Council, which met regularly at the elite Metropolitan Club of New York, was a leading example of the trend.[16]

Reorganization's vogue in the 1920's was not solely a creation of the field of public administration. Several developments in the business sector joined together to create the vogue and, in turn, present business as a fit model for government. First, it was a decade of substantial prosperity for most Americans.[17] Second, it was a decade which saw

[15] The provisions of the National Budget Committee's plan were published in a pamphlet printed by the committee and titled, "A Proposal for Government Reorganization." Its provisions were incorporated in a bill introduced by Senator Medill McCormick (Rep., Ill.), but no action was taken.

[16] The Federal Reorganization Council was actually something of a peak association in that it included membership by groups interested in reorganization, such as the National Budget Committee and the National Committee for Governmental Efficiency. It attempted to influence government through the involvement of government officials in its activities. Letter, C. T. Cheney to Herbert D. Brown, November 5, 1920, Bureau of Efficiency, 1.01, RG 51, National Archives, Washington, D.C.

[17] See James Prothro, *The Dollar Decade* (Baton Rouge: Louisiana State University Press, 1954).

the full maturation of modern, managerial capitalism, defined by Alfred Chandler, Jr., as the administrative coordination and allocation of elements within the large, multi-unit firm.[18] Third, it was a decade which created the new businessman, the professional manager.

The essence of the decade is captured by Alfred Sloan, Jr., in his memoir of his career at General Motors. Sloan had led in modernizing GM's organizational structure during the 1920's, introducing divisional autonomy. Sloan noted the key difference between managers like himself and the founders of the great industrial firms. Men like Henry Ford and Durant (GM's founder) were gifted with intuition, but they were "without the discipline of management by method and objective fact."[19] They were replaced by a generation of disciplined managers. If business had solved the problem of managing large, multi-unit organizations, why could not government do the same?

Reorganization Planning Redux

Government's postwar expenditure levels virtually assured the creation of another official, comprehensive reorganization planning episode. But what was less predictable was the form and focus such planning would adopt. If it was to be initiated by Congress, the president's role would perhaps be minimized in a return to a 19th-century reform style. But in light of those precedents of presidential authority over administration set by Roosevelt, Taft, and Wilson, could Harding surrender the administrative realm to congressional dominance?

Following the Republican victory in the 1920 election, Congress created a replica of its own 19th-century reorganization planning efforts. By joint resolution in December 1920, it created a Joint Committee on Reorganization which would be composed of three members from each house, one of whom must be a member of the Democratic minority. The senators appointed to the committee were Reed Smoot (Rep., Utah), James Wadsworth (Rep., N.Y.), and Pat Harrison (Dem., Miss.). Its House members were Representatives C. Frank Reavis

[18] Alfred Chandler, Jr., *The Visible Hand: The Managerial Revolution in America* (Cambridge, Mass.: Belknap Press, 1977), Chap. 14. One indication of the enormous impact of the great manufacturing corporation in American life is the fact that between 1899 and 1929 the value of manufactured goods produced in the United States increased by 650 percent. Merle Fainsod, Lincoln Gordon, and Joseph Palamountain, *Government and the American Economy* (3rd ed. rev.; New York: W. W. Norton, 1959), pp. 11-12.

[19] Alfred Sloan, Jr., *My Years with General Motors* (Garden City, N.Y.: Doubleday, Inc., 1962), p. 4. Also see the discussion of organization management in Reinhard Bendix, *Work and Authority in Industry* (New York: Wiley, 1950), pp. 274-288.

(Rep., Neb.), Henry Temple (Rep., Pa.), and Robert W. Moore (Dem., Va.). The Joint Committee was instructed to recommend the distribution of functions among the various agencies "so that each executive department shall embrace only services having close working relations with each other . . . to the end that there shall be achieved the largest possible measure of efficiency and economy."[20]

Congress acted in a presidential vacuum. The incumbent was politically and physically broken and had only a few more months to serve. His successor had not yet expressed any concrete intentions about the direction of his administration, and he gave every appearance of welcoming a return to a dominant congressional role in government. But upon entering office, President Harding asserted a presidential direction over the Joint Committee, and Congress succumbed to his claim of presidential primacy. Even before it began work, the Joint Committee's makeup changed in response to pressures along the fault line between the separated powers in American national government, beginning congressional and then falling under predominantly presidential influence.

The change of the Joint Committee's makeup and focus suggests the beginning of some routinization of a presidential role in executive reorganization by 1921. Routinization, as used here, means the widespread assent among actors in the political system about the proper locus of responsibility for a particular matter. Clearly, executive reorganization had not yet become fully routinized in this sense. However, when President Harding asserted a presidential place in reorganization planning, Congress submitted to an unusual request without any real protest, as if a president's claim to a leading role in reorganization was privileged.

Constituting Reorganization Planning in the Harding Administration

After his inauguration, President Harding informed Senator Reed Smoot, who was serving as chairman of the Joint Committee, that it would be desirable for the President to appoint a representative to the committee. Senator Smoot agreed to seek this revision of the committee's format.[21] In a later meeting, Harding told Smoot that when Congress approved the change, he would appoint Walter F. Brown, a Toledo attorney and a major figure in the Ohio Republican Party, as

[20] Joint Resolution, 66th Congress, 2d Sess., Chap. 7, Sec. 2 (1920).
[21] Letter, Harding to Brown, March 22, 1921, Box 1, Folder 3, Walter F. Brown Papers, Ohio Historical Society, Columbus, Ohio.

his representative. Harding also told Smoot that he wanted his representative to be designated as the committee's chairman.[22] Smoot advised the President that it would be unwise to propose publicly that the presidential representative be chairman, but he agreed to seek that outcome through discussion among the Republican members of the committee.

Senator Smoot's amending resolution concerning the Joint Committee passed both houses in strong party line votes.[23] Republicans expressed no concern with the hybrid they created; Harding was theirs. What Republican could see in him a usurper of legislative prerogative? The Democrats, however, attacked him for exactly that sin. During the discussion of the amending resolution, one Democratic congressman asked why the Republicans "do not have Executive representation on the Appropriations Committee"?[24] Later, when the Congress moved to pass a resolution stipulating that Walter Brown be paid a salary of $7,500 per year, the Democrats conducted what the *New York Times* called the most successful filibuster of the year, stalling but not killing the action.[25]

Harding's request that Brown be the committee's chairman was a particular bone of contention. While that plan had not been made public, it was alluded to by the floor leader for the resolution. The Democrats lambasted their Republican colleagues for violating the separation of powers. Yet what happened here was more than a Republican congressional majority granting the wish of its inoffensive president. Harding's request was motivated by a view of administration as within his domain. That Congress granted his request signals that members were willing to grant that assumption.

Upon entering the presidency, Warren Harding had initiated his own steps toward executive reorganization, independent of the congressional committee. Even while he was negotiating with Senator Smoot about the Joint Committee, the President set his officials to the

[22] Walter Brown was an influential Toledo, Ohio, Republican who had been long associated with the more progressive wing of the party in that state. In that role he had often clashed with Harding, but they had struck a truce which turned into a friendship. Despite that friendship (and perhaps because of it in part), Brown maintained an independent political base in Ohio, as seen by that fact that even as Harding was negotiating Brown's appointment to the Joint Committee, the President was also delicately negotiating with Brown over federal patronage positions in Ohio. Letter, Harding to Brown, May 2, 1921, Box 1, Folder 3, Walter Brown Papers, Ohio Historical Society.

[23] U.S. Congress, *Congressional Record*, Congressional Record, 67th Cong., 1st Sess., 1921, vol. 61, Part 1, 939.

[24] *Ibid.*, p. 942.

[25] *New York Times*, July 27, 1921.

task of planning reorganizations. The President's first assignment in this regard was to his personal physician, Brigadier General Charles E. Sawyer. He asked Sawyer to study the feasibility of a Department of Public Welfare. Within a short time Sawyer reported favorably, and Harding informed him that he would make that major change a part of the overall reform he would recommend to Congress.[26] A second major departmental level reform that interested the President was the idea of a Department of Public Works, which would combine Interior with parts of War and Agriculture. These two notions, along with five other smaller changes in organization, were major topics of discussions in cabinet meetings in Harding's early months in office.[27]

Reorganization was also addressed with fervor by Secretary of Commerce Herbert Hoover. Hoover was one of the stars of the Harding cabinet. In the presidential campaign Harding had promised to appoint "the best minds" to his administration. Hoover, along with Charles Evans Hughes, was meant as a fulfillment of the promise.[28] He was a leading internationalist, a moderate progressive, and an experienced public administrator. Hoover became the administration's strongest proponent of reorganization, saying: "One fundamental necessity stands out above all others, and that is that the administrative units of the Government must be regrouped so as to give each of the great departments more nearly a single purpose."[29] What Hoover espoused in general he applied with focused concentration to his Commerce Department. Within two months of entering the cabinet, he had devised a basic reorganization scheme for the department.

The Reorganization Planners

With Walter Brown as a seventh member, the Joint Committee on Reorganization held its first meeting on May 12, 1921; it is significant

[26] Transcript, testimony of General Charles Sawyer, joint hearings by Senate Committee on Education and Labor and House Committee on Education, May 11, 1921, File 312:1, Roll 197, Warren G. Harding Papers, Ohio Historical Society, Columbus, Ohio. Harding's position is indicated by his statement to Secretary of Labor James Davis: "I have been trying to commit our forces to the creation of a department of public welfare...." Letter, Harding to Davis, April 30, 1921, File 5-1, Roll 197, Harding Papers.

[27] Cabinet briefing paper on reorganization, March 1921, Bureau of Efficiency, 1.01, RG 51, National Archives.

[28] See Robert K. Murray, *The Harding Era* (Minneapolis: University of Minnesota Press, 1966), p. 179. Murray also provides a good overview of the Harding cabinet.

[29] From Hoover's speech to the Federated Engineering Society, quoted in the *New York Times*, April 17, 1921, p. 19.

that this congressional committee met at the White House. Senator James Wadsworth opened the meeting by nominating Brown for the committee's chairmanship. Senator Pat Harrison, a Democrat, argued the impropriety of a presidential appointee as chairman of a congressional committee. But Brown was elected over Harrison's objections.[30] Next, President Harding spoke to the committee about reorganization; efficient administration was impossible without eliminating the hodge-podge organization of the departments and unifying the departments around common purposes.

After hearing the President's comments the committee discussed its work plan. Earlier, Senator Smoot had arranged for the Bureau of Efficiency to perform studies as they would be needed by the committee.[31] The bureau had been created in 1916 by giving independent status to some operations of administrative investigation in the Civil Service Commission that Congress had funded since 1913. The origin of these activities of the Civil Service Commission had been Congress' wish to keep alive activities of the President's Commission. However, unlike the President's Commission, the Bureau of Efficiency was essentially a congressionally oriented operation. Gustavus Weber said of the bureau that it functioned "largely as a direct agent of the legislative branch."[32]

The fact of presidential representation on the committee caused a striking change in its understanding of its work method. At its next meeting, in mid-June 1921, the committee received a statement from President Harding developed in cooperation with his cabinet. In part, it stated:

Since it is extremely difficult to administer efficiently departments which include wholly dissimilar and unrelated services, and quite impossible to administer economically identical or similar services which are scattered throughout several departments, it would seem necessary at the outset of the work of reorganization to provide a statutory regrouping of governmental activities to the end, as far as practicable, that each department shall be made-up of agencies having substantially the same major purpose, and further, that identical or similar services should be grouped together. This task accom-

[30] Minutes, Joint Committee on Reorganization, May 12, 1921, Box 1, Folder 3, Brown Papers.

[31] Memorandum, Herbert Brown to Senator Reed Smoot, January 6, 1921, Bureau of Efficiency, 1.01, RG 51, National Archives.

[32] Gustavus Weber, *Organized Efforts For the Improvement of Methods of Administration in the United States* (New York: Appleton & Co., 1919), p. 111.

plished, the work of eliminating duplication ... and of devising efficient administration for the several departments could then be taken up in logical order. ...[33]

The Joint Committee decided that it was "entirely in accord" with the administration's statement of principle, and it requested the President to design a program for reorganization in consultation with his cabinet and furnish it to the committee.[34] At that, the committee went into hibernation.

When the Joint Committee surrendered its job to President Harding, Walter Brown became Harding's reorganization aide. Unable to staff his planning assistance to President Harding with outsiders due to lack of resources, Walter Brown requested the Bureau of Efficiency for occasional research support. Herbert D. Brown, the bureau's chief, readily assented. While the bureau was tied to congressional concerns, Herbert Brown was an active participant in the overwhelmingly pro-executive reorganization vogue, and as such he was a frequent contributor to conferences and symposia. The Bureau of Efficiency served two masters; the legislature set a large part of its work agenda through the appropriations process while at the same time the agency's top personnel viewed government organization through the executive-centered lenses of the young discipline of public administration. Like a metallic particle caught between opposing magnets, the Bureau of Efficiency moved toward whichever branch made a stronger claim on it, retaining a capacity to speak the administrative language of either the Congress or the executive.[35]

The memoranda prepared by the Bureau of Efficiency in early 1921 reveals its "split personality." But more than that, these documents are interesting because of their indication of a continuing existence of dual conceptions about administration within the government.

The first of these documents is a memorandum dated January 6, 1921, in which Herbert Brown suggested to Senator Smoot a general approach for the work of the Joint Committee on Reorganization (prior to the addition of Walter Brown to the committee). Herbert Brown outlined a micro-administrative approach, entailing a detailed survey of all of government's administrative activities and aiming very specifically at identifying points of possible economies through the

[33] Letter, Harding to Brown, June 11, 1921, Box 1, File 3, Brown Papers.
[34] *Ibid.*
[35] The Bureau of Efficiency was eliminated in 1933 through merger by Executive Order with the Bureau of the Budget. Symbolically, that merger represents the end of a legislative pretension to a capacity to guide administration.

reorganization of those activities. The memorandum suggested the preparation of what it called a "critical statement" which would assess the waste within each activity studied. Nowhere in the bureau's memorandum to Senator Smoot was there a hint of an overall principle of administration guiding its recommendations, unless penuriousness is considered a principle.[36]

The second, contrasting document prepared by the bureau during the same period was a memorandum addressed to the members of the Harding cabinet and dated April 21, 1921. This memorandum presented to the new administration the need for executive reorganization to overcome three "principal defects" in the executive branch. One, the departments contained agencies performing functions extraneous to the departmental purpose. Two, related functions were scattered throughout the departments. Three, government was bereft of "adequate machinery for the control and management of the executive branch as a whole."[37] The bureau's memorandum continued on to identify the cause for the lack of administrative coordination in the executive branch:

> Under the Constitution the President is responsible for the management of the executive branch of the government, but up to the present, Congress has not seen fit to give to the Chief Executive any machinery with which he can effectively discharge this responsibility. The President's staff consists wholly of a small number of personal secretaries and clerks. The time of this staff is taken up with the consideration of legislative business, the preparation of commissions, appointment matters, and so on. Under these conditions the President is . . . unable to function as an administrative officer.[38]

When Walter Brown called upon the Bureau of Efficiency for aid in the preparation of a reorganization plan, he was mobilizing executive-centered assumptions and biases from this curiously two-faced agency capable of serving legislative and executive masters with a different personality for each.

The tone of the administration's reorganization program was set by those who were the direct, regular participants in it. Harding himself favored it but did not have the capacity or focus to shape a vision of

---

[36] Memorandum, Herbert Brown to Senator Smoot, January 6, 1921, Bureau of Efficiency, 1.01, RG 51, National Archives.

[37] Memorandum, Herbert Brown to Postmaster General, April 25, 1921, Bureau of Efficiency, 1.02, RG 51, National Archives.

[38] *Ibid.*

reform.[39] By far the largest influence in shaping the administration's reorganization program was Secretary of Commerce Hoover. He was the member of the administration who was most interested in reorganization. Given that Harding had no well-wrought view of reorganization and that Walter Brown lacked any administrative experience or background in administrative reform, Herbert Hoover loomed over them and his other colleagues in the cabinet by virtue of his administrative credentials. After a career in mine engineering in which he created a major, international consulting firm in that field, Hoover responded to the plight of civilians in occupied Belgium and France during the First World War by organizing a massive organization for the provision of food and medical relief: the Committee for the Aid of Belgium. After American entry into the war, Hoover was appointed as United States Food Administrator by Woodrow Wilson, responsible for food in the mobilization for war.[40]

But Hoover's influence on the administration's reorganization planning cannot be attributed solely to his experience; he was a most influential member of the administration, and Harding esteemed him as one of his wisest advisers.[41] Also, Hoover was closer to Walter Brown than was any other member of the cabinet; prior to Brown's appointment to the Joint Committee, Hoover had offered him the post of solicitor of the Department of Commerce, which Brown had declined in favor of membership on the committee.[42]

Thus several factors gave Hoover the opportunity to advise President Harding in a way that would have been difficult for any aide to fulfill and impossible for the Bureau of Efficiency, because of its ambivalent situation and its distance from the President. An advisory-teaching relationship such as seen in the Taft-Cleveland relationship and as

[39] Harding's view of the presidency was quite unsophisticated. Francis Russell describes him as viewing the office as largely ceremonial and feeling most comfortable with this aspect of it. Undoubtedly this was connected with his fear of being unsuitable for the office. He told Nicholas Murray Butler: "I am not fit for this office and should never have been here." Francis Russell, *The Shadow of Blooming Grove* (New York: McGraw-Hill, 1968), p. 453.

[40] See David Burner, *Herbert Hoover* (New York: Knopf, 1978).

[41] On the breadth of Hoover's role in the administration, see Joan Hoff Wilson, *Herbert Hoover* (Boston: Little, Brown, 1975), pp. 94-95, 108; also see Burner, *Hoover*, pp. 159-189.

[42] While Harding had recommended Brown to Hoover for the job of Commerce's solicitor, Hoover was so impressed by him that he urged Harding to push Brown into accepting the position. Hoover told Harding that he wanted Brown to serve as "one of the real cabinet of the Department of Commerce in determination of its broad policies." Letters, Hoover to Harding, March 8 and April 2, 1921, President Harding, O.F., C.P., Hoover Presidential Library.

developed between Harding and Hoover required a combination of proximity, trust, and the willingness of a president to grant an adviser independent authority.

Hoover was the rare public servant in that he engaged administration at a conceptual level. Throughout his cabinet service (from 1921 through 1927), he spoke and wrote profusely about the need for building competent public organizations. Harold Seidman cites Hoover as the leading representative of "orthodoxy" in administrative theory.[43] In his classic textbook, *Introduction to the Study of Public Administration*, published in 1926, Leonard White adopted a principle of single-purpose departmentalization, relying upon Hoover's defense of the desirability of organization by "major purpose under single headed responsibility."[44]

Herbert Hoover's leverage over reorganization in the Harding administration was enhanced because he had a clear vision of administration. While Hoover is conventionally identified as a conservative, his notion of government organization was anything but the anti-bureaucratic, minimalist view characteristic of modern conservatives.[45] For example, he stressed organizational efficiency rather than sheer economy in his response to the stringent budget policies of both the Harding and Coolidge administrations. He refused to submit easily to what he saw as mindless cuts to the Department of Commerce's services. He argued that his department and others were engaged in "reproductive" activities in the sense that their actions benefited society out of proportion to their costs. In 1923, protesting another wave of attempted reductions in appropriation requests, Hoover wrote to Coolidge: "The country will welcome a statement from you that in these matters reduction is the worst sort of national economy and that real economy lies in building up our national assets. . . ."[46]

The Harding administration's reorganization planning endeavor began on mixed grounds, without a decisive choice made between opposing conceptions of administration, economy versus efficiency. Both values were present. Congress had created the Joint Committee and

[43] Harold Seidman, *Politics, Position and Power* (2nd ed.; New York: Oxford University Press, 1975), Chap. 1.

[44] Leonard White, *Introduction to the Study of Public Administration* (New York: Macmillan, 1926), p. 66.

[45] I have addressed the contrast between Hoover and most of current American conservatism on matters of administration and organization in Peri E. Arnold, "The Great Engineer as Bureaucrat: Herbert Hoover and Modern Bureaucracy," *Review of Politics* 42 (July 1980), 329-348.

[46] Letter, Hoover to President Coolidge, November 5, 1923, President, O.F., C.P., Hoover Presidential Library.

a president who had been nurtured by that Congress was responsible for formulating a plan. Against that tendency, Herbert Hoover, a handful of organizational experts in the Bureau of Efficiency, and the growingly influential body of ideas of public administration portrayed reorganization as a means for improving government's performance. How would the tension between competing approaches be resolved? The answer lies in the politics of reorganization planning during the Harding administration.

The Politics of Reorganization Planning

It was politics and not administrative theories that occupied Walter Brown's attention as he began to assemble the administration's reorganization plan. The administration's first several months were filled with political jockeying amongst the agencies aiming to protect or enlarge their domain. For example, Philander Claxton, the Commissioner of Education, actively lobbied Congress for a cabinet-level department of education, an idea opposed by President Harding. In a surprising expression of strength, Harding asked for and received Claxton's resignation, but this case was distinguished only by the brazenness of the lobbying effort.

As Brown began the planning task, he impressed upon Harding the importance of controlling bureaucratic lobbying; it would destroy any chance for reorganization before the plan for a reform was even completed. On June 14th, President Harding informed the department heads that he would dismiss any bureau chief who used Congress to work against reorganization.[47]

Walter Brown began by specifying a research agenda for the Bureau of Efficiency; he requested that it prepare reports on thirteen specific agencies as well as on the administration of overseas territories, on the federal role in radio communications, and on federal activities in education. Most of these reports were completed during the summer of 1921.[48] His next step was to direct the cabinet-level departments to formulate their own reorganization proposals. This, of course, threatened to further stoke bureaucratic-political conflicts. It is one thing to expect the members of the cabinet to agree on principles, but it is quite another matter to gain agreement on the concrete changes to be instituted. Principles of efficient organization premise a universe in which organizational units can be shifted about to match an abstract, deductive blueprint. But in the real world, organizational po-

---

[47] *New York Times*, June 15, 1921.

[48] Memorandum, "Progress of Work for the Joint Committee on Reorganization," July 18, 1921, Bureau of Efficiency, 1.01, RG 51, National Archives.

sition has political importance, and structural changes disrupt carefully nurtured alliances which protect agencies.[49]

A most important feature of the planning process instituted by Walter Brown was that it occurred in the absence of a disinterested planning center for addressing politically charged matters. Recall the concerns in the Taft administration that reorganization planning be conducted at some remove from the agencies. The planning format adopted by Brown did not provide that independence, and the departments themselves became the primary forum for planning. Those most interested in the outcome of reorganization planning were invited to do the planning. This opposite approach to Taft's threatened to be disablingly conflictual.

The period of most concentrated departmental planning activity was the last half of 1921. During this exercise, Walter Brown served as a combined consultant and referee. In particular, he had to step into the role of referee among members of the cabinet. The most aggressive department in this process was Commerce. Hoover began planning for reorganization of Commerce early.[50] The plan that he created was grandiose; not only would the organization of the existing Department of Commerce be changed but chunks of the Departments of the Interior, Agriculture, Treasury, State, War, and Labor would be added to it. Hoover's intention for Commerce was to transform it into the center of government's activity regarding industry, trade, and transportation. He envisioned a departmental reorganization that would create three separate divisions, one for each of these broad areas. In the reorganization plan that Secretary Hoover presented to the President, all or part of seventeen bureaus were identified for transfer to Commerce along with parts of two independent commissions.[51]

Following the preparation of reorganization plans by the departments, Brown envisioned a period of rational discussion and agreement from which an overall reorganization plan for the executive branch

[49] The view of organization is derived from the institutional school of organization theory, which has made the greatest contribution from among the range of work on organizations to our understanding of the relationship between the functions of organizations and their political settings. A leading example of this approach is Phillip Selznick, *TVA and the Grass Roots* (Berkeley: University of California Press, 1949). A classic statement on positional politics in bureaucracy is Norton Long, "Power and Administration," *Public Administration Review* (Autumn 1949): 257-264.

[50] Secretary Hoover sketched an outline of a reorganization plan for Commerce in a letter to Elliot Goodwin, an official of the Chamber of Commerce, May 16, 1921, U.S. Chamber of Commerce, O.F., C.P., Hoover Presidential Library.

[51] Letter, Hoover to Walter Brown, October 20, 1921, File #80553/4, RG 40, National Archives; Memorandum, Hoover to Brown, December 8, 1921, Misc'l-1921, O.F., C.P., Hoover Presidential Library.

would be formulated. Necessarily, because it was by far the most ambitious of the departments' plans, Commerce's proposals held center stage as Brown attempted to manage these negotiations. Also, they received the most attention because these plans fit the spirit of the administration as one dedicated to fostering prosperity. That they were Hoover's plans gave them legitimacy that no other department's proposals could have had.

However, obtaining agreement on Hoover's recommendations was a very different problem. In December, Walter Brown assured Secretary Hoover that it would be possible to recommend to Congress his suggested transfers of relatively small units dealing with surveys and research from War and Navy to Commerce, but Hoover's hopes for major acquisitions from Interior, Agriculture, and Labor ran into deep resistance.[52] Hoover desired to move the U.S. Land Office and the Geologic Survey from Interior, the Bureau of Markets and the Bureau of Public Roads from Agriculture, and the Bureau of Labor Statistics from Labor. These departments had substantial political constituencies and a capacity to launch trenchant defenses of their organizational integrity.[53]

By the first month of 1922 all of the departments had submitted to Walter Brown their own plans for reorganization, and he began to shape the overall plan that would go to the Joint Committee. Brown's first effort incorporated many of Hoover's recommendations, but omitted any transfers to Commerce from Interior or Labor. But for all of its spirited defence, the Department of Agriculture suffered heavily in the plan, with recommendations that the Bureau of Markets go to Commerce and that the Forest Service be shifted to Interior.

Beyond these decisions that came with more or less negotiation with the cabinet members, the plan contained several decisions that were made independently by President Harding and Brown without being proposed by cabinet members. These were recommendations for a wholly new department, Education and Welfare; a merged and renamed department, Defense; and an expanded and renamed department, Communications.[54]

[52] Letter, Walter Brown to Hoover, December 8, 1921, Bureau of Efficiency, O.F., C.P., Hoover Presidential Library.

[53] For example, heated protests came to the administration concerning the possible diminution of Agriculture. A case in point is Letter, A. F. Woods to Walter Brown, October 10, 1921, Reorganization-General #1, 21.1, RG 51, National Archives; Letter and press release, Agricultural Legislative Committee of California to Hoover, January 17, 1922, Reorganization of Government Departments, O.F., C.P., Hoover Presidential Library.

[54] Memorandum, Walter Brown to Harding, January 21, 1922, Box 1, Folder 4, Brown Papers.

A Defense Department as well as an Education and Welfare Department were recommended in two of the more prestigious private reorganization plans of the period.[55] Also, both of these ideas had been on the agenda of Taft's commission a decade earlier, although the defense proposal was not formalized prior to the commission's death. That these cabinet-level reforms had a good lineage may have masked their political dangers. Walter Brown was a newcomer to Washington. He exhibited more than a little naivete in his remark in defense of this initial plan of reorganization: "I am convinced that substantial success can be attained only by first determining a sound principle . . . and then following wherever that principle leads."[56]

With the plan completed, President Harding opened it for discussion in the cabinet. Two major elements came in for the most criticism, a unified Defense Department and the transfer of the Forest Service (to Interior). The former violated the long traditions of cabinet-level representation for the military services. The latter pricked sensitivities that went back to the Glavis-Ballinger dispute of the Taft administration and the recollection that Interior was an undependable trustee of the nation's forests.[57]

President Harding was caught in a deadlock by the cabinet opposition. He wanted to support the plan, but he appeared incapable of forcefully defending a position. In regard to the proposed merger of War and Navy, he told Navy Secretary Edwin Denby: "I do not know . . . what recommendation will be made to the Joint Commission [sic]. . . . there are many advantages to be gained by amalgamation. I can see numerous objections. . . ."[58] The cabinet could not make a final decision on the plan because the President was unwilling to press for that decision. The *New Republic*'s pre-inaugural prediction for Harding seemed accurate: "The new President will prefer harmony, but he will not know how to get it."[59]

The opposition to a merged War and Navy was mild compared to the reaction to transferring the Forest Service. After all, the defense idea was sensible; it had been around for over a decade in discussions

---

[55] National Budget Committee, *Proposal for Government Reorganization* (New York: National Budget Committee, 1920); W. F. Willoughby, *Reorganization of the Administrative Branch of the National Government* (Washington: Brookings Institution, 1923).

[56] Memorandum, Walter Brown to Harding, January 21, 1922, Box 1, File 4, Brown Papers.

[57] See Wayne Rasmussen and Gladys Baker, *The Department of Agriculture* (New York: Praeger, 1972), Chap. 10.

[58] Letter, Harding to Derby, January 12, 1922, file 303-3, roll 196, Harding Papers.

[59] *New Republic*, November 10, 1920, quoted in Andrew Sinclair, *The Available Man* (New York: Macmillan, 1965), p. 177.

of federal departmental reorganization, and it was difficult to attack on any ground but that of the separate traditions of the services. On the contrary, the proposal to shift the Forest Service flew in the face of the interests of a strong clientele department, Agriculture, and it dredged up the old hash about the mismanagement of the national forests when they were in the care of the Interior, prior to 1905. Thus while the administration had only to cope with a relatively late developing and narrow (even if intense) opposition to the Defense merger, it had an explosive and broad response to the Forest Service proposal. At the height of the controversy, Gifford Pinchot, the founder of the Forest Service, publicly denounced the threatened move as a veiled attempt to return the forests into the hands of those who would use them selfishly.[60] Secretary of the Interior Albert Fall did not help matters as he criticized the Forest Service for discouraging economic development, particularly in the Alaskan forest reserves.[61]

Four months after the cabinet began considering the reorganization plan, the administration was still no closer to resolving its own central conflicts in reorganization planning. This indecision continued into the fall of 1922. The break came with the congressional election of 1922; the Republican Party took a significant defeat, losing seventy-nine seats in the House and reducing its House majority to twelve. After the election, Charles Dawes, who had left the administration after a year as budget director, publicly attacked the cabinet for dragging its feet on reorganization.[62] The implicit thrust of Dawes's point was that unless the Republican administration acted decisively, the GOP would lose power. Responding to Secretary of War Sinclair Weeks's complaints to him about Dawes's attack, President Harding admitted that the administration had to act. He told Weeks that he was due shortly to report to the full Joint Committee on Reorganization, and he wrote: "I do . . . hope to make some report . . . I think it is desirable to make some show of progress toward reorganization."[63]

---

[60] See the letter by Pinchot, *New York Times*, December 23, 1921, and editorial, December 24, 1921. Also see the *Times* editorial, "A Menace to Forestry," December 15, 1921.

[61] *New York Times*, March 12, 1922.

[62] Dawes spoke to the National Budget Committee on October 13, 1922; his comments about the cabinet and Congress were so politically charged that they were the next day's headlines and the subject of glowing editorials on the following days. *New York Times*, October 14, 1922; *New York Herald*, October 15, 1922.

[63] Letter, Harding to Sinclair Weeks, November 28, 1922, file 303, roll 196, Harding Papers. Francis Russell wrote that the 1922 election results forced Harding to an increased level of activity. F. Russell, *The Shadow of Blooming Grove*, pp. 551-553.

The cabinet members could no longer stall the administration's major reform effort. Harding pushed his reorganization plan through the cabinet on December 13, 1922. The following day he met with the Joint Committee and announced that his plan would be quickly forthcoming. However, he confessed to the committee that he had not achieved unanimous cabinet support for it. After a year and a half that the administration had been working on a reorganization plan, the secretaries of War, Navy, Agriculture, and Interior remained opposed to parts of it.[64] In fact, the cabinet bickering over reorganization continued, and Harding did not supply the Joint Committee with his plan of reorganization recommendations until February 13, 1923. In the interim, the President made adjustments to reduce opposition by Agriculture and Interior. It was decided to leave the Bureau of Markets in Agriculture. Also, there were a number of last-minute additions in the plan aimed at strengthening Interior, particularly in its public works role.

The Administration's Reorganization Plan

Despite late changes, the overall plan the administration presented to the Joint Committee on Reorganization in early 1923 was the plan prepared by Walter Brown for the President. The recommendation for a Department of Defense remained in it as did the recommendation for a Department of Education and Welfare. Commerce remained the department that would benefit most from comprehensive reorganization.

At first glance the administration's plan was a mix of vogue and politics. The recommended new departments could not be understood as politically motivated. If anything, the reforms would create controversy, but they were legitimated by the contemporary mood about reorganization. Emboldened by a post-1922 conviction to lead, Harding embraced that mood and decided to push ahead with broad recommendations.

Other of the administration's recommendations were politically viable. For example, the expansion of the Department of Commerce was supported widely in the business community. On the other side of the coin, the Department of Labor was slated to lose the Women's Bureau and the Children's Bureau to the new Education and Welfare Department. Earlier, Labor had been left unscathed in the plans, but by early 1923 organized labor as a political force had diminished

[64] *New York Times*, December 14, 15, 1922.

within the administration. During 1922 protracted coal and railroad strikes had led President Harding to view its leadership as obdurate. In addition, the Labor Department's secretary, James J. Davis, was by far the weakest member of the Harding cabinet.[65]

The leitmotif of the administration's plan was increased presidential strength. Three elements in the plan speak to that end. First, it proposed that the Bureau of the Budget be transferred from its location in Treasury to be attached directly to the presidency.[66] It also proposed that the General Accounting Office be transferred from independent status (aligned with Congress) and placed into the Treasury.[67] This transfer of the Bureau of the Budget was consistent with the role played by that bureau; it was understood to be a presidential agency. What was radical about the recommendation was the treatment of the General Accounting Office, an agency that was created to protect Congress' power of the purse as a new budget authority was bestowed on the presidency. The administration's plan would end that independent congressional counterbalance to presidential budgeting and spending powers. The defence for the recommended transfer was that the G.A.O.s operation ought to be "amenable to the control of the President."[68]

A second presidency-strengthening element of the administration's reorganization plan was its adoption of the principle of organization by purpose. The logic behind the recommendations for a unified Defense Department, a Department of Education and Welfare, and the expansion of Commerce, along with most of the smaller changes, was the purification of organizational purposes. The purpose of reorganization was to make departments more manageable from the top. Writing at the same time that the Harding administration was preparing its reorganization plan, William F. Willoughby described the virtues of departmental reorganization by purpose:

> It correlates the several operating services of the government into one highly integrated and unified piece of administrative mechanism;

[65] Francis Russell, *The Shadow of Blooming Grove*, pp. 536-548; Andrew Sinclair, *The Available Man*, pp. 186-187.

[66] The evidence is that this transfer was urged on Harding by Hoover. Letter, Hoover to Harding, May 11, 1921, President Harding, May-June 1921, Hoover Presidential Library.

[67] On the beginnings of the General Accounting Office and its legislative history, wherein the question of independent status against Treasury location was debated, see Frederic C. Mosher, *The GAO: The Quest for Accountability in American Government* (Boulder: Westview, 1979), pp. 43-61.

[68] "Memorandum Describing the Reorganization Plan Recommended by the President and his Cabinet," December 19, 1923, Box 11, Folder 5, Brown Papers, p. 80.

it ensures the establishment of an effective system of overhead administration and control; it makes definite the line of administrative authority and responsibility. . . .[69]

To reorganize the departments was to rationalize their organization, and rationalized organizations were assumed to be more easily surveyed, understood, and directed from the top.

A third presidency-strengthening element of the administration's reorganization plan was its conception of the need for a continuing presidential reorganization authority; this went to the heart of an executive-centered view of administrative organization. The desirability of presidential discretion to initiate reorganization follows from the premise that the president is responsible for administration. This issue was most sensitive since it treaded upon congressional sensibilities. Thus the administration's reorganization plan did not put this matter into a direct recommendation. Instead, the memorandum explaining the recommendations closed with a statement that constituted an informal recommendation that reorganization authority be vested in the president:

The mere shifting of executive agencies from one department to another will of itself be of little benefit. The real reorganization must come later, as the result of executive action. . . . This authority should be comprehensive enough to permit the transfer of work from one departmental subdivision to another, the elimination of agencies which may be found superfluous, and the consolidation of agencies whose work can best be performed under single direction.[70]

CONGRESS AS REORGANIZATION PLANNER: THE JOINT COMMITTEE REAPPEARS

After receiving the administration's plan, the Joint Committee for Reorganization was responsible for presenting recommendations to Congress. But three factors rooted in different strata of legislative politics impeded the committee's work; these suggest how difficult a task reorganization planning poses for the Congress. The first factor was within the committee. This was discernible early on, with the Democratic attack on the inclusion of a presidential representative. Partisan conflict was aggravated by the process of reorganization planning in the administration and further by the political possibilities

[69] W. F. Willoughby, *Reorganization of the Administrative Branch of the National Government*, p. 10.

[70] "Memorandum Describing the Reorganization Plan Recommended by the President and His Cabinet," pp. 83-84.

raised by the Republican defeats in the 1922 election. In the aftermath of the 1922 election, the committee's Democratic senator, Pat Harrison, denounced Walter Brown for ignoring the Joint Committee and violating what he claimed was the operating assumption that anything Brown did within the administration would be discussed in the committee. Instead, Harrison charged, the reorganization planning process had been monopolized by the administration with Brown's cooperation.[71]

A second factor impeding the Joint Committee was rooted in a deeper stratum of legislative politics, that point at which bureaucratic interests intermesh with legislative interests and create political support for what Anthony Downs calls "bureau territoriality."[72] Agencies defend their responsibilities and organizational position as animals defend territory. Typically, agencies can call on supporters among interest groups and within Congress for aid. Thus when the administration's recommendations were given to the Joint Committee, the conflicts that had been papered over in the cabinet broke out again in a new arena.

A third factor coloring the Joint Committee's work was the separation of powers. Originally, Congress had created the Joint Committee on Reorganization in anticipation of it formulating recommendations for making government more economical. Now, through an unanticipated process, presidential domination of a congressional initiative, a plan was emerging which invoked executive control values instead of governmental economy. Principles more than substance triggered congressional opposition to the administration's plan.

The administration's reorganization plan became a political problem for the Joint Committee. Yet, at the same time, it was stuck with the process it had created, and the presidential plan was a product of that process. After the Harding plan had been given to the committee on February 16, 1923, not one of its Republican members publicly defended it. Back in 1921, when the Joint Committee was created, Senator Reed Smoot had declared a target figure of $300,000,000 in

---

[71] *New York Times*, November 16, 1922. That Senator Harrison's attack was not simply hyperbole can be seen in a memo written by the budget bureau's counsel, C. W. Collis, profiling the background and activities of the Joint Committee, as of May 1923. He wrote: "The Joint Committee itself has made no report whatever and apparently has never met for the consideration of the question of reorganization." Memorandum, Collis to Lord, May 14, 1923, Reorganization-General #1, 21.1, R11, RG 51, National Archives.

[72] Anthony Downs, *Inside Bureaucracy* (Boston: Little, Brown, 1967), pp. 212-216.

savings that he expected the committee's work to produce.[73] Having publicly committed himself to an economy-oriented reorganization program, how could Senator Smoot regard the administration plan's disregard for economy *per se?*

Warren Harding's death in August 1923 and Calvin Coolidge's succession to the presidency threw into doubt the prospect of continued leadership in executive reorganization; Coolidge's positions on reorganization in general and the Harding plan in particular were unknown. While Coolidge did embrace most of his predecessor's reorganization plan, he reopened some of the cabinet-level conflict that Harding had earlier overridden. In late October, President Coolidge informed his cabinet officers that he was not pleased with the proposal to merge War and Navy. Finally, in his State of the Union Message, he gave his approval to the plan, with the exception of the proposed Department of Defense and several minor details.[74] But the fact that Coolidge devoted only a couple of sentences of his message to the subject of reorganization signalled more about his interest in the committee's work than the substance of those sentences.

The Joint Committee began its hearings in January 1924, providing a forum for airing the cabinet opposition to features of the Harding plan. There was a string of witnesses to denounce the proposed merger of War and Navy. Also, Secretary of Interior Hubert Work appeared to attack the proposed transfers from his department. Outrightly flaunting the plan, Work proposed a reorganization of Interior that would include a new division of public welfare. Secretary Mellon also appeared, attacking the proposed transfer of the Bureau of the Budget from Treasury; Mellon argued his position on the basis of organizational coherence, demonstrating that administrative theory's sword had two edges. Even a recommendation so simple as the slight expansion and renaming of the Post Office was attacked by Postmaster General New.[75]

Under Coolidge the reorganization episode had lost its energy. Harding was not an activist president, but Coolidge was even more passive. Furthermore, Harding had been motivated about reorganization by two men he trusted, Hoover and Walter Brown. Coolidge was not close to either man. Finally, the parade of Coolidge administration officials testifying negatively before the Joint Committee about a reorganization plan that President Coolidge had endorsed demonstrates

[73] *New York Herald,* April 24, 1921.

[74] *New York Times,* October 27, 1923.

[75] U.S. Congress, Joint Committee on the Reorganization of the Administrative Branch of the Government, *Hearings,* 68th Cong., 1st Sess., 1924.

that the President was exercising no discipline. The appearance was that reorganization was of no importance to him.

The Joint Committee was in a politically difficult position. With melting presidential support, there was little chance that a major reorganization program would find support in Congress. Yet the committee had no leeway; it had tied itself to a presidential reorganization plan as the foundation for its own recommendations. The unexpectedly long gestation period for the Harding plan further limited the committee's freedom. It had to obtain an extension of its reporting date simply to have time for hearings. The committee had no time for creating an alternative plan, and, anyway, it lacked the staff for such a task. Finally, the Republican Party had promised major administrative reorganization since 1920, and 1924 was an election year. The Joint Committee was the instrument through which the party had to appear to be taking seriously the project of comprehensive reorganization.[76]

The weight of time, resource scarcity, political considerations, and its own procedures forced the committee to report to Congress recommendations that looked much like the Harding plan. But the impetus behind such an outcome involved more than muddling through. Even while the administration now seemed uncertain about the plan, the most prestigious voices concerning administration, both inside and outside the administration, weighed heavily in favor of it. Most notably, Herbert Hoover and W. F. Willoughby gave fervently supportive testimony in front of the Joint Committee.[77]

In early summer 1924 the committee reported to Congress.[78] Its recommendations were the Harding plan less the proposed merger of War and Navy. Congress had created the Joint Committee on Reorganization to achieve "the largest possible measure of efficiency and

[76] In its 1920 platform, the GOP stated: "We advocate a thorough investigation of the present organization of the Federal departments and bureaus, with a view to securing consolidation, a more business-like distribution of functions, the elimination of duplication, delays and overlapping of work and the establishment of an up-to-date and efficient administrative organization."

In its 1924 platform, more specifically, the GOP stated: "We favor a comprehensive reorganization . . . along the lines of a plan recently submitted by a joint committee of the Congress which has the unqualified support of President Coolidge."

Kirk Porter and Donald Johnson (eds.), *National Party Platforms: 1840-1956* (Urbana: University of Illinois Press, 1956), pp. 233, 259.

[77] U.S. Congress, Joint Committee on the Reorganization of the Administrative Branch of the Goverment, *Hearings*, pp. 86, 349.

[78] Senate Document No. 128, U.S. *Congressional Record*, 68th Cong., 1st Sess., 1924, vol. 65, part 10, 10,248-10,271.

economy." The recommendations reported in 1924 did not explicitly fulfill this goal of economy. How did the Joint Committee present and justify its recommended plan?

The committee's report identified three central problems of the executive branch: "First, the presence . . . of bureaus . . . which perform functions having little or no apparent relation to the major departmental purposes; second, the maintenance by two or more departments of agencies which do work in the same . . . fields of activity; and third, the existence of a considerable number of government agencies outside the ten executive departments."[79] Would the correction of these conditions produce a reduction in federal expenditures? Would their elimination produce better management in the executive branch?

While the Joint Committee's report carefully avoided choosing between a straightforward economy approach and a managerial perspective, it could not avoid the appearance of having made a choice for the managerial perspective, given the fact that the Harding plan had a strong executive thrust and basically disregarded the possibility of expenditure reduction. Thus the committee could not fulfill its mandate by specifying to Congress the amount of money that could be saved by adoption of these recommendations. In its discussion of the consequences of the problems it had diagnosed within the executive branch, the committee's report signals the degree to which a managerial perspective informs its plan.

Three observations in the report suggest the consequences of the problems identified; they all concern good management. First, in discussing departments containing unrelated functions, the report observed that effective supervision becomes difficult.[80] Second, the report noted that overlapping functions cause wasteful duplication of work. This apparently concerns economy, but the committee added a strong caveat here: it is not easy to separate necessary from wasteful duplication. Good administration may require some duplication. Third, the report observed that the large number of independent agencies led to unsupervised and uncoordinated activities; in cases where the independent agency performs similar functions or works "in the same direction" as a department, the committee recommended that it be transferred to that department. Exception was made for the quasi-judicial aspects of independent commissions.[81]

The fact that the essentially executive spirit of the Harding plan was

[79] *Ibid.*, p. 10,255.
[80] *Ibid.*
[81] *Ibid.*

unchanged while the plan itself was transmuted into the proposals of a congressional committee shines through in the report's last recommendation; it is lifted almost verbatim from the memorandum prepared to accompany the Harding report. The Joint Committee concluded: "The real reorganization must come later, as the result of executive action."[82] Thus the committee embraced a preliminary form of the idea of presidential reorganization authority.

That the Joint Committee had not fulfilled Congress' original intent for it did not go unremarked. In a minority report, the committee's two Democratic members observed: "It has become evident that the expectation of reaching results which would bring about any considerable economies will not be realized."[83] It may have been that many members of Congress of both parties shared this view, for, despite Republican Party platform promises, the proposals lay untouched by the Congress. Without the promise of real economy, there was no incentive for Congress to pass these reforms into law. And lacking crisis, why would Congress strengthen the president as a manager?

An answer to this question had been evolving among those dedicated to executive enhancing reorganization. Executive reorganization was simply not politically viable as long as it was starkly a means for shifting the center of administrative authority away from Congress and toward the presidency. Beginning with Frederick Cleveland, the supporters of an enhanced presidential managerial capacity argued that real reorganization would enhance the Congress' capacity to make informed policy choices at the same time that it rendered the President more capable. Congress' traditional role in administration was one of detailed control. The reorganizers' response was that what might appear as a weakening of legislative authority was really an enhancement of the legislative role because effective management would present Congress with greater information, clearer choices, and full disclosure of the consequence of those choices. As Herbert Hoover said in his testimony to the Joint Committee, the savings that might result from reorganization were not nearly as important as the coherence that reorganization would lend government: "Whatever these reductions of expenditure may be they are not . . . as important as the . . . ability of Congress to handle expenditures with better comprehension and long view policies."[84]

[82] *Ibid.*, p. 10,261.

[83] *Ibid.*

[84] U.S. Congress, Joint Committee on the Reorganization of the Government, *Hearings*, p. 349.

The Fate of the Joint Committee's Recommendations

None of the Joint Committee's large-scale recommendations were given serious consideration by Congress, and between 1924 and 1927 only a few of the bureau-level changes recommended by it were effected. These attest to the political influence of Herbert Hoover, for the most important bureau-level changes took place in the Department of Commerce.[85]

But to assess the importance of this episode of comprehensive reorganization planning, it must be placed within the context afforded by its predecessor planning efforts in the Taft administration and the reorganization effort addressed in the next chapter: the attempts at administrative reform under the New Deal. The efforts of the 1920's are grounded in a developing tradition or "school" of administrative thought. An overall view of the problems of large government and the need for centralizing guidance to administration become the themes of reorganization planning.

The obvious difference between the recommendations of the President's Commission and the Joint Committee was that the former stressed the executive budget while that reform was an accomplished fact for the latter. However, both planning enterprises saw the rationalization of department organization as a necessary step in making government amendable to management, and both pointed to the necessity for strengthening the president's staff resources as a means for providing the presidency with managerial reach. The President's Commission's version of this was its recommendation for a presidential bureau of administrative control; the Joint Committee addressed this matter with its recommendation for the transfer of the Bureau of the Budget from Treasury to a direct organizational connection to the president.

Looking ahead into the 1930's, one finds equally strong continuities. There is a shift in tone between the 1924 report of the Joint Committee and the 1937 report of the Brownlow committee. But underneath that shift remains a strong, steady focus on the managerial centrality of the presidency in the executive branch, and the Brownlow report shares in the continuity of concerns with budgeting, departmental organization, and presidential staff resources.

---

[85] Two major agencies were transferred from Interior to Commerce in 1925; both transfers had been suggested by the Joint Committee's 1924 report and had been in the Harding plan. Interestingly, both transfers were effected through executive orders. On March 19, the Patent Office was transferred to Commerce, and on June 3 the Bureau of Mines was moved to the same department.

To place the comprehensive reorganization planning of the 1920's into this larger context shows its meaning and importance beyond the short-term failure of its recommendations. There are several characteristics of the Harding administration-Joint Committee episode which demarcate its individual importance and its contribution to the evolution of a managerial conception of the presidency. First, the similarities between this episode's perspective and that of the earlier President's Commission suggest that reorganization in the 1920's served a routinizing role in the development of an intellectual-political structure of reorganization planning within the executive branch. That the planning episode of the 1920's began as an economizing congressional initiative and became a presidentially-oriented planning exercise makes the experience a positive test for the routinization of comprehensive reorganization.[86] In repeating the presidency-enhancing patterns of the President's Commission, the planning episode of the 1920's established comprehensive executive reorganization as a major weapon in the modern presidency's managerial armory.

Connected to this process of routinization is a second important characteristic of this episode of the 1920's. As it reflects the routinization of a set of perspectives on management and reform in the executive branch, so it also served to carry forward a set of specific values and recommendations about administration in the executive branch. In light of this episode of the 1920's, a continuing reorganization agenda appears to be developing, offering a menu of reform to the future. Finally, the reorganization effort of the 1920's taught that Congress cannot plan reorganization, although that lesson would be hard for some members to retain.

[86] Undoubtedly an important stage in the routinization of comprehensive reorganization planning was its wide adoption as a reform tool for state governments during the decade after the work of Taft's Commission on Economy and Efficiency. See A. E. Burk, *Reorganization of State Governments in the United States* (New York: Columbia University Press, 1938). For an excellent recent analysis of the variety of experiences of the states with comprehensive reorganization, see James Garnett, *Reorganizing State Government* (Boulder: Westview, 1980).

Chapter Four

MANAGING THE NEW DEAL: REORGANIZATION AND THE PROBLEM OF PRESIDENTIAL GOVERNANCE

"The President needs help."[1]
Brownlow Committee

Executive reorganization had different purposes at different parts of the New Deal. It was first used to economize, and only later was it used for managerial ends. But what distinguished the use of executive reorganization planning in the New Deal was that it was thoroughly a presidential tool. For the first time in the history of reorganization planning, its goals were those imposed solely by a president. For this autonomy Franklin Roosevelt was indebted to the developing tradition of reorganization planning.

THE THREAD OF REORGANIZATION

In his first annual message President Hoover argued that there is "no hope for . . . sound reorganization . . . unless Congress be willing to delegate authority . . . to the Executive. . . ."[2] During the 1932 presidential campaign Hoover spoke repeatedly about reorganization, mentioning it in two dozen of his messages and speeches.[3] Accentuating Hoover's long-standing interest in reorganization was its potential for addressing problems posed by the Great Depression. In that pre-Keynesian era it was assumed that government ought to restrict spending during an economic downturn.[4] But, Hoover was caught between

[1] President's Committee on Administrative Management, *Report* (Washington: Government Printing Office, 1937), p. 5.

[2] *Public Papers of the Presidents: Herbert Hoover, 1929* (Washington: Government Printing Office, 1974), p. 432.

[3] Louis Fisher and Ronald Moe, "Delegating With Ambivalence: The Legislative Veto and Reorganization Authority," in Congressional Research Service, *Studies on the Legislative Veto* (Washington: Government Printing Office, 1980), p. 173.

[4] Herbert Stein, *The Fiscal Revolution in America* (Chicago: University of Chicago Press, 1969), p. 173. For an excellent and salient discussion of change in theoretical frameworks in economics, see John Hicks, "Revolutions in Economics," in Hicks (ed.), *Classics and Moderns* (Cambridge, Mass: Harvard University Press, 1983), pp. 3-16.

reduced revenues and increased expenditures. Seeing political advantage as early as June 1930, Franklin Roosevelt attacked Hoover for government's deficits.[5]

In the mid-1920's Hoover had identified economy as a minor goal for reorganization, but with few other available tools, it would have to serve that end. Hoover asked Congress to grant reorganization authority to the president, and Congress did so in the Economy Act of 1932.[6] The act gave the president permanent reorganization authority, subject to veto by either house of Congress within sixty days of an executive order for reorganization. No departments could be created nor renamed under these provisions. Hoover's first chance to use the reorganization authority came after his electoral defeat. In December 1932 he sent to the lame-duck Congress orders effecting changes in fifty-eight governmental activities.[7] Many of these changes enacted recommendations of the Joint Committee. But the House of Representatives vetoed the defeated President's executive orders. Hoover's reaction was strong and prophetic; he told Congress:

> Either Congress must keep its hands off now or they must give to my successor much larger powers of independent action than given to any President if there is ever to be reorganization. And that authority to be effective should be free of the limitations in the law passed last year which gives Congress the veto power, which prevents the abolition of functions, which prevents the rearrangement of major Departments. Otherwise, it will, as is now being demonstrated in the present law, again be merely make believe.[8]

In effect, Congress granted Hoover's criticism, amending the presidential reorganization authority in the Economy Act of 1933.[9] Passed after Roosevelt's inauguration, the act limited the congressional veto by requiring that it be invoked through a bill of disapproval. Thus the instrument of veto had to pass both houses and was subject itself to presidential veto.

Franklin Roosevelt turned this generous grant of authority to picayune purposes. In the campaign he said: "We can make savings by

[5] Frank Freidel, *Franklin D. Roosevelt: The Triumph* (Boston: Little, Brown, 1956), pp. 138-140.

[6] 47 Stat. L. 413-15.

[7] U.S. Congress, *Congressional Record*, 76th Cong., 2d Sess., 1932, vol. 76, part 2, 2,254.

[8] *Public Papers of the Presidents, Herbert Hoover, 1932-33*, "Statement About Reorganization of the Executive Branch," January 3, 1933, p. 923.

[9] 47 Stat. L. 1519.

reorganization of existing departments, by eliminating functions, by abolishing many of those innumerable boards. . . ."[10] In an executive order of June 10, 1933, Roosevelt specified a number of small changes, most of which had been prepared by the director of the Bureau of the Budget, Lewis Douglas. These reforms differed markedly from those that Hoover had earlier proposed. Whereas Hoover's aimed at organization by purpose, Roosevelt's order was a grab bag of small organizational changes. It abolished some minor commissions, cut back the Department of Commerce, and reduced support to the extension operations of the Department of Agriculture.[11] Three months after entering the presidency, Franklin Roosevelt boasted that he had saved a "billion dollars . . . through lopping off of functions."[12] Of course, while claiming these savings, Roosevelt was spending new billions on the emergency programs which were the main focus of his attentions. Through this expansion of government's activities the President was creating the very conditions of organizational complexity that he would later address through reorganization planning, seeking ends other than economy.

Even in his first year in office Roosevelt mixed into his economizing references to reorganization some asides about reform's rewards in increased efficiency rather than economy.[13] Is there a "real" Roosevelt within this appearance of conflicting positions? Scholars often label the economizing Roosevelt as symbolic rather than real.[14] Other students take both sides of Roosevelt equally seriously. Freidel has written: "Although subsequently Roosevelt felt that reorganization was primarily important as a means of obtaining greater effectiveness in the government, in March 1933 he planned it as a means of cutting costs."[15]

Franklin Roosevelt's pre-presidential political career contains elements which suggest the basis for both of his views on reorganization: economy and efficiency. As assistant secretary of the Navy under President Wilson he garnered organizational experience and a sense of government's administrative shortcomings. Like most reform-minded people of his period, Roosevelt was an avid supporter of an executive

[10] Frank Freidel, *Franklin D. Roosevelt: Launching the New Deal* (Boston: Little, Brown, 1973), p. 241.

[11] Executive Order 6133.

[12] Quoted in Freidel, *FDR: Launching the New Deal*, p. 251.

[13] *Ibid.*, p. 252.

[14] Richard Polenberg, *Reorganizing Roosevelt's Government* (Cambridge, Mass.: Harvard University Press, 1966), pp. 6-8.

[15] Frank Freidel, *FDR: Launching the New Deal*, p. 241.

budget. Later, as Governor of New York, he benefited from a broadly reorganized state government, Al Smith having rationalized state government by building eighteen more or less coherent departments out of 187 agencies.[16] But there are elements in his background which give reason to take at face value his narrower, economizing perspective. Despite his proximity to reorganization during his career, Roosevelt had never instituted administrative reform. Also, one should not overlook Roosevelt's conservatism, or perhaps one might say conventionalism, in fiscal matters.

What pushed him from his early emphasis on economy through reorganization to his later emphasis on management? Two elements in his experience suggest an explanation. First, the tasks of leading and coordinating a rapidly expanding executive branch presented Roosevelt with a managerial problem that could not be addressed through an economizing conception of administration. Second, among Roosevelt's advisers were individuals whose outlook was that of a managerially oriented public administration theory.

ADMINISTRATIVE THEORY COMES OF AGE

In the 1930's the study of public administration gained the characteristic trappings of "big-time" social science, manifested by elite professional committees "governing" the discipline, associations, foundation funding, and government contacts.[17] Scientism and pragmatism were the two main intellectual themes within the public administration of the 1930's. Its earlier crude empiricism had transformed into a concern with the development of administrative principles.[18] Yet the scientism of students of public administration was qualified. Marshall Dimock wrote that administration's abstract principles had to be tempered by the practical: "Admitting that the formulation of

[16] For a review of New York's reorganization under Governor Al Smith consult Finla G. Crawford, "New York State Reorganization," *American Political Science Review* 20 (February 1926), 76-79.

[17] An overview of the social science establishment of the 1930's as well as biographical background on Franklin Roosevelt's reorganizers can be had in two books by Barry Karl, *Executive Reorganization and Reform in the New Deal* (Cambridge, Mass: Harvard University Press, 1963), and *Charles Merriam and the Study of Politics* (Chicago: University of Chicago Press, 1974).

[18] The work of Frederick Taylor was the model for that early scientism in public administration. On the scientific claims of Taylorism, see Georges Friedmann, *Industrial Society* (Glencoe, Ill.: The Free Press, 1955), pp. 37-66; for a provocative discussion of the claims and assumptions within Taylor's science, see Judith Merkle, *Ideology and Management* (Berkeley: University of California Press, 1980).

hypotheses and principles is necessary . . . , the worker in the field of public administration should be constantly on his guard against generalizations which bear no close relation to the solution of the particular problem which he is exploring."[19] These administrative scientists were finally pragmatists at heart.[20] But pragmatism also came to public administration congenitally, so to speak, it being the underlying philosophic orientation of the progressive movement.[21]

Administrative Thought in the 1920's and 1930's

The leading textbook of public administration prior to the Second World War was Leonard D. White's *Introduction to the Study of Public Administration*. It was published in 1926, and its second edition appeared in 1939.[22] Given this text's prominence—and quality—the opportunity to compare two editions, thirteen years apart, offers an excellent means for tracing intellectual changes in the study of public administration over a decade.

White's 1926 edition is dominated by the metaphor of administrative organization as a machine, and its tone is conditioned by that metaphor's abstractness. After an opening chapter on the importance of administration in the modern state, White offers four chapters on "The Administrative Machine." The first of these carries that title, and the following three chapters concern the abstract relationships within the machine—centralization, and integration. Later in the book White addresses topics such as executive reorganization and personnel in the spirit of assessing them as engineering applications of these abstractions.

Conceptually, the 1926 book shares a great deal with Frederick Cleveland's view of administration. The same mechanistic understanding of administration informs both views: good administration is defined as the product of the properly structured organization. But there was a fly in the ointment; a basic problem that had been recognized

[19] Marshall Dimock, "The Meaning and Scope of Public Administration," in John Gaus, Leonard White, and Marshall Dimock, *The Frontiers of Public Administration* (Chicago: University of Chicago Press, 1936), p. 4.

[20] Dwight Waldo, *The Administrative State* (New York: Ronald, 1947), p. 178.

[21] Eric F. Goldman, *Rendezvous With Destiny* (New York: Vintage Books, 1960), pp. 119-124; Robert H. Wiebe, *The Search for Order: 1877-1920* (New York: Hill and Wang, 1967), pp. 151-152. On the relationship between efficacy and change in pragmatism see Phillip Wiener, *Evolution and the Foundations of Pragmatism* (Cambridge, Mass: Harvard University Press, 1949).

[22] Leonard D. White, *Introduction to the Study of Public Administration* (New York: Macmillan, 1926), and (2nd ed., New York: Macmillan, 1939).

by Cleveland remained unsolved in the 1920's. Underlying the availability of a notion of what constituted good administration was an assumption that there was an authoritative decision maker who could apply this notion to administration. Yet, in 1926, White did not feel comfortable with that assumption. He wrote:

> Finally the greatest uncertainty prevails as to the ultimate role of the chief executive. His authority and prestige are clearly now rapidly expanding; but whether he is to become primarily an administrator, or primarily a political leader . . . remains in the laps of the gods.[23]

White's 1926 edition reads as an antique, albeit one of excellent quality. But the 1939 edition seems modern. The machine metaphor of the earlier edition is washed out of the later one, and in its place is a richer view of agencies and their political environments. The 1939 edition assumes that to understand administration one must understand specificities of organization and politics. The text shows how that view can operate through a number of new chapters devoted to specific organizational forms. Beyond chapters on staff agencies and departments, it treats independent regulatory agencies and government corporations. White opens the 1939 edition's preface by stating: "The decade which has passed since the first edition of this book has shaken the economic and political foundations of the contemporary world."[24]

Consistent with a shift in focus from the mechanical to the political, White gives greatly increased attention to the chief executive in the later edition. After several general opening chapters on public administration's scope, context, and subject, White offers a chapter titled "The Chief Executive as General Manager." White's view of the executive's competency has changed as well; admitting that the presidency still lacks the means to control administration, he sees the balance shifting from the legislature to the chief executive. He writes that the presidency "still lacks many essential means, but despite these severe handicaps Woodrow Wilson, Herbert C. Hoover, and Franklin D. Roosevelt . . . expanded greatly the administrative influence of the office."[25]

---

[23] *Ibid.* (1926), p. 204.

[24] *Ibid.* (1939), p. vii.

[25] *Ibid.* (1939), p. 51. Leading political scientists of the 1930's began to view the president's relationship to administration in terms of a struggle that the executive was beginning to get the edge within. Unlike their predecessors of the 1920's and earlier, they did not view the president's managerial problem as simply equivalent to that of the private sector manager, understanding that the president faced a far greater and

White's 1939 edition exhibits two elements which pervade the study of public administration in the 1930's. First, the text struck a balance between the scientific and practical approaches to administration; White combined a flexible notion of the desirability of a scientific approach with a strong sense of the role of prudence in governmental affairs. Second, White's 1939 edition decides in favor of the chief executive's dominance of administration, rendering canonical what had been doubtful in the 1926 edition and had been outrightly avant garde when argued by Frederick Cleveland a dozen years before that.

The Public Administration Establishment

Another characteristic of the study of public administration in the 1930's must be noticed to understand its symbiosis with executive politics. During the 1920's a conjunction formed among some elements of the social sciences, private philanthropy, and the federal government to the end of encouraging what today could be called a policy science. This development began in 1924 with the founding of the Social Science Research Council, its membership drawn from the major disciplinary associations of the social sciences. The leader in organizing the SSRC was Charles E. Merriam of the University of Chicago. While president of the American Political Science Association, Merriam accomplished the inter-disciplinary negotiations to launch the council; his financial support came from the Laura Spelman Rockefeller Memorial, an affiliated fund of the Rockefeller Foundation.[26] The first great accomplishment of the Social Science Research Council was its success in convincing President Hoover of the need for a presidential-level research effort on national "social trends." In 1929 Hoover created the President's Research Committee on Social Trends headed by the economist Wesley C. Mitchell, who was also director of the Social Science Research Council; the committee's financial support was provided by the Rockefeller Foundation and funneled through the SSRC.

Parallel to the SSRC as an interdisciplinary organization of the social sciences, the different associations of public administrators were brought together in 1930 in the Public Administration Clearing House. The financial angel in this affair was also the Spelman Fund (as the Laura Spelman Rockefeller Memorial was renamed). In fact, the Spel-

---

finally insurmountable challenge in the size of the executive branch combined with its political character. See Marshall Dimock, "Executive Responsibility, The Span of Control in the Federal Government," *The Society for the Advancement of Management Journal* 3 (January 1938), 22-28.

[26] Barry D. Karl, *Executive Reorganization and Reform*, p. 50.

man Fund was more than the financial backer of a new network organization for administrative practitioners; it was instrumental in developing, selling, and then funding the idea. The idea began in 1926 with Louis Brownlow, then city manager of Knoxville. Brownlow interested Charles Merriam in his plan and together they took it to Beardsley Ruml, executive officer of the Spelman Fund. Ruml and his fund then became the prime forces in moving Brownlow's idea to reality.[27] In the summer of 1930 the Public Administration Clearing House was created across the Midway from the University of Chicago, the Spelman Fund supporting the center with a half million dollars over a period of ten years. The location adjacent to the University of Chicago was chosen on the assumption that the clearing house would establish close ties with the university, which was fast becoming the nation's leading center of graduate education and research in the social sciences.[28]

In 1930, Leonard White's chairmanship of the SSRC's public administration committee terminated, and Luther Gulick replaced him. Gulick was director of the Institute for Public Administration in New York (the successor organization to the New York Bureau of Municipal Research). He was also (along with Richard S. Childs, president of the National Municipal League, and Brownlow) one of the legal incorporators of the Public Administration Clearing House, and his institute in New York and the new clearing house had a majority of their trustees in common. Through this network of people and organizations, a newly influential social science-public administration network was created, offering a strongly executive-centered perspective on problem identification, policy design, and problem solving in the public sector. The motivating ambition behind the formation of this establishment was the idea of social science in the public service. Roosevelt's New Deal offered a promising opportunity for putting this ideal into practice.

EFFORTS AT MANAGEMENT: 1933-1935

Franklin Roosevelt's first year in the presidency was a virtuoso performance of political improvisation. He had found an economy in disarray, a gross national product which had fallen almost by half since 1929, and a level of total federal revenue for fiscal year 1933

[27] Louis Brownlow, *The Autobiography of Louis Brownlow*, Vol. II: *A Passion for Anonymity* (Chicago: University of Chicago Press, 1958), p. 229.

[28] *Ibid.*, p. 254. See T. V. Smith and Leonard D. White (eds.), *Chicago: An Experiment in Social Science Research* (Chicago: University of Chicago Press, 1929).

that was less than half the total figure for fiscal year 1930. At the same time, federal spending for 1933 would be more than twice the expected revenues.[29] Roosevelt did not have a fixed plan, but he was to try a wide variety of different programs aimed at addressing one or another problem.[30]

Coordination Through Supercabinets

In his first year in office Roosevelt created a spate of agencies, some for the emergency's duration and others to be permanent. Also most of the established domestic departments, such as Labor, Interior, and Agriculture, received substantial new duties.[31] Roosevelt was like a juggler with a dozen balls in the air. Initially he wowed the electorate with his boldness, and administering the New Deal was not yet a pressing problem.[32]

Coordinating his creations was the President's next task. Overlap and redundancy ran through the new programs. For example, in the area of public works, the Public Works Administration, the Civil Works Administration, the Works Progress Administration, and Tennessee Valley Authority competed among themselves and with other established agencies like the Corps of Engineers and the Bureau of Reclamation.

President Roosevelt's attempts to build a means for coordination of his domestic emergency apparatus began six months after he took office. During the first term he focused on bringing together agencies with overlapping policies. The Executive Council was Roosevelt's first mechanism for coordination, created by executive order on July 11, 1933.[33] From the start the council was doomed by its design. It was composed of the whole cabinet plus the heads of the emergency agencies and the budget director, and it failed for the same reason the

[29] U.S. Bureau of the Census, *Statistical History of the United States* (New York: Basic Books, 1976), pp. 1,106, 1,114.

[30] In the months after his inauguration, Roosevelt's advisers were taken with ideas of "planning" and overall approaches to problems. Roosevelt used the term "planning," but by it he seems to have meant nothing more than a kind of common-sense orderliness in policy and administration. On the notion and practice of planning during the 1930's, see Otis L. Graham, Jr., *Toward a Planned Society* (New York: Oxford University Press, 1976), Chap. 1.

[31] On the array of early New Deal agencies, consult Arthur Schlesinger, Jr., *The Coming of the New Deal* (Boston: Houghton and Mifflin, 1958), Chaps. 1, 2, 4, 5; and Freidel, *FDR: Launching the New Deal*, Chaps. 4, 15, 18, 20, 25.

[32] Freidel, *ibid.*, p. 499.

[33] Executive Order 6202A.

cabinet fails as an instrument of policy coordination.[34] It was too diverse, with responsible officials interested only in their own concerns and uninterested in cooperating with others.

The President's next attempt at policy coordination was his National Emergency Council, created by executive order on November 17, 1933.[35] The new council contained three design improvements over its predecessor. It was smaller, it was more homogenous, and it was more centralized. From the cabinet the new council included only the heads of Agriculture, Commerce, and Labor; the heads of the New Deal agencies provided the remaining membership. The council's director was authorized "to execute the functions and to perform the duties vested in the Council by the President through such persons as the Executive Director shall designate. . . ."[36] The director was also given resources to build a secretariat. At the National Emergency Council's first meeting, on December 19, 1933, the President said that his intention "in organizing this Emergency Council is to centralize the work of putting the country back on its feet. . . ."[37] But all too quickly, as its transcripts show, the council became a discussion group. At one level this was important in that discussion aired policy preferences and problems, but the council was not an apt mechanism for resolving the problems that arose between agencies.[38]

In the summer of 1934 Roosevelt fashioned a smaller group still, the Industrial Emergency Committee. But in October 1934 he returned to a rejuvenated National Emergency Council. The coordinating mechanisms failed. On the other hand, Roosevelt was able to use what some called "the five ring circus" to keep loose tab on the emergency

[34] On the limits of the cabinet for coordination, see Richard Fenno, *The President's Cabinet* (Cambridge, Mass.: Harvard University Press, 1959), pp. 141-154. On coordination in administration and the contraints on coordination from the top, see Harold Seidman, *Politics, Position, and Power* (3rd ed.; New York: Oxford University Press, 1980), chap. 8, and Allen Schick, "The Coordination Option," in Peter Szanton (ed.), *Federal Reorganization* (Chatham, N.J.: Chatham House, 1981), pp. 85-113.

[35] Executive Order 6433A. For a discussion of the NEC's role and a complete transcript of its sessions see Lester Seligman and Elmer Cornwell, Jr. (eds.), *The New Deal Mosaic: Roosevelt Confers With His National Emergency Council* (Eugene: University of Oregon Press, 1965). A secondhand view of Roosevelt's hopes for the NEC can be had from a letter of Bernard Baruch to the President in which he recalls an earlier conversation the two had had about the NEC. Baruch wrote: "The plan you mentioned in our talk . . . would eliminate many of the difficulties which beset you, give you more time for contemplation and leave less room for conflict." Letter, Baruch to Roosevelt, November 14, 1934, President's Personal File, 88, Baruch, 1932, Roosevelt Library.

[36] Executive Order 6433A.

[37] Transcript of meeting in Seligman and Cornwell, *New Deal Mosaic*, p. 2.

[38] See Seligman's introduction in *ibid.*, pp. xxii-xxvii.

agencies. But something more was necessary for a president facing growing complexity in government. In assessing the National Emergency Council from the perspective of its purported purpose, Lester Seligman suggests that its failure became a watershed point in Roosevelt's understanding of his office:

> By 1935 ... the crisis atmosphere had abated somewhat. It was obvious to all that NEC was no precedent for a permanent solution. The "super cabinet" method had shown that coordination and clearance could be better accomplished perhaps by the strengthening of the President's personal staff rather than by collegial bodies.[39]

An Alternative Strategy for Administrative Coordination

Roosevelt was ripe for the advice of the public administration establishment. Its members had been eager to help from the beginning. For example, in April 1933 Louis Brownlow offered to use the Public Administration Clearing House's connections and budget to provide expert consultants for government when public funds were unavailable for that purpose.[40]

The highest-placed agency in the administration in which a social science viewpoint predominated was a planning committee for natural resources created in 1933. Its initial title was the National Resources Board, changing to the National Resources Committee and then the National Resources Planning Board. Its original purpose was to consider developments that would affect the nation's environment and natural wealth. However, this mission quickly became broader and vaguer as was the tendency of "planning" activities during the New Deal. By 1935 this body had taken to itself the problem of overall, large-scale planning.[41] The group's members were Frederick Delano, the President's uncle and a well-known city planner; Wesley C. Mitchell, a Columbia University economist and former director of the Social Science Research Council; and Charles E. Merriam of the University of Chicago and the Social Science Research Council. These were not natural resource planners, and they actively sought a redefinition of their role. Roosevelt was favorable to this request because he was at the same time groping for some order in government's chaos.[42] In June

[39] Seligman and Cornwell, *ibid.*, p. xxvi.

[40] Letter and accompanying memorandum, Louis Brownlow to Louis Howe, April 27, 1933, President's Official File, 285-C, Franklin D. Roosevelt Library, Hyde Park, New York.

[41] Otis Graham, Jr., *Toward a Planned Society*, pp. 52-58.

[42] Arthur Schlesinger, Jr., *The Coming of the New Deal*, p. 350.

1935 the National Resources Board presented Roosevelt with a dissenting view to his supercabinet approach to managerial coordination. It suggested a body of five "disinterested" individuals reporting directly to the President, each taking responsibility for a segment of New Deal programs.[43] The board's recommendation was not taken by Roosevelt, yet it sparked the move to a change in his approach.

During the summer of 1935 Roosevelt met several times with the National Resources Committee (the board's new name) to discuss what was beginning to be called top-level management. In light of these meetings, Charles Merriam drafted a working paper proposing a study of "Management in the Federal Government." It would aim at "recommendations which would lead to more effective overall administrative management . . . , a better integration of the activities of the administrative departments . . . , and a reduction of the jurisdictional conflicts which are inherent in an organization of such great size." Its focus would be "the staff which the Executive should have to exercise over-all management," the organization of that staff and the role it would play in relation to the agencies.[44] Merriam asked, how could the public administration establishment's stature be mobilized in support of a study that would enhance the presidency? "Should the NRC request the Public Administration Committee of the Social Science Research Council to make a study of management in Federal Administration?"[45] This is the course that Merriam himself favored because of the intellectual resources available to the Public Administration Committee.

Louis Brownlow, current chairman of the Public Administration Committee, was also a regular, if unofficial, participant in National Resource Committee meetings.[46] Brownlow organized a conference of leading students of public administration to propose the scope of a study and the composition of the study team. The study would deal with the provision of sufficient staff so as to enable "the President to exercise executive supervision. . . ." Should there be time, it might also engage "the broad question of the functions of the departments and their relations with the President."[47] The study group, it was proposed,

[43] Telegram, Delano, Mitchell, and Merriam to Roosevelt, June 25, 1935, President's Official File, 26-Cabinet, Roosevelt Library.

[44] "Proposed Study of Management in the Federal Government," October 1935, President's Committee on Administrative Management, A-II-1, Roosevelt Library; this is reproduced in Brownlow, *A Passion for Anonymity*, pp. 327-328.

[45] *Ibid.*

[46] *Ibid.*, p. 326.

[47] Memorandum, "Notes on a Conference on a Study of Over-all Management in

would include Brownlow; Harold Dodds, a public personnel expert and Princeton's president; Luther Gulick, director of the Institute of Public Administration; Lewis Meriam, head of the Brookings Institution's Institute for Government Research; and Lindsay Rogers, professor of political science at Columbia.[48] That plan was presented to the Public Administration Committee, which met after Christmas 1935 in Atlanta; it added its formal approval, and the Rockefeller Foundation promised that funds would be available to support the study. Brownlow sent to President Roosevelt a belated Christmas present, a high-powered study to solve his administrative coordination problem, with study design, personnel, and funding all provided.

Creating the President's Committee

With the management study proposal in hand, Roosevelt hesitated. The experts who had proposed (and would staff) the study waited expectantly. For example, Luther Gulick accepted no new long-term assignments in the early weeks of 1936, expecting to be called by Roosevelt. Hearing nothing, he finally contracted for a management study for the New York State Board of Regents.[49] Then the President called.

Roosevelt had seen two complications to the study as proposed. First, it was too prefabricated; it bound him to a process beyond his control. Second, he was sensitive to the auspices under which such a study would proceed, and he feared the connection of the Rockefeller Foundation to the proposed study.[50] Louis Brownlow addressed these concerns, producing a memorandum for Roosevelt which spelled out the purposes of the proposal:

> What is needed is a careful study of the managerial and administrative relationship of the President to all the farflung . . . agencies. . . . After all the President is responsible in fact if not always in law and cannot escape that responsibility. The recognition of this fact makes it impossible to devolve his prerogative.[51]

---

the Federal Government," December 16, 1935, President's Committee on Administrative Management, A-II-3, Roosevelt Library.

[48] *Ibid.*

[49] Luther Gulick, interview with James Garnett, November 30, 1976. I am grateful to Professor Garnett for making available to me the transcript of this interview.

[50] These concerns are reflected in a memorandum reporting a meeting of the National Resources Council with the President on February 20, 1936; it is reproduced in Louis Brownlow, *A Passion for Anonymity*, pp. 333-334.

[51] Louis Brownlow, "Rough Notes on Kind of Study Needed," February 1936, President's Committee on Administrative Management, A-II-6, Roosevelt Library.

Brownlow's memo stressed the importance of staff support for the presidency, because the president can fulfill his responsibility for "control and direction" only through staff.

On March 4, 1936 Brownlow met with President Roosevelt and accepted his invitation to lead a study that would be publicly financed. But the delay created competition in the field of federal administrative studies. In February the Senate created a select committee to study reorganization of the executive branch, with Senator Harry Byrd (Dem., Va.) as chairman. Reorganization was one of the senator's major interests. As governor of Virginia he had overseen a reorganization of state government conducted by Luther Gulick and the Institute for Public Administration. A reorganization study also gave Senator Byrd a way of hedging the President's activities. Luther Gulick notes: "Harry and FDR were not sympathetic individuals, and Harry tried very hard to run the ball on government reorganization as his major issue. . . ."[52]

The potential for competition was the largest problem posed for Roosevelt by the Byrd committee. While that competition could (and would) have significant political consequences, its initial expression was over personnel and scope. Senator Byrd sought as staff for his study the same people that the President had chosen to conduct his. The same day that Brownlow was asked by Roosevelt to head his study committee, he had been invited by Senator Byrd to join his committee's advisory group. Brownlow explained that he was in the midst of developing a presidential study but that he would be happy to cooperate with the senator's study. Brownlow left the meeting thinking that Byrd would cooperate with the presidential study.[53] Later in the day, Brownlow told Roosevelt "it might be possible for his committee to work on the main problems of mangement . . . and devolve upon the Senate committee . . . the more detailed examinations into the overlappings and conflicts."[54] Senator Byrd approached Luther Gulick to head his research staff. Gulick did not accept the job, still assuming that the President was going to invite him to join his study. As Gulick recalls: "We felt the job should really be done by the executive and not by the legislative branch."[55] Senator Byrd then contracted with the Brookings Institution to serve his subcommittee's research needs.

[52] Luther Gulick, interview with James Garnett.
[53] Louis Brownlow, memorandum for files, March 4, 1936, President's Committee on Administrative Management, A-II-y, Roosevelt Library.
[54] Louis Brownlow, *A Passion for Anonymity*, p. 338.
[55] Luther Gulick, interview with James Garnett.

At their March 4th meeting, the President and Brownlow discussed membership of the study group. Roosevelt desired a small committee, suggesting Frederick Delano and Charles Merriam along with Brownlow for its membership. Delano adamantly refused membership.[56] Ultimately, Roosevelt decided for a four-member committee made up of Brownlow, Merriam, Gulick, and Frank Lowden, a former Republican governor of Illinois. However, due to his health, Lowden declined to serve, and the committee was launched with three members.

On March 22nd, the President informed the Speaker of the House and the President of the Senate of his new committee. His letter to them conveyed presidential primacy in administrative reform. He wrote: "Last October I began holding some conversations with interested and informed persons concerning what appealed to me as the necessity of making a careful study of the organization of the Executive Branch. . . ."[57] The President's letter also stressed the need for cooperation between the presidential and the congressional reorganization studies, "in order that duplication of effort . . . may be avoided."[58]

Brownlow, who had drafted the letter, worried afterward whether the strong commitment to cooperation would hamper the freedom of the presidential study.[59] But Roosevelt decided to pursue cooperation, and he seemed to think of a strategy of open cooperation as a means for covert control. Thus he encouraged both Brownlow and Gulick to accept Senator Byrd's invitations to join his advisory board. Similarly he urged them to serve as advisers to a House select committee which had been created a bit later than but parallel to the Byrd committee. Roosevelt seemed to bank on the possibility that Brownlow and Gulick would be the dominant figures for the two congressional committees, eliminating problems of duplication and competition.[60]

THE BROWNLOW COMMITTEE AT WORK

Roosevelt gave his committee freedom to organize as it thought best. Although the President had rejected the proposal of the Social Science Research Council as the medium for the study, to ask Brownlow,

[56] Letter, Delano to McIntyre, March 4, 1936, President's Personal File 72, Roosevelt Library.

[57] Letter, Roosevelt to Vice President Garner, March 22, 1936, Bureau of the Budget, 21.1, R-11, Reorganization General #2, RG 51, National Archives.

[58] *Ibid.*

[59] Letter, Brownlow to Roosevelt, March 6, 1936, President's Committee on Administrative Management, A-II-10, Roosevelt Library.

[60] Louis Brownlow, *A Passion for Anonymity*, p. 341.

Merriam, and Gulick to organize a study was to rely upon the networks centering on the council. Roosevelt promised that the committee's report would be presented to Congress in January 1937. At the same time, while Roosevelt retained the right to censor its recommendations, he left the committee to its own devices; he wanted no contact with its substantive work until after the presidential election of November 1936.[61]

Organizing the Committee

In late March, the committee began to build a research staff. Failing an attempt to attract Clarence Dykstra, a prominent city manager, Joseph P. Harris, a political scientist, was offered the post of staff director. On April 1 the committee held its first formal meeting; the initial decision of that meeting was to name the endeavor the President's Committee for Administrative Management.[62] During April the committee assembled a staff from among political science and public administration experts at leading American universities. At a meeting on May 9 and 10 at the New York office of the Social Science Research Council, the committee and its staff discussed its working plans. In attendance were fifteen of the eventual twenty-six members of the staff along with Stacy May and Guy Moffett of the Rockefeller Foundation. An outline of the topics that ought to be addressed by the committee had been circulated. Several of the prospective staff members had also circulated memoranda on the topics they would address.[63]

Louis Brownlow opened the meeting, addressing the concept most closely associated with the committee—top-level management. An indication of the effect of the months of discussion among the leaders of the public administration establishment about a study of the top-level management was that those who had been privy to those discussions understood that what was meant was the president's capacity to coordinate and control administration. But those who had not participated understood the term only in a structural context—reshaping organizations.[64] Thus a major task for the two-day meeting

[61] Ibid., p. 353.

[62] Ibid., pp. 346-347.

[63] These were memoranda by Floyd Reeves (on personnel management), James Hant (administrative rulemaking), William Y. Elliot (cabinet reform), and Arthur Holcombe (the general staff concept); "Outline for the New York Conference," President's Committee on Administrative Management, A-II-21, Roosevelt Library.

[64] Louis Brownlow, A Passion for Anonymity, p. 352.

was to establish a shared understanding of the study's scope: Brown-low explained the mission in these terms:

> It must be remembered that the President is held responsible po-litically in many situations where the legislature has limited his control devices. The executive is relatively defenseless against in-vasion by the legislative and judicial branches. The problem is to give him controls commensurate with his responsibility.[65]

It was evident that the group did not share a terminology. The standard terms of public administration were understood differently by those whose primary research interests ranged across the fields of public administration, American politics, and public law. This dilemma occasioned the production of Gulick's and Urwick's now classic *Papers on the Science of Administration*, a group of essays gathered to provide a common language for the staff.[66] An additional purpose of the col-lection was to provide a tool kit of administrative principles. As Louis Brownlow said to those gathered for the committee's meeting on May 9th: "The President hopes for a report on principles, not methodology. There is danger that . . . disputes over details would bury public interest in the principles."[67]

Beyond the tactical issue of how to shape the reports, the committee faced the necessity of accomplishing a major study in less than nine months. There would be no time for data collection.[68] Brownlow said that the staff had been selected for their capacity for reflection and for their expertise; they were chosen because they were capable of skimming "the cream off the top of their own memories."[69]

Roosevelt had told his committee that while "over-all management" was a problem shared by any advanced society, the particular con-stitutional institutions of the United States required a solution fitted to American needs.[70] The committee's job was to find a solution that could co-exist with the peculiarities of the separation of power system; obviously such co-existence was a prerequisite for its recommenda-tions' political viability.

What can be done for the presidency? This was the question that

[65] Minutes, Meeting of May 9 and 10, 1936, President's Committee on Administrative Management, A-II-5, Roosevelt Library.

[66] Luther Gulick, interview with James Garnett. See L. Gulick and L. Urwick, *Papers on the Science of Administration* (New York: Institute of Public Administration, 1937).

[67] Minutes, Meeting of May 9 and 10, President's Committee.

[68] *Ibid.*

[69] *Ibid.*

[70] *Ibid.*

drove the Brownlow Committee, and the committee brought impressive resources to bear on this question. If its method was to "skim the cream off the top of . . . memories," then the committee and staff had a generous supply of that cream. The moving forces in the committee's work were its three members. But the research staff provided a number of high-quality individual studies along with the important resource of discussion among differing, excellent minds comprising a community within which ideas could grow, unexpectedly, serendipitously. The staff's quality can be seen in the fact that among the thirty individuals comprising it and the committee, there were six past or future presidents of the American Political Science Association. The list of staff members reads like an honor role of distinguished scholars in American political science, although most of these researchers had yet to make their reputations.[71]

During the summer of 1936 the staff began its work while Brownlow and Merriam travelled in Europe, attending administrative conferences and examining European administrative practices. Gulick was also off the scene, finishing his work for the New York Board of Regents. Joseph Harris was charged with working out remaining financial details for the committee's support. What was expected to be simple final arrangements, however, turned into a crisis. The President intended to support his committee through emergency funds. But Comptroller-General J. Raymond McCarl declared that to be an illegal use of appropriated funds.[72] Consequently a congressional appropriation had to be obtained. In late June, Congress appropriated $100,000 to support the committee, but the appropriation entailed a significant complication.

[71] The research staff of the committee had the following membership: Joseph P. Harris (director), G. Lyle Belsley, A. E. Buck, Laverne Burchfield, Robert H. Connery, Robert E. Cushman, Paul T. David, William Y. Elliot, Herbert Emmerich, Merle Fainsod, James W. Fesler, Katherine Frederic, Patterson H. French, William J. Haggerty, James Hart, Arthur N. Holcombe, Arthur W. MacMahon, Harvey C. Mansfield, Charles McKinley, John F. Miller, John D. Millett, Floyd W. Reeves, Leo C. Roston, Spencer Thompson, Mary C. Trackett, Schuyler C. Wallace, Edwin E. Witte.

[72] John Raymond McCarl was the first Comptroller-General, appointed to his fifteen-year term as fixed by statute in the first year of the Harding administration. McCarl had been an aide to Senator George Norris prior to the First World War and subsequently served as director of the Republican Congressional Campaign Committee. More than any later appointment to the position of Comptroller-General, this was a partisan, patronage appointment. McCarl, in office, used his authority imperiously and frequently stymied spending initiatives of the Roosevelt administration. For a full exploration of the early years of the General Accounting Office, see Harvey C. Mansfield, Sr., *The Comptroller General* (New Haven: Yale University Press, 1939), and also see Frederick Mosher, *The GAO* (Boulder: Westview, 1979), Chap. 3.

The Brownlow Committee's funding problem gave the Congress potential influence over its direction. At the center of this financial arrangement was Representative James Buchanan (Dem., Texas), chairman of the House Appropriations Committee as well as chairman of the House's select committee to study government organization. His appropriations committee had produced the bill, and he shaped it to fit his plans for reorganization. Those plans entailed the old congressional economizing view; agency overlap was to be reduced to achieve economy. Through amendment, Buchanan had attached that theory of reorganization to the appropriation bill; it stipulated the purpose of the President's Committee to be ascertaining "whether the activities of any such agency conflict with or overlap the activities of any other . . . and whether in the interest of simplification, efficiency and economy any such agencies should be coordinated . . . or abolished or the personnel thereof reduced. . . ."[73] This provision of the appropriation bill was objectionable to the administration, and to no avail Roosevelt had requested that Buchanan drop it.[74] The bill passed both houses.

Buchanan offered the Brownlow Committee a way out of the dilemma. He proposed that the examination of overlap and duplication be considered part of the responsibility of the Byrd Committee. In effect, the Brownlow Committee would commission the select committee to conduct that part of the work, paying to it $10,000 from its own appropriation, which would be added to the $40,000 already appropriated to support the congressional select committees. Guided by telegrammed communications with Brownlow in Europe, Joseph Harris agreed to this arrangement, finally obtaining an appropriation, or at least nine-tenths of it.[75]

Skimming the Cream of Memory: Formulating the Brownlow Report

Brownlow and Merriam's European trip provided a normative foundation for their committee's report. Visiting Europe in 1934, Brown-

[73] Quoted in letter, Harris to Brownlow, June 18, 1936, President's Committee on Administrative Management, Correspondence-Brownlow, Roosevelt Library.

[74] Letter, Harris to Gulick, May 18, 1936, President's Committee on Administrative Management, Correspondence-Gulick, Roosevelt Library.

[75] Telegram, Harris to Brownlow, June 25, 1936, President's Committee on Administrative Management, Correspondence-Brownlow; Letter, Harris to Fred Powell (of Brookings), June 30, 1936, President's Committee on Administrative Management, A-II-15a, Roosevelt Library.

low had seen the fragility of the democracies. In 1936 he found he features of fascism more sharply etched on the continent and more threatening. At the international meetings on public administration that Brownlow and Merriam attended during the summer they were shocked by the behavior of the delegations from the fascist states, attempting to dominate meetings and producing resolutions favoring "the Fuhrer principle" as a doctrine of administration. At the Warsaw meeting of the International Institute of Administrative Sciences, Brownlow found that "a feeling of fear permeated the atmosphere; that there was a sense of impending great change that, for some, was the elation of dominance soon to be realized, of power . . . soon to be theirs, for others, a sense of impending doom, of deepening darkness."[76] In light of what Brownlow and Merriam saw as an impending storm in Europe, the problem of the president's capacity to lead became all the more pressing.

The Brownlow Committee assumed the president's administrative primacy. In this it was heir to predecessor reorganization efforts and the administrative theories which informed them. The three members of the Brownlow Committee were unanimous in their view of the president's role in administration, although there were slight differences of perspective among them reflecting differences in background.[77] Brownlow had come to his current eminence among administrative practitioners through city management. He was a practical and canny person with a mind that left him comfortable in the company of academicians. Charles Merriam was a leading figure in American political science whose scholarly interests were in American political theory and, growingly, the development of an applied political science. Luther Gulick was a product of the tradition that grew out of the New York Bureau of Municipal Research. Of the three members of the Brownlow Committee, he was the only one with experience in large-scale executive reorganization, having been a principal in many of the reorganizations of state governments from the 1920's and on. Of the three, he was the most concerned with the relationship between organizational structure and managerial leadership. But in the light of the task at hand, the agreement shared by these three men far outweighed their differences. In what could be the committee's credo, Charles Merriam said:

> The organizational development and position of the American Executive is one of the great contributions of American genius. . . .

[76] Louis Brownlow, *A Passion for Anonymity*, p. 367.

[77] See the autobiographical sketches of Brownlow, Merriam, and Gulick in Barry Karl, *Executive Reorganization and Reform.*

It is important, however, that the Executive office be developed on the side of management and administrative supervision as well as on the political side if its full possibilities are to be realized. . . .[78]

After the problem to be solved was specified, strengthening the president as manager, the task was to find specific recommendations that would achieve that solution. Two rather different answers were apparent. The first approach would strengthen administration by making the cabinet departments more manageable. The second approach would strengthen the presidency itself, with the aim of empowering its role over the agencies. On their face, these approaches could be founded on pragmatic differences: what will work best? But they could spark more fundamental disagreements. The first approach is consistent with congressional primacy, depicting the president's role as ministerial. Edward Corwin, a leading proponent of this view wrote:

> Certainly, to conceive of the President as a potential "boss of the works" save in situations raising broad issues of policy would be both absurd and calamitous; and for such issues the legislative process is still available, a field in which presidential leadership is today a more vital factor than ever before.[79]

The second approach is consistent with a view of the president as the primary authority over administration, a view seen above, in Frederick Cleveland's functional theory of the presidential administrative role. Underlying these two views of the presidency is yet a more fundamental difference over an understanding of the Constitution. In Corwin's view the Constitution was given and complete. For Cleveland the formal Constitution was not the sole guidance on fundamental questions within the American regime.

Within the committee's staff discussions, the cabinet reform position was reflected in arguments for coordination through the cabinet.[80] The direct, presidency-strengthening position's proponents argued for giving the president authority and tools over administration.[81] The prac-

[78] Memorandum, "Proposed Study of Management in the Federal Government," October 1935, President's Committee on Administrative Management, A-II-1, Roosevelt Library.

[79] Edward Corwin, *The President: Office and Powers* (4th ed. rev., New York: New York University Press, 1957), p. 98.

[80] This perspective is best exemplified in the study paper written by William Y. Elliot, "The President's Role in Administrative Management," and follow-up memorandum he prepared, President's Committee on Administrative Management, G-I-2, 3, 4, Roosevelt Library.

[81] This position is exemplified in a memorandum by Herbert Emmerich, "Possible

tical character of the staff discussion is exemplified by a memorandum that Lewis Meriam wrote for the committee. Meriam was a member of the Brookings Institution and would direct the Byrd Committee's study, becoming a strong critic of parts of the Brownlow recommendations. But Meriam wrote a friendly memorandum for the Brownlow Committee which identified the problem to be addressed as the president's administrative incapacity.[82] Presumably, Meriam was comfortable with a position that was so strongly in agreement with the Brownlow Committee's view because he entertained that issue only at a technical level.

Between April and November 1936, the Brownlow Committee had no contact with the President or Congress. Roosevelt did not meet with his committee until after the 1936 election, and the congressional committees were inactive, awaiting the Brookings Institution's study. President Roosevelt had placed the Brownlow Committee under a restriction of confidentiality, but the committee's members kept passing research papers to outside experts for their judgment. In one instance of this, later political conflict was intimated in Lewis Meriam's technical comments on A. E. Buck's paper, "Financial Management by the President." Meriam objected to Buck's call for limiting the Comptroller-General's control over expenditures.[83]

Between August and November the committee drafted a report. The focus of activity was on the three members, although Joseph Harris frequently met with them. The committee's members also met frequently with officials, trying out ideas on veterans of the administrative wars. They needed outside intelligence and information: what were the available mechanisms for strengthening presidential managerial capacity? How could fiscal integrity be insured while making auditing a centralized part of governmental administration? How could independent commissions be integrated into the broad stream of governmental policymaking? Once possible solutions to these puzzles were in hand, the committee had its more difficult task, the one it had to face alone. It had to commit an act of statesmanship: weighing alter-

Organization of Presidential Staff," November 5, 1936, and in an unsigned memorandum prepared about the same time, "Tentative Outline on Administrative Management in the National Government," President's Committee on Administrative Management, A-II-39, Roosevelt Library.

[82] Lewis Meriam, memorandum titled "An Executive Staff Agency," President's Committee on Administrative Management, A-II-2, Roosevelt Library.

[83] Memorandum, Lewis Meriam to Joseph Harris, n.d., President's Committee on Administrative Management, D-IV, Roosevelt Library.

natives and deciding what reforms would meet government's needs and win acceptance as well.

The judgment required of the committee had three different elements. First, it had to consider the role of the presidency in the American regime, but this was the easiest step because its work had begun with the premise that the presidency needed strengthening. Next, the three committee members had to call upon their individual experiences with government and politics to decide which reforms had the greatest chance for success in practice. Finally, the committee had to concern itself with the President as well as the presidency. It had to consider what was appropriate for Franklin Roosevelt and not just what changes were appropriate for the role. Running beneath all of these specific concerns was a sense of crisis. As Brownlow described it: "Not one of us harbored a single doubt that our task amid the gathering world storm was to strengthen the presidency that the President of the United States might be better equipped not only to manage the affairs of the government but to defend the freedom of the American people."[84]

The Committee's Recommendations

The recommendations that the committee presented to the President after the November elections were consistently executive strengthening and centralizing. Their overall spirit can be garnered from the opening lines of Brownlow's covering memorandum. He wrote that the report's underlying assumption was "that managerial direction and control of all departments and agencies of the Executive Branch ... should be centered in the President; that while he now has popular responsibility for this direction ... he is not equipped with adequate legal authority or administrative machinery to enable him to exercise it. . . ."[85]

Meeting with Brownlow and Gulick (Merriam could not get to Washington) on November 14, President Roosevelt approved almost all of the committee's recommendation. The only major one that he rejected called for a White House secretariat with specific assigned duties. This proposal was changed into the recommendation for the Executive Office of the President and six presidential assistants without specified duties.[86] The committee returned to a period of intensive

[84] Louis Brownlow, *A Passion for Anonymity*, p. 371.

[85] Memorandum, Louis Brownlow to President, November 5, 1936, President's Committee on Administrative Management, A-II-33 Roosevelt Library.

[86] Letter, Joseph Harris to William Y. Elliot, December 17, 1936, President's Committee on Administrative Management, Correspondence-Elliot, Roosevelt Library.

drafting and editing. On December 22 Roosevelt discussed the substance of the committee's report with the cabinet.[87] On January 2, 1937, the report in page proofs received Roosevelt's final approval.

The *Report* made recommendations in six areas: I, White House Staff; II, Personnel Management; III, Fiscal Management; IV, Planning Management; V, Administrative Reorganization of the Government; and VI, Accountability of the Executive to Congress. Its introduction linked together problems relating to governmental machinery, administrative efficiency, presidential capacity, and democracy itself. The committee intended the *Report* to be more than an essay on administrative principles; it was to address the link between administrative competency and democratic politics. The introduction closed with a fine flourish that expressed the committee's understanding of reorganization's ultimate purpose:

> Too close a view of machinery must not cut off from sight the true purpose of efficient management. Economy is not the only objective, though reorganization is the first step to savings; the elimination of duplication and contradictory policies is not the only objective, though this will follow; a simple and symmetrical organization is not the only objective, though the new organization will be simple and symmetrical. ... There is but one grand purpose, namely, to make democracy work today in our National Government; that is, to make our Government an up-to-date, efficient, and effective instrument for carrying out the will of the Nation.[88]

In its recommendations on the White House, the *Report* focused on increased support for the president, proposing six new assistants to be assigned at presidential discretion. It also recommended discretionary funds that would enable the president to acquire more help when needed. Finally, this section proposed a major organizational addition to the presidency, the Executive Office, with the Bureau of the Budget as its centerpiece.[89]

Under the category of personnel management the *Report* proposed changes aimed at increased centralization in the public service while increasing protection from partisan considerations in employment. It called for abolition of the Civil Service Commission and the creation of a central personnel agency headed by a single administrator an-

[87] Letter, Francis Perkins to Louis Brownlow, December 23, 1936, President's Committee on Administrative Management, Correspondence-Brownlow, Roosevelt Library.

[88] President's Committee on Administrative Management, *Report* (Washington: United States Government Printing Office, 1937), p. 4.

[89] *Ibid.*, pp. 6-7.

swerable to the presidency. It also recommended the extension of the merit system to cover almost all federal positions, with an independent citizen watchdog board given the sole responsibility of overseeing the merit principle.[90]

The *Report*'s main thrust under fiscal management was to pull into the Treasury Department the currently divided fiscal controls of government. Under the Budget and Accounting Act of 1921 the Comptroller-General had authority to prescribe and supervise government's accounting systems. These duties, the committee urged, should be lodged in Treasury. Also it recommended that authority over disbursements be placed in the secretary's hands, with the Attorney-General given authority to judge their legality. If implemented, these recommendations would strip the Comptroller-General of his functions short of the final audit of governmental expenditure. In line with this, the committee recommended that this position be retitled the Auditor-General, with its agency becoming the General Auditing Office (instead of the General Accounting Office).[91]

Regarding planning management, the committee recommended the expansion of the National Resources Board to five members and its strengthening as a central planning agency for the president. Planning was treated briefly by the committee, with only one major recommendation offered. However, the subject of planning had high priority for the committee. It assumed that planning would provide an ambitious president with the ability for comprehensive packaging of policy, simultaneously giving greater unity to the executive branch's activities and more coherent leadership to Congress.[92]

The *Report*'s longest section conveyed recommendations for organizational change in the executive branch. Extensive departmental reorganization was recommended, along with the creation of three new departments, Conservation, Social Welfare, and Public Works.[93] This section also recommended the permanent renewal of the lapsed presidential reorganization authority, and it proposed a radical reorganization of the independent regulatory commissions; they would be organizationally divided between their policy-administrative opera-

[90] *Ibid.*, pp. 11-12.

[91] *Ibid.*, pp. 24-25.

[92] *Ibid.*, pp. 27-30. On the idea of planning behind this recommendation, see George A. Graham, "Reorganization—A Question of Executive Institutions," *American Political Science Review* 13 (August 1938), 708-718. Also see Otis Graham, *Toward a Planned Society*, pp. 59-64.

[93] President's Committee on Administrative Management, *Report*, pp. 31-47.

tions and their quasi-judicial role. The former would be joined with the appropriate cabinet-level department.

Finally, the *Report* turned to the most sensitive of its topics: the presidential accountability to Congress. The omnipresent issue for reorganizers is congressional authority. How can increased presidential authority be justified within a separation of powers regime, and how can that change be made politically palatable? The Brownlow *Report*'s response to this problem was similar to Frederick Cleveland's nearly twenty-five years earlier. It suggested that a coherent executive branch and responsible president are more easily held accountable by the legislature. The formula the *Report* adopted for presenting this conception invoked a separation of political choice and administration. In its view, once Congress fulfills its obligation to designate policy ends and appropriate the funds necessary for their implementation: "... the responsibility for the administration of the expenditures under that appropriation is and should be solely upon the Executive."[94] This passage is the only part of the *Report* which clearly embraces a dichotomous view of administration and politics. Given how interested the committee was in strengthening the presidency as a force in administration, it would have been disingenuous to rely too heavily on the separation of administration and politics.

The *Report* closes with a strong statement of the committee's view of the reasons for presidential efficacy:

> Those who waiver at the sight of needed power are false friends of modern democracy. Strong executive leadership is essential to democratic government today. Our choice is not between power and no power, but between responsible but capable popular government and irresponsible autocracy.[95]

The committee's report was an eloquent call for presidential authority. Yet, in none of what it recommended was the committee simply a conduit for Roosevelt's views. The coincidence of Roosevelt's reorganization planners' intellectual perspectives with the President's political interests is exemplified in the committee's controversial recommendation for the independent regulatory commissions. Even the committee's staff member who had prepared the study paper on the independent regulatory commissions (which the committee had ignored in its recommendations) attacked the *Report*'s recommendations

[94] *Ibid.*, p. 50.
[95] *Ibid.*, p. 53.

on the independent commissions as an instance of presidential cooptation.[96] This was a misperception. Luther Gulick observes:

> It was not my sense that FDR was pushing us around. I think
> that Merriam from the . . . broader political science side . . . felt
> that the independent regulatory commissions were standing in the
> way of a national mandate in the field of regulatory performance.
> And Brownlow felt the same. I think my position was that I was
> pushing at all costs for a great strengthening of executive responsi-
> bility and that I wanted to see all the agencies . . . so set up that a
> President with a mandate or a new approach could carry it out. . . .[97]

The Brownlow Committee devised recommendations that reflected
Roosevelt's interests for a combination of reasons, the character of
administrative theory, the political sophistication of its members, their
admiration of Roosevelt, and their sense of a crisis for democracy.
But to presume that the specific details of the committee's recommendations could have been specified beforehand by Roosevelt conflicts
with the facts of his past record in administrative coordination. None
of his earlier, failed efforts had been akin to the approach taken by
the Brownlow Committee.

THE POLITICS OF THE BROWNLOW REPORT

The first audience to receive the full Brownlow *Report* was the Democratic leadership of Congress, meeting at the White House on January
10, 1937. Roosevelt had asked his committee to have its recommendations put into a draft bill.[98] He presented the leaders with the bill,
holding back copies of the *Report* until after the meeting. The congressional leaders had not been consulted in the development of the committee's recommendations, and they had no reason to expect that they
would be so broad. Perhaps overstating the uniqueness of the inter-
branch confrontation (William Howard Taft after all had stepped into
a similar role), Louis Brownlow spelled out the drama of the confrontation he witnessed that afternoon in the White House:

> For the first time in the history of the great American Republic, a
> President of the United States, deeming himself in fact as well as in
> name the head of the executive branch of the government, had come
> to close grips with the leaders of the legislative branch, who from

[96] Luther Gulick, interviewed by James Garnett.
[97] *Ibid.*
[98] Louis Brownlow, *A Passion for Anonymity*, pp. 388–389.

the beginning of the government had considered themselves responsible for the control, confinement, bridling, and ultimate determination of the organization of all branches of the government.[99]

Two days after the meeting, the President formally sent his reorganization bill to Congress.

To understand the fate of that bill it is necessary to understand the political context within which it sought passage. Two different strata of problems would affect the course of reorganization. First, there were politically sensitive recommendations within the committee's report, among them the abolition of the Civil Service Commission and the diminution of the Comptroller-General's authority. Second, there was Franklin Roosevelt's attempt to enlarge the membership of the Supreme Court by appointing new justices for each sitting justice over the age of seventy—"court packing."[100] By association with the simultaneous "court packing" fight, the reorganization effort was tarred with the charge of Roosevelt's seeking change to aggrandize power. The 75th Congress was an unlikely instrument for blunting the President's ambition. Roosevelt's landslide reelection had created a two-thirds Democratic majority in both houses. Roosevelt sought to use the consequent leverage to effect reform. In his inaugural address he said: "... we recognized a deeper need—the need to find through government the instrument of our united purpose to solve for the individual the ever-rising problem of a complex civilization."[101]

In both administrative and court reforms, Roosevelt adopted what appears to be an impolitic secrecy.[102] These two plans were literally sprung on Congress. What moved this normally wily presidential politician to adopt this style in early 1937? One can only speculate about an answer, but it is likely that Roosevelt's strategy was set in reaction to the scale of his political triumph in 1936. That great victory could easily be seen as more Roosevelt's triumph than it was the Democratic

[99] *Ibid.*, p. 392.

[100] For a balanced understanding of this issue, see Robert Scigliano, *The Supreme Court and the Presidency* (New York: The Free Press, 1971), pp. 45-54. Claiming an interest in increasing the efficacy of the federal courts, in February 1937 Roosevelt proposed a new law mandating the president the authority to appoint an additional member to the federal courts when a specific court's judge reached the age of seventy. Under the President's proposal, the maximum size of the Supreme Court would have been raised to fifteen justices.

[101] Franklin Roosevelt, "Second Inaugural Address," January 20, 1937, in Davis N. Tott (ed.), *the Inaugural Address of the American Presidents* (New York: Holt, Rinehart and Winston, 1961), p. 237.

[102] James M. Burns, *Roosevelt: The Lion and the Fox* (New York: Harcourt, Brace and World, 1956), pp. 293-294.

Party's. Or, more properly said, with that election it appeared that the President and his party had become one. If this view fits, then it is easy to see that Roosevelt's triumph would lead him to a combined plebiscitary and energized view of the presidency. The presidency seemed to have become the focus of both the nation's political life and its governing needs. In turn, this creates an injunction for a government more directable by the president. Circumstantially linked to this conception of his opportunities and responsibilities must have been Roosevelt's assumption that with huge Democratic majorities in both houses of Congress, he could be assured of comfortable levels of support for major reforms.

But, in fact, Roosevelt's legislative resources were spread too thin. In late February he remarked that because of the judiciary plan he had not "discussed reorganization with anybody for three weeks. . . ."[103] Consequently, the President divided responsibility for these two reform plans, asking his son James to shepherd the reorganization program while he gave primary attention to the judiciary plan. In practice, the everyday work of defending the President's interests in reorganization fell to the members of the Brownlow Committee.

The legislative year that began with enormous promise for the President ended in defeat or deadlock on his two major reform programs. By the end of the year, the House of Representatives passed an attenuated form of the bill, dropping most of the Brownlow Committee's recommendations but providing the President with six assistants and reenacting the reorganization authority which had lapsed in 1935. But on the Senate side the reorganization bill had not come up for a vote. At least the President could take satisfaction in the fact that his reorganization program remained alive. His judicial reform program suffered a worse fate, being defeated in the Senate Judiciary Committee and recommitted by the Senate as a whole.

It was more than coincidental associations with "court packing" which made the reorganization program subject to charges of power grabbing. The Brownlow Committee's frankness in its *Report* helped spark that political attack. The *Report* was perceptive, direct, intelligent, even at times eloquent. The committee itself defined the field of battle. To support the strong presidency is to support the reorganization program; to reject that vision of the office was to reject the program. The issue of presidential power came to a head concerning those recommendations regarding government's fiscal operations.[104]

---

[103] Quoted in Richard Polenberg, *Reorganizing Roosevelt's Government*, p. 43.
[104] President's Committee on Administrative Management, *Report*, pp. 15-26.

The thrust of these was to reduce the independent power of the Comptroller-General, reasoning that a division of responsibility over spending hampered executive efficacy and obscured congressional interest in quick information about administrative actions.[105] The nub of the issue was the Comptroller-General's authority to disallow expenditures made by authorized administrative agents. The committee recommended that all prior controls over spending be internal to the executive branch, with the Comptroller-General's authority limited to the final audit.

The Brownlow Committee had called for reform in the government's accounting and auditing system for eminently practical reasons; it was not simply guided by some abstract doctrine of executive authority in reaching its fiscal recommendations. The process of fiscal management had become terribly convoluted. Orders for expenditures by the agencies had to meet approval by the General Accounting Office at two different points, without taking into account the final audit. Also, the expenditure control system seemed irrational in that while the Comptroller-General's staff was hindering normal administrative spending actions, his agency lacked consistency and speed in its final auditing responsibility. Thus the agency was failing in its duty of maintaining overall congressional responsibility for the expenditure of appropriated funds. An unstated criticism of the General Accounting Office entailed the personality and behavior of the man who had served as Comptroller-General from 1921 through 1935, J. Raymond McCarl.[106] McCarl had used the office's authority as a bludgeon, imposing his traditional economizing views about the proper purposes of governmental expenditure onto agency spending decisions. Protected as he was by his fifteen-year fixed term, McCarl had become a kind of final authority in government.

The Brownlow Committee's recommendations for integrating all but the final audit into the executive branch contrasted with the report that the Brookings Institution had prepared for Senator Byrd's reorganization committee.[107] But not only was the substance of the Brookings report in opposition to the Brownlow Committee's recommendations; the Brookings Institution itself entered the resulting political fray. With this development, the appearance of a unified public administration establishment was shattered.

[105] For a discussion of the Comptroller-General's authority and role, see Frederick C. Mosher, *The GAO*, pp. 65-97.

[106] See note 70 above.

[107] U.S. Congress, Senate, Select Committee to Investigate the Executive Agencies of the Government, *Report*, 75th Cong., 1st Sess., 1937, part V, pp. 108-109.

In its style and focus, the Brookings Institution's report for the Senate select committee differed greatly from that of the Brownlow Committee.[108] Where the committee's report was terse and sharply focused, the Brookings report was turgid with data and dispersed in its focus. In contrast to the Brownlow Committee's fix on management at the top, Brookings work for Senator Byrd had aimed at determining sites of overlap and inefficiency in government's operations through the massive accumulation of data. Its view was from the bottom.

Beyond differences of style and focus between the two reports, there was an important substantive difference in recommendations for reform of fiscal management.[109] Both reports recommended changes from the existing domination of fiscal management by the Comptroller-General. But in contrast to the Brownlow Committee's call for a sharp break between the executive and legislative dimension of fiscal management, the Brookings report recommended a larger executive role over accounting, but maintained the necessity for a continuing involvement of an independent auditing authority in the process of disbursement—continued disallowance powers and an expanded pre-audit. Behind this technical disagreement was a major political issue. The control over expenditure was a legislative instrument, and its presence in fiscal management signalled a legislative presence within administration.

The Brownlow Committee's best defense for its recommendations lay in their connection to principles of good administration. However, where the Brookings Institution disagreed with the committee's recommendations, the appearance of a theoretical conception of good administration underlying those recommendations vanished. Thus it became easy to portray the Brownlow recommendations as arbitrary preferences, dependent on one's view of executive power for their legitimacy rather than on administrative theory.[110]

[108] Ibid., parts I-V.

[109] Compare the Brownlow Committee's *Report*, pp. 15-25, to part 5 of the Senate Select Committee's *Report*, pp. 103-110.

[110] Speaking to his fellow students of administration through a leading scholarly journal, Lloyd Short sounded a plaintive note about the controversy between the two reports. He said: "The writer cannot refrain from expressing the regret which is shared by many that the divergent views of the President's Committee and the Brookings Institution on certain matters should have been permitted to figure so prominently in congressional committee hearings and debates in the press, thus obscuring the many points upon which both groups were in substantial agreement and the fact that the two reports were complementary rather than conflicting." Lloyd Short, "An Investigation of the Executive Agencies of the United States Government," *American Political Science Review*, 23 (February 1939), 66.

There were two different bases to the Brookings Institution's role as an exponent of congressional authority in the area of fiscal management. The first was intellectual, founded in its view of legislative authority over administration. The second was opportunistic; Brookings was on contract to Senator Harry Byrd, who was set on an anti-Roosevelt course.

The intellectual side of the Brookings defense of the Comptroller-General's role was informed by W. F. Willoughby's views. Of course, as discussed earlier, Willoughby had argued in favor of Congress' delegating its administrative authority to the president, allowing him to function as a general manager. Willoughby had argued that the Comptroller-General's authority over disbursements could easily be justified on the basis of Congress' administrative authority. In fact, Willoughby admitted that there was a strong argument against the intrusion of the Comptroller-General on the grounds of sheer efficiency. But in the end, viewing Congress as the source of all administrative authority, he thought that the principled rather than pragmatic perspective must dominate.[111]

But to understand the full motivation for the conflict between the Brookings Institution and the Brownlow Committee, Senator Harry Byrd's purposes have to be considered. Byrd was by this time an enemy of Roosevelt and the New Deal. His principled position in the reorganization controversy was that of the traditional economizing view of government. But, as governor of Virginia in the 1920's, Byrd had overseen a reorganization of state government planned by Luther Gulick and the Institute for Public Administration that had aimed at enhancing the executive's power—Byrd's power. But the power to be enhanced by the Brownlow Report was Roosevelt's power, and Byrd had a good political reason to opt for the opposing congressional view of reorganization.

The strife between the White House and Senator Byrd was heightened by the failure of the President and Brownlow to consult Senator Byrd.[112] This problem came to a head in January 1937, when Senator Byrd was not included among those who were briefed on the Brownlow Committee's *Report*. The Senator submitted to some embarrassment by having to call Brownlow on January 9th to request a briefing on

---

[111] William F. Willoughby, *Principles of Public Administration* (Washington: Brookings Institution, 1937), pp. 631-633.

[112] Richard Polenberg suggests that Senator Byrd's original agreement to cooperate with the President's Committee rested heavily on an implicit understanding that the senator would be consulted during the course of the investigation. Polenberg, pp. 32-33.

the forthcoming recommendations.[113] When Brownlow and Gulick met with the Senator on January 11th, Capitol Hill was already abuzz with word of the previous day's meeting at the White House.[114]

Senator Byrd objected most strongly to the Brownlow recommendations on fiscal management. Gulick expressed his surprise to Byrd in a letter he wrote to him following the meeting, reminding him of his support of reorganization in Virginia:

> The thing that we are recommending here in Washington is exactly what we recommended in Virginia as to the essential principles and is the plan which you introduced there. You will remember that under the Virginia plan the settlement of claims is handled by the Comptroller who is a member of the finance department and is an auditor who does not keep the accounts and is not responsible to the Governor but is selected by the legislature.[115]

Further evidence for this failure of consultation in conditioning Byrd's opposition is presented by a letter that the Senator sent to Roosevelt two days after his meeting with Brownlow and Gulick and after the reorganization bill had been presented to Congress. Stating his opposition, Byrd implied that the recommendation and his response to it might have been different had he been consulted before they were made public.[116] After one attempt to placate Byrd, at a meeting with him on January 22nd, Roosevelt made no further effort to enlist his cooperation.

The Brownlow Committee vs. Brookings Institution debate over fiscal management became something of a tempest in a teapot. What was symbolically and thus politically important had been the initial disagreement and Senator Byrd's use of it. As the debate continued between the two sets of reorganization planners, it became academic. Yet even as an academic debate it is worth noting because it became

[113] Memorandum, Brownlow to McIntyre, January 9, 1937, President's Official File, 285-C, Roosevelt Library.

[114] The day of the meeting, Byrd delivered a radio address that put him on record as opposed to the direction of the Brownlow recommendations. The thrust of the talk can be gathered from the following: "Retrenchment . . . is always unpopular. . . . Efficiency is always exacting. The economical way is the hard way in anything. But there are times in the histories of governments when these things must be brought about if we are to continue in the pursuit of the national happiness. Such a time is upon us." U.S. Congress, *Congressional Record*, 75th Cong., 1st Sess., Vol. 81, Part 9, p. 26.

[115] Letter, Gulick To Byrd, January 11, 1937, Correspondence-Gulick, President's Committee on Administrative Management, Roosevelt Library.

[116] Letter, Byrd to Roosevelt, January 13, 1937, President's Official file, 285-C, Roosevelt Library.

a reagent highlighting the public administration establishment and its institutions. After several months of a sometimes heated correspondence between Brownlow and Harold Moulton, the director of the Brookings Institution, Moulton, prepared a memorandum justifying the Institution's position, and attempting to suggest that its work had not been conditioned by the political considerations of its Senate employer.[117] Moulton sent this memorandum to the members of the Social Science Research Council and the program officers at the Rockefeller Foundation.[118]

President Roosevelt achieved only some of the benefits of his reorganization planning efforts and only after two congressional sessions of failure.[119] Finally, in 1939, Congress passed a Reorganization Act which delivered to the President the bare bones of what he wanted in his reorganization bill of 1937.[120] It delegated reorganization authority to the president for a two-year period, subject to numerous qualifications, and gave the president the authority to employ six presidential assistants. Roosevelt immediately used the reorganization authority to achieve another recommendation of the Brownlow Committee; in Reorganization Plan No. 1 of 1939 he created the Executive Office of the President and moved into it the Bureau of the Budget, the Central Statistical Board, and the National Resources Planning Committee, redesignating it the National Resources Planning Board. Immediately after Reorganization Plan No. 1, Roosevelt issued an executive order specifying the organization and responsibilities of the expanded presidency.[121] Through this order, Roosevelt designated the formal relationships in the Executive Office, the White House Office with its new assistants, the Bureau of the Budget, and the remaining components of the new presidential establishment.

The Reorganization Act of 1939 did not seem a victory for Roosevelt, lacking as it did most of the President's 1937 bill. It was on its face a congressional product, drafted under the guidance of Repre-

[117] There is an extensive correspondence between members of the Brownlow Committee and officials of the Brookings Institution. High points of the controversy can be seen in Memorandum, Brownlow to Moulton, March 11, 1937, President's Committee on Administrative Management, A-II-45a, Roosevelt Library.

[118] Memorandum, n.d., President's Committee on Administrative Management, A-II-45c, Roosevelt Library.

[119] On the legislative failure of Roosevelt's reorganization plan see Richard Polenberg, *Reorganizing Roosevelt's Government*, Chaps. 6-9; and William E. Leuchtenberg, *Franklin Roosevelt and the New Deal*, 1932-1940 (New York: Harper and Row, 1963), pp. 277-278.

[120] 53 Stat. L. 36.

[121] Executive Order No. 8,248.

sentative Lindsay Warren (Dem., N.C.) as a way of short-circuiting the intense, negative connection between presidential strength and the reorganization program. However, Roosevelt, Brownlow, and Gulick had consulted on the bill, and it gave Roosevelt the core of the Brownlow Committee's recommendations for presidential managerial needs.[122] The Brownlow *Report* speaks to almost every realm of public administration. But the essential view that led the committee to all of its recommendations was an interest in strengthened top-level management. The committee's doctrine was the inseparability of good administration and executive leadership. Thus the Reorganization Act's inclusion of only two elements of the Brownlow recommendations was a success of some measure, because it made possible those reforms which were aimed at supporting the president and extending his authority over administration.

Throughout the legislative battle over reorganization the Brownlow Committee's members worked for the President's (and the presidency's) interests. With the passage of the Reorganization Act the committee served Roosevelt in designing the early use of the authority granted under it. In early spring of 1939, Roosevelt wrote to Luther Gulick that he wished to see all three members of the committee, "just as soon as the Reorganization Bill passes."[123] Gulick then wrote to Brownlow and Merriam:

> F.D.R. plans to call us down the moment he signs the reorganization bill (you notice I spell that with a small "r") because he wants to introduce one or more reorganization orders shortly before the adjournment of Congress. Did you ever see such a matador?[124]

THE BROWNLOW COMMITTEE AND ITS PREDECESSORS

It is a convention of scholarly treatment of the history of executive reorganization to attribute to the Brownlow Committee the initiation of modern comprehensive reorganization's agenda. One prominent author writes: ". . . the most original contribution of the President's Committee . . . was the formulation of a new concept of the admin-

[122] Correspondence, Roosevelt and Lindsay Warren, November 16 and December 5, 1938, President's Secretaries' File 140, Congress; and President's Personal File 2412, Roosevelt Library.

[123] Letter, Roosevelt to Gulick, March 20, 1939, President's Personal File 4307, Roosevelt Library.

[124] Letter, Gulick to Brownlow and Merriam, March 21, 1939, President's Committee on Administrative Management, Current Correspondence, Roosevelt Library.

istrative position of the Chief Executive."[125] As this chapter has shown, it is beyond question that the president's administrative capacity was foremost on the collective mind of the committee. However, fitting this case in with two preceding cases of comprehensive reorganization planning, one is unlikely to see the committee's contribution as wholly innovative. The Brownlow Committee is best understood as distilling a tradition of thinking in public administration that reached back to the work of the President's Commission during the Taft administration. The presidency was central to the work of Frederick Cleveland and his associates just as much as it was at the core of the work of Brownlow, Gulick, and Merriam.

The Brownlow Committee is distinctive in several respects, but these are derivative from an already established reorganization tradition.

One element of distinctiveness about the Brownlow Committee's work was its attention to presidential staff support. Neither the President's Commission nor the Joint Committee considered the topic of White House staff. Yet the commission had seen the need for staff support for an administratively active president, recommending a bureau of administrative control. Where the Brownlow Committee differed was in the more personal cast of its recommendations. The President's Commission recommended a staff organization to serve the presidency in budgeting, whereas the Brownlow Committee sought six presidential assistants to serve as extensions of the president in any area where that was useful.

Another apparent difference between the Brownlow Committee and its predecessors is its greater attention to "top-level management." At a casual glance one might think that the Brownlow Committee had rejected the organizational concerns of its predecessors for an approach aimed solely at the top of the executive branch. But realizing that the thrust of organizational reform for Taft's President's Commission and the Joint Committee of the 1920's was to make governmental agencies more manageable from the top, one understands that what was distinctive about the Brownlow Committee was not so much its fundamental concerns but its perspective. And, of course, the Brownlow Committee by no means rejected organizational rearrangements for the purpose of making government more manageable, as its detailed recommendations for organizational change make clear.

The Brownlow Committee also differs from its predecessor planning episodes in its boldness. The President's Commission and the Joint

---

[125] Herbert Emmerich, *Federal Organization and Administrative Management* (University, Alabama: University of Alabama Press, 1971), p. 58.

Committee spoke softly and obliquely about the link between administrative reform and enhanced presidential authority. On the other hand, the Brownlow Committee spoke more directly to this point. It packaged its recommendations in a single neat *Report* which received very wide distribution. And, at the *Report*'s beginning, as if to make sure that no one missed the point, the committee stated its doctrine in bold language: "The President needs help."[126]

Finally, the Brownlow Committee differs from its predecessors in its relationship to a president. More than earlier reorganization planning efforts, it connected its work to the needs of its patron. Here may be the most important developmental aspect of this case; the committee's ability to be Roosevelt's instrument is symptomatic of the development of the managerially central presidency. Even while the President's Commission had been "presidential" in fact, its guise and language suggest an independent, neutral status of ultimate concern for good administration. But the Brownlow Committee assumed that the interests of good administration and the President's interests were overlapping if not identical.

[126] President's Committee on Administrative Management, *Report*, p. 5.

Chapter Five

THE FIRST HOOVER COMMISSION AND THE MANAGERIAL PRESIDENCY

[Hoover's] big accomplishment in the . . .
Commission [was that] he really contributed to
something approaching a workable theory on the
fundamental nature of the Presidency.[1]

Don K. Price

Modern war is profligate in its use of money as well as lives. By 1945 the national debt had increased six times over its level in 1940.[2] The war's end left a huge debt and a tangle of wartime organizational apparatus and policy. Paradoxically, the end of wartime's frantic spending brought with it a fear that the end of its economic stimulus would cause a return to the depression.[3] Government welcomed peacetime, but no one wanted to return to a "normalcy" of economic depression.

RECONSTRUCTION AND REORGANIZATION

Just as reorganization planning was the tool adopted by office holders to meet the dislocations of the war's end in 1919 and those of the depression in the early 1930's, so both the President and Congress chose reorganization planning as a tool to deal with post-war adjustment in the 1940's. President Harry Truman's initial move in the area of reorganization was consistent with a developing pattern of presidential primacy, viewing reorganization planning and implementation as within the executive domain.[4] But the complication to this as-

---

[1] Don K. Price, "Oral History Interview," Hoover Library, p. 15.

[2] U.S. Bureau of the Census, *The Statistical History of the United States* (New York: Basic Books, 1976), pp. 1,102, 1,114, 1,117.

[3] Alonzo Hamby, *Beyond the New Deal: Harry S. Truman and American Liberalism* (New York: Columbia University Press, 1973), Chap. 1. Predicting peace's dire economic impact, John W. Snyder, head of the Office of War Mobilization, wrote to Truman in August 1945: "In a sense, we have exchanged lives which would have been lost in battle for sharp unemployment at home." Quoted in Cabell Phillips, *The Truman Presidency* (New York: Macmillan, 1966), p. 103.

[4] For a detailed account of Truman's interest in and use of reorganization, see William Pemberton, *Bureaucratic Politics* (Columbia: University of Missouri Press, 1979).

sumption was that Truman was without reorganization authority. The Reorganization Act of 1939 had lapsed in 1941. During wartime, President Roosevelt had used a more sweeping reorganization authority under the First War Powers Act of 1941.[5] But with the end of hostilities that authority vanished.

The main influence on President Truman's estimation of executive organization as a presidential instrument was Harold D. Smith, director of the Bureau of the Budget since 1939. In his unpublished diary, Smith described his advice to Truman on reorganization:

> Congress on its own could never do a reorganization job—in fact, the Congress had never done one successfully in the history of the Government. . . . I took occasion at this point to emphasize the fact that in any event this was an executive function. . . . I pointed out that the reorganization legislation previously in force . . . was the best scheme ever devised. To this the President heartily agreed. I said that the legislation could be brought into force merely by changing the effective date, but that I would suggest the limitations on it be removed. Then with some audacity, I tried to say diplomatically as I could that I thought this was a strategic time to present such a request to Congress. . . . He requested that we prepare a strong message. . . .[6]

On May 24 Truman sent to Congress a message requesting that the reorganization authority be renewed without limitations.[7]

Congress did not grant Truman's request until December 1945, and the Reorganization Act of 1945 contained eleven qualifications on the president's authority to order organizational changes.[8] While Congress finally accepted the same veto mechanism as contained in the Reorganization Act of 1939—veto by concurrent resolution—there was substantial support for a one-house veto. Also like the 1939 act, this delegation of authority was limited to two years, expiring on April 1, 1948.

Armed with reorganization authority, Truman used the Bureau of

[5] 55 Stat. L. 838.

[6] Diary of Harold D. Smith, May 4, 1945, Truman Library. Also see entries for April 26, May 16, and May 21.

[7] *Public Papers of the Presidents: Harry Truman, 1945* May 24, 1945, pp. 71-72.

[8] 59 Stat. L. 613. For a brief legislative history of the Reorganization Act of 1945 see Louis Fisher and Ronald Moe, "Delegating With Ambivalence: The Legislative Veto and Reorganization Authority," in Congressional Research Service, *Studies on the Legislative Veto* (Washington: Government Printing Office, 1980), pp. 196-204.

the Budget to prepare a reorganization program.[9] Director Smith proposed that any reorganization ought to address one or more of the following objectives: (1) reducing the number of agencies reporting to the president; (2) grouping together related functions; (3) strengthening the heads of departments and the internal organization of the departments; (4) achieving more effective groupings of agencies; and (5) strengthening the machinery at the top of the executive branch for improved leadership. Essentially, the bureau's advice was that reorganization's agenda should aim at strengthening presidential management.[10]

On May 16, 1946, President Truman sent three reorganization plans to Congress. Plan No. 1 made permanent some temporary changes which had earlier been ordered by authority of the War Powers Act of 1945. Plan No. 2 transferred social welfare related activities to the Federal Security Administration; the President's message described these changes as a step toward the ultimate transformation of FSA into a cabinet-level department. Plan No. 3 ordered a number of reforms within five departments, none of these being interdepartmental transfers.[11] The House of Representatives passed resolutions of disapproval for each of the plans, but two, Plan Nos. 1 and 3, survived the Senate. Acting budget director Paul Appleby attributed the administration's defeat in the House to the lack of effective leadership in support of the administration.[12] And things were to get worse as the congressional election of 1946 brought Republican majorities in both houses.

A Congressional Approach to Reorganization Planning

The Republican victory in 1946 augured ill for the Democrat's chances in the 1948 presidential race. President Truman's most astute White House assistant, Clark Clifford, recalls of that election: "It pointed up more clearly than anything else could that there was no clear direction, no political cohesion to the Truman program. . . . And it pointed to two more years of frustration and final defeat for Mr.

[9] Letter, Truman to Harold Smith, December 20, 1945, Official File, 285-A, Truman Library.

[10] Memorandum, Smith to President, February 8, 1946, President's Secretary's Files, General File-Reorganization, Truman Library.

[11] U.S. Congress, Senate, Committee on the Judiciary, Hearings, 79th Cong., 2nd Sess., pp. 1-24.

[12] Memorandum, Appleby to Truman, June 27, 1946, Official File, 285-A, Truman Library.

Truman in 1948."[13] Presuming that their party would hold the White House after 1948, the Republicans of the 80th Congress set out to use executive reorganization for quite different ends than those sought by President Truman, essentially ignoring the President's claims and initiatives in the area.

Through identical bills introduced in both houses in January 1947, Senator Henry Cabot Lodge (Rep., Mass.) and Representative Clarence Brown (Rep., Ohio) proposed a commission to plan for organization of the government.[14] In the Senate, Lodge introduced the bill with the following statement: "This Commission will find the places where economies can be effected and the places where there is overlapping and duplication."[15] This traditional, economizing approach to reorganization passed unanimously through both houses of Congress in July, presumably made acceptable by its generalized appeal to economy and its bipartisanship. The Commission on the Organization of the Executive Branch would have twelve members appointed in a tripartite fashion, four by the president, four by the Speaker of the House, and four by the president pro tempore of the Senate. In each set of four appointments, two were to be private citizens and two public officials, and the four were to be evenly divided in party affiliation. The commission would elect its own chair.[16]

The administration was cool to the Lodge-Brown bill; the new budget director, James Webb, expressed strong reservations about a congressionally initiated commission, but he promised full cooperation.[17] Frederick Lawton, assistant budget director, testified at committee hearings that the administration preferred the continuing process of presidential reorganization authority to a "one-time approach" such as that of the Lodge-Brown bill.[18]

Ironically, the strongest defense of presidential primacy in reorganization was made by an agent of Congress, Comptroller-General Lindsay Warren. Warren, a former member of Congress, had been floor leader for the Reorganization Act of 1939 and had consequently been appointed by Roosevelt as Comptroller-General. Warren described the Lodge-Brown bill as pointless, arguing that there was already a re-

[13] Quoted in Cabell Phillips, *The Truman Presidency*, p. 163.

[14] H.R. 775 and S. 164.

[15] U.S. Congress, *Congressional Record*, 80th Cong., 1st Sess., 1947, Vol. 93, part 1, p. 268.

[16] 61 Stat. L. 246.

[17] Letter, Webb to M. C. Latta, Clerk of the White House, July 3, 1947, BOB, E 11-1/47.1, RG 51, National Archives.

[18] U.S. Congress, Senate, Committee on Expenditures, *Hearings*, 80th Cong., 1st Sess.

organization agenda based on widely accepted principles of government organization; there was no need to reinvent an approach to
reorganization. And, he argued, the means for effective reform was
presidential reorganization authority.[19]

At first appearance the Lodge-Brown bill presented the traditional
congressional doctrine of economy through reorganization. But the
Republican Congress sought more than economy. Beneath the Lodge-
Brown bill's facade of bipartisanship lay a sharply etched ideological
mission. That real intention of the Republican 80th Congress' use of
comprehensive reorganization is seen in the process of forming the
Commission on the Organization of the Executive Branch.

ORGANIZING THE HOOVER COMMISSION

Speaker of the House Joseph Martin (Rep., Mass.) made the most
important appointment to the new commission, former President Herbert Hoover. The appointment was symbolically charged; resurgent
Republicans mandated their last president, and the New Deal's foremost critic, with the task of reassessing the national government. By
private agreement between Hoover and the Republican congressional
leadership, he accepted the appointment on the condition that he
would be made chairman.[20]

During the brief negotiations over his appointment, Hoover remained in New York City and was represented in Washington by his
friend and former associate at the Department of Commerce, Julius
Klein. Something of the spirit of the GOP leadership can be gathered
from Klein's telegram to Hoover on the day of his appointment to the
commission: "Decent folks here all delighted your selection. . . . New
Deal bureaucratic units however much alarmed. . . ."[21] Shortly after-
wards, Klein gave Hoover a description of Representative Clarence
Brown's plan for the commission:

> Brown plans to get into the matter very aggressively and asked me
> to pass along the word to you in strict confidence that he put in the
> provision that the Commission should report *after* November 1948

[19] Letter, Warren to Rep. Clare Hoffman, May 21, 1947, Official File, 285-A, Truman
Library.
[20] Telegrams, Klein to Hoover, Hoover to Klein, July 18, 1947; Letters, Klein to
Hoover, July 18 and 24, 1947, First Hoover Commission, General Management of the
Executive Branch, Correspondence-Klein, Hoover Library.
[21] Telegram, Klein to Hoover, July 18, 1947, *ibid.*

... so as to lay the groundwork for the expected complete house-cleaning that will be necessary at that time.[22]

By July 18 the other commissioners had been named. President Truman appointed Dean Acheson, James Forrestal, George H. Mead, and Arthur S. Flemming. The president pro tempore of the Senate Arthur Vandenburg appointed Joseph P. Kennedy, Senator John McClellan (Dem., Ark.), Professor James K. Pollock, and Senator George D. Aiken (Rep., Vt.). Aside from Herbert Hoover, Speaker Martin named James H. Rowe, Jr., Representative Carter Manasco, and Representative Clarence J. Brown. Julius Klein sent Hoover a capsule political description of the Democrats appointed. He told Hoover that they looked more promising than might be expected. Carter Manasco, a congressman from Alabama, "is a first class conservative," and James H. Rowe, Jr., "is a former F.D.R. assistant but less friendly to the New Deal in recent years."[23] With Joe Kennedy, whose conservative stripes were clear by this time, the bipartisan split did not seem to hamper the likelihood of a conservative majority. However, Klein warned, on the Republican side, it would be necessary to keep an eye on Senator Aiken and George Mead, a paper manufacturer from Dayton. Aiken had liberal tendencies and Mead was not to be counted upon because he was a favorite of the administration for bipartisan appointments.[24]

What Is To Be Studied?

The commission's first meeting was held at the White House on September 29, 1947; Hoover was elected chairman, and Dean Acheson was elected vice-chairman. The only substantive matter taken up was the means for implementing the commission's recommendation.[25] Having assumed a Republican president after 1948, Congressman Brown argued that the best way to get action was through presidential reorganization plans. The effect of this discussion on the commission was to convince its members of the importance of recommending the renewal of the reorganization authority, due to lapse on April 1, 1948.

[22] Letter, Klein to Hoover, July 18, *ibid.*

[23] Thirty-two years later, Rowe's response at hearing Klein's judgment of him for the first time was a tart "He was wrong." James Rowe, Jr., interviewed by author, October 23, 1979.

[24] Letters, Klein to Hoover, July 18 and October 6, 1947, First Hoover Commission, General Management of the Executive Branch, Correspondence-Klein, Hoover Library.

[25] Minutes, September 29, 1949, Hoover Commission Minutes, Pollock papers, Michigan Historical Collection, Bentley Library, Ann Arbor, Michigan.

With Hoover in its chair, the commission became the Hoover Commission, and Hoover treated it as his. With a remarkable vigor—he was 72 in 1947—Hoover developed an organization and agenda for his commission. In early October he circulated a "preliminary outline" of work among the members. It suggested zeroing in on government's functions in a three-stage process: (1) identify the parts of government by function; (2) determine the most important of those functions; (3) organize groups of experienced people to investigate those functions. Hoover decided that the research should be done by specialist task forces; consequently the commission's staff itself could be assigned to administrative and support roles.

Hoover's approach to the commission's work was close to his reorganization experiences of the 1920's. On his list of functions to be examined he included "presidential direction and control," but by this he meant only the issue of the president's span of control.[26] The presidency figured in Hoover's view of reorganization much as it had in reorganization in the 1920's. He was set on making organization more manageable rather than in making the president a more effective manager; therein was an intellectual seam—the difference in perspective—between the Joint Committee and the Brownlow Committee.

It was on the topic of presidential management that Hoover received the most response from commissioners. James Pollock, a distinguished political scientist at Michigan and a Republican who had known Hoover for a decade, gently urged that the agenda be broadened "to make clear that a study is needed of the function of the whole office of the President, which had expanded so greatly." Also Pollock suggested some attention be given to "tools of management as well as . . . functions. . . ."[27] Commissioner James Forrestal also suggested a focus on top-level management. He agreed with Pollock that managerial tools ought to be examined—fiscal management, personnel policy, etc. But more important, he thought, the commission should address the idea of a cabinet secretariat.[28] Forrestal, who as Secretary of the Navy sat in Truman's cabinet, was fascinated by the possibility of adapting aspects of collective decision making in the British cabinet system to presidential government. Dean Acheson observed that this idea "possessed his mind."[29]

[26] Letter, Hoover to Pollock, October 3, 1947, Hoover Commission, Correspondence-Hoover, Pollock Papers, Michigan Historical Collection.

[27] Letter, Pollock to Hoover, October 9, 1947, First Hoover Commission, General Correspondence-Pollock, Hoover Library.

[28] Letter, Forrestal to Hoover, October 30, 1947, First Hoover Commission, General Correspondence-Forrestal, Hoover Library.

[29] Transcript, "Princeton Seminars," July 2, 1953, p. 8, Dean Acheson Papers, Truman

Pollock's and Forrestal's views were that the Hoover Commission should pick up the unfinished task of the Brownlow Committee in strengthening top-level management. This position was reinforced by a third voice joining the discussion, that of Director of the Budget James Webb. Hoover turned to the bureau with a pressing problem. Having been away from government since 1933, he needed guidance in traveling the labyrinth of the contemporary executive branch. He also needed access to information, and the bureau was the best source of information about the executive branch. But it was also an agency with one client, the president. If Hoover was to rely upon it, it would have to be within a context that was acceptable to Truman. This was the setting for a meeting on October 6 between Hoover and Webb.[30]

Discussion began with Hoover's request for assistance on the commission's study relating to the presidency, which Hoover would conduct himself. After hearing Hoover's plans and views, James Webb decided that this was "a happy development." As Webb later wrote to Truman:

> As you know, numerous proposals bearing directly on the Presidency are being advocated. . . . The evaluation of such proposals by persons who have not either occupied the Presidential office itself, or worked in extremely intimate relationship with it, is extraordinarily difficult. From my several conversations with Mr. Hoover, I am convinced of his appreciation of the difficulty and delicacy of dealing with the whole problem.[31]

As if to guarantee the direction of the commission's study on the presidency, Webb recommended an assistant for Hoover who would bring a Brownlowian perspective to the subject. This was Don K. Price, then working with Herbert Emmerich, Brownlow's successor as director at the Public Administration Clearing House. Hoover arranged to borrow Price, while reimbursing the Clearing House for his

---

Library. In this seminar Acheson also described the following example of Forrestal's passion for cabinet government. During the summer of 1946 Forrestal had attempted to keep the cabinet active while Truman was away from Washington. He arranged luncheons to which the cabinet was invited and attempted to convince White House staff member Clark Clifford to serve as informal secretary of the cabinet group. Upon learning of this development, Truman ordered his staff to have nothing to do with it, and he ordered the cabinet to meet only in his presence.

[30] Memorandum, Francis Brassor to Hoover, October 3, 1947, First Hoover Commission, General Correspondence-Brassor, Hoover Presidential Library. Also present at this meeting were Assistant Budget Director Donald Stone and chief of the bureau's government organization section, Arnold Miles.

[31] Memorandum, Webb to Truman, n.d. (mid-October 1948), Webb papers, Truman Library.

salary.[32] Consequently, the bureau cooperated with the commission. As one assistant director Frederick Lawton later recalled: "Whatever type of informational service they wanted, we'd endeavor to supply them . . . tell them who were the people they should contact. . . . We had talked to Mr. Hoover generally about our views on . . . the Presidency."[33]

There was a deeper base to Hoover's apparently benign view of the modern presidency than an instrumental relationship to the Bureau of the Budget. Hoover was an ex-president who must have been impressed by the expanded capacities of the office under his Democratic successors. In addition, the curiously emotional tie that developed between Hoover and Truman helped shape the former's view of Truman's presidency. Truman welcomed Hoover back into the White House after decades of exile. Even before the commission came along, Truman called Hoover back to national service for work on his Famine Emergency Committee. The import of all this for Hoover shines through a note that he wrote to Truman in 1962:

> When the attack on Pearl Harbor came, I at once supported the President and offered to serve in any useful capacity. . . . I thought my service might again be useful, however there was no response.
>
> When you came to the White House within a month you opened the door to me to the only profession I knew, public service, and you undid some disgraceful action that had been taken in the prior years.[34]

The Two Faces of Hoover's Agenda

Seemingly at odds with Hoover's favorable view of the Truman presidency was his ideological ambition for the commission. From a Republican perspective the commission's task was preparation for the coming Republican administration. The "housecleaning" that Congressman Brown had mentioned did not mean enhancing the president's capacity; it meant hacking back at the expense and activities of the Democrat's government. Thus there was tension between these tendencies, mirrored in Hoover himself. On its face, the choice to put

[32] Don K. Price, "Oral History Interview," Hoover Library, p. 3.

[33] Frederick Lawton, "Oral History Interview," Truman Library, p. 15.

[34] Letter, Hoover to Truman, December 19, 1962, President's Secretary's File, General File-Hoover, Truman Library. The "disgraceful action" to which Hoover refers must have been Franklin Roosevelt's decision to change the name of the Hoover Dam, construction of which began in 1931, to the Boulder Dam. In 1947 President Truman ordered it renamed the Hoover Dam.

Hoover at the head of the commission seemed perfectly consistent with the ambition for the commission that Brown represented. Hoover had spent the last two decades excoriating the evils of the New Deal, Democrats, and socialism. But there was another side to Hoover which James Webb saw; this was the Hoover of the 1920's, the Hoover who had grappled with the problems of the presidency and executive branch. Thus Hoover brought to the commission a kind of split view of its agenda. In regard to the presidency and centralized management, he was a friend of continuing modern tendencies, but in regard to the policies of government, "functions," his anti-governmental side dominated.

That other side of Hoover was expressed in the second meeting of the Hoover Commission, on October 20, 1947. Chairman Hoover raised an issue that was to remain unsettled until the 1948 election and even crept into parts of the commission's final reports. This was the issue of whether or not the commission's mandate included the responsibility for assessing the soundness of policies as well as the efficacy of organizations. The Lodge-Brown Act mandated to the commission the responsibility to assess policy. The act offered five means through which the commission was to go about promoting "economy, efficiency and improved service." The first three related to organizational reform and expenditure reduction, but points four and five entailed the assessment of policy. Point four stated that these ends could be achieved by "abolishing services, activities, and functions not necessary to the efficient conduct of government," and point five stated that they could be achieved by "defining and limiting executive functions, services and activities."[35]

Chairman Hoover convinced a majority of commissioners that they had a license to assess policy. He drafted a "policy statement" to this effect which was adopted by the commission on October 20, 1947.[36] This action was crucial because that meeting was to launch the process of investigation; thus the consideration of the place of "policy" in its work took the form of a discussion of the principle upon which task forces would be constituted. The "policy statement" asserted that the commission was "not confined to recommending management or structural changes but is . . . directed to exploring the boundaries of government functions in the light of their cost, their usefulness, their

[35] 61 Stat. L. 246, section 1.
[36] Minutes, October 20, 1947, Hoover Commission Minutes, Pollock Papers, Michigan Historical Collection.

limitations, and their curtailment or elimination."[37] It glossed this with the observation that:

> At no time has there been such a public desire for a complete reconsideration of the province of the Federal government and overhaul of the business methods of Federal administration and their relationship to the citizen. The need is much greater than at any time in the past. The huge expansion of the executive branch during the past 20 years has been made in an atmosphere of hurry and emergency which now calls for calm challenge.[38]

Defending the interests of the Truman administration, Dean Acheson argued against any evaluation of policies "except when they are clearly so subordinate as not to endanger by their disappearance programs which have been given Congressional or Presidential approval."[39] The only profitable concern for the commission, he continued, was enhancing the executive's capacity to administer government. Acheson saw the choice of direction for the commission as entailing a choice for Republican or Democratic interests in the next election.[40]

But Hoover saw no contradiction in pursuing an executive enhancing inquiry, on the one hand (in the study regarding the presidency), and conducting a critique of government's intrusion into the private sector, on the other hand. One might argue that to pursue these two purposes at once was to strengthen the central instrument of governance for the modern state while favoring destruction of the state's capacity and works. But Hoover thought that each inquiry was distinct; management and policy substance pertained to different aspects of government.

Hoover's sympathy for executive enhancement stemmed from a view of these matters as procedural. All organizations must be managed, regardless of their function. Therefore, management was itself a politically neutral concept. On the other hand, the functions performed by these organizations were political. The national government created by the New Deal was wasteful and intrusive. This was not just partisanship; it was Hoover's political credo. He was not a laissez-faire

---

[37] "Policy Statement Adopted at Commission Meeting on October 20, 1947," Commission on Organization of the Executive Branch, Executive Director-Misc'l Correspondence-Policy Statement, RG 264, National Archives.

[38] *Ibid.*

[39] Memorandum, Acheson to Hoover, n.d. (November 6, 1947), p. 16, Confidential File, Truman Library.

[40] Transcript, "Princeton Seminars," July 2, 1953, p. 19, Acheson Papers, Truman Library.

conservative. More than anything else, he was Wilsonian, believing in an economy of small units coordinated by cooperation, with businessmen and citizens alike protected by governmental regulation in those few areas where it was necessary, such as public utilities' rate-making.[41] To Hoover, the New Deal's social-welfare policies and its forays into public power and resource development were an anathema.

Hoover thought that government needed greater coherence and central executive capacity, while he also thought that major parts of government's functions were undesirable and inefficient. He could not examine the presidency without engaging the first view, and he could not examine the activities of the departments without engaging the second view. He could be "liberal" and "conservative" at the same time, concerned with strengthening the presidency and critical of big government, as long as he was able to maintain separate intellectual compartments wherein presidential managerial capacity was confined to one and public policy was kept solely within the other compartment.[42]

Chairman Hoover held the two missions of his commission in separate compartments, and he appointed staff and delegated tasks in ways that fit into one or another compartment. Hoover began organizing the staff during late summer 1947. In early September, he acquired an assistant in the person of Dr. Arthur Kemp, an economist at the New York University School of Business. Kemp's viewpoint was consistent with Hoover's own anti-New Deal position. His first assignment demonstrated Hoover's use of an ideological test in appointing some of the staff. Hoover asked Kemp to research the literature of public administration for the names of experts who might be called upon to serve the commission. To this end, Kemp examined the recently published *Elements of Public Administration*, edited by Fritz Morstein Marx, a group of essays written by leading young scholars of the field.[43] In reporting to Hoover, Kemp found all the authors who had contributed to the volume (James W. Fesler, George Graham, V. O. Avery Leiserson, Harvey C. Mansfield, John D. Millett, Don K. Price, and Wallace S. Sayre, among others) to be "a list of people to keep out of any work of the Committee [*sic*] on Government Organization

---

[41] The most consistent treatment of Hoover as a progressive is Joan Hoff Wilson, *Herbert Hoover: Forgotten Progressive* (Boston: Little, Brown, 1975).

[42] On this tension in Hoover's action and ideas, see Peri E. Arnold, "Ambivalent Leviathan: Herbert Hoover and the Positive State," in J. David Greenstone (ed.), *Public Values and Private Power in American Politics* (Chicago: University of Chicago Press, 1982), pp. 109-138.

[43] *Elements of Public Administration* (New York: Prentice-Hall, 1946).

. . . each of these gentlemen has essentially the New Deal approach."[44] Parenthetically, it is a testament to the paradox of the commission's maintenance of two categories of work that several of these experts black-listed by one side of the commission's "personality" turned up as important contributing members to the work of its other side.

Another instance of Hoover's ideological bias in staff considerations appears in his search for a secretary for the commission. Julius Klein conducted the search for him in Washington. While the result was fruitless, his attempt to recruit G. Lyle Belsley for the position exemplifies ideological considerations. Belsley was an experienced Washington "hand" who had been a member of the Brownlow Committee's research staff and worked in government during the war. He was nominated for the commission staff by Admiral Lewis Strauss, an old friend of Hoover's and a prominent Republican. After thoroughly checking on Belsley, Klein assured Hoover that he showed "not a trace of New Deal or other unfavorable political contacts."[45] Through September, Hoover, Strauss, and Klein importuned Belsley to take the job, but he stood firm in declining it. At that, Hoover used his appointment power to name Francis Bressor to the job without any consultation with the commission.

Other activities of Julius Klein reflect the political character of the search for staff members. From late July on, Klein gathered names of those who might serve as staff researchers and investigators. A major source of recommendations was Representative John Taber (Rep., New York), a devout conservative and chairman of the Appropriations Committee in the 80th Congress. Taber had a corps of investigators to poke into the spending habits of agencies, and he insured the trustworthiness of his sleuths through checks by the Federal Bureau of Investigation. Taber recommended that Hoover borrow some of these people for his staff, providing FBI reports on his staff to pass on to Hoover.[46] Finally Hoover was imperious in his selection of an executive director. At the commission's October meeting he mentioned to vice-chairman Dean Acheson that he was considering Sidney Mitchell, a banker of Hoover's long acquaintance, for the post of director; Acheson protested, recommending against the appointment. At the commission's next meeting Hoover announced Mitchell's appointment.[47]

[44] Memorandum, Kemp to Hoover, September 9, 1942, First Hoover Commission, General Correspondence-Kemp, Hoover Library.

[45] Loretta Carp (Hoover's secretary) to Klein, September 13, 1947, and Klein to Hoover, September 18, 1947, First Hoover Commission, General Management of the Executive Branch, Correspondence-Klein, Hoover Library.

[46] Letter, Klein to Hoover, July 31, 1947, *ibid.*

[47] This incident was related to presidential assistant John Steelman by Acheson; Steel-

Building Task Forces

Hoover dominated the commission's meetings of October 20 and November 18, 1947, with his recommendations for potential areas of study for task forces. At the November 18th meeting Hoover also offered a large number of names to his fellow commissioners as potential task force appointments.[48] In fact, Hoover had already contacted a number of those mentioned, with requests that they either head or join one of the task forces. Hoover's power in task-force selection was secured by the passivity of his fellow commissioners, producing an unquestioning majority.

Hoover's conservative policy biases were ingrained into his view of the world. They were, he thought, the views of a sensible man. The following gives some flavor of how he approached policy areas that were fraught with political traps. He announced:

> I would like to make an inquiry by this Commission by some perfectly unbiased people as to certain business operations of the government, whether those operations are better conducted by government than by private enterprise. I would like to know which is which. . . . We can take some of these government agencies that are actively in the field and examine them in their relative situation vis à vis private enterprise as to whether they are doing a better, more economical, and more just service . . . , and what the balance is in favor or against. I would like to see it done. If you gentlemen want me to, I will try to fish around and see if I can find some people to suggest.[49]

The commission approved this plan, as it routinely approved Hoover's suggestions. It is interesting to see what Hoover meant by "unbiased" in the selection of task force leaders.

For his task force on "Federal Business Enterprises," Hoover wound up contracting with two major accounting firms to produce reports, Haskins and Sells, and Price, Waterhouse. However, the firms in this case were a secondary consideration; the commission wound up with them because Hoover approached principals in the firms with the request that they lead task forces, and these principals countered by offering their firms' services. In the case of Price, Waterhouse, Hoover

---

man reported it to a White House staff conference on November 5, 1947. Eben Ayers Diary, p. 172, Truman Library. Mitchell had served in Hoover's Committee for Belgian Relief and had long been a Hoover loyalist.

[48] Transcripts, October 20 and November 18, 1947, Commission on Organization of the Executive Branch, Secretary's Office-Transcripts, RG 264, National Archives.

[49] Transcript, November 18, 1947, Commission on Organization of the Executive Branch, Secretary's Office-Transcripts, RG 264, National Archives.

had approached Paul Grady, a partner of that firm. Grady had been recommended by Lewis Strauss, James Forrestal, and Sidney Mitchell, Hoover intimates who shared his economic conservatism.[50]

Another example of Hoover's tendencies can be seen in the task force on "Natural Resources." Throughout late November and much of December, Commissioner James Rowe, Jr., himself a westerner, sought some influence on the selection of members for this task force. He feared the appearance of political bias in the make-up of the task forces and expressed that fear to Hoover in mid-November.[51] Consequently, he attempted to broaden the "Natural Resources" task force by suggesting prominent Americans connected with the conservation movement who were not involved in natural resources either as businessmen or as politicians with pork-barrel interests. Rowe urged upon him people such as Bernard De Voto, the writer, and Charles Mckinley, a political scientist specializing in natural resources policy.[52] None of Rowe's suggestions was taken by Hoover. Rowe recalls that none of the commissioners had any real influence on appointments of staff or task force members.[53]

Thus, Hoover efficiently built into several of the task forces a bias which matched his own view of politically sensitive areas. Another interesting case of this was in the task force on "Federal-State Relations." Hoover appointed Thomas J. Coolidge to head it; he was chairman of the United Fruit Company. The members of the task force were drawn from business and state governments. Rowe, who was particularly active in following these matters because he spent almost full time on the commission's work, protested, writing to Hoover the following:

> Since the release yesterday of the names of the committee on Federal and state relationships, I have heard considerable criticism in government circles that the committee appears to be top-heavy with states' rights men. I am inclined to agree with this criticism at least in one sense—that there is no man on the committee who has any experience with the federal point of view. . . .[54]

[50] Paul Grady, "Oral History Interview." Hoover Library, p. 3.

[51] Letter, Rowe to Hoover, November 12, 1947, Commission on Organization of the Executive Branch, Executive Director-Misc'l Correspondence-Rowe, RG 264, National Archives.

[52] Correspondence, Rowe and Hoover, December 12, 20, 23, 26, First Hoover Commission, General Correspondence-Rowe, Hoover Library.

[53] James Rowe, Jr., interviewed by author, October 23, 1979.

[54] Memorandum, Rowe to Hoover, December 19, 1947, Commission on Organization of the Executive Branch, Executive Director, Task Force Files—Federal and State Relations, RG 264, National Archives.

However, in this glance at the organization of the task forces to aid the commission, it would leave a distorted impression to mention only the political bias that Chairman Hoover built into several of them. There were, after all, thirty-four different study teams working on twenty-three organizational and policy areas.[55] The study groups which developed reports within these different areas were not all, properly speaking, task forces. Fifteen of the thirty-four studies were contracted out to research and consulting firms. The organizations brought into the commission's work in this manner included the Brookings Institution (transportation and welfare), the Institute of Public Administration (budgeting), Klein and Saks (federal field services), the National Bureau of Economic Research (statistical services), Haskins & Sells (federal business enterprises), Price, Waterhouse & Co. (federal business enterprises), and Cresap, McCormick & Paget (personnel management).

The Hoover Commission's size and scope of operations dwarfed earlier reorganization planning operations. Among its task forces were many who were committed to careful and objective work. Chairman Hoover's political biases in some appointments should not obscure the fact that over all it was a distinguished group that served the commission. In fact, it is the over-all distinction of the group that highlights the less distinguished and partisan character of Hoover's selections in some areas.

Hoover's choices of staff to aid him in the report on the President's role within the general management of government reflected an acceptance of big government. At the commission's November 18th meeting, Hoover announced that he would conduct the study on the president's relationship to government organization and that Don Price would assist him. Price was one of those who Arthur Kemp had suggested be kept out of the commission's work. As if for good measure, Hoover also arranged for the help of another contributor to the *Elements of Public Administration*, John D. Millett of Columbia University. Hoover also asked James Rowe to work on this project; Rowe

[55] A list of subject areas and individual study groups as well as the personnel of all the groups can be found in *The Hoover Commission Report* (New York: McGraw-Hill, 1949), pp. 505-524. The titles of the different studies are as follows: 1. General Management of the Executive Branch; 2. Budgeting and Accounting; 3. Statistical Services; 4. Records Management; 5. Federal Supply Activity; 6. Personnel Management; 7. Foreign Affairs; 8. National Security Organization; 9. Treasury Department; 10. The Post Office; 11. Department of Agriculture; 12. Department of Interior; 13. Department of Commerce; 14. Department of Labor; 15. Medical Activities; 16. Veterans' Affairs; 17. Federal Business Enterprise; 18. Independent Regulatory Commissions; 19. Social Security and Education; 20. Indian Affairs; 21. Overseas Administration; 22. Federal-State Relations; 23. Federal Research.

was the only other commissioner who had worked in the White House. However, Hoover so dominated the commission's work regarding the presidency that Rowe's role was minimal.[56]

The commission developed two different circles or coalitions: one to deal with matters relating to presidential organization and one to deal with governmental functions. In effect, the commission as a whole took on Hoover's own bifurcated view of government. On those issues amenable to an anti-big-government perspective, the commission typically split nine commissioners to three, Hoover leading eight commissioners against the liberal minority of Acheson, Pollock, and Rowe. When the issue under consideration related to the presidency, these three liberals had inordinate influence, joining with Hoover and several other commissioners to carry the day for presidency-strengthening recommendations.

The commission's liberals' major resource was their assistants. Each commissioner chose one assistant, and Acheson and Pollock brought to the commission two of its most effective staff people. Acheson used Charles Aiken, an assistant professor of political science at Berkeley, and Pollock chose Ferrel Heady, a young political scientist at Michigan. These able, hard-working assistants and the three liberal commissioners provided a focal point for a continuing conversation about the presidency into which Don Price entered as another key participant.

Mention of political scientists working with the Hoover Commission deserves an aside, given the apparent differences between the Brownlow Committee and the Hoover Commission. The former has the appearance of being a foray into planning by liberal academicians, and the latter appears as a solid group of sober, practical men. But interestingly, behind the facade of the Hoover Commission was a covey of political scientists equivalent in size to the research staff of the Brownlow Committee. Excluding the two commissioners who held Ph.D.'s in political science, Flemming and Pollock, twenty-nine political scientists served the commission in one role or another.[57] Predictably, where their influence was most felt was on the problem of presidential management.

THE HOOVER COMMISSION IN OPERATION

The Hoover Commission operated in a highly decentralized manner in which different of its parts were influenced by different forces. Consider the commission as a set of concentric circles. The center

[56] James Rowe, Jr., interviewed by author.

[57] "Political Scientists Connected with the Commission on Organization of the Executive Branch," box 39, file 12, Pollock Papers, Michigan Historical Collection.

circle holds Chairman Hoover and his staff; in the next circle are the other commissioners and their assistants, with some of the commissioners and assistants closer to the center than others, and in the third circle is the commission's study groups. This device of concentric circles dramatizes the separation between the commission's operating levels. Perhaps isolation is a better term; frequently the outer circle operated with very little guidance from the core.

That isolation had the effect of granting great freedom to the task forces. The groups had two different problems, given the broad nature of their charters to examine and recommend reforms within the areas to which they were assigned. The first problem was that the expectations for the kind of report they would produce were not clarified. The second problem was that instead of encouraging study groups working on related problems to coordinate their work, Hoover initially discouraged such communication through what Acheson's assistant, Charles Aiken, called the "task force non-intercourse policy."[58]

Chairman Hoover's original view on the study groups is that one could appoint experts (exercising the kind of personnel selectivity that would pre-determine the general orientation of the groups) and leave them on their own. Several months into 1948, it became evident that this approach was short-sighted. In March, Dr. Howard Rusk, chairman of the Agriculture task force, told Hoover that his task force was in some quandary over the exact scope of its inquiry and ends.[59] By May it was clear that Hoover would have to find means for giving more guidance to the study groups, and he conducted several "coordination dinners" in New York to which he brought together members of related groups.[60] These dinners did not squelch the demand for coordination. After one of the coordination dinners, Robert Moses, chairman of the Public Works task force, requested that several meetings be arranged between himself and chairmen of other study groups.[61] In creating a format for coordination, Hoover attempted to retain full control over it, conducting the dinners at his Waldorf-Astoria suite and combining the role of host and chairman of the post-dinner meeting. Yet the task forces' needs for coordination went be-

[58] Memo, Aiken to Acheson, July 3, 1948, Commission on Organization of the Executive Branch, Aiken Memoranda, Acheson papers, Truman Library.

[59] Letter, Rusk to Hoover, March 4, 1948, Commission on Organization of the Executive Branch, Executive Director, Task Force Files-Agriculture, RG 264, National Archives.

[60] Memo, Aiken to Acheson, June 18, 1948, Commission on Organization of the Executive Branch of the Government, Aiken Memoranda, Acheson Papers, Truman Library.

[61] Memorandum, Aiken to Acheson, July 3, 1948, *ibid.*

yond those that could be served by an instrument so easily controlled by the chairman.

There was also isolation between the commission's core and its first circle—between the chairman and the commissioners. Hoover was a domineering man and a solitary worker. With the exception of Don Price, he had surrounded himself with a worshipful personal staff to which he was "the Chief." He had always been intolerant of multi-headed organizations so, regardless of the commission's structure, he was set on running it as his organization.[62] Just as he took upon himself the commission's personnel authority, so he considered it his prerogative to generate policy guidelines for the task forces when it became clear they were needed. The commissioners were virtual outsiders in this process, dependent on rumors to keep track of the chairman's actions. In one of his unfailingly clever memoranda, James Rowe spoke to Acheson of Hoover's style. He observed that Hoover:

> . . . will tell the task force leaders what he wants them to put in their reports and he will not give his fellow Commissioners any time to prepare adequate rebuttal material. He has done it since 1921 and he has gotten away with it. Objectively I admire the technique, but . . . I don't happen to be objective in this deal.[63]

Distrust was one result of the semi-isolation of the commission's parts. Another was that the different parts of the commission's work fell under the influence of external forces. Its processes and final recommendations were heavily shaped by cooptations that, on the whole, tended to improve the product.

The Commission's Environment

Five elements had constant proximity to the commission's work and influenced its recommendations. Three of these were official institutions within the national government, the president (largely represented by the Bureau of the Budget), the federal departments and their

---

[62] Throughout his administrative career, Hoover had considered multi-headed organizations as inappropriate vehicles for "doing" as opposed to "judging." It is likely that this perception on organization is related to Hoover's autocratic behavior on the commission. In 1929 he said of commissions: "There is no worse agency of government . . . for executive action," and he viewed them solely as deliberative bodies. But, as chairman of the Hoover Commission he was concerned with action, producing reports, forming task forces, prodding them to act, etc. Thus his conception of organization tends to justify his behavior. Quote from Ray Lyman Wilbur and Arthur M. Hyde (eds.), *The Hoover Policies* (New York: Scribners, 1937), p. 43.

[63] Memorandum, Rowe to Acheson, April 16, 1948, Commission on Organization of the Executive Branch, Rowe Memoranda, Acheson Papers, Truman Library.

agencies, and the Congress. The fourth force of obvious, potential importance is singular only as an abstraction; it is the collective of interest groups and professions that had a stake in the commission's recommendations. The fifth element is the presidential election of 1948.

There is no direct evidence of consistent interest group pressure on the commission; the records contain only indications of scattered letters from interest groups. James Pollock offered several possible explanations for the absence of pressure. Speaking to the 1949 meeting of the American Political Science Association, he said: ". . . we operated at such an Olympian height, or pressure groups decided not to take us seriously until we reported, or they figured that to intervene was risky—for one or all of these reasons, our work was not subject to the usual kind of annoying or even helpful pressure which is so usual in government."[64] There is another hypothesis worth entertaining; it may be that the foxes were not scratching at the commission's gate only because they were already inside. Typically, the task forces were composed with an eye toward including the most powerful interests regarding their topic area in the membership.

Consider three task forces: public works, medical services, and veterans' affairs. The three are a fair sample in that only the first produced recommendations which were conflict-producing. The other two groups produced what were considered among the better reports, and while they contained some controversial proposals, they were generally unobjectionable. Do the membership characteristics of these task forces suggest that the hypothesis might be sustainable under closer examination?[65]

The public works task force was chaired by Robert Moses, New York's legendary builder of highways, parks, bridges, and ports, and it contained sixteen members, seven of whom were businessmen with construction interests, two who were public sector highway officials, two who were directors of state departments of public works (one from New York), one academic engineer (from New York University), the head of the New York Port Authority, and the president of the National Federation of Federal Employees, and a former Secretary of the Army. This group represented those who had a large stake in public construction, and it was loaded with members of Robert Moses' New York public works empire.[66]

[64] James Pollock, "Some Thoughts on the Hoover Commission," box 43, file 8, Pollock Papers, Michigan Historical Collection.

[65] The following membership identification is drawn from The Hoover Commission Report, pp. 505-524.

[66] The extraordinary saga of Robert Moses' public works career in New York State

The medical services task force was headed by Tracy S. Voorhees, an Assistant Secretary of the Army, and had fifteen members, eleven who were physicians. Among the four laymen was a chairman of the board of a major Chicago hospital, the former vice-president in charge of medical affairs at the University of Pennsylvania, and two members of the financial community. In all, this was a distinguished group and represented the top strata of the medical profession, with academic medicine and the medical officers of major teaching hospitals represented. It was not likely that organized medicine in the form of either the American Medical Association or the American Hospital Association had reason to feel unrepresented by the task force.

The veterans' affairs task force was much smaller than the aforementioned groups. It had a chairman and a three-member advisory committee, with a number of insurance executives attached to consult on the insurance aspects of veterans' policy. The chairman of the group was the former national commander of the American Legion who was also a former chairman of the board of the Prudential Life Insurance Co. His three-member advisory committee was made up of the presidents of three major life insurance companies. This group combined sympathy for veterans with representation of the industry with whom government was a major competitor in its veterans' insurance programs. At the same time, the insurance industry might be able to provide the best advice on how the government insurance programs were being conducted. It all made excellent sense.

Among the three governmental institutions that would seem likely candidates for influence over the commission—the presidency, the departments, and the Congress—it was the president who was most influential. But it was not President Truman who influenced the commission so much as his Bureau of the Budget. The Hoover Commission operated in the midst of the golden age of the bureau. The bureau's leadership from 1939 through 1952 was of remarkable quality; in no other period of similar length in its history has it had a line of directors to equal Harold Smith, James Webb, Frank Pace, and Frederick Lawton.[67] Also, the White House staff was relatively small and disorganized, offering no competition to the bureau's professional staff.

---

and in the city of New York as well is told in a book nearly as monumental as the man's accomplishments, see Robert Caro, *The Power Broker* (New York: Knopf, 1974). A sense of Moses' style and political skills can be gotten from Chaps. 25, 28-31, 35, and 46.

[67] On the budget bureau's golden era, see Larry Berman, *The Office of Management and Budget* (Princeton: Princeton University Press, 1979); also see Hugh Heco," OMB and the Presidency—the Problem of Neutral Competence," *The Public Interest* 38 (Winter 1975), 80-98.

When Hoover met with Budget Director Webb on October 6, 1947 to establish a working relationship, he knew he needed the bureau. Webb found Hoover full of plans to uproot government's recent bad tendencies. Webb recalled that "there weren't enough votes in Congress to pass a single proposal he was making and that . . . he had two years of work and he had two million dollars . . . , and he could either devote it to a report that would gather dust or he could use his time and effort . . . so that something substantial could be accomplished."[68] Webb's view of the meeting's result was that Hoover came around to a view that his mission would be to achieve workable, politically acceptable reforms.

There are good reasons to qualify Webb's view of the degree of Hoover's surrender to necessity in October 1947. A strong streak of more grandiose ambitions for fundamental policy changes remained in him, but the meeting taught Hoover that if he was going to gain cooperation from the Bureau of the Budget, then on the projects for which he needed cooperation he would have to take an apolitical, managerially oriented approach. So the primary role of the bureau in the commission's work was in cooperation with the study group working on the presidency and questions of departmental management. In effect, Hoover was this study group, aided by Don Price, John D. Millett, and H. Struve Hensel, a corporate attorney and former Assistant Secretary of the Navy.

There was also a more covert influence of the bureau upon the commission. As well as aiding Hoover on the study of presidential management, it served the liberals on the commission who needed skilled, intensive staff work for the analysis of task force reports, drafts of commission recommendations, and for the preparation of dissenting opinions. The bureau provided that service, preparing brickbats to be launched at Hoover even while it was sweetly cooperating with him on the presidency study. The link between the commission's liberals and the bureau was James Rowe and his assistant, Walter Pincus. Rowe had worked with the budget staff back when he was a White House aide, and Pincus had been on the bureau's staff. The budget connection gave Rowe (as well as Acheson and Pollock) quick access to analysis of any material that troubled them. Rowe describes the bureau as having been his staff agency. He said of the bureau personnel: "We used them a great deal, far more than anybody on the Commission knew."[69]

[68] James Webb, interviewed by author, June 4, 1980.

[69] James Rowe, Jr., interviewed by author. It is evident that Rowe's quickly prepared and expert analytic memoranda and alternate drafts of reports confounded Hoover and his minions. It is also evident that they did not realize Rowe's dependence on the Bureau

A third source of institutional influence affected the task forces. The task forces developed close ties to the agencies they were studying, and this relationship had a formative effect upon many of the study groups. While the task forces may have started with diverse views on the organizations they were commissioned to study, contact with the federal agencies impressed upon the study groups the view of matters from the agency perspective. Not surprisingly, that perspective often came to make sense to the members of the task forces. As Don K. Price observed about this process, while the task forces looked quite conservative at the outset, "in actual practice, each specialized group . . . when put closely in touch with the department that it was interested in, fell in love with its presumed victims."[70]

The commission's relationship to the Congress was potentially intimate; senators and congressmen composed a third of its membership. But for two different reasons this was not as potent an arrangement as it might sound. First, the congressional members, with the exception of Senator Aiken, were prone to follow Hoover, whom they saw representing an economizing approach to government. The congressional members reacted negatively as a group to only two of the final reports, Business Enterprises and Medical Activities. In different ways, the task forces in both areas had entered deeply into a discussion of congressionally mandated policies and the fact that all four congressional commissioners dissented or added reservations to these reports suggests that they saw congressional turf that needed protection. The second reason for less congressional influence than might be expected through these members is the simple fact that none of them attended so closely to the commission's work that they became major forces. None of the congressional members saw fit to use their assistants to fullest possibility, and their tendency was to detail an aide from their congressional office to oversee their responsibilities on the commission. As a result, no congressional member's assistant devoted the time to the commission or became as influential as assistants for Hoover, Acheson, Kennedy, Pollock, or Rowe. In some personal notes about the commission that James Pollock wrote immediately after the end

of the Budget for aid in the production of these documents. As late as July 1949, Hoover and his people were guessing that "the carefulness and the quality" of Rowe's work resulted from his connection to a "left wing" research organization, the Public Affairs Institute. Letters, Robert McCormick to Hoover, July 21, 1949 and Hoover to McCormick, n.d., First Hoover Commission, Correspondence-McCormick, Hoover Library.

[70] Don K. Price, "Oral History Interview," Hoover Library, p. 18.

of his service on it, he described it as "poorly served by the congressional members."[71]

Senator Aiken and Congressman Brown should be exempted from the strongest of this criticism, Aiken because he was less dogmatic than his fellow commissioners from "the Hill" and Brown because he was willing to moderate his first appearance of dogmatism. James Rowe describes Brown as a man with whom he could talk out differences. As he put it: "Clarence and I got along very well; we were always quite startled."[72] The clearest manifestation of Congressman Brown's flexibility was his willingness to temper Chairman Hoover's greatest excesses.[73] In this he was a sometime ally with the liberals of the commission. His role in encouraging revisions in an early draft of the report on presidential-departmental relations is a case in point. At the outset, the commission was presented with two very different drafts of that report, one by Hoover and the other by Dean Acheson. Their differences were both stylistic and substantive. In a letter to Pollock, Acheson remarked of the Chairman's draft: ". . . it is terrible and shocks one's sense of competence, professional pride, and sometimes the fundamentals of literacy."[74] In this dispute, while the rest of the congressional members sided with Hoover, Clarence Brown attempted to finesse the conflict by having Acheson's draft joined with Hoover's, so that cosmetically it would appear to remain Hoover's general product but in a cleaner version.[75]

More important than its congressional members in aligning the commission's work with Congress' intent was Hoover's relationship with the Republican congressional leaders. Throughout the life of the commission, Hoover attended closely to the views of a handful of key Republicans, in particular, Senators Henry Cabot Lodge and Robert Taft (Ohio) and Representatives John Taber and Clarence Brown.[76]

[71] Memorandum, "Reflection on the Organization and Work of the Commission . . . ," n.d., box 43, file 8, Pollock Papers, Michigan Historical Collection.

[72] James Rowe, Jr., interviewed by author.

[73] Ibid.

[74] Letter, Acheson to Pollock, December 29, 1948, box 38, file 2, Pollock Papers, Michigan Historical Collection.

[75] Ibid. At about the same time, Representative Brown joined Rowe in cautioning the chairman and the rest of the commission on the loose practice of attaching dollar figures of estimated savings to recommendations. This is all the more interesting an alliance when one remembers that Brown's view of reorganization was that it was essentially economizing. Memorandum, Brown and Rowe to Commission, December 13, 1948, Commission on Organization of the Executive Branch, Executive Director, Misc'l Correspondence-Coordination, RG 264, National Archives.

[76] For example, Letter, Hoover to Lodge, May 6, 1948, First Hoover Commission, Correspondence-Lodge, Hoover Library.

Only in the latter instance was a member of the commission also an influential Republican congressman. From staffing through assessing final reports, Hoover was attentive to suggestions from these leaders. Days before the 1948 presidential election, Hoover asked for a meeting with Senator Taft and Representative Taber; he told them that the commission's investigations were about completed and he now desired "to discuss the whole reorganization matter with you."[77] Of course, as Chairman Hoover wrote those words he assumed that the next president would be Thomas Dewey, and he was concerned with positioning the commission so as to produce recommendations consistent with the aims of his party.

With that assumption in mind, Hoover had looked beyond key Republican members of Congress for guidance as to Dewey's intentions. In late June 1948, Chairman Hoover asked Governor Dewey, who had just received the Republican nomination, to designate a person who "we could take into the circle of our organization who might represent any ideas you may have and who could interpret our ideas currently back to you."[78] Dewey designated his counsel, Charles D. Breitel, for this role, and through the months until the election Hoover sent copies of all the commission's confidential material to Breitel.[79] Hoover attempted to create an even closer relationship as the election drew nearer and the commission began to make final substantive decisions. At the September 13 meeting, Hoover announced that he had invited Governor Dewey's representative to sit in on the commission's meetings. This created the rare partisan split in the commission. Senator McClellan objected, saying that the right to sit in the meetings would then have to be offered to representatives of all the candidates for the presidency. Forrestal asked whether the chairman had also invited the States' Rights Party candidate, Strom Thurmond, to attend meetings. Representative Brown worried that the Progressive Party candidate Henry Wallace, or the Socialist, Norman Thomas, might also ask to join the commission.[80] Hoover's proposal was dropped in

[77] Letter, Hoover to Lodge and Taber, October 31, 1948, First Hoover Commission, Correspondence-Taft, Taber, Hoover Library.

[78] Letter, Hoover to Dewey, June 26, 1948, First Hoover Commission, Correspondence-Deb to Dov, Hoover Library.

[79] Correspondence, Hoover and Breitel, July through October, 1948, First Hoover Commission, Correspondence-Breitel, Hoover Library.

[80] Transcript, September 13, 1948, Commission on the Organization of the Executive Branch, Secretary's Office Transcripts, RG 264, National Archives. Details of this incident were also described to the author by Robert H. Connery, Professor of Government, Columbia University, and a consultant to the task force on national security and the Hoover Commission.

the heat of this response. However, the informal relationship continued, and Hoover had Don Price act as the commission's liaison to Breitel.

But, of course, the 1948 election did not fulfill conventional expectations, bringing instead Truman's reelection and a solidly Democratic Congress to boot. That the election result shaped the commission's direction was evident even from the character of the meetings in its wake. Dean Acheson recalled that they "were rather different than before!"[81] James Rowe describes Chairman Hoover as shifting perceptibly on his insistence that policy was included in the commission's mandate. After the election, the conflicts between the three liberals and the chairman became less frequent and sharp. Rowe notes that Hoover seemed to decide "no more policy after the election."[82]

Until the election, the liberals were powerless in opposing Hoover's control of agenda and staff. But its results gave them leverage. The election did not reshape Hoover's political beliefs. What it did do was confront him with the fact that if he wanted to bring the commission's work to a successful conclusion, he was going to have to adopt a direction that would not prove offensive to President Truman and Congress.

Budget Director James Webb reassured Hoover that there was no reason to fear for the commission's future, if the commission was really on a course toward producing serious recommendations for the improvement of the government. Webb himself had little doubt that it could be put on such a course and kept on it.[83] Don K. Price had sought out James Rowe on the day after the election and discussed the possibility of getting President Truman to reaffirm his support for the commission. Rowe approached Webb and found he had the same thoughts on the matter.[84] Webb presented his recommendation to Truman, and the President agreed, asking that Webb draft a letter to that effect. Accompanying that letter, Webb also sent a memo to Truman which spelled out Webb's view of why Truman should nurture the Hoover Commission. Webb saw this as an important moment in the development of the presidency. "The Republican Party," he noted, "has historically been against Presidents."[85] But now the President had

[81] Transcript, "Princeton Seminar," July 2, 1953, pp. 19-21, Acheson Papers, Truman Library.

[82] James Rowe, Jr., interviewed by author.

[83] James Webb, interviewed by author.

[84] James Rowe, Jr., interviewed by author.

[85] Memorandum, Webb to Truman, November 5, 1948, Webb Papers, Truman Library.

an opportunity to build a solid base of bipartisan support for "the kind of Chief Executive office that will have enough authority and the right kind of organization to do the most difficult of jobs." How could this be accomplished? Webb explained:

> Based on my relations with Mr. Hoover, as your liaison representative, I believe there is now a possibility of getting the last Republican President to urge you to accept an implementation of and organization for executive responsibility that the Republican party has historically denied to Presidents. If that can be managed, you will undoubtedly be able to achieve—with at least a show of bipartisan agreement—a new level of Presidential leadership and effectively discharge responsibility for administration unknown in our history.[86]

Truman's victory presented Hoover with a new reality.[87] Now the commission's work, and what Hoover thought would be his last chance at great public service, depended to a large extent on Truman's support.

Before the election, liberal commissioners had been on weak ground in arguing that the commission could not consider policy. They were disadvantaged by statute, which gave the commission authority to look into policy as well as administration. Also, they were disadvantaged by having the weaker side of an argument. They argued that policy was a matter for Congress and that the commission's focus should be on administration. Thus the liberals embraced the separation of policy from administration, while Herbert Hoover—often described as a living monument to that administrative tradition—countered with an argument for the fusion of administration and policy. He told the commission that "as to structural versus policy questions there has never been any doubt in my mind that policy is involved in almost every study."[88] To Dean Acheson's argument that the commission could not recommend the elimination of policies without intruding on Congress' domain, Hoover responded that while it would be difficult to demarcate in abstract the line at where the commission should not

---

[86] *Ibid.*

[87] On November 12, 1948, the White House released a letter from Truman to Hoover which read, in part: "Today I too occasion to reaffirm the importance which I attach to the work of the commission. . . . The field in which the commission is working is one which calls most pressingly for action." Letter, Truman to Hoover, November 12, 1948, Post-Presidential Individual-Truman, 41-48, Hoover Library.

[88] Letter, Hoover to Rowe, May 9, 1948, Hoover Commission, Correspondence with Rowe, Pollock Papers, Michigan Historical Collection.

cross in recommending elimination of congressionally mandated policies, "the difficulty is not so great in practice as it is in theory."[89] Hoover's argument also broke the liberal block; James Pollock, certainly aware of the recent literature in political science attacking the politics-administration dichotomy, suggested to his liberal partners that the separation of administration from policy was untenable.[90]

Incidences during late 1947 and early 1948 indicated that Hoover was manipulating some task forces toward conservative conclusions. Rowe learned that Hoover had called in the task force leader for the Post Office study and been rather plainspoken about what he wished the report to conclude.[91] Similarly, there were indications of manipulation of the Medical Services task force. At the commission's March 22, 1948 meeting, Hoover stated the view that the treatment of non-service-related illnesses in Veterans' Administration hospitals was "socialized medicine." Hoover then mentioned the members of the Medical Services task force who were "sound," and he reassured his fellow commissioners that "knowing some of these men here, we only have to tip them off."[92] But after November 1948, the commission sailed an altered course.

Formulating Recommendations

The task forces did not have the last word. It was their duty to report to the commission, which could adopt whatever recommendations it wished. This process required detailed consideration by the commissioners of the task force reports. The procedure for considering task force reports required their distribution to commissioners, along with a summary of their contents. Also, staff members prepared a memo for each report, showing how it fit into or conflicted with other reports already submitted. Finally, arrangements were made to prepare draft legislation that could be submitted to Congress along with the commission's own reports.[93]

[89] Letter, Hoover to Acheson, August 28, 1948, First Hoover Commission, Correspondence-Acheson, Hoover Library.

[90] Letter, Pollock to Aiken, September 7, 1948, box 38, file 2, Pollock Papers, Michigan Historical Collection.

[91] Letter, Rowe to Acheson, January 22, 1948, Commission on Organization of the Executive Branch, Memoranda to Acheson from Aiken and Rowe, Acheson Papers, Truman Library.

[92] Transcript, March 22, 1948, Commission on Organization of the Executive Branch, Secretary's Office-Transcripts, RG 264, National Archives.

[93] Memorandum, "Procedure for Task Force Reports," August 18, 1948, box 38, file 5, Pollock Papers, Michigan Historical Collection.

Such was the plan, but the reality was less smooth. Commissioners complained about disorderly operations. Members attributed commission inefficiency to the low quality of staff and its poor use. Commissioner Rowe complained to executive director Sidney Mitchell that the staff's job should be to keep the commissioners abreast of the progress of task forces. He went on to virtually charge Mitchell with incompetence, stating: "I do not think the staff has been of much help to me. . . . Perhaps it is because we do not see eye-to-eye on this duty of the staff."[94] The liberals feared that staff incompetence was compounded with a tactical use of inefficiency.[95] By crippling the commissioners' abilities to assess each task force report, Hoover could dominate the discussions and recommendations of the commission.

But the 1948 election created a new dispensation under which the liberals could affect the commission's direction. One consequence was that the tensions within the commission increased because the liberals were no longer without power, and they went on the attack. James Rowe best expressed the new mood when, in explaining to Dean Acheson why he had sent a combative memo to Hoover, he said: "I have wearied of playing mouse to a toothless old lion."[96]

Rowe's metaphor was apt; Hoover was weakened by the election. He would still attempt to fit his biases into the commission's recommendations, but the changed mood and the crudeness of the most biased of the task force reports stymied his attempts. A good case of this is to be found in the Federal Business Enterprises report. Hoover's first draft was so blatant that it was rejected by a majority of the commission; for the first time the liberals put together a majority, pulling to their side Commissioners Aiken, Forrestal, Manasco, and McClellan. The most divisive aspect of the report concerned public power, and Hoover's draft reflected a task force report that decidedly favored federal withdrawal from the production of electric power and absolutely rejected the retailing of electric power by the government.[97]

The commission's response to this draft forced Hoover to accommodate. The most influential person in redrafting was James Landis, a leading expert on federal regulation and administrative law who

[94] Memo, Rowe to Mitchell, March 3, 1948, Commission on Organization of the Executive Branch, Memoranda-Rowe, Acheson Papers, Truman Library.

[95] James Pollock, "Reflections on the Organization and Work of the Commission on the Organization of the Executive Branch," box 43, file 8, Pollock Papers, Michigan Historical Collection; James Rowe, Jr., interviewed by author, October 23, 1979.

[96] Letter, Rowe to Acheson, December 3, 1948, Commission on Organization of the Executive Branch, Memoranda-Rowe, Acheson Papers, Truman Library.

[97] Text of oral message, Rowe to Acheson, February 21, 1949, Commission on Organization of the Executive Branch, Business Enterprises #1, Acheson Papers, Truman Library.

was acting for Joseph Kennedy in the latter's absence.[98] Hoover's redraft was less passionate on public power issues, yet Landis thought that Hoover was still "courting controversy. . . ."[99] He offered another set of criticisms and suggestions for revision which were reflected in a third, still milder version of the report.[100] The passions became so high over these drafts that the meeting of February 23, 1949 broke into a childish struggle in which Hoover ignored James Rowe.[101] However, the outcome of the meeting was that Hoover consented to removing the political biases from the report.[102]

The other report which engendered extensive conflict in the commission was the one dealing with the Department of the Interior. It combined issues which enraged two of the commission's congressional members and forced the liberals to prepare a dissenting opinion. McClellan and Manasco were horrified that the majority report recommended transfer of the Army Corps of Engineers to the Department of Interior.[103] For their part, the liberals saw the majority report as weakening a task force they admired, which, to their surprise, had recommended a Department of Natural Resources and heartily endorsed federal involvement in natural resources development.[104]

Given the ideological agenda with which the Hoover Commission began, its final reports were models of moderation. Hoover and his allies on the commission had been moderated by several forces among which were their relationship to the Bureau of the Budget and the political realities introduced by the election of 1948. James Rowe, Jr., looks back at the reports with a sense of accomplishment. To Rowe they were successful because they made "Washington and part of the country aware of government organization as no study had done. . . ."[105]

[98] Landis was particularly influential in this instance because his role was stipulated in a bargain between Hoover and Kennedy in which Kennedy gave his proxy to Hoover but designated Landis as his voice in formulating some of the reports. Letters, Kennedy to Hoover, January 11, 1949, First Hoover Commission, Correspondence-Kennedy, Hoover Library.

[99] Letter, Landis to Hoover, February 21, 1949, *ibid.*

[100] Letter, Hoover to Landis, February 26, 1949, *ibid.*

[101] Letter, Pollock to Hoover, February 23, 1949, First Hoover Commission, Correspondence-Pollock, Hoover Library.

[102] *Ibid.*

[103] For a discussion of the Corps of Engineers' fight against reorganization, see William Pemberton, *Bureaucratic Politics*, pp. 99-106.

[104] Compare the commission's recommendations regarding the Department of Interior with the *Task Force Report on Natural Resources* (Washington: Government Printing Office, 1949).

[105] James Rowe, Jr., interviewed by author.

THE COMMISSION AND THE PRESIDENCY

While Chairman Hoover's energy and presumption affected everything about the commission, on the subject of the presidency he was utterly dominant; Herbert Emmerich said of him: "He constituted himself the task force for the treatment of the Presidency."[106] The primacy of the report on the presidency among all the reports is itself a datum for the shift in Hoover's mind toward the presidency as a focal point of the commission's work. The first report issued by the commission was "General Management of the Executive Branch." Without mentioning the Brownlow Committee, Hoover effectively embraced its urgent assertion that "the President needs help." This report manifested the essential spirit that Brownlow and his colleagues had brought to the problem of "top-level management" in the late thirties.

Ironically, in light of his position on policy as part of the commission's mandate, Hoover cast the problem of the presidency vis à vis the executive branch into the syntax of the politics—administration dichotomy. In the introduction to the report, Hoover described the administrative problem of the executive branch in these orthodox terms:

> The President, and under him his chief lieutenants, the department heads, must be held responsible and accountable to the people and the Congress for the conduct of the executive branch. Responsibility and accountability are impossible without authority—the power to direct. The exercise of authority is impossible without a clear line of command from the top to the bottom, and a return line of responsibility and accountability from the bottom to the top.[107]

The commission's report charged that the executive branch was unmanageable. Its lines of communication and authority were unclear, and it lacked tools at the top for developing policy.[108] The report suggests reform in three major areas. First, barriers to vertical responsibility and authority must be removed; the major discretionary authority within departments should be vested in the department heads rather than in the bureau chiefs. This recommendation was prompted

---

[106] Herbert Emmerich, *Federal Organization and Administrative Management* (University, Alabama: University of Alabama Press, 1971), p. 86. James Rowe, Jr. and Harold Seidman, then with the Bureau of the Budget, both recall Hoover's dominance in drafting the report on "General Management." Harold Seidman, "Oral History Interview," Truman Library, 1970, pp. 12-13; James H. Rowe, Jr., "Oral History Interview," Hoover Library, pp. 12-13.

[107] *Hoover Commission Report*, p. 3.

[108] *Ibid.*, 3-5.

by Congress' practice of vesting statutory powers directly in bureau chiefs; department heads were more easily held responsible to the President. Second, clarity of direction and greater control can be achieved by grouping the executive branch agencies into departments "as nearly as possible by major purposes in order to give a coherent mission to each department."[109] Third, the president's staff must be enlarged and the president's freedom in dealing with his staff, giving it shape, and choosing its members, must be absolute.[110]

Hoover envisioned a solution to the problems of the presidency through an orthodox, hierarchical model of organization. As an ardent believer in orthodox administrative doctrine he knew that an executive manager must be given authority equal to his responsibility. The presidency, for Hoover, became an organizational problem and was disassociated from the ideological problems of the New Deal. Once Hoover performed that intellectual alchemy, he was able to organize his study of the presidency on what he would call an expert rather than a political basis. Additionally, Don K. Price offered Hoover the perspective of an intellectual community of scholar-public servants who were, beginning in these years, developing a new model of the strong presidency.[111]

The impact of Price, other political scientists, and the pro-presidential commissioners on Hoover can be seen in the considerations of alternative recommendations for staffing the White House. One idea that had strong support among American academicians, and some people associated with the commission, was an American variant of the British cabinet secretariat.[112] Forrestal was an advocate of such a reform, and Budget Director Webb was interested in the commission considering the idea.[113] This issue was given careful attention, and Don K. Price did the major work in developing memoranda on the concept. By summer 1948 an informal group of staff members and commissioners began to talk about the details of increased support

[109] *Ibid.*, 29-51, quote on 34.

[110] *Ibid.*, 11-28.

[111] During the late 1940's and early 1950's scholarship accommodated an expanded view of the presidential role. See, for example, Wilfred Binkley, *The President and Congress* (New York: Knopf, 1947), and Clinton Rossiter, *The American President* (New York: Harcourt Brace, 1956). For a critique of this model of the presidency, see P. E. Arnold and L. John Roos, "Toward a Theory of Congressional-Executive Relations," *The Review of Politics* 36 (July 1974), 410-429.

[112] On the development of support and coordinating mechanisms in the British cabinet, see Hans Daalder, *Cabinet Reform in Britain, 1914-1963* (Stanford, California: Stanford University Press, 1963).

[113] James Webb interview with author.

for the President through a secretariat. The group profoundly affected Chairman Hoover's view of necessary reforms in the presidency. The commissioners involved were Pollock, Rowe, and Acheson; Forrestal was interested but less involved. The staff people in these discussions were Price, John D. Millett, Charles Aiken, and Ferrel Heady.

Don K. Price, and the others, played an important role in leading Chairman Hoover to consider the weaknesses of the presidential office in light of inadequate organizational supports. Originally, Hoover saw the problems of the presidency as functions of the organizational "irrationality" of the executive branch. His concern with the presidency was that it was incapable of directing and controlling the executive branch. As a result of the continuing discussion of staff assistance and the secretariat, Chairman Hoover abandoned his sole stress on line agency reorganization as a means for aiding the President. He announced, at a meeting on November 8, 1948, that he favored a presidential agency for coordination among the departments. Hoover described this agency: "The idea was that whoever headed this service would become a sort of chairman of a committee more or less representing different departments." He did not want to call this operation a secretariat, but he admitted that it might be preferable to use that name because "any other term we are likely to get confused with administrative offices."[114]

Lest the chairman favor a secretariat arrangement too quickly, Don K. Price cautioned him about the possibility of cabinet coordination. He advised that the cabinet had no tradition of unity and that it is normally torn apart by individual interests. Price argued that a cabinet secretariat could become too powerful and decrease the president's flexibility. Price observed, as early as December 1947, that "the President should not be required to handle a policy problem through any set procedure, or to consult any fixed group of officials, or to take up problems except at the time he chooses."[115] A secretariat might reduce the flexibility with which he could direct his subordinates. At the same time, Price offered Hoover a strong argument for increased aid and presented the Bureau of the Budget recommendations for the uses of expanded, institutionalized staff: "This staff would (1) supplement for the President the views and the advice of the operating departments in the formulation of policy, (2) help the President execute policy by

[114] Transcript of November 8, 1948 meeting, Commission on the Organization of the Executive Branch of the Government, Secretary's Office, Transcripts, RG 264, National Archives.

[115] Memo, Price to Hoover, December 3, 1947, First Hoover Commission, General Management of the Executive Branch, Cabinet Secretariat, Correspondence, Hoover Library.

(a) coordinating programs, (b) developing administrative machinery, (c) coordinating the gathering of information, and (d) helping to establish policies to improve the personnel of the government."[116]

The discussion of institutionalized staff assistance moved away from any direct role with the cabinet and toward a notion of a "presidential secretariat" functioning as a personal extension of the president. In a conversation on August 30, 1948, Price and Commissioner Pollock agreed that the secretariat might well not involve the cabinet at all and instead be a career staff agency at the sole and total service of the president.[117] The idea of a secretariat, and the kind of reliable expertise a career staff could lend the president, had taken firm hold of many of the participants in the Hoover Commission's work. The point at issue among the secretariat's proponents was the proper organizational position for such an agency; about duties there was wide agreement. For example, James K. Pollock presented the functions of a presidential secretariat to Hoover in terms that would fit the chairman's own plan of November 8, 1948. Pollock proposed:

> The secretariat would act as the normal channel through which policy matters would flow from the departments to the President. Similarly, orders, directives, and policy decisions of the President would pass down through the secretariat and out to the departments concerned. . . . It would not make decisions . . . but it would facilitate the making of decisions, and give to the President a more orderly, time-saving, and efficient device than he has hitherto had for coordinating executive matters of high level concern.[118]

In the commission's report, Hoover accepted the basic logic of the presidential secretariat but refused to limit the president within a particular organizational form. The report on the executive office recommended increased support for staff along with complete presidential discretion over how that staff will be used. Interestingly, Hoover moved beyond his own administrative orthodoxy and then saw any fixed staff format as too limiting on the President.

THE FATE OF THE HOOVER REPORTS

The reports of the Hoover Commission were sent to Congress during the first several months of 1949. In range and number of its recom-

[116] Memo, Price to Hoover, *ibid.*

[117] Pollock's notes on discussion with Price, August 30, 1948, box 41, file 1, Pollock Papers, Michigan Historical Collections.

[118] Memo, Pollock to Hoover, November 17, 1948, First Hoover Commission, General Management of the Executive Branch, Pollock Proposal, Hoover Library.

mendations there had been no equal to the commission. It also surpassed its predecessors on another count in that a far larger part of its recommendations were adopted.

The Acceptance of the Recommendations

In all, there were 277 specific recommendations ranging across government's organization and activities. No single theory of administration motivated all 277 recommendations. However, many of them presumed values of coherence in governmental organization, hierarchical control, centralized authority, and organization by purpose. Consider some of the major recommendations. It recommended that the recently lapsed presidential reorganization authority be renewed. It called for a decrease in the president's span of control by reducing by two-thirds the agencies that reported directly to him. It recommended that all departments be organized by major purpose, that departmental administrative regions be made more comparable in geographic terms, and that department heads, under the president, be given the authority vested by statute in their departments. The commission also recommended that administrative activities in government be centralized and pooled where appropriate and that a central agency for administrative housekeeping services be established. It suggested budget reforms to bring the budget format closer to the policy-related activities of government, and it recommended that control over fiscal accounting be centralized in the Treasury. The commission also made a number of recommendations for major changes in the organizational placement of activities, calling for an independent United Medical Administration to house all governmental medical activities, a new Department of Social Service and Education, and major reorganizations in Agriculture, Interior, and Commerce. In Interior, the commission recommended that all power and water resource activities be joined together, with the civil functions of the Army Corp of Engineers relocated from Defense. It further recommended that all land management responsibilities be placed in Agriculture, avoiding the old problem of transferring Forestry out of Agriculture to Interior as a way of centralizing land management activities. Finally, the commission proposed major changes in Commerce, with it becoming the location for all federal non-regulatory, transportation activities.

Because the recommendations vary greatly in their importance, and because there can be disagreement over what actually constituted implementation, box-score counts of success do not tell the whole story. However, by any count the Hoover Commission was more successful than its predecessors.[119] Even before the process of consideration and implementation of the recommendations was over, Herbert Hoover estimated that "55% of the commission's recommendations have been placed into effect. . . ."[120] More conservatively, Herbert Emmerich reckoned that about 100 of the 277 recommendations had been effected.[121] By either count, the results were impressive.

Among the recommendations implemented are a number that are among the most important ones made by the commission.[122] The reorganization authority was renewed, albeit with a one-house veto.[123] The recommendations for increased presidential staff support and discretion in the use and organization of the Executive Office were widely accepted and, in effect, reaffirmed changes and growth already ongoing in the development of White House organization.[124] After the passage of the Reorganization Act, President Truman effected changes consistent with the commission's recommendations in many of the departments and independent commissions, although Congress vetoed plans that would have effected some of the departmental-level recommendations. However, following the commission's recommendations, the Post Office, and the Departments of Interior, Commerce, and Labor were reformed through reorganization plans, as was the National Security Council and a number of independent agencies, such as the Civil Service Commission, the Federal Trade Commission, Federal Power Commission, the Securities and Exchange Commission,

[119] A fairly complete picture of action upon the commission's recommendations as of January 1952 is available in U.S. Senate, "Reorganization of the National Government," Senate Document No. 91, 82nd Cong., 2d Sess., 1952.

[120] Letter, Hoover, to Senator Styles Bridges, February 2, 1952, First Hoover Commission, Correspondence-B, Hoover Library.

[121] Herbert Emmerich, *Federal Organization and Administrative Management*, p. 97.

[122] Harold Seidman, who worked with the commission as an officer of the Bureau of the Budget, observes that one of the Truman administration's main accomplishments was its "follow-through from the Hoover Commission." Harold Seidman, "Oral History Interview," Truman Library, 1970, p. 12.

[123] The intensity of lobbying by Hoover Commission members in attempting to retain a strong presidential reorganization authority can be seen across the commission's records. For example: Letter, Vandenberg to Hoover, February 26, 1949, First Hoover Commission, Correspondence-Vandenberg, Hoover Library; Memorandum, Rowe to Clifford, Acheson, Murphy, Pace, and Webb, March 16, 1949, Official Files, Clifford Files, Commission on Organization of the Executive Branch, Truman Library; Letter, Pollock to Vandenberg, March 23, 1947, Hoover Commission, Correspondence-Vandenberg, Pollock Papers, Michigan Historical Collection. For a description of the legislative history of the renewal of the reorganization authority, see William Pemberton, *Bureaucratic Politics*, Chap. 8.

[124] Stephen Hess, *Organizing the Presidency* (Washington: Brookings Institution, 1976), pp. 57-58.

and the Civil Aeronautics Board. Some recommendations were effected through statute, the most prominent examples being the creation during 1949 of the General Services Administration, the transformation of the National Defense Establishment into the Department of Defense, and the reorganization of the State Department.

The Political Campaign for the Hoover Reports

The Hoover Commission was unparalleled in the history of executive reorganization in the breadth of its political support. Like every predecessor reorganization effort, the commission's recommendations drew the president's support. But unlike earlier episodes, these recommendations also drew substantial congressional approval and widespread public support.

Truman's support was enormously vigorous, and he developed the habit of referring to the commission as "his." As the commission issued its reports, Truman acted quickly to move the government toward adoption. In mid-March 1949, he ordered agency heads to study the recommendations that could be introduced immediately, and he stated: "Where this is the case, it is my wish that you weigh the practicability of the recommendation and that you advise me of the action which you contemplate."[125]

Upon receiving the commission's final report, Truman embraced the whole enterprise: "I personally concur in the recommendation that the administration of the Executive Branch be considered the responsibility of the President and, under him, the Department heads."[126] Truman went a step further and created an Advisory Committee on Management Improvement for the purpose of furthering the program of administrative renewal. His reason for the committee rested on the view that: ". . . improvement in the . . . administrative arrangements of the Executive Branch are essential to efficient conduct of Federal programs," but: "Responsible officials must follow through to see that potential improvements in Government operations are actually realized."[127] In the two years following the commission's reports, Truman submitted thirty-five reorganization plans.

[125] Letter, Truman to cabinet members and agency heads, March 14, 1949, Official File, 285E, Truman Library.

[126] Statement by the President, May 26, 1949, President's Secretary's File, General File-Reorganization, Truman Library.

[127] Statement by the President, July 29, 1949, *ibid*. In his notes for presenting the Advisory Committee to the cabinet, Truman's first point read: "In support of the Hoover Commission recommendations I have submitted proposed legislation and reorganization

Beneath the Hoover Commission's broad support was Hoover's ingenuity at public relations. With a genius for public relations that he had earlier demonstrated as a food relief administrator and as Secretary of Commerce, Hoover created a grass-roots organization to press for implementation of the commission's recommendations.[128] It would seem unlikely that a fervent crusade could be sparked by administrative reorganization, but Hoover did it.

The Citizens Committee for the Hoover Reports was Hoover's creation and an instrument of his will. He chose Dr. Robert Johnson, president of Temple University, as chairman of the organization. Johnson suggested that it be named The Citizens Committee for the Support of President Truman's Commission on Reorganization; Hoover chose the pithier title, also keeping first things first.[129] For the leadership, Hoover called upon his band of loyalists, many who went back to his work in European relief and in the Department of Commerce. The general appearance of the organization was neutral and non-partisan, but as Julius Klein wrote to Hoover: "I think we have lined up a pretty good inside set-up of loyal friends. . . ."[130]

The Citizens Committee built a crusade around the Hoover Commission reports. In addition to being a national organization, the committee divided into state and local units. It plastered the country with effective advertising, pushing the idea that through the commission's reports the United States would improve its economy, make government better, and improve its strength in the world. Advertising was handled at no charge by the J. Walter Thompson firm, and its appeals were everywhere. By 1951, the committee "had developed a publicity campaign that included free space in hundreds of newspapers and magazines, fifty thousand cards in buses and streetcars, and frequent spot announcements on radio. By March 1951, 389 newspapers were using 3,087 advertisements ranging from single columns to full pages."[131] The committee also organized prominent public figures, including the Hoover Commission's members, into a speakers' bureau.

The style adopted by the Citizens Committee for the Hoover Reports

---

plans to the Congress." Memorandum for President, n.d., Files of Clark Clifford, Truman Library.

[128] On Hoover's talents as a publicist, see Craig Lloyd, *Aggressive Introvert* (Columbus: Ohio State University Press, 1972).

[129] Letter, Johnson to Hoover, February 21, 1949, First Hoover Commission, Correspondence-Johnson, Hoover Library.

[130] Letter, Klein to Hoover, May 19, 1949, First Hoover Commission, General Management of the Executive Branch, Correspondence-Klein, Hoover Library.

[131] William Pemberton, *Bureaucratic Politics*, p. 110.

was self-consciously folksy. As the committee's style sheet instructed, the message was to be practical, citing waste in the form of what it called the "eternal verities." The committee's motto was: "Better Government at a Better Price."[132] Some suggestions of ideological criticism of "big government" crept into this happy and non-partisan atmosphere. It was impossible to avoid the establishment of a conservative perspective in the committee, if just as a minor theme. Circumstances had forced the Hoover Commission away from exorcizing big government. But as the committee blossomed in numbers and influence, Hoover had some thoughts about its serving as a platform for a renewed attack on big government and its works. Noting that the committee was "going like wild fire," Hoover told George Mead: "I do not believe our New Deal opponents will have a chance before the sweep this committee will make in the country."[133] The committee's style was itself conducive to drawing into it elements which saw reorganization as a conservative cause. It stressed the goals of simplicity and economy in government; these were widely saleable items in American political culture, and at their heart they contained elements which fuel a distrust of large government. In this light, consider a speech Robert Johnson made about the Hoover Commission on the ABC radio network. It was titled, "You and the Ten-Cent Dollar"; Johnson told Americans that:

> You, as a citizen, want to stop the national drift towards financial disaster. You want to know what you can do to help.
> Fortunately there is an answer. . . . We have before us the Report . . . of the Commission on Organization of the Executive Branch of the Government.[134]

Meanwhile the Truman administration viewed the committee with caution. Some of Truman's staff understood that the Citizens Committee could present a substantial political problem. Thus while the administration worked with the committee it also carefully watched its activities.[135]

[132] Citizens Committee for the Hoover Report, "Do's and Don'ts on Preparing Material About the Hoover Report," Official File, 285E, Truman Library.

[133] Letter, Hoover to Mead, March 15, 1949, First Hoover Commission, Correspondence-Mead, Hoover Library.

[134] Transcript of Speech, First Hoover Commission, Correspondence-Johnson, Hoover Library.

[135] For example, two memoranda document ideological attacks on the administration under Citizens Committee auspices; "Propaganda by Citizen's Committee for the Hoover Report," June 19, 1950, Official File, 285E, Truman Library.

Even when the suspicion rose that the Citizens Committee was not an unmixed blessing, the Truman administration had no choice but to work with it. One, it was simply too powerful and popular to ignore. Two, in a curious way, the Citizens Committee took on a mantle of orthodox legitimacy as the Hoover Commission's interpreter. With Hoover's blessing, along with his behind-the-scenes guidance, the committee became the oracle of the commission's reports. That the committee played an important role in the Truman administration's reorganization activities is clear in the following memo from Elmer Staats at the Bureau of the Budget to John Steelman, a Truman aide. Staats informed Steelman that he had set up a meeting with several officials of the administration's reorganization program for the next session of Congress; Staats then observed:

> The Citizens Committee has been formally extended through next May. We think it is important . . . that we have a meeting of minds with Johnson as to the approach which their Committee will take. The principal issue which we have in general is the extent to which they are going to insist on a literal construction of the Hoover Commission recommendations as the basis for their support for reorganization actions.[136]

In case the President forgot that he had to deal with the Citizens Committee, it kept the political pressure on him through its frequent campaigns that were comparable in some respects to the intense activities of evangelical religion. On September 21, 1950, sixteen months after the last report of the Hoover Commission was issued, and during one of those campaigns, the White House mail room received 45,600 pieces of mail requesting favorable action by the President on the Hoover Commission recommendations![137]

The committee's grip over Congress had the same basis as its effectiveness in dealing with the administration. But in its dealings with Congress the committee's mask slipped a bit, and it became clear who was the power within the organization. When reorganization business had to be done with the key Republicans in Congress, Hoover entered the picture. Hoover continually "worked" the Republican pastures in Congress, again and again urging the senators and representatives of his party to take a bold stand on the Hoover Commission proposals. Hoover was impassioned by the recommendations and fervently

---

[136] Memorandum, Staats to Steelman, October 18, 1951, Official File, 285A, Truman Library.

[137] Memorandum, White House mail room to White House file room, September 21, 1950, Official File, 285E, Truman Library.

sought to increase the commission's box score of recommendations adopted. When Senator George Malone (Rep., Nevada) attacked the Truman administration for attempting to use Herbert Hoover in its grab for power, Hoover chided the senator as if he were an errant child. He reminded Malone of the Citizens Committee's status:

I do not see anything the matter with the Reorganization Plans *as proposed by the Commission* which should be opposed by Republicans. They ought to be for them.

The various Citizens Committees are seemingly better informed on them than the very overburdened men in Congress. They have relied upon, studied and expounded the documents. Literally, tens of thousands of the Commission's reports have been circulated and the leaders of these groups all have them.[138] (emphasis in original)

What Made the Commission Presidential?

The Hoover Commission was less dominated by a presidentially imposed agenda than its predecessors, yet its major recommendations were consistent with theirs. A commission with a conservative bias created recommendations that were Brownlowian, and a grass-roots lobbying group with a bias against big government made possible the implementation of recommendations for managing big government.

Among the several factors that turned the Hoover Commission into a virtual presidential endeavor in its outcomes were political elements such as President Truman's dramatic political revival, the Bureau of the Budget's efforts to protect the presidency, the trenchant fight by the commission's liberals against its conservative tendencies, and the cooptation of some of the task forces by their bureaucratic objects of study. There were also personality factors that affected this transition almost as much as did those political factors. Foremost was Herbert Hoover's respect for the presidency, combined with his regard for President Truman. Then there was the role of Don K. Price in serving Hoover's positive inclinations toward the presidency with contemporary ideas out of political science and public administration.

Finally, there was a conceptual factor in shaping the commission's outcome. Herbert Hoover's perspective on the presidency as solely a managerial problem allowed him to treat the presidency in expansive terms without engaging his political conservatism. Thus Hoover personifies the abstract role that managerial depoliticization plays within

[138] Letters, Hoover to Malone, May 30, 1950, First Hoover Commission, Correspondence-Malone, Hoover Library.

the development of reorganization planning in the 20th century. At one and the same time, reorganization planning aimed at strengthening the presidency while presenting the issue of enhanced presidential capacity as merely managerial and irrelevant to politics. Herbert Hoover and his commission of 1947-1949 present perhaps the most successful application of that logic within reorganization planning's history.

Chapter Six

REORGANIZATION AT THE CROSSROADS I: EISENHOWER, PACGO, AND THE SECOND HOOVER COMMISSION

Eisenhower . . . preferred results to publicity
when strategic and tactical maneuvering was
required. He deliberately cultivated the
impression that he was not involved even in the
most successful of the maneuvers in which he
directly participated. . . . He employed his skills
to achieve his ends by inconspicuous means. . . .[1]
Fred Greenstein

The Democrats' use of national government was at issue in the election of 1952 but not the expanded, managerial presidency that had evolved during their years of power. The notion that the president was responsible for management in the executive branch was widely shared, and the Hoover Commission had bestowed its imprimatur of bipartisan legitimacy upon the managerial presidency. Consequently Dwight Eisenhower's coherent approach to organization matched rather neatly the contemporary conception of the office he won in November 1952.[2]

THE PRESIDENCY AS AN ORGANIZATIONAL PROBLEM

Eisenhower's post-election preparation for the presidency was the most-organized transition up to that time.[3] It contained four opera-

---

[1] Fred Greenstein, "Eisenhower as an Activist President," *Political Science Quarterly* 94 (Winter 1979-1980), 597.

[2] Eisenhower's military career was the basis for his sophistication about managing organizations. Much of his career was spent in staff positions, and in his role as Supreme Commander during the Second World War Eisenhower was as much concerned with poltics and management as he was with military strategy. Thus he evolved a subtle understanding of both the management and politics of organizations. See Stephen E. Ambrose, *The Supreme Commander: The War Years of General Dwight D. Eisenhower* (Garden City, New York: Doubleday, 1970). In particular, notice the impact upon Eisenhower of General George C. Marshall's conception of delegation (Ambrose, pp. 6 and 53-54).

[3] For a detailed description of the 1952-1953 transition, consult Laurin Henry, *Presidential Transitions* (Washington: Brookings Institution, 1960), pp. 455-703.

tions. First, Joseph Dodge, a prominent Detroit banker, and Senator Henry Cabot Lodge (Rep., Mass.) headed a small group tracking the activities of the agencies, particularly in budgeting, foreign affairs, and national security.[4] Second, Eisenhower appointed his campaign assistant, ex-governor of New Hampshire Sherman Adams, to coordinate building a White House staff. Third, under Herbert Brownell, a New York attorney, and General Lucius Clay, a search was begun for cabinet and sub-cabinet appointments. A fourth operation in the transition team was an organizational reform planning committee of three members, Nelson Rockefeller, Arthur Flemming, and the president-elect's brother, Milton Eisenhower.

Organizing the Eisenhower White House

The Eisenhower White House would be both larger and more functionally specific than Truman's staff.[5] It gave flesh to the concepts of the presidential support staff that had been evolving within reorganization planning. But while Eisenhower organized his White House along lines of specialization, his inclinations were toward a looser form of leader-staff interchange. This is exemplified by his tendency to blur the role boundaries of his organization when it seemed useful. For example, James Hagerty, Eisenhower's press secretary, and Gabriel Hauge, his White House economics specialist, both became influential over a wide range of matters in the White House inner circle.

Another innovation of Eisenhower's was a secretariat to organize the cabinet, comprising a presidential assistant and a small staff. This secretariat established a system of agenda setting, information gathering, and decision tracking for the cabinet. The secretariat reflected Eisenhower's desire to use his department heads for collective consultation and decisions. The cabinet was an important locus for consultation for him, and he trusted those in it.[6] Speaking of the members of his cabinet in a confidential letter to a friend, Eisenhower wrote:

> The average level of ability, dedication and integrity is invariably higher in the Cabinet than it is among the politicians, where we find so many demagogues. . . . So it is lucky for a President that he is

[4] A view of the transition from the perspective of one of the main participants can be had in Henry Cabot Lodge, *As It Was* (New York: Norton, 1976), Chap. 1.

[5] Stephen Hess, *Organizing the Presidency* (Washington: Brookings Institution, 1976), pp. 68-71.

[6] On Eisenhower's use of the cabinet, see Fred Greenstein, *The Hidden Hand Presidency* (New York: Basic Books), pp. 113-123.

enabled to associate much more intimately with his own Cabinet than he does with politicians in general.[7]

The Special Advisory Committee

The White House and cabinet could be molded by the President-elect. But the executive branch posed a different problem; it was fixed and difficult to change. Yet Eisenhower's outlook presumed it was his obligation and right to seek change in the executive branch agencies. Reorganization was a natural element in his perspective.

What Eisenhower sought for the executive branch was not large-scale reorganization; the dust had just settled from the reforms inspired by the Hoover Commission. There was no reason to launch another large-scale reorganization planning effort, and Eisenhower created a very different kind of consultive group on reorganization, a committee of experienced advisers who would serve him in a confidential relationship.[8] This was a job for people who were trusted by Eisenhower and knowledgeable about governmental organization. Eisenhower knew Washington at its highest level through years of work with presidents and Congress, but he lacked recent experience with the permanent government. Shortly after his election victory Eisenhower asked Rockefeller, Flemming, and his brother Milton to constitute what he called a Special Advisory Committee on Government Organization. Rockefeller had served in State during the war; Flemming had been a Civil Service commissioner, worked in defense mobilization under Truman, and been a member of the Hoover Commission. Milton Eisenhower, then president of Penn State University, had begun his working life as a civil servant in the Department of Agriculture, and he had consulted in every administration since Coolidge's.

The committee's major transition assignment was to review the administrative reform literature and recent reorganization planning episodes to recommend means for improving central management in the executive branch. The committee took objectives that were characteristic of presidentially centered reorganization. It sought to strengthen presidential authority over the agencies, clarify internal departmental organization, improve government-wide administrative

[7] Letter, Eisenhower to Duke Hazlett, December 8, 1954, DDE Diary, Dec 54 (2), DDE Diary Series, Papers of Dwight D. Eisenhower as President, Eisenhower Library.

[8] Arthur Flemming described the relationship of the committee to the President as follows: "If Ike had an idea or problem he would bring it to the committee. If the committee had an idea or saw a problem, it would bring it to Ike." Arthur Flemming, interviewed by author, April 24, 1981.

processes in optimal grouping of activities, and eliminate activities and organizations that had outlived their purpose.[9] The committee was also expected to brief appointments at cabinet and sub-cabinet level to the organizational issues they would confront.

More than any earlier reorganization planning vehicle, the advisory committee was an instrument of the intentions of an incumbent president and a part of his own household. The committee had no other client than Eisenhower. It had no connection with Congress, nor were any of its members beholden to executive branch agencies. Moreover, none of its members were professionals in administrative science, so, unlike the Brownlow Committee, the advisory committee had no responsibilities to professional guilds in administration. Through the advisory committee, reorganization planning was meant to be internal to the President's organizational support system.

Because of his respect for its members, and his intimate relationship with the committee, Eisenhower was able to have it address politics as well as organization.[10] The most sensitive issue with which it worked during the transition was that of domestic security. This issue was both troubling and profitable for Eisenhower. He had benefited politically from it during the campaign.[11] On the other hand, Senator Joseph McCarthy (Rep., Wis.) and his allies built a crusade out of the issue, threatening the governmental organization for which Eisenhower was now responsible. The committee's unimplemented suggestion for defusing the issue was the creation of a high-level investigating commission of individuals who were, in the committee's language, "familiar with due process and with the rules of evidence;" recommendations for members included names such as Learned Hand, John Davis and Laird Bell.[12]

Between December 1952 and April 1953 the committee delivered twenty memoranda to Eisenhower, each dealing with one agency or organizational issue.[13] Eisenhower consequently entered the presi-

[9] Memorandum on duties of the Special Advisory Committee on Government Organization, January 13, 1953, 10-3 A-2, Official File, White House Central File, Eisenhower Library.

[10] Memorandum on duties of the Special Advisory Committee on Government Organization, January 13, 1953.

[11] Herbert S. Parmet, *Eisenhower and the American Crusades* (New York: MacMillan, 1972), pp. 126-134.

[12] Memorandum, Advisory Committee to Eisenhower, December 21, 1952, Rockefeller (6), Administration Series, Papers of DDE as President, Eisenhower Library.

[13] Memorandum, n.d., file 24, PACGO, Eisenhower Library. The confidentiality of the committee's work was conditioned by a fear that congressional knowledge of its specifics would endanger Eisenhower's ultimate reorganization program. Letter, Joseph

dency with a reorganization agenda in hand. He successfully presented ten reorganization plans to Congress in his first year—six of the most important of these within three months of the inauguration. Among them were the creation of the Department of Health, Education, and Welfare and major changes in Agriculture, Justice, and Defense.

Along with its recommendations, the advisory committee suggested a general strategy on reorganization.[14] Just as the Joint Committee had concluded in the 1920's, the committee urged that administrative reform be viewed as "a perpetual, day-after-day job." In this light it stressed the necessity for monitoring the administrative capacities of agencies, the importance of an improved public service, and the dangers of what it called, "bureaucratic warlordism." However, it is noteworthy that instead of denouncing governmental bureaucracy, the committee attributed "warlordism" to the characteristics of large organizations, be they public or private, and it encouraged Eisenhower to develop means through which administrators would cooperate rather than confront one another in jurisdictional disputes. In its remarks on the public service as well, the committee was distinctly positive; it praised the quality of the public service even while stressing the importance of continued improvement.

Where the committee's overall view of reorganization was most distinctive was in its explicit linkage of administrative reform and public policy. It stressed that more than administrative principle was involved in reorganization; organizational change must be conceived in light of the policy ends sought from an agency. Finally, the committee urged the importance of foresight, understood as predicting organization or management problems entailed in the administration's policy aims. It put the issue simply: "A Government must be able to think as well as act."[15]

Acting on its advice that his administration would need "to think"— President Eisenhower transformed his advisory committee to permanent status. Four days after the inauguration, the President issued an executive order giving it official status and renaming it the President's Advisory Committee for Government Organization (PACGO).[16] The committee's first task in its new status would be to work with the Bureau of the Budget on the administration's initial group of reorganization plans. However, the uncertain status of the presidential

---

Dodge to Rockefeller, December 2, 1952, 103-A (1), Official File, White House Central File, Eisenhower Library.

[14] Preface to committee's recommendations, memorandum, *ibid.*

[15] *Ibid*, p. 4.

[16] Executive Order no. 10,432.

reorganization authority impeded the quick initiation of Eisenhower's reorganization program.

Renewing the Reorganization Authority

The reorganization authority would expire on April 1, 1953. Many in the administration hoped that the securely Republican Congress would give to the first Republican president in twenty years a generous renewal, hoping at least for a full four-year renewal and retention of the 1949 act's provision of a one-house veto by a constitutional majority.[17] There was even some ambition in the Bureau of the Budget to seek a return to the 1945 Reorganization Act's two-house congressional veto.[18] But the administration's ambitions were stymied by the President's own misstep.

Six days after the inauguration, Eisenhower met the Republican congressional leadership. The leaders expressed a preference for a one-house, simple majority veto. Eisenhower stated that he had no objection to the change.[19] Unaware of the President's remark, the next day Joseph Dodge, now budget director, testified to the House Committee on Government Organization that the administration desired a four-year renewal with retention of the one-house congressional veto by constitutional majority.[20] Congressional questioners asked Dodge whether this was his own position or the administration's.[21] Later that same day, both the House and Senate committees approved a two-year extension with a one-house veto by a simple majority. The committees' action threatened the most serious weakening of the presidential reorganization authority since its inception in 1932.[22]

[17] Letter, Dodge to Rockefeller, December 2, 1952, 103-A (1), Official File, White House Central File, Eisenhower Library.

[18] Memorandum, William Finan to Dodge, January 28, 1953, Director's Office, 52-60, Bureau of the Budget, 51.2 RG 40, National Archives, Washington, D.C. See Louis Fisher and Ronald Moe, "Delegating with Ambivalence," in Congressional Research Service, *Studies on the Legislative Veto* (Washington: Government Printing Office, 1980), p. 217.

[19] Memorandum, "Notes on the President's Meeting with Congressional leaders," January 26, 1953, Legislative Meeting Series, 1953 (2), DDE. Papers as President, Eisenhower Library. At this meeting the only presidential assistant present was General Jerry Persons, whose area of responsibility was congressional liaison.

[20] Memorandum, Dodge to Adams, January 27, 1953, 103-A (2), Office File, White House Central File, Eisenhower Library.

[21] Memorandum, Finan to Dodge, January 28, 1953, Director's Office 52-60, BOB, 51.2 RG 51, National Archives.

[22] The importance of the difference between a constitutional majority and a simple majority can be seen in the case of the House of Representatives. With 435 members,

To save President Eisenhower's ability to use reorganization, the Bureau of the Budget and the White House informed the congressional leadership that the President had misspoken, and that he sought retention of the constitutional majority provision.[23] The administration called upon outside help to seek amendment of the committees' bills in the final floor votes. Herbert Hoover wrote to the relevant committee chairmen, stating: "President Eisenhower's powers in matters of reorganization . . . should not be reduced below those the Congress gave to President Truman."[24] He also reminded the legislators that the Hoover Commission had recommended a two-house veto for the reorganization authority.

The administration achieved its goal in winning reorganization authority in the form of a renewal of the 1949 Reorganization Act. However, that end was not achieved without a floor fight. That this uproar could have been avoided was made clear by Senator Margaret Chase Smith (Rep, Me.), chairman of the Subcommittee on Reorganization of the Government Operations Committee. She admitted to leading her committee to the decision against the constitutional majority only because she understood that the President favored that action.[25] Once it learned his wishes, Congress followed Eisenhower, but he expended resources unnecessarily through confused directions.

REORGANIZATION ON PARALLEL TRACKS

The formalization of the advisory committee into permanent status after the inauguration was a logical culmination of the presidential-centeredness of reorganization planning. The President's Advisory Committee on Government Organization was designed to advise only the President, and to speak to him frankly and confidentially. The implication of this arrangement was that presidents are wholly responsible for overseeing management and planning its forms. Confounding this understanding of reorganization planning, the Republicans in Congress sought a more aggressive congressional role in reorganization planning than that envisaged for it by the administra-

---

a constitutional majority is 218. However, during the 82nd Congress, 1950-1952, the average number of members in attendance for roll calls was 357, a majority of whom would be 179.

[23] Memorandum, Finan to Dodge, January 28, 1953, Director's Office, 52-60, BOB, 51.2, RG 51, National Archives.

[24] Letter, Herbert Hoover to Margaret Chase Smith, January 30, 1953, 103-A (2), Official File, White House Central File, Eisenhower Library.

[25] Letter, Smith to Hoover, February 3, 1953, 2nd Hoover Commission-Correspondence, H.R. 992, Hoover Library.

tion. Just as PACGO was finding its niche in the administration, a wholly separate reorganization planning mechanism was initiated by Congress.

Creating the Second Hoover Commission

Except for the interlude of the 80th Congress (1946-1948), the Republicans had not organized Congress for two decades prior to January 1953. The Republican 83rd Congress had a strong potential for trouble with Eisenhower because its leadership was by habit a leadership in opposition. After decades of attacks on big government and spending, the Republicans found themselves in charge of the same expanded, expensive national government they had been criticizing. After experiencing difficulty with congressional leaders over some potential appointees, Eisenhower observed in his confidential diary: ". . . the Republicans have been so long in opposition to the Executive, Republican Senators are having a hard time getting through their heads that they now belong to a team that includes rather than opposes the White House."[26]

But ideology as well as habit shaped Congress' inclinations during 1953. Particularly high on the legislative agenda of some Republicans was a replay of the Hoover Commission, this time with the assurance that such a mixed commission would not be sidetracked from its mission to cut government. In December 1952 Representative Clarence Brown (Rep., Ohio), a sponsor of the bill to create the first commission and eventually one of its commissioners, discussed with Herbert Hoover the requirements for a second commission.[27] Hoover urged that such a new bill should be very specific about the commission's mandate, and he suggested that there be no statutory requirement for bipartisanship. He also proposed that the law should require some carry-over membership from the first commission. At the opening of the 83rd Congress, Representative Brown and Senator Homer Ferguson (Rep., Mich.) presented a bill incorporating these suggestions.

The Brown-Ferguson bill followed the form of the earlier Hoover Commission, with the addition of Hoover's recommended changes. The bill specified that the new commission would identify desirable reductions in spending, the cutback or elimination of services, and, in

[26] Diary entry, February 7, 1953, DDE Personal 53-54, D.D.E. Diary, Papers of DDE as President, Eisenhower Libary.

[27] Letter, Hoover to Brown, December 3, 1952, and drafts of bill and accompanying letter, Brown to Hoover, December 13, 1952, Second Hoover Commission-Correspondence, H.R. 992, Hoover Library.

an apparent challenge to presidential authority over administration, that it would have the duty to define the responsibilities of executive branch officials. The commission's twelve members would be appointed, four each, by the president, President of the Senate, and the Speaker of the House. Two of each group of four would be drawn from public life, with one of each group of four having served on the First Hoover Commission. The commission was given the same official title as its predecessor, the Commission on the Organization of the Executive Branch of the Government.

The Brown-Ferguson bill was a major topic in an unusual preinaugural meeting of the President-elect with his advisers and intended cabinet appointees. The meeting occupied the weekend of January 12 and 13, 1953, and it took place at Eisenhower's headquarters, New York's Commodore Hotel. On that Saturday morning, Brown and Ferguson met with Eisenhower to discuss their bill, and on Saturday afternoon Eisenhower took up the matter with his cabinet and staff. The administration-to-be was entirely negative about a new commission. Eisenhower reported that he had told Brown and Ferguson that their idea "was an error and . . . gave . . . specifically as reasons that if we wait for the report of a commission we will never get any reorganization done."[28] However, instead of opposing the bill, Eisenhower adopted an approach to it that fits Fred Greenstein's portrayal of Eisenhower as practicing a "covert or hidden hand leadership."[29] According to Greenstein, Eisenhower characteristically sought desired political outcomes through indirect means which left an appearance of his non-involvement in those outcomes.

Eisenhower and his colleagues believed that it would be impossible to dissuade Brown and Ferguson from pursuing their bill. Henry Cabot Lodge, who had been a sponsor with Brown of the first Hoover Commission, told the meeting that Brown "has . . . hitched his wagon to that . . . star," and that his personal political stake in a second commission was too large for Brown to back down.[30] The action adopted was to get Brown and Ferguson to put off passage of the bill and then to encourage them to create a second commission that would be as policy-involved as its sponsors desired. The purpose of this strategy was to keep the second commission out of the administration's concerns with reorganization and reform of executive branch organiza-

[28] Cabinet Meeting-Commodore, January 12 and 13, 1953, Cabinet Series, Papers of DDE as President, Eisenhower Library.

[29] Fred Greenstein, "Eisenhower as an Activist President," *Political Science Quarterly*, 575-599.

[30] Cabinet Meeting-Commodore.

tion, while hoping that the vast terrain of policy might be swampy enough to swallow the commission. Budget director-designate Joseph Dodge expressed the strategy this way:

> I think there is some possibility of using the commission with a limited charter ... and divert it along the lines of function, the elimination, consolidation and decentralization of function, which is a long-range study and which they can't come up with an answer for a year, perhaps.[31]

Thus the administration assented to a policy-oriented commission as a means of leaving open the immediately more important field of government organization.

The symmetry of the administration's notion of using a policy approach as a way of sidetracking the commission and the Republican congressional intention of using that approach as a means for cutting back upon government set the second commission onto a different course than that of its predecessor. The first commission was caught in a web of political tensions, its statutory requirement for bipartisan membership being only the most obvious example of that. The Truman administration understood that there were major political stakes in the work of the Hoover Commission, and it used its resources to direct the commission in ways acceptable to the Democratic administration. On the other hand, President Eisenhower's choice to establish conditions under which the second commission would be placed out of the way meant that there would be little resistance to its ideological goals.[32]

It was a certain conclusion that the new enterprise would be another Hoover Commission. Even though he was 78, Hoover remained the Republican with the greatest stature in executive reorganization, even as he was also the most eminent member of the party's right wing. As in 1947, Hoover placed conditions on his accepting appointment; he would have to be chairman.[33] He also insisted that he be one of President Eisenhower's appointments.[34]

---

[31] *Ibid.*

[32] Comparing Hoover's relationships with Truman and Eisenhower, Arthur Flemming observes that Truman had something to give that the latter hungered for—access to the White House and honorable recognition as an ex-president. Eisenhower, on the contrary, had very little to give Hoover and was less able to keep him leashed. Arthur Flemming, interviewed by author.

[33] Letter, Brown to Hoover, February 4, 1953, Second Hoover Commission, Correspondence, H.R. 992, Hoover Library.

[34] Memorandum of telephone conversation, Hoover and Flemming, July 12, 1953, Second Hoover Commission, General File Correspondence, Flemming, Hoover Library.

Hoover's conditions were met, and he had a large voice in recommending the commission's other members. Hoover proposed names to each of the officials charged to appoint commissioners; of the eleven members in addition to himself, six were people he had recommended.[35] Eisenhower's four appointees were Hoover; Herbert Brownell, the Attorney-General; James A. Farley, Roosevelt's old political adviser and postmaster-general; and Arthur Flemming, a member of PACGO and the first commission. Hoover had recommended Flemming. Vice-President Nixon named Senators Homer Ferguson and John McClellan; Solomon Hollister, dean of Cornell's School of Engineering; and Robert Storey, dean of Southern Methodist's law school and president of the American Bar Association; Hoover had recommended Ferguson and Hollister. Speaker of the House Joseph Martin named Representatives Clarence Brown and Chet Holifield (Dem., Ca.); Joseph Kennedy, a member of the first commission; and Sidney Mitchell, executive director of the first commission. Hoover had recommended Brown, Kennedy, and Mitchell.

The second commission's members were closer to Herbert Hoover's ideological inclinations than those of the first. There was only one liberal in the group, Representative Holifield, and only two of the members could be considered moderates, Herbert Brownell and Arthur Flemming. In choosing individuals to recommend for appointment, Hoover had screened them for their political reliability. For example, because Hoover knew Solomon Hollister only by reputation, he asked a friend on Cornell's board of trustees, Neal Dow Becker, to "see if Hollister agrees fully with my power speech," referring to a recent speech Hoover had made attacking publicly financed and marketed electric power.[36] Hoover also expected the second commission's members to defer to him, and he requested each member to sign a proxy statment that would give their vote to Hoover should they be absent from a meeting.

A consequence of the commission's ideological homogeneity was that it was easily dominated by Hoover. For reasons of age and stature, blending with personality characteristics that had always been present, Hoover had become superbly imperious; he treated the commission as his tool and the mission of reorganization as his personal crusade.

[35] Letter, Hoover to Brown, July 11, 1953, Second Hoover Commission, General Nominees for New Commission, Hoover Library; memoranda of telephone conversations, Hoover with Nixon and Ferguson, July 12, 1953, Second Hoover Commission, General File Correspondence, Flemming, Hoover Library.

[36] Memorandum of telephone conversation, Hoover & Mitchell, July 12, 1953, Second Hoover Commission, General File Correspondence, Flemming, Hoover Library.

His personalization of the enterprise shows through his language in a note to Dr. Fordyce B. St. John, asking for advice concerning the make-up of a task force on medical activities. Hoover wrote: "Having agreed to reorganize the United States again, I am in need of help and advice."[37]

Chairman Hoover's haughty mien dominated the commission, but it further distanced him (and the commission) from the White House. Personal relations between Hoover and Eisenhower were cool, making it difficult for the President to influence the course of the commission. Eisenhower seemed to be constantly irritated by Hoover's presumptuous style. To illustrate, two weeks after the commission's first meeting, Hoover asked Arthur Flemming to make sure that the administration made no policy or organization changes in areas under consideration by the commission. Hoover listed for Flemming the areas that should not be touched, and they included: water development and power policy, governmental personnel, regulatory commissions, and the Interior, Agriculture, and Commerce departments. Hoover then listed the reforms that he would approve the administration's undertaking immediately. He thought it would be acceptable to have reorganization plans transfer the Rio Grande and St. Lawrence Boundary Commissions to Interior, to transfer the National Capitol Housing Authority to the District of Columbia, and to transfer forest land in the jurisdiction of the Bureau of Land Management to the Forest Service.[38] It was hardly a list of heroic reforms that Hoover would allow Eisenhower. The President ignored Hoover's request.

President Eisenhower and his staff could not but also notice that Herbert Hoover revived the politically potent Citizens Committee for the Hoover Report at the outset of the second commission. By mid-fall 1953 there was sufficient reason to suspect that the President's "hidden hand" strategy had loosed a cannon upon the administration's deck.

PACGO and the President: 1953-1955

After its intensive work between late 1952 and April 1953, President Eisenhower allowed PACGO to shift to a slower pace.[39] Established

---

[37] Letter, Hoover to St. John, September 12, 1953, 2nd Hoover Commission, TF on Medical Service, Misc. Corresp.-McCormick, *ibid.*

[38] Letter, Hoover to Flemming, November 12, 1953, Second Hoover Commission, General File Correspondence, Flemming, Hoover Library.

[39] Letter, Eisenhower to Rockefeller, April 23, 1953, DDE Diary 52-53 (3), Papers of DDE as President, Eisenhower Library.

as a permanent committee on organization, it would have three different responsibilities. Most immediately it would consult with the administration and the Bureau of the Budget on implementation of the reorganization plans it laid out in its transition documents. Second, its longer-range responsibility would be to scan the organized presidency and the executive branch with an eye toward fruitful reforms. In this role it would fulfill one of its own transition recommendations. It had stressed that organizational monitoring must be a full-time activity within government. The committee's intention had been for the Bureau of the Budget to expand into that role.[40] But the bureau's budget and legislative responsibilities always overloaded its limited resources.[41] Thus it was simpler to charge PACGO with that monitoring role, even though it had the disadvantage that it was not connected to channels of communication—such as the budget process—which would enhance its capacity to oversee the operation of administration. Third, the committee became the administration's monitor of the second Hoover Commission, and after the commission's demise it had a major responsibility for handling the touchy question of what should be done with its recommendations.

For Eisenhower to maintain the committee's existence was a sensible course of action. The committee had proved its mettle in the transition. Also, its intimacy with Eisenhower meshed well with his organizational style. His attentiveness to organization required that a continuing capacity to think about organization be built into his closest circle of advisers, and by virtue of its membership PACGO was within that circle. As one of PACGO's few staff members described the committee's relationship to the President; its

> pattern . . . is different from that used before or since. . . . Here were three citizens, one of whom is the brother of the President, a trusted confidant, thinking aloud with him . . . on the whole business of the structuring of the administration. At any point if they wanted to informally check the President . . . they just did it, or Milton did it overnight and back the next day they were in business.[42]

[40] Preface to recommendations, n.d., file no. 24, PACGO, Eisenhower Library.

[41] On the recurring problems in the bureau's role in management support, see Larry Berman, *The Office of Management and Budget* (Princeton: Princeton University Press, 1979). In 1953 and 1954 the bureau was even more limited in its capacity to work for management improvement in the executive branch because of Joseph Dodge's insistence that its budget be pared back consistent with the administration's overall policy of budget reduction. *Ibid.*, p. 53.

[42] Jarold Kieffer, interviewed by author, October 31, 1979.

PACGO operated on a part-time basis. Its members were all occupied with other assignments. Rockefeller, its chairman, was undersecretary of the new Department of Health, Education and Welfare.
Flemming was director of the Office of Defense Mobilization as well
as a member of the Hoover Commission, and Milton Eisenhower had
recently assumed the presidency of Penn State University. The committee worked intermittently, operating through telephone conversations among the three members and meetings of one or two of them
with the President. PACGO held no formal meetings through the last
half of 1953, and to keep it running Rockefeller hired a full-time staff
director, Arthur Kimball, who had been deputy director at the United
States Information Agency.[43]

But PACGO's members took on a reorganization planning task in
1953, working under another label. During the transition period the
advisory committee had not addressed defense organization. But in
mid-1953 President Eisenhower asked Nelson Rockefeller to chair a
committee formally titled the Committee on Department of Defense
Organization. In fact, it was an extended PACGO; joining Rockefeller
were Arthur Flemming, Milton Eisenhower, General Omar Bradley,
Vannevar Bush, Robert A. Lovett, and David Sarnoff.[44] The defense
committee prepared recommendations for reorganization of the Defense Department which became the single 1953 reorganization plan
that did not originate in the advisory committee's recommendations.

PACGO's success cannot be judged only by the 1953 reorganization
plans. It offered recommendations for restructuring presidential organization that were effected without reorganization plans. The more
important of those was the designation of a presidential assistant as
an adviser on national security matters (a post filled initially by Robert
Cutler); reform of the budget process pertaining to the Executive Office, with the designation of single subcommittees in both houses to
deal with all but National Security Council and Office of Defense
Mobilization budgets; the creation of a cabinet secretariat (a post
initially filled by Maxwell Rabb); the establishment of ad hoc cabinet
committees to cover particular policy areas; and changes in the re-

[43] Arthur Kimball Oral History Interview, Eisenhower Administration Project, Columbia University Oral History Research Office, 1968.

[44] For the committee's report see U.S. Congress, Senate, Committee on Armed Services,
Report of the Rockefeller Committee on Department of Defense Organization, 83rd
Congress, 1st Sess., 1953. For an excellent treatment of the committee and its recom-
mendations in the context of the organizational development of the Department of
Defense, see John C. Ries, *The Management of Defense* (Baltimore: Johns Hopkins
University Press, 1964), pp. 147-162.

sponsibility of the chairman of the Civil Service Commission, designating him the president's chief adviser on civilian personnel matters in the government.[45]

PACGO's success in defining the administration's 1953 reorganization agenda could not be duplicated for 1954. The peculiarity of the 1953 agenda is that it was prepared during the transition when the committee faced no competition. But, beginning with the inauguration, the committee had a rival in the Bureau of the Budget. As William Finan of the bureau's management division said to Budget Director Dodge, the issue was "whether the Bureau has the initiative in proposing a reorganization program or whether, as was the case this year, the initiative rests with the Committee."[46] After some discussion with Dodge and Rockefeller, Finan drafted a memo which envisaged a relationship between the bureau and the committee that would leave to the bureau the basic job of planning the administration's reorganization program.[47] According to Finan's proposal, the bureau would have primary responsibility for the 1954 program. The committee, on the other hand, would have three responsibilities. One, it would continue work to implement its original reorganization recommendations. Two, it would advise the President and the budget director on reorganization. Three, it would undertake special assignments given to it by the President.

William Finan's attempt to finesse the committee's dominance of reorganization might have worked, were it not for the second Hoover Commission. The bureau had two marked advantages over the committee, despite its limited resources and the committee's status. One, it was at the apex of an information system which gave it a capability of addressing organizational needs that was far greater than PACGO's. Two, PACGO's attention was limited by the part-time status of its members and by its tiny staff composed of a director, a staff assistant, and two secretaries. But the Hoover Commission enhanced PACGO's importance. The bureau had no significant role in the Hoover Commission's work, while PACGO provided the best link between the White House and the commission. That link was forged by the fact that Arthur Flemming was a member of both bodies. It was strengthened by the fact that Flemming's designated assistant at the commission, Jarold Kieffer, was PACGO's staff assistant. In the fall of 1953,

---

[45] "Committee Recommendations Accomplished or Substantially Accomplished," box 5, file no. 29, PACGO, Eisenhower Library.

[46] Memorandum, Finan to Director, September 15, 1953, Director's Office, 52-60, BOB, series 51.2, RG 51, National Archives.

[47] Memorandum, Finan to Director, October 30, 1953, BOB, series 54.1, F2-80, RG 51, National Archives.

Milton Eisenhower suggested to his brother that the committee oversee the administration's interests in the Hoover Commission's work, in particular consulting with and advising the administration's two members on the commission, Herbert Brownell and Arthur Flemming.[48] Increasingly, this assignment occupied PACGO's attention.

While the Bureau of the Budget was not able to dominate PACGO, after 1953 a more equal if not trouble-free relationship developed. An important development enabling this partnership was the administration's realization that it could trust the Bureau of the Budget as an agency of professionals able to adapt to Eisenhower's goals.[49] When a program for reorganization for 1954 was presented to Eisenhower, it was presented as a joint product of the bureau and the committee.[50] The program was trivial in comparison to that of 1953. Seven items were recommended for immediate action through reorganization plans; they included shifting some of the Reconstruction Finance Authority's responsibilities to Treasury as the RFA was terminated, consolidating the International Claims Commission and War Claims Commission, and transferring responsibilities of the Arlington Memorial Amphitheater Commission to the Department of Defense. As Dodge and Rockefeller said to Eisenhower in describing their recommendations, these were "proposals deemed worthwhile but involving comparatively minor functions in the executive branch."[51] President Eisenhower chose to submit only two reorganization plans during 1954; these merged the claims commissions and moved functions from the Reconstruction Finance Corporation. But the administration's main organizational focus during 1954 was on a different target than small-scale organizational changes. It had become increasingly concerned with the possibility of reshaping organizations in the light of its developing policy preferences.

PACGO's role in stimulating the President to reexamine an organizational-policy nexus is demonstrated by its work on water resources policy. In the spring of 1954 the committee prepared a memorandum on water resources that argued a need for overall policy coordination among the several relevant agencies.[52] In water policy the committee saw a set of problems that could be addressed only at the highest level.

[48] Jarold Kieffer, interviewed by author.

[49] Larry Berman, pp. 48-52.

[50] Memorandum, Dodge and Rockefeller to Eisenhower, February 17, 1954, BOB, 54.1, F2-80, RG 51, National Archives. After 1953, PACGO and the Bureau of the Budget joined together in preparing an annual set of reorganization recommendations.

[51] *Ibid.*

[52] This memorandum was presented to the cabinet on May 12, 1954 by Sherman Adams; box 19, file 154, PACGO, Eisenhower Library.

These included questions about the purposes of water policy, the fact that the President could hold no single member of his cabinet responsible for this area, and the great resistance to change from established interests. The committee saw that these were not problems easily addressed through a one-shot reform and recommended a cabinet committee to confront these intertwined policy and organizational problems. Consequently, President Eisenhower created his Advisory Committee on Water Resources Policy. In PACGO's view, cabinet committees promised a format wherein a unified administration position might develop while coopting relevant agencies to that position through their participation in them.[53] During 1954, PACGO recommended the formation of a presidential advisory committee on Transport Policy and Organization and a presidential advisory committee on Telecommunications Policy and Organization, both of these recommendations being adopted by the President.[54]

After 1953 PACGO's meetings suggest an intertwining of the committee and the Bureau of the Budget. Officials of the bureau were always present at those meetings; the typical meeting would include the budget director and the assistant director in charge of management and organization. Frequently others from the bureau would also join the meetings; during the life of the Hoover Commission, Edward Strait of the bureau would join those meetings because part of his responsibility was to act as that agency's liaison to the commission. The bureau's presence at PACGO's meetings was far from perfunctory; its officials were active participants in the whole array of issues discussed by the committee. However, PACGO retained an edge over the bureau. President Eisenhower had charged PACGO with long-range planning, while the Bureau of the Budget, by the nature of its link to the annual budget cycle, was tied to the immediate and the short term. To force the bureau into long-range planning would have demanded of it resources it could ill afford, as well as a manner of operation that would disrupt its routines. In fact, toward the end of the Eisenhower administration, to the bureau's discomfort, PACGO raised the issue of the bureau's incapacities for organizational analysis and planning.[55]

[53] For a study of the Ford administration's use of a similar mechanism, see Roger Porter, *Presidential Decisionmaking* (New York: Cambridge University Press, 1980).

[54] Bernard Shanley, memorandum for the record, August 11, 1954, Whitman Diary Series, August 1954 (3), Papers of DDE as President, Eisenhower Library; and Summary of the Principal Activities of PACGO, n.d., box 4, file 25, PACGO, Eisenhower Library.

[55] Minutes of Committee Meeting, December 14, 1954, Box 2, file 18, PACGO, Eisenhower Library.

THE SECOND HOOVER COMMISSION IN OPERATION

Organizationally the Second Hoover Commission replicated its predecessor. Task forces conducted its investigations, the commission devising its reports on their basis. The staff was small, excluding clerical personnel and the commissioners' assistants, never larger than eight persons. Its executive director was John B. Hollister; later a deputy was appointed in the person of W. Hallam Tuck. Francis Brassor, who was the first commission's executive secretary, performed the same role in the second, and Harold Metz, who had been a staff person on the earlier commission, became director of research this time around. Neil MacNeil was brought in midway as editorial director, supervising two other editorial staff members. At the end of the commission's work, a legislative draftsman was added to the staff.

While the form was similar, the staff assembled for the second commission differed in an important respect from the first; it was without academicians or research-oriented public administration specialists. The second commission staff was without any equivalent to figures like Don Price or Charles Aiken. The only person similar to a Price or Aiken on the staff of the second commission was Flemming's assistant, Jarold Kieffer, who had finished a Ph.D. in political science at Minnesota in the late 1940's. Another difference between the analytic capacities of the first and second commissions was the greatly reduced role of the Bureau of the Budget in the second commission's work. The strong, unchallenged policy orientation of the second commission would, under any circumstances, create tension with the bureau's presidential support role. In particular, the bureau's professional staff was wary of the lack of bipartisanship on the commission.[56] Consequently, Hoover was informed "that the Bureau was in no position to provide for the new Hoover Commission the kind of assistance . . . provided to its predecessor."[57]

Hoover's Ideological Agenda and the Task Forces

Because the second Hoover Commission lacked the first commission's diversity, Hoover was able to dominate its agenda with little oppo-

[56] This is clear in the bureau's analysis of the Brown-Ferguson bill, prepared by Arnold Miles. Memorandum, Miles to Finan, January 28, 1953, BOB, 53-1, F2-70, RG 51, National Archives.

[57] Memorandum, Miles to Sutton, describing an oral communication to Ross Huddleston on the commission's staff, August 21, 1953, BOB, 53.4, F2-70, RG 51, National Archives.

sition. At the commission's first meeting he outlined the areas that he thought needed investigation and asked the commissioners to authorize him to create task forces to address those areas. Hoover's request was granted without a dissenting voice; as the meeting's minutes put the decision, the task force members were "to be appointed at his sole discretion."[58]

Six weeks later Hoover announced to his fellow commissioners that he had created seven task forces, picked their chairmen and had assembled nearly their full memberships; these were the task forces on budget and accounting, food and clothing, lending, medical service, personnel, real property, and water and power resources.[59] In the next several months more task forces were added at the suggestions of the commissioners. For example, Commissioner Storey suggested a task force on legal services, and the proposal was adopted, with Storey given authority to organize it.[60]

The commission's fourteen task forces were a mixed bag of purposes and personnel. With few exceptions, they were more conservative than those of the first commission. But some of the task forces operated with little or no ideological coloration, instead tackling narrow or technical problems with substantial expertise. The reports of the task forces on budget and accounting, paperwork management, real property, and surplus property were competent, technical, and non-controversial.

Addressing more controversial issues, the task force on personnel and civil service was extremely professional, and its report is a milestone in the development of the idea of an American public service. This task force was distinguished from all the others of the second commission in that it brought together leading business people with major academic specialists. It was chaired by Harold W. Dodds, a political scientist and president of Princeton, and among its nine other members were the leading student of American public administration in his generation, Leonard White, and a groundbreaking thinker about decision making in organizations, Chester I. Barnard. The task force's staff director was a younger scholar on American public service and administration, George A. Graham of Princeton. Joining these academic specialists was a group of very successful men whose work was particularly germane to public personnel problems, such as Robert Ramspeck, formerly a congressman and member of the Civil Service

[58] Minutes, September 29, 1953, Commission on Organization of the Executive Branch, 1953-55, Office of the Secretary, Minutes, RG 264, National Archives.
[59] Minutes, November 16, 1953, *ibid*.
[60] *Ibid*.

Commission (then an airline vice-president); Devereux C. Josephs, vice-president in charge of personnel at a New York City bank; and Don G. Mitchell, a chairman of the board of a large manufacturing firm and a director of the American Management Association. Finally, this task force was distinctive in its outlook, being the only one to consciously accept a perspective "from the standpoint of top management."[61]

All the task forces were not so expert or balanced as those on paperwork management or personnel and civil service. A thread runs through perhaps half of them which, in turn, becomes a theme for the second commission—the attack on big government. The formation and work of the task forces on medical services and water resources exemplify the ideological thrust of the commission's work.

The task force on medical services was dominated by physicians, although its chairman was a layman. Herbert Hoover had originally sought a physician, Dr. James Miller, Northwestern University's president, to take the job.[62] After Miller declined, Hoover offered the position to Chauncey McCormick, a Chicago businessman.[63] McCormick's qualifying experience for heading one of Hoover's task forces may have been his service in Eastern Europe in 1919-1920 as an agent of Hoover's American Relief Commission. In addition to McCormick, only one other member of the twenty-five-member medical task force was not an M.D., Otto Brandhorst, D.D.S., dean of Washington University's dental school. The members of the task force were drawn from the health profession's elite; they were of the faculties of major medical schools, directors of large teaching hospitals, and alumni of war-related governmental medical activities. The group also contained current and former officers of professional associations, including the current heads of the boards of psychiatry and surgery, as well as officers of the national associations of medicine, dentistry, and hospital administration.[64]

That this task force felt comfortably aligned with the medical es-

[61] Memorandum, "Summary of Scope of Activities of Task Forces," and accompanying letter, Hollister to Adams, October 1, 1954, OF 103-A-1, 1952-54 (2), White House Central File, Eisenhower Library.

[62] Letter, Hoover to F. B. St. John, September 12, 1953 and memorandum, St. John to Hoover, September 17, 1953, 2nd Hoover Commission, TF on Medical Services, Misc'l Correspondence-McCormick, Hoover Library.

[63] After McCormick's death on September 8, 1954, he was succeeded by Dr. Theodore G. Klumpp, a member of the task force.

[64] Membership lists of task forces along with brief biographies can be found in, Commission on the Organization of the Executive Branch, *Progress Report* (Washington: Government Printing Office, 1954).

tablishment is attested to by the fact that the American Medical Association loaned to it the secretary for its division dealing with federal medical services.[65] Its relationship to the establishment is further demonstrated at its first meeting. Dr. Edward Churchill spoke on the work of the first Hoover Commission's task force on medical services, of which he had been a member. Churchill told his colleagues on the new task force that the earlier one had been warned to have nothing to do with what Churchill called the "Chicago organizations," meaning the American Medical Association and the American College of Surgeons. In the transcript of the first meeting of the task force, Churchill is quoted as saying: "We were told . . . to keep any identity with Chicago organizations at a very low visibility because that would be the one thing that would be suspect on capitol hill."[66]

The commission's mission was addressed more directly at the next meeting of the medical services task force when the question was raised about whether the task force could consider policies as well as the organization of medical services. Dr. Paul Hawley, formerly medical director of the Veterans' Administration, wondered if it was clear that the task force was free to "get into government policy."[67] Chauncey McCormick responded that the task force was charged to prepare "a full report" for the commission, meaning a report which spoke to all the factors considered relevant by the task force in improving federal medical services. Dr. Walter Martin added the view that this had been where the first commission's task force had gone astray, its recommendation for a non-cabinet federal medical administration failing to draw support "because that did not deal with the basic fault of continued growth of the federal service." Martin's opinion was backed, so to speak, by the voice of authority. At this juncture in the meeting's discussion, the task force's director of research, Dr. Edwin Crosby, produced a copy of the congressional act creating the second commission. But the last word was had by Dr. Michael DeBakey, who reminded his colleagues of Herbert Hoover's informal comments to the task force at its first meeting. DeBakey said: "Mr. Hoover pointed this out himself in talking to us, that the law this time was written definitely different, and they learned their lesson from the previous time where they were specifically concerned with operations of the executive branch . . . and not with policy."[68]

[65] Transcript, November 11, 1954, Commission on Organization of the Executive Branch, 1953-55, TF on Federal Medical Services-Transportation, RG 264, National Archives.

[66] *Ibid.*

[67] *Ibid.*, February 11, 1954.

[68] *Ibid.* Describing Hoover's instructions to the task force at that first meeting, Theo-

The recommendations of the medical task force bespeak the success of Hoover's personnel selection strategy. Among its recommendations were several for the enhancement and further autonomy of professional medicine in the federal establishment. The first of these was for the creation of a Federal Council of Health in the executive Office of the President on which would sit "ten persons of distinguished competence in the health field as broadly defined. . . ." Its job would be to advise presidents on health policy and to evaluate ongoing federal activities in the health field. The second of these was the creation of a National Library of Medicine, and the third of the profession-enhancing recommendations was for federal research grants to medicine to drop their project specificity and become long-term (five-year) block grants to research institutions, supporting a research agenda at the institution's discretion.[69] Once the task force got beyond tending its garden professionally, it issued recommendations for the cutback of federal medical services, suggesting that military dependents in the United States be covered through medical insurance rather than military medicine, proposing that veterans with non-service-related ills not be treated without charge by the Veterans' Administration, and recommending the end of federal health services to merchant seamen.[70]

The second Hoover Commission's largest and most expensive task force was the one on water resources; it had 26 members supported by the largest staff of any task force, and it spent $336,892 between fall 1953 and May 1955. However, the water resources task force is memorable more for its political coloration than its scale. It was probably no more conservative, but its operation and recommendations drew the sharpest controversy of any of the task forces' reports. It differed from other, equally conservative task forces in the status of its subject of investigation and in its chairman's character.

This task force was focusing on a foundation issue on which the progressive-liberal coalition had formed in American politics between the 1920's and the Second World War. Lenin defined communism as electrification plus the Soviets. An American wag might have echoed him in suggesting that New Deal liberalism was public power plus the

dore Klumpp remembers his telling the members that the legislation creating the second commission, in Klumpp's words, "authorized the task forces and the Commission to examine the legislative aspects of the executive departments, and we were free to make our recommendations in any way we sought. There were no barriers . . . there was a gleam in Mr. Hoover's eyes when he told us that no holds were barred. . . ." Theodore G. Klumpp, M.D., Oral History Interview, December 2, 1969, Hoover Library.

[69] Commission on Organization of the Executive Branch, *Task Force Report on Federal Medical Services* (Washington: Government Printing Office, 1955), pp. 7-23.

[70] *Ibid.*, pp. 25-50.

Democrats. To attack public power was to attack the foundations of Democratic national policy. To rub salt in the wounds left by the attack, Herbert Hoover selected a curmudgeon to lead the task force, Admiral Ben Moreell.

Ben Moreell became chairman of the board of the Jones and Laughlin Steel Co. after an engineering career in the Navy. But Hoover drafted more than an engineer and manager in bringing Moreell to the task force's chairmanship. Moreell recalled the conversation he had with Hoover about the appointment:

> He seated me, and said, "There's no use beating around the bush. I want you to be chairman of the second Hoover Commission Task Force on Water Resources and Power." I said, "I'm surprised, Mr. Hoover. You know I have the reputation of being very conservative, one might even say reactionary, with respect to governmental operation." . . . He said "I know all about you. I've probably read every speech that you've made that has been published." I said, "Then we understand each other."[71]

The task force formed under Moreell included engineers (14), lawyers (6), and several businessmen. Only one of the engineers was currently employed by a governmental unit, the chief engineer for the Los Angeles Water District. Three engineers had worked in the past with the Army Corp of Engineers and three with the Bureau of Reclamation, and most of the engineers had worked with or consulted for government during their careers. Given the fact that these were professionals whose careers had developed during the 1930's and 1940's, having worked for government was far more an indication of where in the American economy capital investment had originated than a sign of satisfaction with the public sector. The only members of the task force ultimately supportive of public power were Harry W. Morrison, formerly director of the Bureau of Reclamation, and Harry Polk, a North Dakota publisher. Both dissented from the task force's report.[72]

The only instance of a commissioner challenging Chairman Hoo-

[71] Admiral Ben Moreell, Oral History Interview, 1970, Hoover Library. At one point in this interview Moreell relates that one of his prize possessions was given by "the Chief." It was Volume II of the House Committee on Un-American Activities' 1940 hearings. Moreell stated that Hoover gave it to him saying that in it he would find, in Moreell's words, "a very complete account of the Communists in the administration of the T.V.A." Commission on the Organization of the Executive Branch, *Progress Report* (Washington: Government Printing Office, 1954).

[72] For the dissents to the task force recommendations, see Commission on the Organization of the Executive Branch, *Task Force Report on Water Resources and Power*, Vol. I (Washington: Government Printing Office, 1955), pp. 227-231.

ver's task force personnel selections arose over the water resources task force. At the commission's November 16, 1953 meeting, Representative Chet Holifield, a liberal and westerner, asked that the minutes record his objection to the absence of public power advocates on the task force. He moved that five members fitting that description be added to it. Hoover brushed aside the complaint, explaining "that the members were leading men in their fields, that none of them were connected with private power, and one or two were connected with public power."[73] Hoover had obviously assumed that consulting for and representing private power companies did not constitute being "connected" with them.

At the commission's meeting of January 11, 1954, Holifield again attacked the bias of the water resources task force, urging the necessity for balance on it through additional appointments.[74] This attack launched Hoover into a more straightforward defense of the personnel selections for the task force, a defense that is revealing of Hoover's overall appointment strategy. No longer stressing the professional eminence and neutrality of the task force members, Hoover wrote to fellow commissioners the explanation that the statute creating the second commission specified that it should seek to reduce government's activities, especially those competitive with private enterprise. He said: "There is *no* direction to increase activities which are competitive with private enterprise" (emphasis in original). Thus, Hoover reasoned, it would violate the law and thwart congressional intentions to appoint individuals to the task forces "whose purpose is the direct opposite of the Act."[75]

What Hoover expected of Admiral Moreell's group is clarified in a memo he sent to Moreell about a month before the task force's first meeting.[76] The memo suggested guidelines for the task force's work. Hoover urged the development of a "yardstick" of evaluation by which federal activities such as maintaining the navigability of rivers, providing irrigation, reclaiming land, and generating power could be assessed. But larded into this discussion of essentially concrete measures of economic performance are strong ideological judgments offered as if they were of the same status as the factors making up a relatively

[73] Minutes, November 16, 1953, 2nd Hoover Commission, General File, Correspondence, Holifield, Hoover Library.

[74] Minutes, January 11, 1954, *ibid.*

[75] Memorandum, Hoover to Hollister and Mitchell, January 12, 1953, 2nd Hoover Commission, Task Force on Water Resources and Power, Hoover Library.

[76] Memorandum, "Development of Water Resources and Water Power," 2nd Hoover Commission, TF on Water Resources and Power, Hoover Library.

objective economic assessment. For example, in suggesting that Moreell's task force keep in mind the overhead cost of the federal administrative apparatus required to conduct land reclamation and irrigation projects, Hoover simply concluded: "The State governments could do a better job of administration than the remote control from Washington." Later in the memo, Hoover listed a series of nine questions the task force should entertain. The list swings from a relatively technical question to a blatantly ideological proposition put in the form of a question. So, the first question concerned accuracy of the cost estimates to Congress on major projects. But the second asked: "Whether there has been coercion or bureaucratic tyranny over competitive private enterprise." Questions followed about whether monopolies had been created and whether the federal government should be in the business of producing power. The list closes with the most extraordinary question to ask of a task force. Hoover wondered: "Whether parts of the present operations are unconstitutional."[77]

Policy and the Task Forces: The Case of Water Resources

Because of the symbolic importance of federal public power policy to Democratic liberalism, the Republicans who took over in 1953 had to find an alternative policy position on public power and water resources. The search for a new policy took on the character of a struggle within the Republican Party. At PACGO's suggestion, Eisenhower created a cabinet-level committee on federal water and power policy within a year of taking office.[78] But the administration had little freedom for movement, the second commission's task force on water resources becoming the medium through which the Republican right attempted to impose its perspective on national policy.

The spirit of the administration's approach to water and power policy was established in a memorandum prepared by Budget Director Dodge. Dodge denounced the doings of past administrations without recommending that the Republican administration abandon the large-scale development of water resources. Instead he urged that national, not just local, interests should be weighed in deciding upon federal investment in a project, and he specified the need for a more active mix of state and local governments as well as the private sector into water resource projects.[79]

[77] Ibid.

[78] Draft memorandum, Rockefeller to Eisenhower, December 4, 1953, file 153, PACGO, Eisenhower Library.

[79] Memorandum, Dodge to Eisenhower, December 14, 1953, Dodge 53-55 (2), Administrative series, Papers of DDE as President, Eisenhower Library.

After seeing Dodge's memorandum, President Eisenhower requested a revision, stressing the lack of overall planning in water and power policy. The President insisted that the key change in water resource development must be an increase of rationality in government's action.[80] The final version of Dodge's paper can be taken as the moderate Republican—and the President's—stance on water resources policy. It admits to an active federal role and shares the long-term liberal concern with resource planning. On the other hand, this position differs from the Democratic practice in its stress on intergovernmental and public-private partnerships in water resource development.

While the administration was developing its stance toward water resources, major power projects awaited decisions. The most prominent of these was the upper Colorado River project, involving the construction of three high dams. This project would supply both water and electric power at the projected construction cost of a billion dollars. The Truman administration had supported it, and in January 1954 President Eisenhower informed its legislative backers that his administration would also favor it.[81]

Learning of the administration's support for the upper Colorado project, Hoover attempted to convince Joseph Dodge that the project's power production should be given over to private utilities through fifty-year leases, but Dodge rejected that means for tying government's hands.[82] Next Hoover went to the President, asking Eisenhower to "promote harmony in the work of the Reorganization Commission, Executive Agencies and the Congress. . . ."[83] Observing that the commission's mandate was to investigate the activities of the government and recommend new policies, Hoover stated:

> What I am asking is that no more such proposals [for new projects] should be given the Administration's backing until my colleagues and I should have an opportunity to express our views. Better still, that Congressional leaders be advised that authorization of all such projects should be deferred until the next Congress. . . .[84]

Between late April and June 1954, Hoover and Moreell carried their campaign repeatedly to Eisenhower, through letters and several meet-

[80] Memorandum, Eisenhower to Dodge, December 17, 1953, *ibid.*

[81] Elmo Richardson, *The Presidency of Dwight D. Eisenhower* (Lawrence: Regents Press of Kansas, 1979), pp. 48-49.

[82] Letter, Hoover to Dodge, April 4, 1954, 2nd Hoover Commission, TF on Water Resources, Correspondence-Moreell, and memorandum, Resources and Civil Works Division of the Bureau of the Budget to Director, April 14, 1954, Hoover Library.

[83] Letter, Moreell to Hoover, April 23, 1954, *ibid.*

[84] Letter, Hoover to Eisenhower, April 23, 1954, *ibid.*

ings at the White House. With his famous short temper showing, Eisenhower observed to Sherman Adams that:

> It does appear strange that after all these years of study and investigation into this particular project, there should be such violent disagreement in conclusions among individuals who are not only of our own political party, but are presumably of the same political philosophy in the field of conservation and use of water resources.[85]

Their failure to win over Eisenhower did not stop Hoover and Moreell. They took Eisenhower's decision to stick with the upper Colorado project as a license to voice their disagreement with the administration on water policy. In early June, Admiral Moreell stated to the press that his task force had no commitment to the President regarding Eisenhower's campaign promises to maintain the Tennessee Valley Authority; the commission, as Moreell pointed out, was a creature of the legislature. For Hoover's part, he appealed to Eisenhower privately again on June 21, 1954, even presuming to offer a draft of a statement the President could issue to postpone all water resource projects.[86] Eisenhower of course refused and Hoover testified at a congressional hearing on the legislation for the Colorado River project, asking Congress to postpone its legislation until his commission reported.[87] Hoover evidently saw no conflict between his role at the Hoover Commission and his active endeavors to stop the Colorado River project's legislation. After his congressional testimony, he planned quiet lobbying activities in the Senate to try to keep the bill in committee, using his personal assistant at the commission, Lawrence Richey, as his agent in this matter.[88] Because of such opposition, the upper Colorado basin project did not gain congressional approval until 1956, and then only because of strong Democratic support.

In early 1955 the water resource task force issued its report. Its published report is 1,781 pages long and contains a mountain of data on federal water projects.[89] Yet there is only a loose fit between this voluminous documentation and the task force's recommendations. Recall the recommendations of the medical services task force. In a

[85] Memorandum, Eisenhower to Adams, June 18, 1954, Hoover (2), Administrative Series, Papers of DDE as President, Eisenhower Library.

[86] Letter, Hoover to Eisenhower, 2nd Hoover Commission, TF on Water Resources, Colorado River Project, Hoover Library.

[87] Draft statement, June 26, 1954, *ibid.*

[88] Memorandum, Hoover to Richey, June 29, 1954, *ibid.*

[89] Commission on the Organization of the Executive Branch, *Task Force Report on Water Resources and Power*, 3 volumes (Washington: Government Printing Office, 1955).

short report, that task force stated its recommendations with relatively brief explanations and with no attempt to suggest that its policy judgments could be validated by a larger collection of data. That task force, for example, recommended against continued treatment without cost for veterans whose ills were not service-related. The task force could observe that the adoption of this recommendation would produce savings, but presumably it understood that what it was recommending was a policy choice. The water resources task force attempted to escape the appearance of making policy choices by accumulating massive data on federal water projects. This strategy fit the task force's secondary thrust, which was to argue that federal water resource projects were often uneconomic. But the task force's main thrust was political. The "findings" offered prior to the recommendations signal this to the most casual reader.[90] Among these was the observation that there is a need for a clear definition of the federal role in water policy limited to the framework of national interest in conservation. The report also offered the view that the federal role had grown larger and larger, dominating water resource activities which should be outside the federal realm. Also, the task force found that the federal government "has used water resource projects, which should be undertaken exclusively for economic purposes, to accomplish indirect social and political ends." The findings continued on in this spirit.

The general findings paved the way for the task force's specific recommendations.[91] Foremost among these was the recommendation for the creation of a Water Resource Board and an affiliated board of review to be placed in the Executive Office for the purpose of coordinating and authoritatively reviewing all federal water projects. The resource board would have five public members and the secretaries of the Army, Agriculture, and Interior, along with the chairman of the Federal Power Commission, as the other voting members. The review board would be composed of only public members, appointed to long and overlapping terms. They would be, the task force envisioned, distinguished and knowledgeable in the field of water resources, and they would have a virtual veto over public works projects in the water area.

Preparing the Hoover Reports

As the Hoover Commission received the task force reports, its method for analyzing them and drafting a commission report was to assign a

---

[90] *Ibid.*, pp. 1-27.
[91] *Ibid.*, pp. 83-110.

committee of commissioners to the task. This committee, composed usually of three commissioners designated by Hoover, aided by their assistants and commission staff, would draft a report that was meant to incorporate whatever seemed desirable from the task force report and represent the formal recommendation of the Hoover Commission. This draft report was then circulated among the commissioners, whose responses were then considered by the original committee of commissioners and the report revised in light of them. The revised report was then recirculated among the commission and placed on the agenda for final consideration at the next commission meeting.[92]

In preparing its reports, the second Hoover Commission was necessarily more self-reliant than the first Hoover Commission had been. The first commission had the luxury of staff support from the Bureau of the Budget which was absent in the second commission's work. The bureau had backed up several of the task forces of the first commission as well as Chairman Hoover's own study of the presidency and departmental management. Furthermore, for the first commission the bureau had participated in the process of assessing task force reports, expanding the perspective of the commission. The second commission was without this very important resource. Thus the assessment of task force reports and their translation into commission reports was dependent upon the limited resources of the second commission itself.

But the Bureau of the Budget was not totally absent from the activities of the second commission. The bureau supplied one staff member, Edward Strait, as a liaison on a part-time basis between the commission and the bureau; Strait would attend the meetings of the commission and attempt to help it with basic informational needs and governmental contacts. The covert but larger role the bureau played in the commission's reports was through Arthur Flemming's liaison function between the commission and the administration. From Flemming and Herbert Brownell the bureau acquired copies of draft reports, and it would arm Flemming and Brownell with analysis to help them seek revisions in reports.[93]

[92] This procedure was established at the meeting of January 7, 1955; Minutes, January 7, 1955, Commission on Organization of the Executive Branch, Office of the Secretary, Minutes, RG 264, National Archives.

[93] Flemming's assistant, Jarold Kieffer, was one of the most able of the commissioners' assistants. Thus Hoover called upon him for a number of staff assignments for the commission. For example, he drafted and edited the commission's reports on personnel, surplus property, and budgeting. Kieffer's job as Flemming's assistant also entailed his bootlegging copies of draft reports, when one could be obtained, to the Bureau of the Budget for analysis, so that Flemming and Brownell could be directed to represent an administration position, once one was determined. Jarold Kieffer, interviewed by author.

A consequence of the second Hoover Commission's limited staff support was that it was more closely tied to its task forces than the first commission. The commission's report on water resources exemplifies this. Its first recommendation was an omnibus restatement of the task force's points. The federal government should participate in water projects only when the national interest was involved. It should encourage and aid other levels of government and private interests in developing water resources. Projects would be approved only when economically desirable, etc. The report also called for a Water Resources Board as described by the task force, but it stopped short of approving the review board recommendation, asking instead for a strengthening of the Bureau of the Budget's capacity to review projects. On the question of federal electric power development and generation, perhaps the most politically sensitive topic in this realm, the commission report recommended reduction in the federal role in power generation and its limitation to hydroelectric generation. The report also rejected the use of electric power policy and pricing for social policy or regional development ends. The distribution and pricing of power should be done through non-federal means if at all possible and no matter what agency distributed and priced policy, it ought to be on a "sound" economic basis with no other policy purposes.

Similarly, the commission's medical services report adopted the major recommendations of the task force on medical services, including the call for a cut-back in medical services for non-service related illness, the end of federal health care for seamen, and the substitution of health insurance in place of government health service for military dependents in the United States. Also, the commission adopted the profession-regarding stance of the medical task force in recommending a Federal Advisory Council on Health and the establishment of a National Library of Medicine.

This pattern of commission adoption of task force recommendations continued across the board. The legal services task force report was embodied almost whole into the commission report, including its narrow, profession-regarding perspective. That perspective can be seen in the recommendation for a legal career civil service and the call for a substantial increase in the middle and upper salary scale for attorneys in federal employ. Also in this category was the commission's adoption of the task force's recommendation that each department's or independent agency's legal staff be organized under an assistant secretary for legal affairs or under a general counsel. Perhaps the most important recommendation of the task force from a policy perspective was the call for a creation of an administrative court which would take over the judicial-like functions of the regulatory agencies. This recommendation, posed in terms of abstract assumptions about the necessity for maintaining the separation of governmental functions, would have a huge impact on the development and implementation of regulatory policy if implemented. Yet the task force gave no attention to this side of the problem, nor did the commission as it adopted this recommendation.

A large majority of the commission found its political view reflected in the task forces' reports. But there were dissents to the reports. Virtually all of the eighteen different reports submitted to Congress by the commission drew dissents. Many of them amounted to statements of disagreement, with only one or a few of the recommendations adopted by the commission. But the water resource report in particular drew overall dissents from commissioners Brownell, Farley, Flemming, and Holifield. The pattern of dissents across all the reports reveals both the commission's conservatism and its dominance by Chairman Hoover's viewpoint. Two of the commissioners lodged no dissents at all, Senator Ferguson and Robert Storey. The commissioner with the most dissents was Representative Holifield, who dissented with 196 of the Commission's 315 recommendations.[94] The next commissioner in frequency of dissent was Farley, with 53. The mean average number of dissents for a commissioner was 36.9. But, more important, the commissioners cluster in their dissents. Hoover, Solomon Hollister, Kennedy, and Mitchell all had twenty dissents, and they were dissents to the same twenty recommendations in the legal services report. Flemming and Brownell also dissented on these twenty recommendations, each of them dissenting to a number of other recommendations as well. Senator McClellan offered just four dissents and Representative Brown six. Senator Styles Bridges (Rep., Vt.) joined the commission in January 1955, to replace Senator Ferguson after his retirement, and he issued only four dissents.[95]

Thus the second Hoover Commission's reports were consistent with Chairman Hoover's intentions for his commission.[96] Nothing had swayed him from the course upon which he set the commission—no

[94] Representative Holifield, the commission's most vigorous dissenter, even entered a strong dissent in the commission's *Final Report to Congress*. Therein he questioned the utility of a commission with the legislative mandate given to the second Hoover Commission. Commission on the Organization of the Executive Branch, *Final Report to the Congress* (Washington: Government Printing Office, 1955), pp. 26-31.

[95] Data on dissents compiled in a staff document, "Dissent from Commission Reports," n.d., 2nd Hoover Commission, Commission Reports, General, Hoover Library.

[96] For an excellent overall discussion of the second commission's reports, see James W. Fesler, "Administration Literature and the Second Hoover Commission Reports," *American Political Science Review* 61 (March 1967), pp. 135-157.

significant opposition on the commission itself and no pressure from the White House. In early January 1953 President-elect Eisenhower and his advisers expected the policy orientation of what would become the second Hoover Commission to give them the time to address the organizational reforms that were their highest priority. As the commission's reports were issued, it remained to be seen what price the administration would pay for the choice made in early 1953 to allow it freedom to roam where it chose in the fields of public policy.

Chapter Seven

REORGANIZATION AT THE CROSSROADS II: EISENHOWER, PACGO, AND THE SECOND HOOVER COMMISSION

Having agreed to reorganize the United States again, I am in need of help and advice.[1]
Herbert Hoover

Herbert Hoover invested his ego in the second commission, and after its reports were issued he invested his reputation on the degree to which they were implemented. Hoover attempted a political crusade in support of those reports and in doing so he threatened Presidential primacy over administrative reform.

THE POLITICS OF THE HOOVER REPORTS

The water resources report best exhibits Herbert Hoover's political and personal investment. Chairman Hoover moderated the water resources report in what he understood to be an agreement with Sherman Adams. Hoover thought that, in return for dropping opposition to the upper Colorado project and making no recommendation to close the Tennessee Valley Authority, the President was supposed to support the water resources report.[2] Hoover took the votes of commissioners Flemming and Brownell on the report as his test of the administration's support.

Arthur Flemming had passed early drafts of the water resources report to the Bureau of the Budget and to the cabinet committee on water resources.[3] The response of both the bureau and the committee

[1] Letter, Hoover to Dr. Fordyce St. John, September 12, 1953, Task Force on Medical Services, Misc. Corresp.—McCormick, 2nd Hoover Commission, Hoover Library.

[2] Hoover described this arrangement to some of the commission's staff and to Admiral Moreell. Jarold Kieffer, interviewed by author, October 31, 1979; Admiral Ben Moreell, Oral History Interview, Hoover Library, pp. 25-28.

[3] Having refused Hoover's request that he serve on the drafting committee, Arthur Flemming agreed to let his assistant Kieffer serve on it. But he insisted that Kieffer's service could in no way bind Flemming's support to the committee's product. He obtained the draft reports through Kieffer. Jarold Kieffer, interviewed by author.

was negative. When the finished report came up for vote in the commission, Flemming and Brownell both voted against it.[4] They also jointly dissented from the report, citing ten of its fifteen separate recommendations as highly objectionable.

Chairman Hoover had not been magnanimous about dissents in the first commission, and he was less welcoming of them this time. But his reaction to the dissents on the water resources report was particularly extreme. The dissents were printed in a volume separate from the report itself, the only instance where a report and dissents were separated. In a bitter fight over this matter with Commissioner Holifield, the commission's editorial director, Neil MacNeil, explained that the combination of the report and the dissents would create a volume too large to print.[5] Such a volume would have been 218 pages in length. While the longest volume for a commission report was "Business Organization of the Defense Department" at 148 pages, several published volumes of task force reports were much longer. To some it seemed that Hoover was attempting to hide the dissents. He also made clear his displeasure in a prefatory statement to the dissents:

> The members of this Commission are of course free to record their separate views which depart from the recommendations of the Commission.
>
> However, in respect to the dissents recorded here, some of them ignore the fundamental purposes for which the Commission was created and the directive which the Commission received from the Congress. Some others indicate a misunderstanding of the recommendations or their implications.[6]

Following Flemming's and Brownell's dissents on the water resources report, Hoover complained to the President of their disloyalty.[7]

---

[4] While Flemming's only strong dissent was to the water resources report, he was opposed in general to much that the commission did, but instead of fighting Hoover, Flemming reduced his participation in the commission. Arthur Flemming, interviewed by author, April 24, 1981.

[5] Jarold Kieffer, interviewed by author, Oct. 31, 1979; Neil MacNeil, Oral History Interview, Hoover Library, 1970; "Statement by Neil MacNeil," 2nd Hoover Commission, General Files, Correspondence-MacNeil, Hoover Library.

[6] Commission on the Organization of the Executive Branch, *Water Resources and Power*, Vol. 2 (Washington: Government Printing Office, 1955), p. 1.

[7] Hoover insisted that he brought the water resources report into alignment with the administration's policy. Thus, Hoover argued, Flemming's and Brownell's dissents entailed a betrayal of the administration as well as a betrayal of the commission. To support his case, Hoover had an elaborate memorandum prepared for Sherman Adams which purported to show the overlap between the commission's water resources report

Then he bundled up all the reports and brought them to Sherman Adams, telling him that the first Republican president in twenty years ought to do as much in implementing recommendations for improving government as did Harry Truman. Hoover threatened that should the administration not satisfy him that it was dealing with his reports in good faith, he would take his case directly to the Republican Party and the people.[8]

The Campaign for the Hoover Reports

Herbert Hoover did not place the fate of his reports solely in Eisenhower's hands. At the outset of the second commission he had reorganized the Citizens Committee for the Hoover Reports. Clarence Francis, president of the General Foods Corporation, became its chairman, and many of those associated with the second commission who shared Hoover's views were placed on the committee's board of directors, including James Farley, John Hollister, Solomon Hollister, Neil McNeil, Sidney Mitchell, Admiral Ben Moreell, and Robert Storey. While the Citizens Committee would do grass-roots propagandizing, more than its predecessor it aimed to lobby the administration on behalf of the second commission. In all of its activities the Citizens Committee was Hoover's weapon, and he told Clarence Francis that this was "the last big fight that he was going to get into."[9] Another of his weapons was the Committee of Hoover Commission Task Force Members. The Citizens Committee was meant to both lobby and propagandize; the Committee of Task Force Members was meant solely for lobbying at the highest levels of government.

The task force committee was formed in summer 1956. It was chaired by Charles Hook, chairman of Armco Steel, and its executive committee included the current or retired presidents or chief executive officers of the Delaware, Lackawanna, and Western R.R.; Kroger Co.; Winthrop Laboratories; Sears, Roebuck & Co., Armstrong Cork; and Johns & Laughlin Steel, as well as the former president of Princeton

---

and the recommendations of the administration's cabinet committee on water policy. In fact, there is sharp disagreement between these two bodies on seven of the commission's fifteen recommendations; on four other recommendations the cabinet committee could be read as lukewarm. "Comparison of Commission's Report on Water Resources and Power with the Report of the Presidential Advisory Committee on Water Policy," 2nd Hoover Commission, General File, Correspondence-Moreell, Hoover Library.

[8] Jarold Kieffer, interviewed by author; Letter, Hoover to Adams, July 6, 1955, OF, 103-A-1, 1955 (3), White House Central File, Eisenhower Library.

[9] These words are Francis', from his diary entry of September 8, 1955, Hoover— 1946-1955, Papers of Clarence Francis, Eisenhower Library.

University; partners in Arthur Young & Co.; Price, Waterhouse & Co.; and a vice-president of Hilton Hotels; and Ford Motor's director of civic affairs. The committee was an excellent instrument for quiet persuasion in high places. The minutes of its executive committee between 1956 and 1960 show that lobbying was the committee's prime activity. The committee's practice was to direct its appeals at the White House and departmental secretaries. Many of the task force members knew their way around the cabinet and sub-cabinet levels of the Eisenhower administration as a result of the investigations conducted by the task forces between 1953 and 1955. Virtually every meeting of the executive committee involved a report by a member of discussions with administrative officials on implementing recommendations.[10]

Increasingly, Hoover saw the Eisenhower administration as a road block to the Hoover reports. Very gingerly, he encouraged public criticism of the administration. The press was one means for spreading this criticism, and the campaign began on May 1, 1956 with a strong *New York Times* editorial which charged:

> The Hoover Commission has been publishing its findings at almost the rate of one a week. . . . Yet almost nothing has been done by way of action on them. The record is particularly depressing when compared with the record of action on recommendations of the first Hoover Commission. . . .[11]

A pack of papers followed on the *Times*'s heels; the *Christian Science Monitor* (May 6), the *Chicago Tribune* (May 11), and the *Philadelphia Inquirer* (May 31). Papers in Buffalo, Columbus, Milwaukee, and elsewhere picked up the theme as well. There is no direct evidence that Hoover and his aides planted the *New York Times* editorial. This snowballing of an editorial position through the American press can be explained as a piece of editorial leadership by a major paper. But Neil MacNeil, the second commission's editorial director and an officer of the Citizens Committee, was a retired editor at the *New York Times*.

The White House received numerous appeals to diligently attend to the recommendations. For example, the executive director of the Massachusetts Federation of Taxpayers Associations wrote to his acquaintance at the White House, Maxwell Rabb, complaining that Eisenhower was not doing as well by the Hoover Commission as had

---

[10] Minutes, 2nd Hoover Commission, minutes of meetings of Task Force members, Hoover Library.

[11] *New York Times*, May 1, 1955.

Truman. Noting that citizens were ready to support the commission recommendations, he said: "As of today these good citizens have nothing to do. . . . Up to now, they have been passive. There are signs that open criticism can break loose at any moment."[12] In early June, Rowland Hughes, who had replaced Dodge as director of the budget, reported to the President a high level of concern about the reports among businessmen:

> I found an almost universal interest among all shades of opinion in these groups in the Hoover Commission reports and what the administration was planning to do about them. There has apparently been a very thorough job done of stirring up a really active interest among the members of the business community.[13]

Demands on the administration to implement the Hoover recommendations were strongest from the right wing of the Republican Party, the Taft wing that Eisenhower had bested at the 1952 convention and in his organization of the administration. But the political danger to him did not lie solely in the threat of an uprising on his right. Rather it lay in the commission's potential appeal to a broader range of citizens within Eisenhower's constituency on the basis of its evocation of values of efficiency and good government.

The Administration's Response

In truth, the administration did not ignore the commission's recommendations. In early spring 1955 a process was established within the Executive Office of the President for reviewing each report, initial staff work being done at the Bureau of the Budget, then the affected agency commenting, with all organizational recommendations then going to PACGO. It was planned that these steps could be accomplished within thirty days of a report's appearance.[14] But the review process was overloaded, due to the rapidity with which the commission issued reports in the spring of 1955.[15] A back-log of unaddressed commission reports presented the appearance of foot-dragging.

By early June the administration had reviewed the first five reports, civil service, medical services, lending agencies, transportation, and

[12] Letter, Norman MacDonald to Rabb, May 14, 1955, OF 103-A-1, 1955 (1), White House Central Files, Eisenhower Library.

[13] Memorandum, Hughes to President, June 9, 1955, BOB, 52.1, F2-2, RG 51, National Archives.

[14] Memorandum to BOB staff, March 15, 1955, BOB, 55.1, F2-72, *ibid.*

[15] Memorandum, Brundage to Adams, April 1, 1955, OF 103-A-1, 1955 (1), White House Central Files, Eisenhower Library.

paper-work management. These contained twenty-six recommendations that could be implemented through reorganization plan, legislation, or executive order.[16] Of the recommendations PACGO approved, only a handful were of major status. In the civil service report it approved a Senior Civil Service and the elimination of patronage in appointment of United States marshals and field officials of the Bureau of the Customs. In the medical services report, it approved the recommendation for a National Library of Medicine. Part of PACGO's mission in analyzing commission recommendations was to produce results with which the administration could demonstrate its interest in the Hoover Commission's work. As the committee worked out its recommendations concerning the first five reports, Sherman Adams urged it to be aware of "the public relations aspects" to its work.[17] So far there were no results to show Hoover and his public, and PACGO had to produce enough to make the administration's effort credible. The effort of subduing Hoover began earnestly on June 8th, when President Eisenhower met with him and Clarence Francis of the Citizens Committee. Sherman Adams, Roland Hughes, Nelson Rockefeller, and Arthur Flemming were also present.

Herbert Hoover quickly got to the nub of the matter as he saw it; there was not enough movement on the Hoover recommendations, and he wanted a larger role for his people in the process. Secretary Charles Wilson at Defense had established a committee staffed by some of the task force members to guide departmental evaluation of the recommendations and oversee their implementation. Hoover wanted to see similar operations established by the other departments. Eisenhower refused, but he managed to win at least temporary favor from Hoover and Francis by agreeing to issue regular progress reports on the administration's work with the reports.[18]

To assess Hoover recommendations that dealt primarily with policy, Eisenhower created the Special Policy Committee, composed of Arthur Flemming, Herbert Brownell, Secretary of Commerce Sinclair Weeks, Deputy Secretary of Defense Rueben Robertson, Joseph Dodge, and Budget Director Rowland Hughes, who served as chairman.[19] That committee and PACGO were to divide their responsibilities between

[16] Memorandum, Kimball to Rockefeller, May 31, 1955, BOB, 55.3, F2-72, RG 51, National Archives.

[17] Memorandum, Kimball to Rockefeller, May 24, 1955, box 24, file 35 (2), PACGO, Eisenhower Library.

[18] Letter, Eisenhower to Hoover, June 17, 1957, 2nd Hoover Commission, Citizens Committee Correspondence, Francis, Hoover Library.

[19] Memorandum to cabinet, November 2, 1955, Cabinet Series, Papers of DDE as President, Eisenhower Library.

policy and organization.[20] When that line could not be neatly drawn, recommendations would remain under PACGO's jurisdiction while being also considered by the Special Committee.[21]

A final part of the administration's apparatus for dealing with the Hoover reports was the appointment of a person whose chief responsibility would be to oversee their evaluation and possible adoption. President Eisenhower had promised to create this post in the June 1955 meeting with Hoover. To fill it the administration needed someone prominent enough to signal that the President was serious about the reports. The job was offered first to John McCone, a prominent New York attorney, who refused it.[22] After more searching, it was given to Meyer Kestnbaum of Chicago, president of Hart, Schaffner, and Marx. Kestnbaum's single best qualification was that he had just pulled the Commission on Intergovernmental Relations out of the shambles it had been left in by its first chairman, Clarence Manion, dean of the Notre Dame Law School. Kestnbaum was assigned Jarold Kieffer as his aide. Kieffer had worked with all of the principals in this matter and could guide Kestnbaum over the territory.

With Kestnbaum's appointment as a presidential assistant, a new procedural order was imposed upon the review of Hoover Commission recommendations. The Budget Bureau would prepare a summary of agency views on the recommendations for Kestnbaum, who would in turn consult with PACGO, the Special Policy Committee, and the relevant agencies in formulating a recommendation for the President. Once the President adopted a recommendation for implementation, responsibility for transmitting that decision to affected agencies and for overseeing implementation rested in the Director of the Budget. Kestnbaum's responsibilities also included the preparation of progress reports on the review process and liaison with Hoover and his Citizens Committee.[23] Circumstances led to an even larger role for Kestnbaum than envisaged because just as he joined the administration President Eisenhower suffered a heart attack. The President's temporary removal from the scene left Kestnbaum solely responsible for making the

[20] Not to be overlooked is the administration's interest in looking busy regarding the Hoover reports, so Rowland Hughes described his committee to Hoover as "a unit to carry forward the consideration of the many useful recommendations in your Commission reports." Letter, Hughes to Hoover, July 14, 1955, 2nd Hoover Commission, General File, Correspondence-MacNeil, Hoover Library.

[21] Memorandum, Kimball to Rockefeller, July 8, 1955, box 24, file 35 (2), PACGO, Eisenhower Library.

[22] Telephone message, McCone to Adams, July 22, 1955, OF 103-A-1-A, White House Central Files, Eisenhower Library.

[23] Memorandum, Hughes and Kestnbaum to Adams, September 28, 1955, box 12, file 74, Kestnbaum Papers, Eisenhower Library.

administration appear credible in dealing with the Hoover recommendations.

PACGO quickly became the organizational context within which Kestnbaum operated. Several reasons account for this. Kestnbaum was dependent on Jarold Kieffer for staff work, and Kieffer was a primary staff person to PACGO. Second, the committee was the locus of organizational perspectives that were most intimate with the President's outlook, and in his absence its opinions could be taken as guidance to the President's preferences. Thus Kestnbaum became a regular at PACGO's meetings when it was discussing Hoover Commission matters, as did Rowland Hughes, director of the Budget. Kestnbaum in turn gave up the original description of his job as the main channel to the President on dealing with Hoover Commission recommendations and instead chose to operate consensually with the committee and the budget director.[24]

Beyond the administration's review of the recommendations, Kestnbaum stressed Congress' role in implementing reforms. Therein was an astute political judgment; it might reduce the heat the administration was taking to have the Hoover Commission's partisans identify the Democratic-controlled Congress (the 1954 election creating a Democratic majority in both houses) as guilty of ignoring the Hoover reports. By channelling his energies into congressional liaison and encouraging the Citizens Committee to target Congress, Kestnbaum sought to divert to Congress at least some of the political burdens carried by the President.

The burden that the second commission posed for Congress was potentially equal to its burden on the executive, if the legislators gave serious consideration to its recommendations. By an estimate of the Citizens Committee for the Hoover Report, 142½ of the commission's 314 recommendations required legislative action.[25] By the beginning of the second session of the 84th Congress, in January 1956, 241 bills aimed at enacting recommendations had been introduced, 109 in the Senate and 132 in the House.[26] Fourteen of these were passed into law; without exception, these treated non-controversial matters, such as providing a detailed classification scheme for postal employees,

[24] Memorandum, Keiffer to Flemming, November 1, 1955, *ibid*.

[25] Citizens Committee for the Hoover Report, "Reorganization Record," January 11, 1956, Box 14, Hoover Commission, Gerald Morgan Files, Eisenhower Library.

[26] U.S. Congress, Senate, Committee on Government Operations, *Action by the Congress and the Executive Branch of the Government on the Second Hoover Commission, 1955-57*, 85th Cong., 2nd Sess., 1958, Dept. 1289; Citizens Committee for the Hoover Report, "Reorganization Record," January 11, 1956, box 14, Hoover Commission, Gerald Morgan Files, Eisenhower Library.

authorizing the Surgeon-General to award grants for research on mental illness, and separating the Home Loan Bank System from the Housing and Home Finance Agency. Two years later, at the end of the first session of the 85th Congress in December 1957, the legislative picture had not appreciably changed. During the first session of the 85th Congress 297 Hoover Commission related bills were introduced. Yet only nine of these bills had passed by the end of the session.[27] As was the case in the earlier Congress, those recommendations acted into law were non-controversial; Congress was clearly unwilling to shoulder the burdens offered by the commission's recommendations.

The primary reason for congressional disinterest in the recommendations was their political naiveté. The recommendations threatened protected congressional policy areas such as veterans' benefits, water resources, river and harbors programs, and federal credit insurance policies for small business, agriculture, and housing. There was no incentive for Congress to undo such programs. Now that the Congress was controlled by the Democrats, the partisans of the Hoover Commission enjoyed reduced congressional influence. But Congress' refusal to move the major elements of the Hoover reports created even more dissatisfaction with the administration's role among Hoover partisans. Congress' failure to see the light could be explained away by Democratic control. However, the administration was Republican, and it ought to fight against waste.

The tense dance between the partisans of the Hoover Commission and the administration did not end in a neat climax; over time it simply ran down to a stop. The mechanism for lobbying the administration remained in existence throughout the 1950's, but the climate of general public support for the Hoover Commission faded. Also, with President Eisenhower's victory in the 1956 election, the Hoover partisans lost whatever political leverage they had. The Republican right wing was no longer the President's problem; he had to continue and improve working relations with the Democratic majority in Congress, and it had no concern for the Hoover Commission's recommendations.

The Adoption of Hoover Commission Recommendations

Given the second Hoover Commission's political orientations, it is quite remarkable that a fairly large number of its recommendations were implemented. The public relations blather issuing from both the

[27] U.S. Congress, Senate, Committee on Government Operations, *Action by the Congress*, pp. 2 and 77.

administration and the Citizens Committee about adoption used raw box-score percentage rates of adoption. So, for example, in February 1958, the administration announced that 77.1 percent of the commission's recommendations had been accepted by the administration and that 76 percent of those were either implemented or in the process of implementation.[28] Given the great differences among the recommendations, it is uninformative to report "success" in such terms. However, such score-keeping served the interests of both the administration and the Citizens Committee because it gave a patina of success to the whole enterprise.

More finely grained data on the adoption of the second commission's recommendations suggest that there were, in effect, two different sets of recommendations. In terms of its attention to the actual number of recommendations along with care in the determination of "adoption," the best source is a report done in early 1958 for the Senate Committee on Government Operations.[29] Herein 519 recommendations are attributed to the commission rather than the 362 it claimed for itself.[30] The Senate report concluded that 61 percent of the recommendations had been adopted, with 88 percent of those either implemented or in the process of same. More interesting, the Senate report looked at the fate of each of the 519 recommendations, and the great differences that emerge among the commission's different reports suggest virtually two different sets of reports.

Table 1 shows the proportion of each report's recommendations which were adopted.[31] Note the characteristics shared by those reports that vary most from the reports' mean rate of implementation—53 percent. Those reports on the positive side of the mean are among the most technical of the second Hoover Commission's reports. The two reports at the negative extreme from the mean are two of the commission's most policy-oriented reports, water resources and legal service.

The substantial rate of implementation for the technical reports did not change Hoover's view of the administration's failure. For him the commission's goal was to address and change the mistaken policies of the last several decades, and not one of the recommendations aimed at this task had been accepted and implemented. This failure was not

[28] Memorandum, Kestnbaum to President and attached press release, February 10, 1958, Box 15, file 95, Kestnbaum Papers, Eisenhower Library.

[29] U.S. Congress, Senate, Committee on Government Operations, *Action by the Congress.*

[30] Commission on the Organization of the Executive Branch, *Final Report to the Congress* (Washington: Government Printing Office, 1955), p. 14.

[31] *Ibid.*, p. 5.

Table 1
Adoptions of the Recommendations of the
Second Hoover Commission

Report Title	Number of Recommendations	Percent Accepted	Percent Implemented
Personnel and Civil Service	41	58	56
Paperwork I	23	91	87
Medical Services	36	67	42
Lending Agencies	54	48	44
Transportation	44	61	47.5
Legal Services	54	28	13
Surplus Property	24	75	54
Food and Clothing	26	85	85
Business Enterprise	36	55	44
Depot Utilization	28	89	89
Research and Develop.	20	85	85
Overseas Economic Operations	28	61	61
Real Property	24	63	50
Budget and Accounting	28	93	84
Bus. Org. of Dept. of Defense	22	54	45
Intelligence Activities	2	50	50
Water Resources	26	19	15
Paperwork II	1	100	100

a fault of the times or circumstances; for Hoover and his minions, this was President Eisenhower's fault. Neil MacNeil recalls a 1961 conversation with Hoover in which "the Chief" denigrated Eisenhower as weak and compared him to Coolidge.[32] In the oral-history recollections of those close to Hoover during the period of the second commission, the theme of Eisenhower's weakness appears repeatedly.[33] It is as if they could see no reason why a Republican president would not throw himself whole hog into implementing the most extreme of the Hoover Commission's recommendations; since there could be no good reason, he must have been weak. What the Hooverites overlooked was the most obvious explanation for Eisenhower's

[32] Neil MacNeil, Oral History Interview, Library, p. 27.

[33] This view is a leitmotif of the oral history interviews with Hoover's associates. See the interviews with Theodore G. Klumpp, M.D., Paul Grady, Solomon Hollister, Clarence Francis, and Neil MacNeil. All of these are in the collection of the Hoover Library.

coolness toward them and their reorganization report; rather than a show of weakness, it was an exercise of political skill by a president who understood where he must obtain support to maintain influence.

PACGO AFTER THE HOOVER COMMISSION

Regarding the Hoover Commission, PACGO's role was reactive.[34] For a time Hoover Commission reports temporarily overwhelmed the administration's capacity for independent planning. But after 1956, PACGO reasserted a reorganization agenda that centered on problems of top-level management, and it addressed them in a style which was particularly sensitive to the character of the Eisenhower presidency.

Four lines of inquiry and discussion occupied PACGO between 1957 and 1960. They are: one, the restructuring of the Executive Office to reduce presidential burdens while increasing managerial capacity; two, the reform of foreign affairs organization; three, further development of central managerial mechanisms in the Department of Defense; and, four, the creation of new domestic departments.

Reforming the Executive Office

PACGO's view of the chief executive's task was best summed up by Milton Eisenhower: "I am absolutely convinced that the task . . . is an impossible one, that the responsibilities cannot be redeemed as the Constitution and the laws require, and this constantly becomes more acute as our country grows . . . and the responsibilities of the President increase."[35] Thus (to recall a phrase heard before in the history of executive reorganization), the president needs help. But PACGO's outlook was also affected by the fact that its President in particular needed help. During his last five years in office, President Eisenhower suffered a heart attack, a temporarily disabling stroke, and underwent major gastro-intestinal surgery.

The President's health problems sharpened an existing interest of PACGO in reducing presidential burdens. The strongest evidence for the association between Eisenhower's health and PACGO's focus on the presidential workload is their chronological juxtaposition. The President was disabled by a heart attack in September 1955, and the

[34] The Hoover Commission was PACGO's "preoccupation" in 1955 and 1956. Arthur Flemming, interviewed by author.

[35] Milton Eisenhower, Oral History Interview, Eisenhower Administration Project, Columbia University Oral History Collection, Microfilm Corporation of America, 1976, p. 18.

first time the issue of reducing burdens on the President became an explicit topic of a PACGO meeting was November 1, 1955.[36] But certainly Eisenhower's administrative style as well as his health encouraged his reorganization planners to address workload issues.

PACGO's thinking on presidential workload began with the crudest possible formulation—the creation of a new position to share burdens with the President—and developed over a three-year period into a sophisticated plan for institutionalizing in the Executive Office management and personnel controls parallel to the budget process. During the end of 1955 and early 1956, PACGO mounted a small-scale study or "audit" of the President's desk, monitoring what went in and out of his office.[37] This study showed that Eisenhower was being swamped with avoidable matters. Between January and March 1956, the committee fashioned the first proposal for reducing that burden.[38] The committee concluded that there were a number of ceremonial functions that could be delegated to the elected vice-president and that an appointive administrative vice-presidency ought to be created by statute to exercise administrative authority delegated to him by the president.[39]

The committee's plan for an administrative vice-president was presented to Eisenhower during the last week of March 1956; Milton Eisenhower had a conversation with the President about the workload problem and the committee's specific suggestions. The President expressed a positive view of the proposal in general, adding the tentative view that he thought it would be useful to create two administrative vice presidents.[40] This was taken as a signal for more intensive planning on this problem.

Even though the notion of statutory, appointive vice-president appealed to the President, this idea evidently sank of its own political weight and dropped off PACGO's agenda. The plan had the great political liability of being open to the interpretation that *this* President needs help, not in the Brownlowian sense of better tools, but because he could not handle his job due to health, age, or style. That the idea

[36] Milton Eisenhower's view was described in Memorandum, Kimball to Rockefeller, May 24, 1955, Box 24, file 35 (2), PACGO, Eisenhower Library.

[37] Jarold Kieffer, interviewed by author.

[38] "Delegation of Unnecessary Presidential Workload," appears as an agenda item for PACGO meetings regularly during this period, beginning, it appears, on January 17. Sherman Adams was a participant in these discussions within the PACGO meetings. Agenda for January 12 and January 17, 1956, OF 103-A-2, White House Central Files, Eisenhower Library.

[39] Memorandum for President, n.d., Box 11, file 64, PACGO, Eisenhower Library.

[40] Correspondence, GF, 6-S-Hoover and GF, 3-A-2, White House Central Files, Eisenhower Library.

was prone to cause embarrassment is demonstrated in a clumsy episode in early 1956 which also had the consequence of further alienating Herbert Hoover from the administration. Aware of the discussion within the President's staff about an administrative vice-president, Herbert Hoover suggested that mechanism as a solution to the president's burden in a public statement on December 11, 1955, and again in hearings of the Senate's Government Operations Committee on January 16th.[41] However, instead of supporting Hoover's recommendation, presumably speaking for the President, Sherman Adams wrote the Senate committee a public letter which announced that the administration saw no need for the reform described by Hoover. Later in January, to lessen Hoover's resulting rage, Adams wrote another public letter addressed to the Senate committee which admitted that the President thought that Hoover's proposal might "have advantages."[42]

Leaving the administrative vice-president idea behind, PACGO sent a memo to the President suggesting a new design for the Executive Office, centered on a director of administration. The committee conceived of such an individual's taking responsibility for: "budget, personnel management, legislative reference and clearance, and responsibility for policy development and coordination in the fields of organization and management, property management, and reporting and statistical management."[43] The director of administration would stand between the president and four different operations within the Executive Office, each conducted through a separate agency, only one of which was presently in existence, the budget bureau. Budget would be joined by agencies for personnel management, planning, and inspections, each headed by directors who would report to the director of administration. This overall organization would be called the office of administration.

PACGO and President Eisenhower's staff, Sherman Adams, Budget Director Percival Brundage, and the chairman of the Civil Service Commission, Phillip Young, easily agreed to the creation of a bureau of personnel management. It would take over the operating functions of the Civil Service Commission, and its head would serve as the president's adviser on personnel policy. This concept was similar to those offered by the Brownlow Committee and the second Hoover Commission.[44] No such unanimity, however, existed on the overall plan

[41] U.S. Congress, Senate, Committee on Government Operations, *Proposal to Create an Administrative Vice President—Report*, 84th Cong., 2nd Sess., May 9 1956.

[42] *New York Times*, December 12, 1955; January 15, 17, 29, 1956.

[43] Memorandum, PACGO to President, January 10, 1957, Rockefeller 56-57 (2), Administrative Series, Papers of DDE as President, Eisenhower Library.

[44] This planned reform of the Civil Service Commission did reach partial implemen-

for an office of administration. The plan's principal antagonist was Budget Director Brundage. At a January 1957 meeting of Eisenhower and his staff with PACGO to discuss reorganization of the Executive Office, Brundage argued against the proposal on the weak grounds of the unadvisability of mixing staff (budget) and operating (personnel) functions. In fact, like most upper-level administrative operations, staff and line aspects are intermixed within both budget and personnel functions, and the President pointed that out to Brundage. But the President feared a change in budget's status for a more solid reason. He saw that the proposed reform could create problems in staffing top levels of the Bureau of the Budget because the reorganization would "tend to downgrade the top men of the Budget . . . who can be obtained now largely only because they have the right to come in to the President."[45]

Instead of organization changes, the President remained attached to the idea of multiple vice-presidents, one for domestic affairs and one for international affairs, as well as one for administrative matters. Indicating a variant of his constant theme that high-level decision makers need time to think, the President observed that the "big problems" of his office bothered him not in the least; it was the little problems that were overwhelming by their bulk and annoyance quotient. The difference between the President's views and PACGO's developing plans is important to clarify because it sheds light on the advising relationship that existed between the committee and its patron. President Eisenhower was thinking of a designated individual to reduce the trivial burdens of his office. The committee sought a means for doing that while always leaving responsibility and visible administrative centrality in the presidency. And, of course, there were other key actors in this advising relationship between PACGO and the President. The budget director particularly had a huge stake in the outcome of this planning process. If Executive Office change did not take the form of expanded capacities placed *within* his agency, BOB would suffer a great fall. To the contrary, Sherman Adams encouraged PACGO to push ahead with plans that would involve new organization subsuming the budget bureau.[46]

Through early 1957 PACGO tried to graft the vice-president idea

---

tation in the establishment of an Office of Personnel Advisor to the President by Executive Order during 1957.

[45] Memorandum on Conference with the President, January 10, 1957 (prepared on January 12), Jan. 57, Goodpaster, DDE Diary Series, Papers of DDE as President, Eisenhower Library.

[46] Minutes of Meeting, February 20, 1957, Box 21, File 2, PACGO, Eisenhower Library.

onto the organizational arrangement it had planned under a director of administration as a way of joining its and the President's views. During this period PACGO strengthened its staff by adding Don K. Price of Harvard's School of Public Administration as a part-time consultant. But by May 1957 the committee's members agreed that there was no possibility that an administrative vice-president could win congressional approval.[47] Consequently, the committee fixed upon a proposal that might be politically more acceptable, would not require legislation, and would thus not have the disability of a presidential subordinate who was made too inflexible (or too independent) by statutory authority. The new proposal was that the President create an assistant for business management. This position would not have direct authority over other units in the Executive Office and would have only a very small staff; however, by delegation, this assistant could handle routine administrative activities. This small change should be accompanied, PACGO recommended, with a reorganization of the Bureau of the Budget and the creation of two other, parallel bureaus in the Executive Office, a Bureau of Inspections and a Bureau of Personnel Management. The recommended change in the Bureau of the Budget would entail upgrading of that agency's management and organizational responsibilities and renaming it the Bureau of Budget and Management.[48]

During July, a draft memorandum on this idea was distributed among the White House senior staff, and Budget Director Brundage responded to it negatively, arguing that the draft memo did not provide "a suitable basis for a discussion with the President."[49] His chief criticism against the new proposal was that it would only clutter the Executive Office with more agencies that would further confuse the process of presidential management. Brundage's argument was that the Bureau of the Budget was responsible for all managerial concerns and that reforms should not undercut that able and professional operation.[50]

Failing to pacify Brundage, the committee pushed ahead to try to sell its program to the President, setting up a meeting with Eisenhower on October 10 from which Brundage was excluded.[51] Eisenhower

[47] Letter, Kimball to Rockefeller, May 3, 1957, Box 2, File 17 (1), *ibid.*

[48] Minutes of Meeting, May 13-14, 1957, Box 3, File 21 (2), *ibid.*

[49] Memorandum, Brundage to Flemming, July 25, 1957, BOB, Office of the Director, General Records, 1952-60, RG 51, National Archives.

[50] *Ibid.*, and Memorandum, September 10, 1957, Box 11, File 69, PACGO, Eisenhower Library.

[51] Letter, Kimball to Rockefeller, September 18, 1957, Box 2, file 17 (1), *ibid.*; Minutes of Meeting with the President, October 10, 1957, Box 3, file 21, *ibid.*

encouraged further development of the committee's proposal, approving it in principle. But he attempted to diminish the area of disagreement between the committee and his budget director by stipulating that the new assistant for administration's responsibilities would bear only upon the management and not the budget activities of the bureau.[52] Just as it appeared that the committee may have found an acceptable solution to Eisenhower's sense of administrative burden, his health again broke.

Eisenhower's cerebral stroke in November was read by PACGO as a signal that it would be a mistake to continue to pursue the partial solution represented by an administrative assistant. Instead, in consultation with Sherman Adams, the committee decided that the time would be now ripe to introduce a full-scale reorganization of the Executive Office with the creation of a cabinet-level officer (a Secretary of Administration) heading an Office of Administration and Management. Eisenhower himself approved this plan, directing the budget bureau to develop the necessary draft legislation and reorganization plans to effect the PACGO proposal.[53] But the Bureau of the Budget was still not inclined to give up its fight to retain primacy in the Executive Office. At a staff level, William Finan communicated to Jarold Kieffer the bureau's objections to PACGO's new plan, criticizing a number of its features and finally arguing for a strengthening of the organization and management activities within the Bureau of the Budget. But less then two weeks after Finan's objection, Budget Director Brundage gave Sherman Adams his requested work-up of the necessary reorganization plans and executive orders that PACGO's reform would entail.[54]

If it appeared in January 1958 that the Bureau of the Budget's opposition to PACGO's Executive Office reform was dead, then the bureau's resurgence several months later was phoenix-like. The force imparting new life to the struggle was Maurice Stans, who took over as budget director in mid-March.[55] Stans quickly took on Sherman Adams over the issue of reorganizing the Executive Office, and he did

[52] Minutes of Meeting with President, October 10, 1957, *ibid.*

[53] Minutes of Meeting, December 5, 1957, *ibid.*; Memorandum, Rockefeller to Adams, January 3, 1958, Box 11, File 69, *ibid.*

[54] Memorandum, Brundage to Adams, January 8, 1958, Box 11, File 70, *ibid.*

[55] Robert E. Merriam described the two budget directors who followed Joseph Dodge as "unhappy choices . . . because they didn't have enough vision. . . ." On the other hand, Merriam observed that while Maurice Stans was an accountant too, "he had a broader perspective. . . ." Robert E. Merriam, Oral History Interview, Eisenhower Administration Project, Columbia University Oral History Collection, Microfilm Corporation of America, 1976, pp. 32-33.

so with a precise and politically clear set of arguments that identified matters that had not been thought through by PACGO or the White House staff.

In a meeting at the White House in late April with Adams, Stans pointed out that the PACGO plan suffered from two flaws.[56] The first was a flaw in its assumptions about the nature of the presidency. Its plan would freeze executive office machinery, imposing a rigid system upon whomever occupied the office. Stans argued that instead of lifting burdens from the president, the plan added a layer of complexity to the organizational context of the presidency. The plan's second grave flaw was political, according to Stans. Without quite saying it, Stans pointed to a problem of PACGO's view of the presidency. He charged that the plan amounted to an indictment of Eisenhower's weakness. Perhaps PACGO was too close to the President to fully sense the point at which its work aimed at long-term, permanent reforms as against personal, short-term characteristics of the incumbent.

The strength of Stans's objection to the PACGO plan, accompanied by the evident unwillingness of the administration to override the new budget director, led to another suspension of the committee's proposal. Following this, Stans, the committee, and Sherman Adams developed another alternative which was a hybrid of the early 1957 PACGO plan, calling for a Director of Administration and an Office of Administration.[57] However, an added element was that the new plan was an expansion of the Bureau of the Budget, retitled the Office of Executive Management, with the director to be called the Director of Executive Managment. Beneath the director would be a deputy director and six assistant directors, responsible for separate divisions like budgeting, organization and management, and personnel.

What Maurice Stans successfully offered as an alternative to PACGO's earlier planning was, in the short run, a victory for the Bureau of the Budget in a planning context which repeatedly threatened its demotion. In the longer run, what Stans successfully managed to sell to PACGO and Sherman Adams was the organizational outline of what, twelve years later, would constitute the major reorganization of the Bureau of the Budget. In the face of criticism, Stans taught the bureau the lesson that it could respond bravely by claiming that its

[56] Handwritten Minutes of Meeting, April 21, 1958, Office of the Staff Secretary, Rockefeller (5), White House Office, Eisenhower Library.

[57] Meyer Kestnbaum figured in this discussion and may have been the first to suggest it to Adams. Memorandum for the Record, April 23, 1958, *ibid.*; Memorandum for the Record, May 12, 1958, Box 3, File 22, PACGO, Eisenhower Library.

failure was a justification for increasing the bureau's responsibilities and its resources.

While PACGO and Sherman Adams agreed to Stans's variation of the committee's plan, the President stepped back from a decision. In a mid-June 1958 discussion with Sherman Adams, in which Adams was trying to set a schedule for sending the Office of Executive Management proposal to the Congress, Eisenhower decided that the administration's legislative agenda was already too heavy. Instead, he told Adams, they would send the proposal up early in the next session of Congress.[58] Eisenhower's postponement of the reorganization of the Executive Office rendered it unlikely that such a reform would be instituted during his administration. The postponement pushed the issue into January, 1959, and, with less than two years left for the administration's tenure in office, large-scale organizational changes seemed unlikely.

By January 1959, even though the cabinet had discussed the Office of Executive Management and assented to it after brief discussion, PACGO developed some hesitancy on the plan.[59] A change of mood developed on the committee, attributable to changes in membership. After his election as Governor of New York, Nelson Rockefeller resigned from the committee, and Arthur Flemming was designated by Eisenhower as chairman. Then to fill the empty seat on the committee, Don K. Price was made a member. Afterward the committee became skeptical of the proposal. On January 28, shortly after the cabinet meeting which approved the plan, Arthur Kimball wrote a negative memo to the members of PACGO. Kimball asked the committee to consider whether the current proposal was a worthy product of the years the committee had spent on the general problem of reorganizing the Executive Office. Kimball wrote:

> Frankly, I fear that we are being out-maneuvered by the Budget staff. They have been unsuccessful in their many attempts to block this project. However, because of procedural problems, they seem to be about to succeed in watering it down to where it will amount to little more than renaming the Budget Bureau.[60]

[58] Memorandum, Kimball to PACGO members, June 18, 1958, Staff Secretary's Office, Rockefeller (5), White House Office, Eisenhower Library.

[59] Minutes of Cabinet Meeting, January 23, 1959, Cabinet Series, Papers of DDE as President, Eisenhower Library; Record of Cabinet Action (meeting of January 23), February 2, 1959, *ibid.*

[60] Memorandum, Kimball to Milton Eisenhower, January 28, 1959, Box 12, File 71 (1), PACGO, Eisenhower Library.

Kimball's new hesitancy was not the only last-minute opposition raised to the plan. Sometime during February and March, 1959, as they saw copies of the reorganization plan drafted by the Bureau of the Budget, several members of the cabinet objected to it. Arthur Flemming and Milton Eisenhower urged that it be submitted to Congress, nonetheless, but on June 12 the President put off that action until the following year, stating that it would be one of his two big reorganization plans for 1960.[61]

PACGO, the Budget Bureau, and the President went through another round of activity during late 1959 and early 1960 in preparation for reorganizing the Executive Office. However, PACGO's time was up. Organizational innovation is not the currency of presidents in their last year in office. Also after June 1, 1959, it would have been more difficult for the President to achieve reorganization because he would have had to seek a statute to achieve the ends sought, the reorganization authority having lapsed. In the end, Eisenhower chose to leave his recommendations as a parting gesture to Congress, and he requested PACGO to draft a statement for that purpose which was sent to Congress as part of the Budget Message of January 16, 1961.

The First Secretary

The foreign affairs organizational problem that occupied the largest part of PACGO's attention between 1957 and the end of 1960 was more closely tied to the characteristics of the Eisenhower presidency than it was to continuing organizational problems in the foreign affairs establishment. In a way that was parallel to his interest in an administrative vice-president, Eisenhower decided that what the government needed was a new high official, holding status equivalent to a prime minister and responsible for coordinating the diverse strands of national policies that bear upon foreign policy. Precisely what that office would look like and what it would be in charge over seemed unclear. Eisenhower thought the government's foreign affairs activities needed better coordination; he wanted a spokesman who could meet as an equal with the heads of government (as opposed to the chiefs of state) of the world, and he also thought that he needed someone to decrease the burden upon him of a constant routine of ceremonial activities. In early spring, 1957, Eisenhower asked PACGO to devise a plan for such a position to be called a First Secretary.[62]

[61] Meeting with the President, June 12, 1959, Box 3, File 23 (2), *ibid*.
[62] The President's views on the First Secretary from Dwight D. Eisenhower, *The White*

Don Price suggested that a new role should not be statutory because a law creating a virtual prime minister would obviously diminish the president's constitutional authority. Rather, the authority of the First Secretary must depend upon presidential delegation. Price suggested an organizational strategy for creating that top foreign policy official to serve the president. He proposed that State become a super-department containing, in effect, three individual departments, the most important of which would be called the Department of International Relations. The head of that department, the Secretary of International Relations, would be a cabinet member, indicating that the Secretary of State's role was not just that of another department head, but a first among equals—a "first secretary."[63]

The committee was enthusiastic over Price's plan, and it seemed that it had quickly solved the problem put to it.[64] At one and the same time, the plan created a kind of prime minister who would be freed of major administrative duties, his department being run really as three different departments, coordinated by his deputy, and he would be able to serve in the White House as the President's foreign affairs assistant. Also, the Secretary of State would provide a continuing presence in Washington at the top of the foreign policy establishment, as the Secretary of International Relations became the negotiator and traveler for government, working at the level of foreign ministers.

At a meeting on May 30 the plan was streamlined, with the notion of three sub-departments vanishing to be replaced by a reorganized State, renamed the Department of International Relations and headed by a Secretary of State, while a Secretary of International Relations would run the department and serve as chief "traveller and negotiator."[65] The committee, accompanied by Don Price and Budget Director Brundage, met with President Eisenhower on June 18, 1957. The President accepted the organizational format of the recommendation, but he insisted upon the title he had originally used; the Secretary of State would be called First Secretary of the Government.[66] The Pres-

House Years (Garden City, N.Y.: Doubleday, 1965), pp. 634-638. Also see Milton Eisenhower, The President is Calling (New York: Doubleday, 1974), pp. 267-268. This description also relies upon Jarold Kieffer, interview with author; and on a memorandum of a conversation between the President and General Andrew Goodpaster, Diary, January 30, 1958, Whitman Diary Series, Papers of DDE as President, Eisenhower Library.

[63] Memorandum, Kimball to Rockefeller, May 3, 1957, Box 2, File 17 (1), ibid.

[64] Minutes of Meeting, May 13-14, 1957, Box 3, File 21 (2), ibid.

[65] Minutes of Meeting, May 30, 1957, ibid. The plan was polished at a meeting between the committee and budget officials on June 12, 1957. Minutes of Meeting, June 12, 1957, ibid.

[66] Minutes of Meeting with President, June 18, 1957, ibid.

ident announced that he would present this reform to the cabinet for discussion.[67] First and foremost, it would have to be discussed with Secretary of State Dulles.

In his memoirs, President Eisenhower relates that Secretary of State Dulles was opposed to the plan for a First Secretary, pushing the plan for foreign affairs reorganization onto the administration's back burner for much of the rest of 1957.[68] But by the end of the year Dulles was more willing to consider the plan. Eisenhower wrote that Dulles "came to agree to the wisdom of such a plan." This may have been an over-statement, but Dulles was willing to discuss the plan and its implications. For example, Nelson Rockefeller reported to President Eisenhower in February, 1958 that in his conversation with Dulles the secretary had been only mildly negative.[69] PACGO's discussions with Dulles continued through 1958, Eisenhower using the committee as his medium for winning him over to the plan.[70]

In light of Dulles' hesitancy, the President instructed PACGO to put aside the First Secretary aspect of the foreign affairs reorganization and to push ahead with the other aspects, expanding the State Department and adding offices at the sub-cabinet level.[71] This led to a report to the President in mid-June that recommended inclusion of the U.S. Information Agency in State, reversing the committee's and the administration's decision of 1953 to create an independent USIA; this report also recommended means for strengthening departmental management.[72] The recommended changes in State were meant to deal with some of the issues of coordination that had sparked the President's interest in the First Secretary concept, and as the committee had shaped that concept, a strengthened department was its foundation. As Arthur Flemming explained to Eisenhower, this proposal would not interfere with the First Secretary as an eventual proposal; it would, rather, pave the way for it.[73] Yet there was not even unanimity on the reorganization plan, minus the first secretaryship. In addition to Dulles' uncertainties

[67] *Ibid.*; also Memorandum for Record, A. J. Goodpaster, June 22, 1957, Office of the Staff Secretary, Rockefeller (1), White House Office, Eisenhower Library.

[68] Dwight Eisenhower, *The White House Years*, p. 637.

[69] Wednesday, February 12, 1958, Whitman Diary Series, Papers of DDE as President, Eisenhower Library.

[70] Dwight Eisenhower, *The White House Years*, p. 637; Memorandum, Kimball to Rockefeller, April 14, 1958, Box 2, File 17 (1), PACGO, Eisenhower Library.

[71] Minutes of Meeting, April 9, 1959, Box 3, File 23 (2), *ibid.*

[72] Memorandum, Flemming to President, June 8, 1959, Foreign Affairs Organization (2), Records of Robert Merriam, Eisenhower Library.

[73] Meeting with President, June 12, 1959, Box 3, File 23 (1), PACGO, Eisenhower Library.

about the whole issue of reform, the talk of moving the Information Agency back to State was itself controversial, raising issues of that agency's proper role.[74]

There was, however, another matter that would affect the course of State Department reorganization. On June 1, 1959, the President's reorganization authority lapsed. These schemes were far too controversial to implement through legislation in the waning days of a presidency. Thus, like the proposed office of executive management, the First Secretary became part of President Eisenhower's swan song, included in his January, 1961, budget message.

Defense Reorganization of 1958

The third major concern of PACGO in the late 1950's was the organization of the Defense Department. It was commonly thought that effective unification had still not developed in Defense and that its secretary was incapable of directing the services. These issues had been addressed by the Truman administration and then by the Eisenhower administration in its reorganization of that department in 1953.

PACGO's focus on Defense Department organization in 1957 was by presidential direction and reflected Eisenhower's own special interest in this part of the executive branch. The President's self-assurance on military matters caused planning in this instance to be more quickly paced and focused than it was in other areas. The President was often vague about what it was he wanted in other areas, as witnessed by the planning experiences pertaining to the Office of Executive Management and the First Secretary.

In Defense organization the President knew what he wanted—as much unification as could practically be achieved. As far back as 1945, General Eisenhower had spoken in favor of ultimate unification of the separate services into one uniformed service.[75] When, in November 1957, Eisenhower charged PACGO to begin working on proposals for Defense reorganization, his statement to the committee comprised a virtual outline of what he wanted a proposal to contain.[76] President Eisenhower told PACGO that he desired removal of the services from

[74] *Ibid.*; also Correspondence, Abbot Washburn to Persons and Milton Eisenhower, April 6 and 10, and related White House interoffice memoranda, Foreign Affairs Organization (1), Records of Robert Merriam, Eisenhower Library. On role of USIA see that agency's 1950's era blueprint for its role, Leo Bogart, *Premises for Propaganda* (New York: Free Press, 1976).

[75] Dwight Eisenhower, *The White House Years*, p. 248.

[76] Notes on Meeting, November 4, 1957, Box 3, File 21, PACGO, Eisenhower Library.

the direct combat command system of the Defense Department. He envisioned a direct command relationship from the Commander-in-Chief through the Secretary of Defense to the Joint Chiefs and down to unified, inter-service, commands. The services would be adjunct supply and training operations. At the heart of Eisenhower's hope for reorganization was a reconstitution of the Joint Chiefs of Staff into a coherent body, freed from inter-service rivalry and supported by a unified staff. The assignment of manpower to commands, the logistical decisions supporting those commands, and the designation of officers over the commands would be carried out by the central line of executive authority in the department without regard to the services.

Between November 1957 and April 1958, President Eisenhower worked closely with PACGO in formulating a recommendation for Defense Department reorganization.[77] At the same time, an advisory committee created by the recently appointed replacement for Defense Secretary Charles Wilson, Neil H. McElroy, addressed reform within the department. However, PACGO became the center of reform planning in that it was the President's committee. An added factor strengthening PACGO's hand was that Secretary McElroy opposed planning for large-scale change, being uncomfortable with reforming an organization with which he was still unfamiliar.[78]

By early December, PACGO with the Bureau of the Budget had prepared a draft plan for Defense reorganization, following the President's outline of early November. What remained to be settled were some specific matters, the most important of which was whether appropriations would be made to the Secretary of Defense rather than to the individual services.[79] That reform would weaken the link between the services and Congress, giving the secretary greater control over those services.

The Defense Department reorganization process went ahead at a pace akin to the reorganization activities of the administration's first year. Even while there were disagreements to PACGO's plans among the members of Secretary McElroy's advisory committee, Eisenhower approved those plans and ordered the Bureau of the Budget to draft implementing legislation. The President used his 1958 State of the Union address to signal his intentions for Defense reorganization. But the speed of events was not enough to avoid controversy over change in the status of the services; senior officers opened a vocal campaign

[77] Dwight Eisenhower, *The White House Years*, p. 244.
[78] Kimball's notes on conversations with William Finan, November 27, 1957, Box 3, File 21, PACGO, Eisenhower Library.
[79] Minutes of Meeting, December 5, 1957, *ibid.*

against any changes in the place of the services in Defense Department organization.[80] Eisenhower counterattacked with a spirited critique of the independent political influence of each of the services. Citing the large congressional liaison staffs and cadres of public relations officers maintained by each service, the President interpreted these phenomena as symptomatic of the disintegration of the military establishment. Central to his point was a not so veiled attack on congressional support of the separate services; Eisenhower believed that Congress should deal with the Secretary of Defense and the Chiefs of Staff, the proper line of executive command in the department.[81]

After his State of the Union speech, the President offered no details of the projected Defense reorganization. He was frequently asked for some details, but, as he told the congressional Republican leadership on January 14, he felt that it was better to let public discussion about the projected changes in Defense proceed without opponents' having exposed targets at which to shoot. Thus he planned to reveal his plan only when presenting it to Congress.[82] Meanwhile, PACGO took the lead within the upper levels of the administration, building the nearest thing that could be achieved to a consensus position. In discussions with Nelson Rockefeller, Budget Bureau representatives, and the President himself, through late February and March, the Secretary of Defense's advisory committee was more or less brought around to some agreement over the reorganization program. But the service secretaries and the Joint Chiefs continued to oppose unification. These officials attacked the removal of services from the military command structure. Admiral Arleigh Burke wondered how long it would take for logistics to be taken away from the services once military command was removed, suggesting that in operating contexts they were intertwined.[83]

In late March, a bill was drafted for the President's examination along with a message to Congress. Even at this last moment one can glimpse the cracks in the unity of the administration on Defense reorganization. While the bill itself was designed by PACGO and the Bureau of the Budget, the draft presidential message was written in Secretary McElroy's office, and PACGO found the effort inadequate. Meeting with Nelson Rockefeller on March 26, McElroy announced

[80] For Eisenhower's private remarks on this campaign, see, January 15, 1958, Whitman Diary Series, Papers of DDE as President, Eisenhower Library.

[81] Dwight Eisenhower, *The White House Years*, p. 245.

[82] Notes on Legislative Leadership Meeting, January 14, 1958, Legislative Meeting Series, Papers of DDE as President, Eisenhower Library.

[83] Memorandum, Coolidge to McElroy, March 7, 1958, with Memorandum, Mitchell to Rockefeller, Box 18, File 36 (1), PACGO, Eisenhower Library.

that he was sending the draft to PACGO for any help it wanted to give before sending it to the White House. McElroy's behavior was a symptom of opposition to reorganization within his department. After the meeting, Rockefeller summed up his impressions as follows:

> Secretary McElroy expects a complete rewrite of the draft message, and that his purpose in developing it is for his own protection within the Department of Defense. Whatever the President does beyond this is OK with him, but he will always be able to say to the Service people that he stood on and fought for the position agreed to in his paper. Therefore, what the President did beyond that was not his responsibility.[84]

On April 3, President Eisenhower sent a message to Congress outlining his reform plans. He said that the purpose of the reorganization he would propose was to make Defense conform with the realities of modern military needs. The military might of the United States, he said, must be "completely unified," and the different components and various weapon systems of that military capability must be "singly led and prepared to fight as one, regardless of service."[85] One of the President's punch lines in the message was: "Our goal must be maximum strength at minimum cost."[86] Thus the virtues of his reorganization program were really twofold. It would effect a militarily desirable authority system in Defense. And, it would do so at a savings.

President Eisenhower sent the bill to Congress on April 16. It was the virtual embodiment of the ideas he had expressed to PACGO in the prior November. Initially, the bill was criticized by the Congress; the senior members who were most closely connected with military affairs attacked it, among them Representative Carl Vinson (Dem., Ga.), Representative John McCormick (Dem., Mass.), and Senator William Knowland (Rep., Calif.). However, President Eisenhower was in a peculiarly strong legislative position in relation to military matters, and to assure added support the White House staff stimulated expressions of support for the bill from a wide range of business leaders.[87] The reorganization bill passed in an impressively short time, Eisenhower getting it for his signature on August 6, 1958.

The 1958 reorganization of the Defense Department stands in sharp contrast to all of the major subjects PACGO worked on in its post-

---

[84] Notes by Rockefeller, March 26, 1958, Box 18, *ibid.*

[85] *Public Papers of the Presidents, Dwight Eisenhower, 1958*, Special Message to the Congress on Reorganization of the Defense Establishment, April 3, 1958, p. 274.

[86] *Ibid.*

[87] Dwight Eisenhower, *The White House Years*, p. 251.

Hoover Commission phase. Planning for the Executive Office and the foreign affairs organization dragged on and on. The Defense reorganization took nine months from the President's first meeting with PACGO on this subject to his signing the bill which gave him much of what he wanted. The difference between this reform and PACGO's other work was the priority placed on the subject by Eisenhower and his decisiveness about it.

In planning the Defense Department reorganization, PACGO functioned in a focused and directed staff relationship to the President. Therein the President made quite clear what he wanted. But, in the cases of the Executive Office and foreign affairs the President had said that he had a problem and wanted help. In these instances, PACGO was not implementing clear directions; it had the job of trying to invent politically suitable mechanisms to deal with what may have been as much an incumbent's problems as they were problems of the institution of the presidency. Also, in formulating those solutions, PACGO was unavoidably in an advocacy relationship with the President, attempting to understand what he felt he needed and trying to, in turn, convince him that what the committee had devised met those needs. A final difference between the Defense reorganization and these other two instances is the fact that the President was unanimously supported among his senior staff in the former, while both Executive Office and foreign affairs reorganization planning produced dissent within that circle.

Planning New Departments

A large portion of PACGO's work in Eisenhower's second term was devoted to the problem of matching departmental organization to government's priorities and policies. Two points must be stressed about PACGO to understand its role in developing and brokering recommendations for new departments. The first and obvious point is that this is why the committee was created. Eisenhower wanted several wise men to identify pressing issues and think through their organizational ramifications. The second point concerns the inclinations of those "wise men." To function as the President intended them, PACGO's members had to be experienced hands in Washington. Thus they would have had to serve in Democratic administrations, and it is likely that their own political views would be left of the Republican Party's center. Certainly, PACGO's three members were friendlier to public sector solutions to problems than most of their colleagues in the administration.

PACGO's role in developing proposals for new departments was a brokering activity. The committee did not invent ideas for new departments; such ideas had a history of their own and abounded within the Democratic Congress.[88] For example, Congress itself gave increasing prominence to urban issues during the 1950's.[89] But PACGO was the natural place in the administration for these ideas to receive a sympathetic hearing.

In December 1956, after several bills had been presented in Congress to create a department for the cities, PACGO sent the President a memorandum on merging the large Housing and Home Finance Administration and the smaller Federal Civil Defense Administration, creating a new cabinet department.[90] While not accepting the plan, Eisenhower encouraged further work. But the committee's momentum was slowed by the President's press conference of June 19. Responding to a question on a proposed White House conference on urban problems, Eisenhower said: ". . . whenever a conference of mayors comes to me to talk about urban renewal, I have the uneasy feeling that the state echelon of government is subject there to a two-pronged attack one from below and one from above; the state is being ignored."[91] Consequently, when a PACGO memorandum recommending a department of urban affairs was sent to Sherman Adams, his response was negative on its "urban" title and the lack of inter-governmental and state-related elements in the department.[92]

PACGO's next step was to refocus its proposal, aiming at a broader department; Adams had suggested the title Department of Rehabilitation and Development, and the committee entertained Housing and Community Affairs as another alternative. PACGO also turned to the Bureau of the Budget staff with the request that it study how inter-governmental elements might be fit into the already conceived urban affairs format of a new department. The bureau pointed out that several other departments had strong inter-governmental involvements, not the least of them the Department of Health, Education and

---

[88] Bills to create a department for urban affairs were introduced in every Congress from the 83rd (1954). There was less concentrated activity to create a Transportation Department during the 1950's, but between 1935 and 1976 seven bills were introduced on that subject.

[89] See Congressional Quarterly Service *Congress and the Nation, 1945-1964* (Washington: Congressional Quarterly, 1965), pp. 459-475.

[90] Minutes of Meeting, December 21, 1956, Box 3, File 20, PACGO, Eisenhower Library.

[91] Excerpt from Transcript of Presidential Press Conference, June 19, 1957, accompanied by memorandum, Kimball to Rockefeller, June 21, 1957, Box 13, File 86, *ibid.*

[92] Memorandum, Kimball to Brundage, July 5, 1957, *ibid.*

Welfare. By the end of the summer of 1957 PACGO dropped the idea of an urban department. Clearly it was in the position of planning and brokering an idea for which the President was not yet sympathetic.

PACGO's brief consideration of a natural resources agency exhibits a somewhat different role than its brokering of an urban department. The suggestion for a Department of Natural Resources was made by Secretary of the Interior Fred Seaton at a PACGO meeting in early 1959.[93] The issue that the committee had been addressing was the possibility of relocating the civil construction functions of the Corps of Engineers, and Secretary Seaton argued to expand the Department of the Interior into a natural resources department, incorporating civil construction. After that meeting, the Bureau of the Budget reviewed the proposal for such a department made by the task force on natural resources of the first Hoover Commission and the minority report of the commission (Acheson, Rowe, and Pollock) which argued that the task force recommendations should have been adopted in the commission's report.[94] The bureau's own recommendation was positive, and Deputy Budget Director Elmer Staats suggested to PACGO that such a department be placed high on the administration's reorganization agenda.[95]

Secretary Seaton, the Bureau of the Budget, and at least one PACGO member, Don Price, saw the proposed department as a solution to the nagging problem of coordinating water resource policy. Thus through 1959 momentum built at the Bureau of the Budget and PACGO for the idea of a reorganization at Interior. However, this solution to the water resources problem was squelched by that PACGO member who had the greatest sensitivity to the political dynamics that had historically accompanied the idea for a natural resources department, Milton Eisenhower. As much as the movement of the civil functions of the Corps of Engineers, the creation of a Department of Natural Resources meant to most observers of administrative politics the transfer of the Forest Service from Agriculture to a reconstituted Interior Department. Milton Eisenhower was attuned to this issue because he had served at high career levels of the Department of Agriculture under the administrations of Coolidge, Hoover, and Roosevelt, and he had later been president of two major agricultural schools, Kansas State and Penn State. In the midst of the accelerating interest in a natural resources department, Milton Eisenhower stressed to his colleagues that he was

[93] Memorandum, Finan to Kimball, March 13, 1959, Box 20, File 165, *ibid.*
[94] Memorandum, Finan to Stans, March 13, 1959, *ibid.*
[95] Notes for June 5 meeting, n.d., Box 3, File 23, *ibid.*

unequivocally opposed to any change that would threaten the Forest Service's position in Agriculture. Furthermore he argued that the danger of such an idea's being attached to discussion of a new department made the department itself too hot to handle.[96]

Consequently, PACGO chose not to carry a recommendation for such a reorganization to the President for even initial approval that would justify further work on it. Instead, it adopted the narrower alternative of recommending just the transfer of the Corps of Engineer's civil construction authority to the Secretary of the Interior; the President adopted this for presentation in his last budget message to Congress.[97] Thus, in considering the possibilities of major organizational changes, PACGO was able to identify and politically filter those reforms that ought to be considered seriously by the White House.

The final, domestic department reorganization considered by PACGO concerned transportation and was an assignment from Sherman Adams. Isolated transportation issues entered PACGO's considerations in 1956 in the form of considering the Department of Commerce as the organizational locus for federal transportation policies.[98] But in May 1957 Sherman Adams suggested that PACGO consider a new department.[99] The Bureau of the Budget did a staff study on the issue. Later William Finan, whose division of management and organization was conducting the study, reported to PACGO that he and his staff were stymied by the problem of relating the transportation regulatory agencies to the program-implementing agencies. Finan reported he was also having trouble with "the broad non-regulatory organizational principles involved."[100]

PACGO faced the problem of a major reorganization of independent regulatory agenices as well as that of pulling together a variety of different transportation-related activities such as the Coast Guard and the federal highway programs. But this was not the limit of the problem; Sherman Adams had asked for more than just a work-up of ideas concerning transportation; he wanted work focused on a combined agency of transportation and communications. The added factor, communications, was similar in some ways to transportation as an area

[96] Letter, Milton Eisenhower to Kimball, March 18, 1959, and Memorandum, Kimball to Flemming and Price, March 19, 1959, Box 20, File 165, *ibid.*

[97] *Public Papers of the Presidents, Dwight Eisenhower, 1960-61*, Annual Budget Message to Congress, FY 1967, January 16, 1961, pp. 944-946.

[98] Minutes, November 12, 1956, Box 3, File 20, PACGO, Eisenhower Library.

[99] Minutes, May 13-14, 1957, Box 3, File 21 (2), and Minutes, July 25, 1957, Box 4, File 25, *ibid.*

[100] Minutes of Meeting, July 25, 1957, *ibid.*

of federal policy, and that was the problem. It too involves both regulatory and policy implementing agencies, and it also spans a number of very different forms of activities in differing communication media.

PACGO's approach to the problem of dispersed agencies and programs in transportation and communications entailed assumptions about the relationship between organizational proximity and policy coherence that had traditionally motivated reorganizers. Observing that federal policies toward transportation were fragmented, Milton Eisenhower commented: "I . . . thought we needed to unify all federal activities relating to transportation, [and] have the new department develop a consistent set of policies and programs. . . ."[101] Unification would create consistency; therein is a root principle of reorganization as a presidential tool. Also, as Milton Eisenhower urged, organizational coherence of a policy area made an official able "to give the President a balanced view of the over-all" policy.[102]

Deciding that the transportation and communication matters could not be dealt with together, PACGO sought a transportation solution by itself. First it entertained the simple solution of a new transportation administration within the Department of Commerce (renamed Commerce and Transportation), headed by an undersecretary. Commerce naturally favored that solution; it already contained agencies dealing with highways and the merchant marine. But the Secretary of the Treasury informed PACGO that while he would not fight the transfer from his department of the Coast Guard, he was sure that that agency itself would oppose the change. Of greater possible consequence, General Elwood Quesada, the President's special assistant for aviation, notified the committee that he would vehemently oppose the transfer of the new aviation agency he was planning, the Federal Aviation Agency, into the proposed department, preferring that it be established as an independent agency directly responsible to the President.[103]

Meeting with Eisenhower in April 1958, PACGO now suggested the organization of transportation organizations into a new department. The committee abandoned its Commerce-based reorganization because of General Quesada's new aviation agency. Quesada placed great weight on cooperation between the federal administration of civilian aviation and the military aviation agencies in Defense.[104] His

[101] Milton Eisenhower, *The President Is Calling*, p. 271.

[102] *Ibid.*, p. 270.

[103] Minutes of Meeting, December 5, 1957, Box 3, File 21, PACGO, Eisenhower Library.

[104] *Ibid.*

argument against inclusion of the projected Federal Aviation Agency in Commerce was that such cooperation could exist only in an agency wherein some military representation could be established. However, a new department might lessen the alienation of civilian aviation programs from the military by allowing the creation of privileged military access. This likelihood was increased by the fact that other modes of transportation also had some natural security implications, suggesting that this new department would, by necessity, establish closer relations with Defense than could other departments.

At its April meeting with the President, PACGO was ready to recommend that the new department be acted on as quickly as possible. But there was a fly in the ointment; the Bureau of the Budget opposed speedy implementation, while it approved of the substantive recommendation. The bureau's position was that it could not prepare the necessary reorganization plans in time for the current session of Congress because of its workload; consequently it recommended that the President plan on the new department's topping his 1959 reorganization agenda.[105] The President followed the bureau's advice, approving the committee's plan for transmittal to Congress in January, 1959.[106]

But as in the other of the committee's projects that were being carried over from one congressional session to another, elapsed time created mutation in recommendations that at first seemed firm. In this instance, when the committee met again with the President in December 1958 to discuss the transportation reorganization, it had reverted back to its more modest proposal of a transportation administration within the Department of Commerce. At this juncture, the committee explained its change of heart as a matter of practical considerations. As to the FAA, it recommended that that agency (which would begin operation as of January 1, 1959) be transferred into the reorganized department over General Quesada's objections. The committee and the Bureau of the Budget further suggested that the administration adopt a target date of April 1 for submitting the necessary reorganization plan to Congress.[107]

Yet neither Congress nor presidential decision would accommodate this plan. It was on that date, April 1, that the President's reorganization authority lapsed. But there was clearly an even greater barrier to the committee's plan; the President was not yet fully sold on it,

[105] Letter, Kimball to Rockefeller, April 14, 1958, Box 2, File 17 (1), *ibid.*

[106] Memorandum, Rockefeller to President, December 6, 1958, Box 14, Transportation Department, Records of Robert Merriam, Eisenhower Library.

[107] *Ibid.*

being indecisive as to whether he preferred an expanded Commerce department or a new department. By the fall of 1959, the President was leaning back to a department of transportation, and a host of inter-departmental political problems had arisen. Having changed secretaries, Department of Commerce was no longer interested in the PACGO recommendation for its expansion. Lewis Strauss, the interim appointment as secretary to replace Sinclair Weeks, had failed of Senate confirmation, and Frederick Mueller had been appointed Secretary of Commerce. Mueller flatly opposed the earlier recommendation. So far as it went, Mueller's rejection was not so damaging. In fact, by this time General Quesada had come around to more or less willingly supporting a Department of Transportation. But the complication was that Mueller and his associates at Commerce demanded that in return for losing their transportation-related agencies they would get the Small Business Administration, an independent agency, a change in the department's name which would include the word "technology," and, on top of it all, they refused to willingly surrender the Weather Service and the Coast and Geodetic Survey, which were considered by the President, the committee, and the Budget Bureau as transportation relevant agencies.[108]

Between Commerce's recalcitrance and the President's indecision in the face of growing political problems attached to this reorganization recommendation, the issue was pushed into 1960 and killed as a viable possibility for a reform that could be instituted during the administration's remaining months. So, like PACGO's other recommendations of this period, this one became part of Eisenhower's legacy of reorganization suggestions contained in his final budget message. In that message the President urged the creation of a full-blown Department of Transportation. What the President, PACGO, and the Bureau of the Budget could not achieve politically in the real time of the administration they could recommend in parting.

PACGO's planning experience for new domestic departments and foreign affairs organization should be considered in light of the committee's work with Defense Department reorganization in 1957. In defense reorganization the President knew precisely what ends he wished to achieve, and he used PACGO narrowly—assigning it a specific task. However, in the domestic and foreign affairs areas the President used PACGO quite differently; it was given very broad tasks and expected to brainstorm problems, with the possibility that it might

[108] Minutes of Meeting, January 22, 1960, Box 3, File 23, PACGO, Eisenhower Library.

convince the President of the desirability and utility of its solution to one or another problem. In defense reorganization the committee was an instrument for effecting the President's will, whereas in the other areas it was a means for proposing options for him. Thus it would misunderstand PACGO's relationship to Eisenhower to judge it successful in defense reorganization and unsuccessful in foreign affairs and domestic department reorganization; these were different roles, each serving the President in different ways.

REORGANIZATION PAST THE CROSSROADS

The 1950's present a contrast between two very different sets of origins, procedures, and purposes in reorganization planning. The second Hoover Commission was congressionally established, of mixed membership, and public. The President's Advisory Committee on Government Organization was created by the President, comprised of individuals of his choice, and confidential.

The second Hoover Commission's overall format was characteristic of an earlier era of reorganization planning. The underlying assumption of a congressionally instituted, mixed commission is that administrative reform is primarily a legislative consideration rather than, first and foremost, presidential. In contrast, the President's Advisory Committee's format had only a loose similarity with earlier reorganization planning vehicles. More than any of its predecessors, PACGO was a staff mechanism of a president. In this PACGO shares some characteristics with President Taft's Commission on Economy and Efficiency and President Roosevelt's Brownlow Committee, but the differences between those earlier episodes and PACGO are marked. The Commission on Economy and Efficiency was mandated by Congress; its chairman rather than the full membership served in a staff relationship to Taft; finally, the commission's reports were public and apparently independently formulated. The Brownlow Committee differs from PACGO in that it was substantially independent of Roosevelt during its period of active planning. In fact, its claim to legitimacy as a planning instrument was its expertise and not its relationship to Franklin Roosevelt. Like Taft's commission, the Brownlow Committee issued a public report.

In its total regard for the presidency, and in its close association of its President with the presidency, PACGO incorporated only one of two, competing themes in the historical dialectic of executive reorganization. Each earlier planning episode entailed a presidential endeavor to resolve the tensions of the separated governmental branches by coopting congressional reform efforts. For example, President Truman resolved that dialectic in his favor by coopting the first Hoover Commission; Warren G. Harding had similarly affected the course of reorganization planning in the 1920's by coopting the Joint Committee on Reorganization. In contrast, President Eisenhower cut through those inter-branch tensions by rejecting the second Hoover Commission. Eisenhower adopted an indirect tactic for dealing with the second commission, thinking it could be set onto a course that would not interfere with the administration's concerns.

Eisenhower's hidden hand style, to use Fred Greenstein's phrase, had mixed results.[109] The President paid a penalty for the second Hoover Commission's independence from the White House. Eisenhower might have killed the commission while it was still a glimmer in Clarence Brown's eye. Even better, he could have followed a Truman-like course aimed at directing the commission's attention and focus. Instead, Eisenhower chose to encourage the commission's proponents to follow their ideological inclinations, trusting that "policy" would occupy Hoover's new commission as a clew of yarn occupies a cat. What Eisenhower failed to see was that, first, the commission would not confine itself to policy without attacking the organizational setting of public policies, and, second, that "policy" as understood by the commission was everything government did, not just a small concern that could be contained in a corner while government went about its business.

Hidden-hand leadership, as exemplified in this case, requires accurate predictions if it is to be successful, and prediction is a damnably difficult art in a political world where information is the most scarce resource. Consider that Eisenhower faced alternative choices in mid-January, 1953. He could have squelched the idea of a new commission and paid a price for thwarting the ambitions of a handful of congressional Republicans. Such an act would have required a prediction about a proximate state, the moment when Eisenhower told those who were pushing the second commission that he did not want it introduced in Congress. This situation is relatively easily predicted; hurt feelings would result that would have to be assuaged quickly through the President's trove of rewards (both concrete and symbolic) so as to ward off the danger of these legislators deserting the President's legislative program.

On the other hand, to not squelch the second commission meant

---

[109] For the full exposition of this view of Eisenhower's style, see Fred I. Greenstein, *The Hidden-Hand Presidency* (New York: Basic Books, 1982).

that the President paid no immediate price, but it required that he predict that there would be no greater political price to pay down the road should the commission come into being. Such a prediction involves many unknowns. While Greenstein's model of hidden-hand leadership seems applicable to the President's behavior throughout this case of reorganization planning, the case itself seems to exhibit some of the possible costs of that style of leadership. To put the costs most succinctly; because hidden-hand leadership tends to rest on fairly distant predictions and a series of indirect relationships, even small variations from the predicted course of events can lead to a different future outcome than the one sought.

On the other hand it is important to underline a possible success of Eisenhower's leadership style regarding the Hoover Commission. If we recognize that the commission gave a home to the right wing of the President's party, it is possible that its existence tapped energy that might otherwise have been used in a more direct frontal attack on Eisenhower's foreign and domestic policies. Even at its most annoying, the commission was a side issue for him, less difficult to handle and less threatening than a frontal attack. The discussions of the January 1953 Commodore Hotel meeting can be read to suggest that this development may have been part of Eisenhower's expectations in dealing with the proposal for the second commission.

Using the metaphor of this chapter's title, one might say that PACGO and the second Hoover Commission collided at the crossroads. But the long diversion of PACGO from President Eisenhower's organizational agenda to the business (and threat) of the commission did not undermine its importance as a model for reorganization planning. In retrospect it is clear that the second Hoover Commission was the last of its species while PACGO was the first pure form of a new format for reorganization planning. As the following chapters will explore, reorganization planning in the 1960's and 1970's would be conducted with no pretense of independence from the chief executive; PACGO and its successors presented a planning model for the managerial presidency ascendant. No longer would administrative reform proceed within an arena of the separated branches of government. The PACGO model symbolized executive dominance, although the question of whether the symbol could be translated into dominance-in-fact remained unanswered.

Chapter Eight

A NEW ORGANIZATION FOR THE GREAT SOCIETY: REORGANIZATION PLANNING IN THE JOHNSON ADMINISTRATION

All this and more can and must be done. It can
be done by this summer, and it can be done
without any increase in spending. In fact . . . it
can be done with an actual reduction in Federal
expenditures and Federal employment.[1]

Lyndon Johnson, 1964

With the creation of PACGO, reorganization planning was internalized into the organized presidency, signalling its transformation from an instrument in the construction of the managerial presidency to a tool of the established managerial presidency. Consequently, reorganization planning also became more subject to the personal priorities of presidents than heretofore. John F. Kennedy presents a case in point of the magnification of the incumbents' impact on the place of administrative reform in the presidency after 1953.

Kennedy brought to the presidency a style of work which downplayed concerns with formality and structure.[2] He seemed to think of concerns with formality in the presidency as if, to quote the words of the political scientist most identified with Kennedy, Richard Neustadt, organizational reforms entertained by PACGO were "a scheme to make the Presidency manageable for an Eisenhower."[3] The Bay of Pigs debacle at the beginning of Kennedy's presidency taught him that big organizations—the CIA, State, and Defense—could be dreadfully mistaken. Theodore Sorenson recalls his chief's reaction to that crisis to be a deep distrust of government's large organizations.[4] Prior to the

[1] *Public Papers of the Presidents, Lyndon B. Johnson, 1965*, vol. 2, August 25, 1965, pp. 916, 917.

[2] Stephen Hess, *Organizing the Presidency* (Washington: Brookings Institution, 1976), pp. 91-92.

[3] Richard E. Neustadt, "Reorganization the Presidency in 1961: A Review of the Issue," prepared for delivery to the 1960 Annual Meeting of the American Political Science Association, New York, September 8-10.

[4] Theodore Sorenson, *The Kennedy Legacy* (New York: Macmillan, 1969), pp. 167-168, 180-182.

Bay of Pigs invasion, Kennedy had created an advisory committee on administration that was in the PACGO mold. To it he appointed four distinguished people: Robert Lovett, former Secretary of Defense and Undersecretary of State; Don K. Price, dean of Harvard's Graduate School of Public Administration; Richard Neustadt, a Columbia University political scientist; and Sydney Stein, Jr., partner in a Chicago investment firm.[5] But after this committee was established it never met.[6] It is as if after his Bay of Pig's failure Kennedy decided that government's large organizations were swamps into which good intentions vanish.

INNOVATION AND ECONOMY: JOHNSON'S STYLE AND GOALS

Lyndon Johnson brought to the presidency goals for which reorganization planning seemed to be an appropriate means. Johnson's style of work and substantive goals were rooted in his thirty-three years of congressional experience. In Congress, one's world is comprised of colleagues and the relatively small body of salient members of one's constituency. The congressional politician's leadership skills are face-to-face. Doris Kearns's description of President Johnson's behavior with his staff offers a glimpse of the skills of the old congressional leader: "In the end, no organization chart could define Johnson's system of White House control. His techniques were essentially psychological. He elevated a smile, a glance, or a courtesy above all political logic."[7]

Two of Johnson's key themes suggest that there was also a substantive imprint left on his presidency by his congressional experience. He promised to squeeze waste out of government and to transform the national government into a great engine for creating new social policy. Johnson saw legislative accomplishment as the *sine qua non* of presidential success. In explaining Johnson's appetite for a landslide victory in the 1964 election, Eric Goldman said:

> LBJ was determined to enact a sweeping Great Society legislative program after the election of 1964. He wanted to carry the nation

[5] White House Press Release, February 10, 1961, PACGO Records, box 1, file no. 3, Eisenhower Library.

[6] Of the committee, Don K. Price said: "It was never given a chance to do anything. White House staff members were a bit jealous of it, and Kennedy wasn't particularly interested." Don Price, interviewed by Harvey Sapolsky, in *News for Teachers of Political Science* (Winter 1981), 29.

[7] Doris Kearns, *Lyndon Johnson and the American Dream* (New York: Harper & Row, 1976), p. 240.

by so large a majority . . . that he would take his program before a House and Senate which was subdued and ready to follow him.[8]

The 1964 State of the Union message was distinctive among those since 1950 in that it gave priority to domestic social policy. Foreign and defense considerations predominate among the messages between 1950 and 1964, with domestic economic policy given priority in four of the sixteen. In his 1964 address, Johnson opened by saying:

> Let this session of Congress be known as the session which did more for civil rights than the last hundred sessions combined; as the session which enacted the most far-reaching tax cut of our time; as the session which declared all-out war on human poverty and unemployment in the United States; as the session which finally recognized the health needs of all our older citizens; as the session which reformed our tangled transportation and transit policies; as the session which achieved the most effective, efficient foreign aid program ever; and as the session which helped to build more homes, more schools, more libraries, and more hospitals than any single session of Congress in the history of our Republic.[9]

The new President gave priority in his address to the most dramatic group of legislative demands made in decades. To put his domestic legislative agenda up front was for Johnson to signal that his presidency would be a machine for making public policy.

Almost as prominent as his social policy goals was Johnson's commitment to economy in government. In a November 30, 1963, memorandum to executive branch officers, Johnson "pledged that the Executive Branch will be administered with the utmost thrift and frugality. . . ."[10] In the 1964 State of the Union, he placed his statement on economy in government immediately following the above-quoted list of policies he wished initiated. But how could government's activities expand into new areas while still economizing? The President observed:

> All this and more can and must be done. It can be done by this summer, and it can be done without any increase in spending. In fact, under the budget that I shall shortly submit, it can be done with an actual reduction in Federal expenditures and Federal employment.[11]

[8] Eric Goldman, *The Tragedy of Lyndon Johnson* (New York: Knopf, 1969), p. 170.

[9] *Public Papers of the Presidents, Lyndon B. Johnson, 1963-64*, Annual Message to the Congress on the State of the Union, January 8, 1964, p. 112.

[10] *Ibid.*, November 30, 1963, pp. 15-16.

[11] *Ibid.*, January 8, 1964, p. 112.

True to his promise, Johnson submitted a FY 1965 budget that held estimated spending slightly below the level of the FY 1964 budget.[12]

Economy was not a will-o-the-wisp for the President. He pursued it, returned to it, and introduced his news conferences with reports of victories over waste. Like his passion for legislation, Johnson's regard for economy was a value fostered by his congressional experience. Economy is a more useful value for legislators than for administrators. Administrators are intensely involved with a limited number of programs. On the other hand, the legislator makes decisions about a huge number of programs but gains detailed knowledge about only a few. In judging among many different programs, simple decision rules like economy in government become handy sorting devices.

While redolent with the traditional interests of Congress, Johnson's evocation of economy and redirected resources was also responsive to a fashionable new concern in American public life, the problem of choice. The 1960 report prepared by a study group of the Rockefeller Brothers Fund proposed:

> ... the future will make heavy demands on our ability to make choices. While we can envisage an era of well-being far beyond present experience, it will not come about automatically ... we cannot do everything at once. To seek to do too much too soon will increase our economic *problems* but not our economic *results*.[13]

But to recognize the necessity for choice is not to have an instrument for effecting choice.

During the early 1960's Robert McNamara introduced a system of budget analysis at the Department of Defense which promised to be an instrument of rational choice. Planning-programming-budgeting seemed to be the method necessary for assessing the utility of governmental expenditures and comparing them to alternative program investments.[14] One expert who suggested that PPB's success at Defense could be generalized to the rest of the government observed:

> The greater part of a federal budget is what it is because what it was. As those programs already made mandatory—such as farm price supports or veterans' pensions—have to be paid for. ... The

---

[12] The outlay of the 1965 budget was 118.4 billion dollars; the 1964 budget's outlay was 118.6 billion dollars. U.S. Department of Commerce, Bureau of the Census, *Statistical Abstract of the United States, 1978* (Washington: Government Printing Office), p. 257.

[13] The Rockefeller Panel Reports, *Prospect for America* (Garden City, N.Y.: Doubleday, 1961), p. 331.

[14] See Virginia Held, "PPB comes to Washington," in James W. Davis, Jr. (ed.), *Politics, Programs, and Budgets* (Englewood Cliffs, N.J.: Prentice-Hall, 1969), pp. 138-149.

region of discretion, then, is distinctly limited. But as in other human affairs, it is those few decisions that are open to conscious choice which cause anguish. And it is to the resolution of such anguish that the new intellectual techniques are directed.[15]

President Johnson extended PPB to all of government's agencies in August 1965. But PPB was a technique for producing information and not itself a system for resolving conflicting claims of different programs over scarce resources. At best, PPB was the beginning of a solution to the problem posed by Johnson's wish to combine innovation and economy. It promised to become a system for aiding decisions that would balance those two values *if* a larger context could be fashioned which would allow the information produced to be considered by the right decision makers at the appropriate time. Thus PPB provided new impetus for rationalizing government's organization.

THE JOHNSON APPROACH TO ADMINISTRATIVE REFORM

Beyond considerations of economy, President Johnson's most pressing administrative problem was the tangle of Great Society programs, most of which entailed the delivery of grants in the inter-governmental system. By Senator Abraham Ribicoff's (Dem., Conn.) count, 150 separate federal agencies plus more than 400 regional and area field offices were providing aid assistance to states, cities, and individuals through 456 different program channels.[16]

In November 1966 James Reston wrote:

As President Johnson starts his fourth year in the White House, one fact is not only clear but undisputed; his Administration is poorly organized to administer the domestic programs he has introduced. . . . This has created something almost unheard of here. Criticism of the system, cries of growing domination by the Federal Government, complaints about administrative confusion and waste are now coming not alone from the Administration's critics or from observers in the state capitals, but from leading officials of the Johnson Administration itself.[17]

Reston blamed the fault on President Johnson's style, charging that "he is still trying to run the Presidency as if it were a Senator's office.

[15] *Ibid.*, p. 140.

[16] U.S. Congress, Senate, Subcommittee on Executive Reorganization, *Hearings: Establishing a Commission on the Organization and Management of the Executive Branch*, 90th Cong., 2nd Sess., 1968, p. 2.

[17] *New York Times*, November 23, 1966.

. . ."[18] But Reston overlooked the alternative hypothesis that the administrative problems of these programs originate in their inter-governmental complexity.[19]

However, the efforts of the Johnson White House on administrative reform suggest that at least part of the problem may have seen as James Reston stated it. There was no overall direction to the search for ways of confronting the two central administrative dilemmas of the administration, economizing—the disinvestment decision problem—and the inter-governmental administration problem. Instead top levels of the administration were caught up in a rush to innovation.

A Rush to Innovation: The Case of the Commerce-Labor Merger

There was a hunger for dramatic innovation in the Johnson White House. Johnson's staff combed the country after new ideas for domestic policy, for example, systematically scheduling meetings with scholars at leading university centers around the country—at Cambridge, New Haven, Chapel Hill, etc.—to collect policy ideas. Dozens of task forces were created to generate new approaches to existing problems. The President's appetite was also whetted for novel organizational changes. One such organization reform was the plan to merge the Departments of Commerce and Labor into a Department of Business and Labor; it appeared in the 1967 State of the Union address and died several months afterward. The development of this reorganization idea reveals a haphazard, random, and hurried character to innovation and reform in the Johnson White House.

While the notion of an eventual merger of Commerce and Labor came out of the administration's 1964 Task Force on Government Reorganization, the idea did not get serious consideration in the White House's inner circle until the fall of 1966. In mid-August of that year, two White House Fellows ending their assignments at the Departments of Commerce and Labor, William Cotter and Harold Richman, prepared a paper suggesting the merger of the departments into a Department of the Economy. Their memorandum made its way to Joseph Califano at the White House.[20]

---

[18] *Ibid.*

[19] The administrative complexity of the inter-governmental system in light of the public policy innovation of the 1960's can be seen in the case study of federal policy at work in Oakland by Jeffrey L. Pressman and Aaron Wildavsky, *Implementation* (Berkeley: University of California Press, 1973); for an overview of the inter-governmental system with stress on its fiscal complexities, see Deil Wright, *Understanding Intergovernmental Relations* (2nd ed.; Monterey, California: Brooks-Cole, 1982).

[20] Memorandum, Cotter and Richman to Connor and Wirtz, n.d., attached to mem-

Califano asked a member of the Bureau of the Budget's staff to join with a staff director of the 1967 task force on government reform to examine the idea. Although a high-level effort at reorganization planning was ongoing in the Task Force on Government Organization, it was not given the proposal. The task force's director, Fred Bohen, was ordered to undertake the assignment "on a completely confidential basis."[21] In a brief memorandum, Bohen and his budget bureau associative detailed the administrative functions that might be included in a merged department and presented some of the issues raised by the merger idea.[22]

The Commerce-Labor merger proposal gained access to the competition for inclusion in the upcoming 1967 State of the Union message. Its attractiveness was enhanced by the fact that Secretary of Commerce John Conner would soon leave his post, it being a bit easier to merge a headless agency.[23] On December 29 President Johnson asked his Civil Service Commission chairman, John Macy, to advise him on the idea; Macy consequently discussed it with Budget Director Charles Schultze and Califano. Later the same day, Califano discussed the idea with Secretary of Defense McNamara. All of these advisers agreed; the merger was desirable.[24] In early January the circle of discussion of the merger plan was widened, and the idea was broached with George Meany and several members of the Business Council.[25] These contacts produced no negative reactions.

---

orandum, Richman to Johnson, August 12, 1966, and to memorandum, Moyers to Califano, August 16, 1966, White House Central Files, Aides, Gaither, container 38, Government Reorganization, Lyndon B. Johnson Library.

[21] The confidentiality maintained on this matter is evidenced by its complete absence from the Bureau of the Budget's formulation of reorganization proposals for 1967, prepared in early November 1966. Memorandum, Harold Seidman to Director, November 5, 1966, White House Central Files, Aides, Gaither, container 318, Government Reorganization, Johnson Library.

[22] Memorandum, Califano to President, n.d. (November or December 1966), White House Central Files, Aides, Califano, container 15, Califano-Labor & Commerce (2), Johnson Library.

[23] Conner's intention to leave his post is mentioned in: Memorandum, Califano to President, November 30, 1966, White House Central File, Executive, container 220, FG 155, Johnson Library. John Macy recalls an association of the upcoming vacancy at Commerce with the timing of the consideration of the merger idea; John Macy, interviewed by author, March 31, 1981.

[24] Memorandum, Califano to President, December 29, 1966, White House Central File, Aides, Califano, container 16, Califano, Labor and Commerce, Johnson Library; John Macy, interviewed by author.

[25] In separate meetings on January 5th, the President spoke to George Meany and officers of the Business Council about the merger proposal. Memorandum, Califano to President, January 5, 1967, Diary Back-Up, Johnson Library.

In his State of the Union address of January 10, 1967, Lyndon Johnson said: "I have come tonight to propose that we establish a new department—a Department of Business and Labor." He explained the need for this innovation with only a sentence: "I think we can create a more economical, efficient, and streamlined instrument that will better serve a growing nation."[26] The preparation of the merger idea had been so rushed that there was very little definite that had been decided about the new department; serious planning would have to follow the public announcement.[27] On the weekend of January 21 and 22, the Task Force on Government Organization discussed the components and functions of the merged department. But as the task force's chairman, Ben Heineman himself, suspected, a large part of the White House's motive in bringing the task force into the merger project at that time was political;[28] its approval would add a patina of administrative rationality to the plan. After the task force's meeting, Heineman wrote a detailed memorandum of support for the merger. In conveying that memorandum to the President, Joseph Califano informed Johnson that the task force had taken up the issue because "it might be helpful to you at some point in getting the Department through the Congress."[29]

Of course Commerce and Labor never merged.[30] It was a politically difficult item; but presidents rarely invest major resources in fights they cannot win. Everything about the conduct of the White House on this proposal makes it appear that the administration thought it could succeed in it. If there was an error in judgment in this case, it

[26] *Public Papers of the Presidents, Lyndon B. Johnson, 1967*, Annual Message to the Congress on the State of the Union, January 10, 1967, p. 4.

[27] Evidently the White House staff had invested enough time in the merger proposal to make it an attractive package without putting in the hard work necessary to make it implementable. In a briefing memorandum preparing the President for his January 5th meeting with George Meany, Joseph Califano referred to the plan as containing "four days of staffing." Memorandum, Califano to the President, January 5, 1967, Diary Back-Up, Johnson Library. In a draft memorandum of late 1966, Califano wrote the President: ". . . it is not necessary to decide what finally gets into the new Department prior to the State of the Union message." Draft memorandum, Califano to President, n.d., White House Central File, Aides, Califano, container 15, Califano-Labor & Commerce (2), Johnson Library.

[28] Ben Heineman, interviewed by author, January 19, 1981.

[29] Memorandum, Califano to President, February 3, 1967, White House Central File, General, container 406, Task Force on Government Reorganization, Johnson Library.

[30] Much as he tried, the President could not win over organized labor to the merger idea. Failing in this, he backed away from the plan, sending it to his Advisory Committee on Labor-Management Policy for "further active development." It was not heard from again. *New York Times*, March 17 and 18, 1967.

rested upon an error in procedure. The quick and incomplete development of the recommendation to merge Commerce and Labor reduced the idea's political viability, and the very limited circle in which it was aired blinded the White House to the plan's likely political reception.

Policy development in the Johnson White House shared two characteristics, speed and secrecy. Eric Goldman defined what President Johnson meant by an "idea" as "a suggestion produced on the spot, or something for him to do tomorrow—a point to be made in a speech . . . a formula to serve as the basis for legislation to be hurried to Congress."[31] As to Johnson's secrecy, Doris Kearns described it as a core element of his personality and rooted deeply in his background. Kearns observes in him "a powerful inner inclination toward secrecy in the acquisition and use of power. . . ."[32] Speed and secrecy insulated the policy development process from important sources of support and information. Notably, the Labor-Commerce discussion seems to have rushed ahead so quickly that no attention was given to the report of the 1964 Task Force on Reorganization, headed by Don K. Price. It recommended that a Department of Economic Development be created from Commerce, with Labor merged into it later. Such a tactical move might have been more successful than the course chosen by the administration. Of course, the participants in this planning process could not easily call on the findings of the report, nor could they rely on it for public justification of the merger recommendation. Like all the Johnson task force reports, it too was secret.

The Task Force Approach to Reorganization Planning

President Johnson created two task forces for comprehensive reorganization planning. The first was the 1964 Task Force on Government Reorganization; Don K. Price, Dean of the Kennedy School of Government, was its chairman. The second was the 1967 Task Force on Government Organization; its chairman was Ben Heineman, president of the Northwestern Railroad in Chicago. These task forces are distinctive in that they constitute points of coherent, overall thinking about reform in an administration in which reform efforts tended to the piecemeal.

While these task forces are distinctive within the administration as centers of coherent reorganization planning, their organizational for-

---

[31] Eric Goldman, *The Tragedy of Lyndon Johnson*, pp. 131-132.
[32] Doris Kearns, *Lyndon Johnson*, p. 50.

mat was the same as dozens of other groups ordered into existence by the administration to study one or another problem.[33] In his search for innovation, President Johnson had turned to outside experts. The task forces issued their reports to the President through a senior presidential assistant. They occupied an ambivalent position; they were neither public like the Brownlow committee nor were they nearly as intimately associated with the President as was PACGO.

It is difficult for any advising group to attempt to serve a president while as far removed from his mind as were the task forces created during the Johnson administration. However, most of them were concerned with policy problems, and it can be argued that they were useful for generating fresh ideas. Ten experts do not need access to the Oval Office to put together an approach to urban problems that might appeal to the President and his staff. But it is not clear that reorganization planning can work so profitably under the same conditions. Comprehensive reorganization planning is systemic. Operating in the constellation of the president, it should look at the executive branch in relationship to him, and the boundaries of this system are in part set by the approach of an incumbent president to his administrative role.

THE TASK FORCE ON GOVERNMENT REORGANIZATION

In his first few weeks in office, President Johnson sought guidance for his economizing ambitions. He could strike out at waste in more or less obvious ways, such as his "Memorandum on the Management of the Executive Branch," of November 30, 1963, ordering agency managers to prepare reports on the ways they are seeking to reduce costs.[34] But his search for improved administration required a blueprint.

Planning for Reorganization Planning

In late November Johnson ordered the Bureau of the Budget to prepare a recommendation for an ad hoc reorganization planning group. On

---

[33] For a description of the Johnson era administrative practices of the federal government, including detailed examination of the design of the new departments of the period, see Emmett Redford and Marlan Blissett, *Organizing the Executive: The Johnson Presidency* (Chicago: University of Chicago Press, 1981); for a study of the Johnson White House's use of task forces for policy innovation, see Harry P. Cain, "Confidential Presidential Task Forces: A Case Study in National Policymaking" (unpublished Ph.D. dissertation, Brandeis University, 1972).

[34] *Public Papers of the President, Lyndon B. Johnson, 1963-64*, p. 15.

December 9, the budget bureau presented Johnson with its prospectus for a committee on efficiency in the executive branch.[35] It had been prepared by a group gathered by Director Kermit Gordon which included old BOB hands at reorganization like Harold Seidman and Elmer Staats, a few of the professional economists who had entered the bureau through political appointment since 1961 like Charles Schultze and the director himself, and several academics such as Richard Neustadt. The group thought it desirable to recommend a committee with a sharply specified economizing goal and a given set of defined problems to examine. However, to give this committee the possibility of added breadth and sophistication, members would be appointed to it who were capable of taking the committee beyond its simple but politically useful terms of reference.[36] As Richard Neustadt observed, its chairman would have to be tied to presidential regarding values either through "deep loyalty to Brownlow Committee—BOB-type values or a deep loyalty to Lyndon Johnson." Neustadt's fear was a chairman who saw the committee's mission in "good government" terms.[37]

In the months following the recommendation for a committee on efficiency, Johnson felt congressional pressure to act on reorganization planning.[38] Regardless of the relative successes or failures of the two Hoover Commissions, their historical image is positive enough so that there is always a group in Congress that are ready to create a third "Hoover Commission." During the Johnson presidency, Senator Abraham Ribicoff of Connecticut, a liberal Democrat, became the chief proponent of a Hoover Commission-like reorganization study.[39] Added to this legislative pressure was a call for a renewal of the Hoover Commission by Herbert Hoover himself and some of his associates

[35] "Prospectus: President's Committee on Efficiency in the Executive Branch," December 9, 1963, BOB, 61.1b, Director's Subject File, Efficiency and Economy, 1963-64, RG 51, National Archives.

[36] "Digest of Comments Received on Draft of Prospectus," December 5, 1963, and "Notes on Executive Management Meeting," n.d., *ibid.*

[37] "Notes on Executive Management Meeting," *ibid.*

[38] An early example of this in the administration was a bill to create a permanent Hoover-type commission, an idea which the Bureau of the Budget fought to discourage. Letter, Staats to Representative Riehlman, February 7, 1964, BOB, 61.1a, file F2-2, RG 51, National Archives.

[39] Senator Ribicoff chaired the Reorganization Subcommittee of the Senate Government Organization Committee, and he used that position to espouse a Hoover Commission-like enterprise. See his comments in U.S. Congress, Senate, Subcommittee on Executive Reorganization, *Hearings: Establishing a Commission on the Organization and Management of the Executive Branch*, 90 Cong., 2nd Sess., 1968.

from the second commission.[40] The threat existed that reorganization planning could be initiated by Congress. President Johnson's decision on a reorganization planning vehicle suggests that he gave very high priority to White House control over the planning process. Rather than creating a distinct and visible committee, in the spirit of the budget bureau's recommendation, he joined reorganization planning to his task force approach to policy development.

Planning Guided by Memory—Again

The President created the Task Force on Government Reorganization in mid-summer 1964, and it held its organization meeting on July 23 and 24. Its chairman was Don K. Price of Harvard. Nine persons were appointed, and a tenth person was added a month later. The initial appointments were Price; Stephen K. Bailey, professor at the Maxwell School at Syracuse University; John Dillon, Secretary of the Navy; Rowland Egger, professor at the University of Virginia; James M. Frey, a career member of the budget staff; Ferrel Heady, professor at the University of Michigan; Richard E. Neustadt; Syndey Stein, Jr.; Robert F. Tufts; the tenth member was Eugene P. Foley, head of the Small Business Administration. Assistant Secretary of Defense Solis Horwitz later replaced Dillon. The secrecy with which all this was done is exemplified by Herbert Emmerich's observation in his *Federal Organization and Administrative Management*, published six years after the Price task force, that he can find no record of its membership and no public disclosure of the recommendations of either of the Johnson task forces on reorganization.[41]

Instead of the group of delimited problems that the Bureau of the Budget suggested, the task force took the biggest questions of top-level organization, departmentalization, and executive-legislative relations as its purview. At its first meeting in July, the task force settled on twelve topics to be examined. These included, health, education and welfare functions, transportation, the Executive Office of the President (including overall coordination and management problems),

[40] Correspondence, Hoover to Johnson and Meyer Feldman to Hoover, April 27 and May 6, 1964, White House Central File-Executive, container 29, FG 999-proposed departments, Johnson Library; correspondence and memoranda, BOB, 61.1b, Director's Subject File: Hoover Commission, Proposals for, RG 51, National Archives. My understanding of the Task Force on Government Organization has been furthered through an interview with Don K. Price, November 4, 1982.

[41] Herbert Emmerich, *Federal Organization and Administration Management* (University, Alabama: University of Alabama Press, 1971), p. 176.

housing and community development (including metropolitan problems), top level personnel, and something the task force called "the
general philosophy of reorganization." Under the latter rubric, the
task force wanted to consider alternative institutionalized mechanisms
for reorganization, including the reorganization authority, and it
wanted to examine legislative-executive relations.[42]

The Price task force met a half-dozen times between August and
November 1964. It had no contact with the President and little with
the White House staff. The budget director was the central administration figure in its operation, and the bureau was its basic staff support. The only regular form of contact with the White House was
through the task force's executive secretary, Herbert Jasper, who kept
both the budget director and Bill Moyers at the White House informed
about the task force's activities.

The task force's mode of operation was contemplative. It instituted
no major studies, relying on the Bureau of the Budget for information.
The bureau might be likened to a memory bank into which the task
force was plugged. Like PACGO and the Brownlow Committee, the
task force assumed that the organizational experience and intelligence
of its members provided its most important resource in generating
recommendations. There is much that is positive about the relationship
between the Price task force and the Bureau of the Budget, particularly
because its division of organization and management was chronically
undermanned. But even if the bureau's analytic capacity on administration was limited, its information gathering and storage capacity
was large. Thus the marriage between it and the task force was sym-
biotic. However, there was a problem; the task force's patron was not
the director of the budget. Its real patron, President Johnson, remained
distant.

Distance from the President left the task force adrift. However, it
could easily reach into the accumulated lore of executive branch reforms. Four of its ten members, Price, Bailey, Egger, and Heady, had
participated in comprehensive reorganization planning in the executive
branch, and two others, Neustadt and Stein, had worked in the White
House. Also, half its members were academicians who specialized in
the presidency and national administration, and the standard perspective of those areas of political science was Brownlowian.

The Price task force sent its report to the President on November
6, 1964. The speed with which it accomplished its mission, producing

[42] Memorandum, Jasper to Moyers, August 6, 1964, BOB, 61.1b, Director's Subject
File, Task Force on Government Reorganization, RG 51, National Archives.

a 116-page document in the process, attested to the support role played by the Bureau of the Budget. More important, it demonstrated the task force's ability to call upon the shared memory and unanimity of its members concerning top-level organization in the executive branch.[43] The report stated two ends to be sought through reorganization. The first end was an increase in the executive branch's ability "to administer policies and programs effectively and economically." The second end was to make the executive branch "be responsive to Presidential leadership in developing new policies and programs."[44] The report presented three different categories of reforms that were meant to produce these results. The first contained recommendations for reorganization narrowly understood, the reconstitution of major agencies. The second category presented more or less procedural reforms at top-level managerial levels. The third category addressed the effect of executive-legislative relations.

The organizational changes proposed under the first category called for a major overhaul in the cabinet-level departments, recommending the creation of three new departments: Transportation, Education, and Housing and Community Development. It also suggested the creation of two departments through merger, Economic Development and Natural Resources. The former would combine Commerce, minus its transportation elements with the Small Business Administration, the Office of Economic Opportunity, and some related economic development programs. Labor would later be merged into it. The latter super-department would be based on a merger of Interior and Agriculture, but the report entertained the alternative of merging just land and water programs from Agriculture into Interior if it were politically impossible to abolish the Department of Agriculture.

The rationale for the departmental level recommendations was specific to the department and functions under discussion and offered no overall principle of departmental organization. Three of the recommendations were for departments that would be organized on the basis of high-priority policy areas, Departments of Transportation, Education, and Housing. The two other recommendations followed a principle of aggregating related functions into larger organizational units seeking coordination and economies of scale. The task force applied these two different principles expediently, using each to address separate problems.

[43] Don K. Price, interviewed by author.
[44] President's Task Force on Government Reorganization, "Report," November 6, 1964, container 1, Task Force Reports, Johnson Library.

In its second set of recommendations, the task force spoke to the Executive Office and the upper ranks of the civil service. In regard to the Executive Office it recommended four goals: "Improvement in its capability for program evaluation and review; the removal of agencies with operating responsibilities; the abolition of the independent status of Cabinet Committees; [and] greater flexibility in Executive Office organization."[45] Much of this is the standard presidential strengthening doctrine of reorganization planning. But, note the appearance of a new element. The Price task force is the first reorganization planning vehicle to present policy analysis as a tool of political management for the presidency. What the task force meant by program evaluation was the combination of analytic tools and administrative procedures that would aid in shifting resources within existing budget limits. Policy evaluation, in the report's language, was:

> . . . the analysis of the comparative costs and comparative benefits of the programs of various departments and agencies, seen in all their complicated relationships. Such analysis can now draw on the modern techniques of economic and operational analysis such as have been used as the basis of the new system of executive direction and control in the Department of Defense. . . .
>
> Such review should include more attention to the recurrent activities of the Departments (as well as their proposed increments) than is now given in the regular Budget review. It should be based on a calculation or estimate of the comparative advantages and costs of the various departmental programs (including those *not* closely related to each other) judged in the light of the President's total. . . .[46]

On the personal system, the task force offered recommendations for greater presidential power over those who administer policy. It recommended that Congress create several cabinet-level positions that would be subject to Senate confirmation but whose use and assignment would be at presidential discretion—secretaries without portfolio. It also recommended that the president have the authority to make political appointments to a percentage of super-grade positions, and that he have authority to move super-grade civil servants among agencies.

The task force's final set of observations and recommendations spoke to an issue that no reorganization planning group had addressed so directly; Congress' impact on administrative centralism and pres-

---

[45] *Ibid.*, p. ii and pp. 13-15.
[46] *Ibid.*, pp. 13-14.

idential managerial authority. The Price task force, because it spoke confidentially, could broach this matter openly. First, the task force observed that congressional committees needed reorganization even more pressingly than did the executive agencies. Second, it attacked: "the tendency of particular executive bureaus to make deals with particular Congressional committees in establishing procedures that protect a limited and specialized interest against the general judgment of the Congress and the president."[47] The task force meant ad hoc informal relations between administrators and congressional committees as well as the more formal arrangements whereby the committees or Congress as a whole are brought into the steps of the administrative process; the legislative veto, for example. Finally, the task force urged the President to seek permanent reorganization authority from Congress. The report's discussion of Congress closed with language that resonated with views of Congress among administrative reformers going back to the beginning of the 20th century:

> The President shares with Congress the Constitutional responsibility for the general organization of the Executive Branch. But he alone has the perspective to visualize the complex problems of Government organization, and to appreciate how greatly the success of his policies depends on the soundness of the administrative system by which they must be carried out. If the Congress will in general support his initiative in the improvement of executive organization and in particular grant him permanent authority to initiate reorganization plans, the Nation will find fewer pitfalls ahead in the path that leads toward the Great Society.[48]

BOB as Gatekeeper in Reorganization Planning

Upon its completion, the budget bureau prepared an analysis of the task force's report.[49] It undermined the coherence of the report, reshuffling it as a deck of cards. It lifted out each recommendation for organizational change, biasing the discussion toward the report's organizational dimension, and it reordered these recommendations in terms of the bureau's view of their desirability and political feasibility. The brief mention that the bureau gave to the task force's discussion

[47] *Ibid.*, p. 19.
[48] *Ibid.*, p. 21.
[49] "Recommendations of the Task Force on Government Organization," November 23, 1964, BOB, 61.1a, F2-1, National Archives.

of congressional-executive relations was to dismiss any action as too controversial.

The major task force recommendations that the bureau endorsed were those for which there was already positive sentiment. Task forces on transportation, urban affairs, and education had all recommended organizational changes at either the cabinet level or in the executive office consistent with the recommendations of the Price task force. Thus the bureau was strongest for approving the recommendations for the departments of Transportation and Housing and Urban Development. The bureau also endorsed a program for bringing together water resource programs, but it opposed the task force's recommendation to merge Agriculture and Interior.

The bureau's analysis gave little attention to that part of the task force's report which pertained most directly to the bureau's role; the discussion of policy evaluation. To make the bureau the gatekeeper to the reports of the various task forces had obvious merit; no other agency serving the president possessed its administrative lore or tools. The bureau, however, also had a substantial stake in the matters discussed by the Task Force on Government Reorganization. The task force's brief discussion of the necessity for increasing the Executive Office's policy evaluation capacities was an implicit criticism of the bureau's work. As reviewing agency for this task force report, the bureau was put in the position of evaluating the applicability of parts of the report to itself. Not surprisingly, the bureau's evaluation of the Price report contained no reference to its stress on the importance of strengthening the Executive Office's capacities for policy analysis.

That the Bureau of the Budget played a gatekeeper role for the report of the Price task force would not, by itself, have lessened the utility of that planning endeavor had there been other access points through which the report passed and received sustained attention. But there were none. The report was sent to President Johnson through his staff, but the indication is that it was given only cursory treatment at that level as part of a scanning process through which the President's staff was continually searching for isolated policy proposals.[50]

The Task Force on Governmental Organization

As the war in southeast Asia demanded increasing resources, the President's stress on economy in domestic policy overshadowed his earlier

[50] In this letter to Dean Don Price thanking him for his service as chairman of the task force, the President wrote: "I regret that my schedule made it impossible for me

passion for innovation. The dream of financing new policies through the redirection of current financial resources evaporated in record budget deficits.[51] This financial bind comprised an important part of the background of President Johnson's next foray into reorganization planning.

In his Annual Budget Message of January 24, 1966, Lyndon Johnson reiterated the appeals to economy of his first year in office. As a new theme, he identified management improvement as a natural second stage to the innovation of new programs:

> In moving toward the goals of the Great Society, the enactment of substantive legislation is only the first step. . . . If these laws are to produce the desired results—effectively and at minimum cost to the taxpayer—we cannot afford to cling to organizational and administrative arrangements which have not kept pace with changing needs.[52]

Through 1965 and into 1966 the administration was busy with reorganization proposals, the most dramatic of which were the successful bills for the Departments of Transportation and Housing and Urban Development. Also in 1965 the administration obtained a three-and-a-half-year extension of the president's reorganization authority and used it to successfully introduce five plans in 1965 and five in 1966.[53] None of these plans directly implemented recommendations of the Price task force.[54]

---

to meet personally with your Task Force." Letter, President to Price, December 15, 1964, White House Central File, General, container 406, Task Force on Government Reorganization, Johnson Library.

[51] Federal budget deficits in FY 1967 and FY 1968 were the largest since the Second World War. 1967's deficit was $8.7 billion; the 1968 deficit leaped to a massive $25.2 billion. U.S. Department of Commerce, Bureau of the Census, *Statistical Abstract of the United States, 1978* (Washington: Government Printing Office, 1978), p. 257.

[52] *Public Papers of the Presidents, Lyndon B. Johnson, 1966,* Annual Budget Message to Congress, FY 1967, January 24, 1966, p. 65.

[53] Consistent with the Price task force report, the administration asked for permanent reorganization authority, but Congress granted a three and a half year extension of it. *Public Papers of the Presidents, Lyndon B. Johnson, 1965,* vol. 1, February 3, 1965, pp. 125-126.

[54] The subjects of these ten reorganization plans were as follows:

    1965   No. 1. Bureau of Customs

                No. 2. created Environmental Science Service Admin.

                No. 3. locomotive inspection service of I.C.C.

                No. 4. abolished a number of statutory advisory committees

                No. 5. abolished eight statutory committees advising the Director of NSF

    1966   No. 1. moved Community Relations Service from Commerce to Justice

Several other reorganization-related activities between late 1965 and early 1967 added pressure upon the administration to begin another exercise in comprehensive reorganization planning. In more or less piecemeal fashion, the administration had instituted through the budget bureau a program of productivity measurement, calling upon the agencies to develop studies of their own productivity, using formats and methods devised by the bureau.[55] Thus a data base was accumulating which could be useful if an overall assessment and evaluation system could be instituted. Through his 1965 order that the federal budget cycle adopt a planning-programming-budgeting format, the President established a process within which such analysis might operate, if it were established. Furthermore, calls for substantial reorganization arose again in the Congress during 1966. In particular, pressure developed to address the confusion of inter-governmental administrative relations created by the mandates and grants within recent federal policy.

Senator Muskie (D., Me) urged the President to reinvigorate the Advisory Commission on Intergovernmental Relations as a medium for untangling the knots in the inter-governmental system.[56] At the same time, members of Congress, with Senator Ribicoff in the lead, continued to urge another Hoover commission. Reflecting the quandary of the administration amid these different currents of reform, the Bureau of the Budget's assistant director for management and organization, Harold Seidman, wrote in a memo to the budget director that:

> While in the past we have been generally negative to proposals to establish another Commission . . . , I believe that we ought to re-

---

No. 2. transferred Federal Water Pollution Control Admin. from HEW to Interior

No. 3. centralized authority in HEW

No. 4. National Zoological Park

No. 5. abolished the National Capitol Regional Planning Council

[55] Memorandum, Seidman and Terleckyji to Director, October 8, 1965, BOB, 61.1a, F1-4, RG 51, National Archives. While BOB was working with the bureau heads on productivity, the President pressured his cabinet members for increased attention to economy, devoting a cabinet meeting on May 17, 1966 to the topic. In the memo announcing the meeting, cabinet members were informed: "The President wants to devote this meeting to brief discussions by each member . . . on new ideas for increasing the creative thinking and planning within the Government; increasing and improving the efficiency of your Department operation and ways and means by which the cost of operation of your Department may be lowered." Memorandum, Kintner to cabinet, May 7, 1966, BOB, 61.1a, E2, RG 51, National Archives.

[56] Memorandum, Semer to President, April 12, 1966, White House Central File, Executive, container 1, Johnson Library.

evaluate our position. ... I am coming around reluctantly to the view that a comprehensive study of the organization of the executive branch and a reevaluation of our organizational doctrine are needed and could provide the conceptual framework on which to build a consistent approach in developing solutions to current problems. At present we seem to be going off in several directions at once.[57]

A Task Force with Clout

In September, 1966, the White House domestic staff recommended a new reorganization task force. In a memo to the President, Joseph Califano wrote that its mission would be "to insure the coordination and effective implementation of federal programs, with particular emphasis on programs designed to meet the problems of the cities."[58] For its members, Califano suggested Ben Heineman, president of Northwest Industries; William Capron, a Brookings economist formally with BOB; Hale Champion, Director of Finance for the State of California; Eugene Foley, Director of the Economic Development Administration of the Department of Commerce; Kermit Gordon, an economist who had been Director of the Budget until June 1966; Charles Hitch, Assistant Secretary of Defense and specialist in systems analysis; Lane Kirkland, George Meany's assistant at the AFL-CIO; Richard Lee, mayor of New Haven; Bayless Manning, dean of Stanford's Law School; Robert McNamara, Secretary of Defense; Harry Ranson, president of the University of Texas, and Charles Schultze, the current budget director. Johnson approved Califano's recommendation and chose Heineman as the task force's chairman, designating for membership Capron, Champion, Gordon, Lee, Manning, McNamara, Ranson, and Schultze.[59] He designated the group as the Task Force on Government Organization.

In mid-October, as a result of discussions with Charles Schultze and Robert McNamara, Califano recommended that McGeorge Bundy, former national security adviser and then head of the Ford Foundation, be added to the task force. Indicating how concerned the administration was that Congress might take away the reorganization planning

[57] Memorandum, Seidman to Director, April 5, 1967, BOB, 61.1a, F2-9, Reorganization, RG 51, National Archives.

[58] Memorandum, Califano to President, September 30, 1966, White House Central File, General, container 406, Task Force on Government Reorganization, Johnson Library.

[59] Johnson's practice was to indicate his decision regarding a memorandum' contents on the document itself and return it to the appropriate staff member for action; *ibid.*

ball, Califano told Johnson that, in addition to getting Bundy's governmental experience, that appointment "will serve another purpose,
namely, pulling the Ford Foundation in the direction it is inclined to
go—toward us, rather than Ribicoff when he starts his hearings on
organization of the government . . . next year."[60] President Johnson
approved this addition and two others as well. In early November Ben
Heineman suggested the addition of Herbert Kaufman, a professor of
political science at Yale and a leading student of organization.[61] In
March, 1967, when some aspects of foreign policy and intelligence
organization were added to the task force's agenda, Nicholas Katzenbach, undersecretary of state, was added.[62]

Most of the members of the task force had been associated in other
organizations and commissions; Heineman, for example, had known
and worked with almost all of his colleagues on the task force, and
he felt, while there were differences among the group in its priorities,
they shared an overall perspective of where the problems lay and the
centrality of the presidency in the midst of these. Two exceptions to
these generalizations were Richard Lee and Hale Champion, who were
included to bring perspectives from city to state government to the
task force. But there was an implicit assumption in the group that the
problem to be solved was organizational and that principles attendant
to large organizations are essentially the same wherever they occur,
national government or state, public sector or private, non-profit or
profit-seeking enterprise.[63]

The second task force differed from the first in several aspects that
created the possibility of its having more influence than its predecessor.
Its membership was of a quite different character from the 1964 task
force. Price's group was composed of prominent academicians and a
few businessmen, none having ready access to the President. The
Heineman task force, in contrast, was weighted heavily toward members who were currently or recently in public service; it included only
one person who was primarily a private sector manager, Ben Heineman, and it included only two members who were primarily academicians, Kaufman and Manning. Of those members who were of the

[60] Memorandum, Califano to President, October 10, 1966, White House Central File,
General, container 406, Task Force on Government Reorganization, Johnson Library.

[61] Memorandum, Califano to President, n.d., and presidential telephone message in
response, November 5, 1966, White House Central File, General, container 406, Task
Force on Government Reorganization, Johnson Library.

[62] Ben Heineman, interviewed by author; Califano to President, February 25, 1967,
ibid.

[63] Ben Heineman, interviewed by author.

public sector, Charles Schultze and Robert McNamara had as good access to President Johnson as anyone in the White House. Furthermore, these two, plus Kermit Gordon and McGeorge Bundy, were familiar with the President's administrative style and his organizational needs. Thus the new task force contained far greater political resources and had more specifically applicable information than did its predecessor.

The Heineman task force also differed from Price's in that it had independent staff resources and more time to accomplish its work. Instead of several months, the Heinemann task force was given between eight months and a year.[64] Also, while Ben Heineman had relatively little say in the selection of the task force's membership, he had a free hand in selecting a staff. He subsequently hired Frederic Bohen, an assistant dean at Princeton's Woodrow Wilson School, to serve as the task force's executive secretary. Four more professionals were added to the staff on a full-time basis beginning on January 2, 1967; they were David Davis, formerly an assistant to Hale Champion in California; Armin Rosencranz, a political scientist who had just finished a congressional fellowship of the American Political Science Association; Arthur Solomon, on leave from a position as a manpower expert at the United Planning Organization in Washington; and Joel Sterns, on leave as New Jersey's deputy commissioner for urban affairs. To this staff nucleus, Heineman and Bohen added two budget bureau staffers on a part-time basis; Howard Schnoor, chief of the bureau's government organization branch, and Peter Szanton, deputy director of the bureau's program evaluation staff.[65] Also, the task force would call upon outside consultants, particularly for the purpose of obtaining working papers.

A final distinguishing characteristic of this task force from its predecessor was its charge. The Price task force had a virtual blank check. The Heineman task force had a broad mandate but with rather specific objectives within it. It was instructed to examine the need for the reorganization of federal agencies and to consider whether a formal coordinating agency ought to be set up in the Executive Office. It was also assigned the task of addressing the problems of inter-governmental chaos. The task force was instructed to formulate "an organizational structure to insure coordination and effective implementation of programs in the field." Finally, at Robert McNamara's suggestion, the

[64] Memorandum, Califano to President, October 10, 1966, White House Central File, General, container 406, Task Force on Government Reorganization, Johnson Library.

[65] Memorandum, Bohen to Califano, December 23, 1966, White House Central File, aides, Califano, container 43, Heineman Task Force, Johnson Library.

President also approved the assignment to the task force of examining organizational aspects of foreign policy implementation and intelligence gathering.[66]

Reorganization Planning as First Aid

The administrative entailments of the Great Society posed the task force's most immediate problems. Programs such as community action, job training, and Model Cities strained the capacity of government to implement policy within an intergovernmental framework. The administrative center of the Great Society was the Office of Economic Opportunity. The administration's embarrassment at the criticism of its proudest accomplishments placed OEO at the top of the task force's agenda.[67] At the same time, the task force confronted what might be seen as the agency of the Great Society more broadly understood, the Department of Health, Education, and Welfare. That HEW joined OEO for simultaneous consideration was not only a result of the task force's choice. Prior to the task force's formation, HEW Secretary John W. Gardner devised a plan for the reorganization of HEW. The White House placed the Gardner plan on the task force's agenda just as it was taking up the case of OEO.

The task force's work on OEO and HEW was rushed; it had the character of first-aid treatment rather than surgery. Within six weeks of its organization the task force delivered brief reports on both matters. It appears that the urgency with which the task force worked was political in the sense that the appearance of administrative weaknesses in the Great Society could be the Achilles heel of the domestic Johnson presidency.

The speed with which the task force produced its first two brief reports, those on OEO and the Gardner reform recommendations for HEW, is a testimony both to its capacity to focus quickly and to the ability of its still incomplete staff. At its first meeting, the task force considered the Gardner proposal for HEW reorganization, with Sec-

[66] "Task Force on Governmental Organization," n.d., White House Central File, aides, Gaither, container 318, Johnson Library; Memorandum, Califano to President, October 10, 1966, *ibid.*

[67] John Macy, chairman of the Civil Service Commission and Johnson's main adviser on personnel, thought that OEO's administrative problem was the single most nagging managerial issue for the President. In 1965, at Macy's suggestion, the President created a study team chaired by Bertram M. Harding, then the Deputy Commissioner of the Internal Revenue Service, to recommend improvements in OEO's operation. In 1966, Johnson appointed Harding to the post of Deputy Director of OEO. John Macy, interviewed by author.

retary Gardner explaining it.[68] The essence of the plan was to re-structure HEW along what he described as a Department of Defense model, creating three sub-cabinet departments within the existing department, each headed by a secretary.[69] The secretary would become a super-secretary over secretaries of Health, Education, and Welfare. The task force questioned the manner in which this reform addressed what they viewed as the central problem of HEW: its inability to evaluate programs and shift resources on the basis of systematic analysis. After his meeting with the task force Fred Bohen wrote to Secretary Gardner:

> If the functions of health, education, and welfare are to remain the responsibility of one member of the Cabinet, the Task Force seeks greater assurance that proposals for change will actually strengthen the hand of the Secretary of HEW for program and policy planning and analysis, for resources allocation and decision making and execution, and for coordination across program lines, both in Washington and in the field.[70]

The task force also raised political questions about the proposed reorganization. Bohen's memo noted that constituency groups of the various agencies of HEW were sensitive to the organizational rank of their agencies. For example, supporters of the Children's Bureau had long been unhappy with its demotion to a lower level of the HEW organization than it had formerly occupied in the Department of Labor.[71] Meeting on December 3, the task force returned to the consideration of the HEW proposal, deciding to recommend against it.[72]

At the same time that the task force was working on the HEW reorganization proposal, it was developing some quick recommendations for the Office of Economic Opportunity. But, unlike the HEW item, which was discussed at length during the first meeting, the matter of OEO and the administration of the War on Poverty was initially sketched out in a staff paper by Fred Bohen and Joel Stern. After the

[68] Task Force on Government Organization, Agenda, November 12, 166 meeting, White House Central File, aides, Gaither, container 284, McNamara Arrangement, Task Force Material, Johnson Library.

[69] Memorandum, Heineman to President, December 31, 1966, White House Central File, aides, Califano, container 43, Heineman Task Force, Johnson Library.

[70] Memorandum, Bohen to Gardner, November 22, 1966, White House Central File, aides, Bohen, container 5, Gordon, Reorganization, Johnson Library.

[71] Ibid.,

[72] Task Force on Government Organization, Memorandum for the President, December 31, 1966, White House Central File, aides, Califano, container 43, Heineman Task Force, Johnson Library.

task force's discussion of that paper at its meeting of December 4, Heineman and staff prepared a draft report which was circulated to the members.[73] A final memo was prepared for the President, conveying the task force's immediate recommendations on the organization of the War on Poverty. That there was a sense of great urgency in submitting this report is indicated by the fact that only one draft of it was circulated among the task force members; the chairman himself took responsibility for reconciling the various individual responses of the members.[74] On December 15, Ben Heineman presented to President Johnson the report, "The Organization of the War on Poverty and the Future of the Office of Economic Opportunity."

The report's assumptions regarding the War on Poverty were that, one, its melange of policies required increased inter-agency coordination, and, two, its heart was represented by the community action program. To speak to these needs, the task force recommended that a presidential special assistant be appointed, with the particular responsibility of coordinating the War on Poverty programs, removing that responsibility from OEO's director. OEO itself should be turned into an agency whose prime responsibility was for the community action program and experimentation in social policy. The report recommended that its existing programs, such as the Job Corp and Head Start, be shifted to appropriate departments, and new programs developed within OEO should be moved as they matured. Finally, the report stressed the need for the remaining, pared down, OEO to improve its instruments for overseeing the financial responsibility of community action programs.[75]

Following delivery of the report on OEO to the President, Joseph Califano discussed it with task force members Charles Schultze and Kermit Gordon.[76] Califano's summary of the task force report for the President gives as much space to Schultze's and Gordon's opinions as to the recommendations themselves. The disposition of the initial Heineman task force reports signalled the task force's influence. The President put off Secretary Gardner's proposal for HEW reorganization. Regarding OEO, the President followed two of the recommen-

[73] Task Force on Government Organization, Agenda, December 3 & 4, 1966 meeting, White House Central File, Files of James Gaither, container 284, McNamara Arrangement, Task Force Material, Johnson Library.

[74] Memorandum, Heineman to task force members, December 15, 1966, White House Central File, aides, Califano, container 43, Heineman Task Force, Johnson Library.

[75] Task Force on Government Organization, Memorandum to the President, December 15, 1966, ibid.

[76] Memorandum, Califano to President, December 15, 1966, ibid.

dations: that management over the community action programs be tightened and that some of OEO's functions be transferred to appropriate departments.[77]

New Routes to Central Management

At its January 21, 1967, meeting, the task force began consideration on the domestic departments and presidential management. Herbert Kaufman and BOB official William Cary discussed the report of the 1965 task force on inter-governmental relations. David Davis of the staff gave a briefing on Senator Muskie's recent hearings on inter-governmental problems. Finally, Joseph Califano and William Carey described the organization of the Executive Office, with stress on its elements aimed at dealing with Great Society programs, inter-governmental relations, and programs planning and evaluation.[78]

The meeting culminated in agreement to consider alternative models for a staff agency for domestic program management within the Executive Office, the predominant thinking at the meeting being that such an agency would be a "twin or parallel to the Bureau of the Budget."[79] Afterward staff members developed different designs for such an agency. Each of the different arrangements for such an agency assumed that the major thrust for it would be to address problems of inter-governmental administration through one or another means, us-

[77] In his message to Congress on March 4, 1967, accompanying the Economic Opportunity Act of 1967, President Johnson called for managerial improvement in auditing, personnel management, and standard setting, and his bill incorporated features aimed at these areas. *Public Papers of the Presidents, Lyndon B. Johnson, 1967*, Vol. I, pp. 331-346. Also, in 1967 some of OEO's job training programs were shifted to the Department of Labor. There would likely have been more such transfers if that issue had not been politicized by the congressional Republicans during 1967, with legislative attempts to strip OEO of its operating roles by moving all of its programs to the appropriate departments. *New York Times*, April 11, June 9, and June 13, 1967.

More direct evidence of the administration's acceptance of the task force's recommendations on OEO is to be found in a statement Califano made to President Johnson: "We plan to adopt several of its tightening recommendations in our bill and your Message." Memorandum, Califano to President, February 25, 1967, White House Central File, General, container 406, Task Force on Government Reorganization, Johnson Library.

[78] Drawn from a summary of the discussion of the January 21, 1967 meeting in a working paper by Fred Bohen, "Five Models for a Domestic Program Office," White House Central File, File of James Gaither, container 249, Formal Approaches, Johnson Library.

[79] *Ibid.*

ing the prestige and resources of the presidency to lend clout to a broad coordination effort.[80]

Another staff paper growing out of the January meeting indicates a second theme in the task force's view: the promise of program evaluation for improving the performance of the federal government.[81] This paper highlighted for the task force the paucity of evaluation of programs in government. It suggested a necessary connection between basic research on social problems and the analysis of program performance. The paper observed that there was virtually no organized effort in government to analyze the social mechanisms of the problems addressed by policy.

Together, the papers on top-level coordination and the evaluation made explicit the connection between an *organization* for improved management and the *intellectual tools* upon which improved management must depend. The Price task force had been the first comprehensive reorganization planning group to even tentatively raise the relationship between these two elements of management. Now these elements were connected plainly and concretely. These ideas developed against the background of PPB's full-scale introduction to the budget process in 1965. PPB would ostensibly provide a regular means through which the data necessary for the evaluation of program effectiveness would be available to the Executive Office of the President. However, as the task force observed, the serious problem remained of the lack of a capacity within the Executive Office to use such data for program evaluation, not to speak of the total absence of any capacity to examine the social problems at which such programs were aimed.

The task force's staff warned against viewing any form of top-level organizational innovation as a panacea, even as it developed papers on a number of different approaches to the problem of top-level coordination.[82] As staff director Bohen put the issue: "The staff has reservations about the desirability, efficacy, and utility (*especially to the President*) of superimposing a Presidential structure on top of a host of rather fundamental weaknesses and problems within the structure of American Government, which the new volume of complex

[80] *Ibid.*

[81] Task Force on Government Organization, "Improving the Evolution of Federal Programs," February 21, 1967, White House Central File, aides, Bohen, container 4, Executive Office Organization, Johnson Library.

[82] Memorandum, Bohen to task force members, February 16, 1967, White House Central Files, Files of James Gaither, container 294, Models for Domestic Program Office, Johnson Library.

THE GREAT SOCIETY | 255

domestic social programs has exposed. . . ."[83] At its February meeting, the task force heard Professor Wallace S. Sayre of Columbia University, who echoed Bohen's view. Sayre offered an overview of new problems of regional coordination of executive agencies and of the interface among levels of government. But, rather than seeing these regional-inter-governmental issues as utterly novel, Sayre saw them as connected to the traditional issue of presidential management:

> The needs of the President require that his leadership over the executive agencies in Washington be greatly improved in strength before he is asked to risk his resources in field coordination of the executive agencies, particularly to equip regional officials with the power of decision.[84]

Sayre, along with its own staff, urged the task force to see that until a means was found through which a president could impose his agenda on the executive branch agencies, the regional and inter-governmental dilemmas would remain unsolvable. Administrative decentralization can follow only after effective administrative centralization.[85] This is the case for two distinct reasons. One, only through such centralization could the president effect a regionally coordinated solution to the field activities of federal agencies. Two, only a centralized executive branch would be relatively uninviting to the temptation on the part of state and local officials to seek at the level of national administration what they could not achieve in the bargaining process that would characterize highly regionalized administration within the federal system.

Consequently, the task force attempted to chart a course which would combine a coordinating organization for the Executive Office with the analytic capacity to endow the president with the centralizing ability to make informed decisions about resource allocation. This ambition is addressed in three different ways in the task force's first large report, "The Organization and Management of Great Society Programs."[86] These were, one, consideration of a means for program coordination; two, identification of a need for program design, de-

---

[83] *Ibid.*

[84] Wallace S. Sayre, "Some Notes on Presidential Leadership of Executive Agencies" (a written summary of remarks made at task force meeting of February 26, 1967) White House Central File, Bohen Office File, container 7, Sayre Material, Johnson Library.

[85] The logic of the discussion in the task force implicitly follows a classic argument about centralization and reform, see Morton Grodzins, "Centralization and Decentralization in the American Federal System," in Robert A. Goldwin (ed.), *A Nation of States* (Chicago: Rand McNally, 1961), in particular, pp. 21-23.

[86] Submitted to the President on June 15, 1967.

velopment, and evaluation within the president's support system; and, three, a proposed reorganization of the executive departments upon the basis of a super-department principle.

The first of these, a mechanism for program coordination, was the most troublesome of the three elements. Improved program coordination was the means through which the task force hoped to engage the problems of field implementation and inter-governmental chaos that were central parts of its assignment. Yet the question remained, how did this issue (and its solution) relate to the basic, presidential-strengthening orientation of the task force? Were inter-agency program coordination and improved field administration inescapably parts of the president's responsibility? Should a mechanism devised to address these problems be located within the Executive Office of the President?

The suggested solution developed in a working paper written by task force consultant I. M. Destler.[87] Destler's formulation of a co-ordinating mechanism began with a set of premises already accepted by the task force, such as the particular need for coordination in the human services and urban policy areas and the need for presidential level coordination because of the policy problems that cut across agency lines. Destler's working paper proposed a coordinating bureau within the Executive Office with an attached field staff. To give it leverage, Destler suggested a clearance system for agency operating regulations similar to BOB's legislative clearance role.

In contrast to Destler's paper, another of the task force's consultants presented a memo which argued against a coordinating agency.[88] Allen Schick took the position that coordination was not a presidential activity. He argued that the coordinating agency idea would result in the imposition upon the president of concerns that pertain essentially to a field or departmental viewpoint. He stated:

> As a presidential agency, EOP's main concern must be with presidential choice, not with the field or departments. The latter become relevant for presidential attention only when they bear on national policy, program decisions, financial choice and other presidential matters. The President cannot be and his direct agents cannot be

[87] I. M. Destler, "Integrating Program Coordination in the Executive Office of the Presidency: Organizational Needs, Problems, and Alternatives," March 27, 1967, White House Central File, Aides, and Alternatives," March 27, 1967, White House Central File, aides, Bohen, container 4, Executive Office Organization, Johnson Library.

[88] Allen Schick, "Preliminary Thoughts on the Evaluation and Coordination of Federal Policy," March 30, 1967, *ibid.*

program managers or field coordinators. The scale and sprawl of federal involvements constrain against such a role.[89]

At the heart of Schick's objection to a centralized coordinating agency was the idea that it centralized the wrong thing. To his mind, "program execution . . . is primarily a non-central function." But decision making about programs is a central concern, Schick asserted, and information pertaining to program function, its evaluation, and an organization to facilitate that decision making within a generally coordinated federal structure belonged in the Executive Office.

A majority of the task force remained unshaken in their commitment to a centralized coordinating agency, and the task force report on "The Organization and Management of Great Society Programs" recommended the establishment of an Office of Program Coordination in the Executive Office. It is not that the task force ignored the argument that specific program coordination is not a presidential function. Rather, it chose to pointedly disagree with it. In the report's discussion of the presidency's institutional weaknesses, the first major point was that the president lacks "institutional staff and machinery":

> . . . to anticipate, surface, assess and settle wasteful program and jurisdictional conflicts between peer Federal departments in Washington; to control and pull together the related programs of Federal departments in Washington and in the field; to mediate problems and disputes between Federal departments in the field; to reflect the presidential perspective in program areas requiring cooperation between Federal agencies and between Federal, State and local government.[90]

Disagreement arose in the task force over the location of an office of program coordination. A minority composed of Heineman, McNamara, and Schultze would have preferred to locate a new coordinating organization and staff within a greatly reorganized Bureau of the Budget. The majority preferred independence from BOB. But the report's language clearly indicated the relative unimportance of this disagreement in stating: "Members of the Task Force unanimously view the need for the creation of this office as far more important than its precise location in the Executive Office."[91]

[89] Ibid.

[90] Task Force on Government Organization, "The Organization and Management of Great Society Programs," June 17, 1967, p. 2, Task Force Reports, container 4, Johnson Library.

[91] Ibid., p. 3 and pp. 7-10.

As a second means to creating stronger presidential management, the task force considered ways to develop a program development and evaluation capacity in the Executive Office. Peter Szanton set the agenda for the task force by conceptualizing the president's program development interests as three-fold: program definition, program design, and program evaluation.[92] Both Szanton and Allen Schick recommended that the logical home for those tasks would be a reorganized Bureau of the Budget. Allen Schick argued that the Bureau of the Budget required transformation, with program evaluation becoming its central activity and perspective.[93]

The task force adopted most of the staff's ideas on program development. It accepted the notion that program development must be seen broadly, that it must include regular, in-depth attention to the causes of social problems, and that it should be located in the Bureau of the Budget. Thus in its report, "The Organization and Management of Great Society Programs," the task force recommended a major reorganization of the Bureau of the Budget. As the report stated, echoing Allen Schick's analysis of the problem: "Reorganization should speed up sharply the bureau's transition from intelligent reaction to departmental demands to active, independent leadership in program development that supports and is responsive to the President and his perspective."[94] This change was to be effected by creating an office of program development within BOB.

The third element of the task force's concept development regarding a strengthened presidency was its recommendation on departmental reorganization. The task force's staff's work substantially broadened the traditional principle of organization by like purpose or function. In a staff paper, David Davis observed that the domestic agencies represented "a curious mixture of economic development, economic analysis, conservation, provision of services to special clienteles, regulation, and preservation or enhancement of the environment."[95] It was as if the departments were each a swirl of intermixed purposes. But, Davis observed, the overall activities of the domestic departments,

[92] Peter Szanton, "Organizing the Executive Office of the President for Better Program Development," March 27, 1967, White House Central File, Files of James Gaither, container 250, Task Force on Government Organization, Johnson Library.

[93] Allen Schick, "Some Budgetary Prerequisites for Program Planning: A Critical Analysis," n.d., White House Central File, aides, Bohen, container 4, Executive Office Organization, Johnson Library.

[94] "The Organization and Management of Great Society Programs," p. 11.

[95] David W. Davis, "Remaining Domestic Executive Departments: Some Organizational Problems and Alternatives," March 28, 1967, White House Central File-aides-Bohen, container 4, Domestic Executive Departments, Johnson Library.

aside from HEW, could be broken into neat categories such as economic development and natural resources, and these categories could become the basis for broad departments spanning a field the way Health, Education, and Welfare spanned human services. Consequently, Davis prepared a set of alternative departmental reorganization plans displaying different degrees of departmental consolidation.

The task force broached departmental organization more gingerly than it had other issues. The task force members were intellectually disposed toward large-scale reorganizations producing super-departments. Heineman and McNamara had extensive experience with successfully managing huge private sector organizations, large even by the standards of federal departments, and McNamara seemed to have succeeded at managing Defense, the second largest of federal departments.[96] But the political barriers to large-scale departmental reorganization seemed too great.

The task force concluded that departmental management is a function of adequate support and not size. In "The Organization and Management of Great Society Programs," it gave high priority to recommendations for strengthening the managerial supports of department secretaries, increasing staff, and improving budgeting, legislative planning, and administrative procedures at the secretary's level. But the report was silent on large-scale departmental change, suggesting only a few medium-scale revisions such as shifting all manpower programs from Labor to HEW. The most extensive organizational change recommended by the "Great Society" report concerned field organization in several domestic departments.[97]

An Uncompromised Recommendation

Noting that its reports so far were attentive to feasibility and that the American political system displayed "a continuing compromise between the dictates of a pluralistic political process and the requirements of orderly management," the task force produced a final domestic report offering a longer-range and less-compromised view of national government. In a report titled "Future Organization of the Executive Branch," it attacked the pluralistic tendency toward more and narrower departments. Consolidated departments would create a level

[96] For a case study exhibiting McNamara's use of managerial tactics, staff, and systems analysis to assert central authority over the services, see Robert Art, *The TFX Controversy* (Boston: Little, Brown, 1968).

[97] "The Organization and Management of Great Society Programs," pp. 12-17.

below the president at which competing interests and broadly related programs could be balanced and coordinated. Therefore, the report stated: ". . . the future . . . organization of the Executive Branch should be shaped over time to provide a small number of appointive deputies (4-6) to manage the full range of Executive departments and agencies short of the President."[98] The report asserted that such a reform would strengthen the president in that it would channel significant administrative decisions into arenas responsive to presidential priorities. The breadth of the aggregated departments, it was assumed, would free the secretaries from their narrow constituencies.

In its final form, the task force added to the report a forceful statement of the relationship between organization and presidential positional power:

> We urge resistance by Presidents to the perpetual political pressures to create more executive departments and independent agencies. Unchecked, these pressures to widen the President's span of control will eliminate the possibility of meaningful direction from, and contact between, the President and the major line officials of his Administration.[99]

In effect, the task force was saying, the president must defend the political integrity of the hierarchical structure of the executive branch, counterposing centralizing management to the decentralizing pressures of the political process. However, the report continued, the present organization of the executive branch was an infirm basis for presidential leadership. It noted that: "The Presidency . . . is not now supported by the line organization required to support its obligations for leadership in policy development or administration."[100] To serve the need for the office and its functional obligations, the line departments must be reconstructed.

To this end, the task force recommended the reorganization of the twelve cabinet departments into seven departments. Four super-departments would be created, Social Services, National Resources, Economic Affairs, and Science and Environmental Preservation. Social

[98] Memorandum, Bohen to Task Force members, August 23, 1967, White House Central File, Files of James Gaither, container 247, Government Organization Perspectives, Johnson Library; draft report, "Future Organization of the Executive Branch," August 23, 1967, *ibid.*

[99] Task Force on Government Organization, "A Recommendation for the Future Organization of the Executive Branch," September 15, 1967, p. 1, Task Force Reports, container 4, Johnson Library.

[100] *Ibid.*

Services would bring together most of HEW with the Veterans Admin-istration, Office of Economic Opportunity, the Equal Opportunity Employment Commission, and the Department of Labor's manpower programs. National Resources and Development would include large parts of HUD, Transportation, Agriculture, and the land, water, and mineral resource programs in Interior and the Corp of Engineers. Economic Affairs would combine Treasury, Commerce, the remaining parts of Labor and regulatory activities from Agriculture and Interior. Finally, Science and Environmental Preservation would be built from National Aeronautic and Space Administration, the Atomic Energy Commission, the Environmental Science Service Administration, and environmental programs currently located in HEW, Interior, and Com-merce. The report also recommended aggregating organization in the foreign affairs and national defense areas, recommending a Depart-ment of Foreign Affairs incorporating State, the Agency for Interna-tional Development, and the United States Information Agency. A proposed Department of National Security Affairs would be built from Defense and the intelligence collection function of the CIA. Of all the current cabinet level departments, only Justice would remain un-touched in the task force's long-range recommendations.

Last Things

The Heineman task force concluded with reports on economic policy and foreign affairs sent to the President in the early fall of 1977. The report on the organization of economic advice suggested that the single best change that President Johnson could effect in the economic policy area would be a Department of Economic Affairs. Such a department, the report reasoned, would overcome: "the existence of several special-interest executive departments, each holding a stake in only part of the national economy, and none now capable of serving as a neutral, Presidential instrument of program or policy on broad-gauged eco-nomic issues or problems that affect 'their' clientele."[101]

But recognizing the dim early prospects for such a department, the task force offered several smaller-scale reforms in the organization of economic policy.[102] It suggested a reorganization of the Department

---

[101] *Ibid.*, p. 3.

[102] The organizational setting of economic policy formulation in the Johnson admin-istration is described by James E. Anderson, "Managing the Economy: The Johnson Administration's Experience," paper presented to the 1980 Meeting of the American Political Science Association, Washington, D.C. For a study of the Ford administration's contrasting efforts at the organizational rationalization of economic policy formulation,

of Commerce identical to that forwarded by the Price task force in 1964. With the administration's proposed merger of Commerce and Labor having collapsed six months earlier, the task force suggested the more modest alternative of building up Commerce into a department of broad economic concerns while weaning it from its close relationship with the business community. The task force also recommended a staff in the Executive Office which would pull together germane data from throughout government and coordinate economic policy. Finally, though the Federal Reserve's relationship to presidentially directed economic policy had been good in the recent past, the task force thought that institutional reforms ought to be instituted at the Fed that would make it more responsive to presidential leadership. Noting the difficulty of lessening its formal independence, the task force recommended that the Federal Reserve's chairman's term be made coterminous with that of the president, that the size of the board be reduced from seven to five, with terms shortened from 14 to 10 years, and that monetary policy be made the direct responsibility of the board, with the Fed's Open Market Committee being abolished.

The last report, "Organization for the Management and Coordination of Foreign Affairs," was a product of a rump group formed largely from the original task force.[103] Four members of the task force were dropped—Hale Champion, Herbert Kaufman, Richard Lee, and Harry Ransom—and one member was added, Under-Secretary of State Nicholas Katzenbach. The organizational problems of the foreign policy system identified by the task force were three: (1) neither White House nor State Department gives overall and continuing guidance to all the agencies within the foreign policy system; (2) there is no single organizational source providing the president with "comprehensive analysis" of foreign afffairs; (3) there is no overall budget review wherein the budgets of all the agencies engaged in foreign policy are looked at "from the perspective of the priorities, commitments and requirements of foreign policy."[104]

The proposed solution to these varied problems lay in establishing a point of continuous and full authority over the foreign policy system. At one and the same time, this authority had to be responsive to the president and yet able to carry the burden of overseeing foreign policy

see Roger Porter, *Presidential Decision Making* (New York: Cambridge University Press, 1980), esp. Chaps. 1-3.

[103] Task Force on Government Organization, "Organization for the Management and Coordination of Foreign Affairs," October 1, 1967, Task Force Reports, container 4, Johnson Library.

[104] *Ibid.*, p. 3.

at one step removed from the president. This authority, the task force decided, should be the Secretary of State, who must, in the words of the task force, "advise him and act for him across the whole range of his international responsibilities."[105] The presidential national security adviser and the National Security Council's staff were dismissed as candidates for this role because it would only create greater conflicts in the foreign policy process (between itself and the Secretary of State) and reduce their utility as a personal presidential advising system.

However, the task force realized, the Secretary of State was severely hampered in playing the role recommended; he was occupied with his own department's administrative problems, responsibility as the government's chief negotiator, prime world traveler, and ceremonial stand-in for the president. Therefore, the task force reasoned, the office itself must be redefined, asserting: "The Secretary of State must become not primarily a diplomat, a defender of policy, or an international negotiator (although he will on occasion be all of these) but preeminently the director and coordinator for and on behalf of the President, of all U.S. foreign and national security policy."[106] The means for doing this would be to establish a new post of Deputy Secretary of State and, perhaps, another position, such as Chief Negotiator. The deputy secretary would reduce the secretary's managerial burdens within State while the establishment of another post (or posts) for negotiations and ceremonial functions would leave the secretary of state to fulfill the new role of overseer of all American foreign policy. All this, of course, will sound more than faintly familiar; the Heineman task force was reinventing the First Secretary concept of the Eisenhower era.

The major Heineman task force reports reached President Johnson at a time that was inauspicious for organizational reforms. By late 1967 the domestic organizational and policy problems that were addressed by the task force had been overshadowed by Vietnam and its domestic political consequences. The consequences of the task force's work can be properly appreciated only when it is remembered that the political end of the Johnson administration was only months away.

REORGANIZATION PLANNING IN THE JOHNSON ADMINISTRATION

The Heineman task force had an immediate influence on the administration's actions. First, it was used to address the two pressing ques-

[105] *Ibid.*, p. 7.
[106] *Ibid.*, p. 8.

tions of reforming OEO and assessing HEW's plan for reorganization. Second, the administration's 1967 Equal Opportunity Act contained some of the task force's recommendations. Another indication of the task force's influence is its relationship to the Bureau of the Budget. The Price task force, like the substantive policy-oriented task forces, was subject to processing and review by the bureau. In contrast, the Heineman task force was independent of the bureau. Its report on "The Organization and Management of Great Society Programs" called for a major reorganization of the bureau so as to reorient it to a program development and evaluation perspective.

Like the rest of its "Great Society" report, the recommendations for the reorganization of the Bureau of the Budget and the establishment of an Office of Program Coordination were not implemented. But Doris Kearns testifies that President Johnson seriously considered establishing the Office for Program Coordination.[107] A month after the "Great Society" report was sent to Joseph Califano he wrote to the President: ". . . the proposals to strengthen the Executive Office of the president are clearly steps in the right direction. Schultze is carrying out his own study of BOB and I will be working closely with him, Heineman, and Kermit Gordon to develop a practical and workable plan to moderate BOB, so it can be an instrument of much greater power and use to you."[108] Following upon the task force report, a large-scale (and defensive) self-study was conducted in the bureau to grab the initiative on reform.

Although the Heineman task force reported at an inauspicious time for administrative reform, in contrast with the earlier Price task force it was by far the more effective planning endeavor. The Price task force was too far removed from the President's concerns to be able to read his managerial needs. Thus the task force could have recourse only to the lore of administrative reform. There was no single reason why the first task force was so far removed from the sphere of its natural concerns; there is no evidence at all that there was an intention to put the task force into a vacuum. The sin was one of omission rather than commission. No one in the administration seemed to have thought about the requirements of a reorganization planning vehicle that would adequately consider the problem of reform in light of the incumbent president's interests. Everything about the Price task force cut against its ability to work on an intimate basis with President Johnson's needs. It was kept at arms length from the White House by

---

[107] Quoted in Doris Kearns, *Lyndon Johnson*, p. 292.
[108] Quoted in Larry Berman, *The Office of Management and Budget*, p. 101.

having to work through the Bureau of the Budget. Its membership included no one who had easy access to the President. Finally, the task force was not given a presidential agenda to work upon; rather, it devised its own working agenda without regard to the President's priorities and problems.

The Heineman task force, by contrast to its immediate predecessor, has some of the qualities of Eisenhower's PACGO. It worked upon several problems that were specifically given to it as high-priority concerns in the Johnson administration. Its membership contained at least two people who had very easy access to the President and who were trusted by him, Robert McNamara and Charles Schultze. The task force also dealt directly with the White House—Joe Califano acting as liaison between the President and the task force—rather than having to filter everything it did through the Bureau of the Budget. Thus in a way that was impossible for the Price task force, the Heineman task force responded to presidential expectations and needs. In this, the Heineman task force stands in a line, a reorganization planning vehicle at the service of the managerial presidency which begins with PACGO and stretches through the 1970's. In contrast, the Price task force is anomalous; its operation and recommendations were secret, yet it had no access to the President's concerns and plans such that the secrecy under which it operated was justified. The Johnson administration appears to have been slow to learn the prerequisites of reorganization planning as an activity within the managerial presidency. Its first attempt was inadequate, and by the time it got around to a second attempt, the administration was beset by problems for which reorganization planning had no solutions.

While there are significant differences in the operation and influence of these two task forces, it is instructive to note their substantive similarities. Operating within three years of each other, they allow one to see into the intellectual substratum beneath reorganization planning during the 1960's. If we compare the recommendations of the task forces, two ideas are tentatively introduced by the Price task force which then receive fuller and firmer treatment by its successor. These notions pertain to policy analyses and departmental organization.

The first task force's report had stressed the need for what it called "program evaluation and review" in the Executive Office, without offering a specific organizational recommendation through which those capabilities might be effected. But, its report praised initial efforts toward program evaluation as represented by joint work between the Bureau of the Budget and the Office of Science and Technology in assessing major capital expenditures for scientific research. The report's unspoken recommendation, therefore, seems to be that the Bureau of the Budget be strengthened as that staff agency for conducting program evaluation. The second task force gave more attention to policy analysis than did its predecessor, and it offered specific organizational recommendations through which the analysis of policy, from its development stage through evaluation of its impact, could be implanted in the Executive Office.

The intellectual substratum of these two task forces was formed by the assumption that public policies could be developed and assessed with analytic devices pioneered by engineering, the information sciences, and the social sciences.[109] To all appearances, a policy science was an idea whose time had come; techniques in diverse disciplines offered building blocks for an applied science of public policy, and the policy commitments that developed in the 1960's produced a heretofore unknown density and complexity of domestic policies. It might be that a government of limited ends could ascertain its policies in terms of a pluralistic political bargaining process, seeing policy choice as a matter of political bargains struck among interests rather than a maximizing decision about the optimal use of limited resources. But in the face of greatly increased governmental ambitions confronting urban decline, poverty, educational crises, etc., many sensible observers hoped Henry Rowen was correct in saying:

> What do I mean by analysis? . . . suffice it to mean an attempt to define objectives, to describe alternative means to these ends, to invent new objectives and new alternative means, to assess benefits and costs, to take account of uncertainties, to quantify what looks useful to quantify, to isolate decisions that can be deferred from those that can't, to create options. All this may appear ordinary. It is, but it is often difficult to do and it hasn't been attempted much in a systematic way on major public decisions. With results in the Defense Department that are impressive; I predict that results throughout other parts of government will, in time, be at least as impressive.[110]

---

[109] Among the leading examples during the 1960's of work aimed at developing a framework for a policy science is Yehezkel Dror, *Public Policymaking Reexamined* (Scranton, Pa.: Chandler, 1968). For a broad-gauged critique of this instrumental view of policy assessment, see Aaron Wildavsky, *Speaking Truth to Power* (Boston: Little, Brown, 1979).

[110] Rowen made this remark in a paper presented to the 1966 meeting of the American Political Science Association, published in excerpted form as, Henry Rowen, "Bargaining and Analysis in Government," in Michael Reagan (ed.), *The Administration of Public Policy* (Glenview, Ill.: Scott, Foresman, 1969), p. 122.

The application of policy analysis to the federal government raised two different questions: the first concerned the methodological issues entailed in a working policy science; the second question concerned the organizational place for such a function within government, assuming the solution to the first questions. Underlining the importance of this second concern, Yehezkel Dror has observed that: "Improving policymaking requires, among other things, improving the various major organizations that make up the public-policymaking system, which in turn requires, besides everything else . . . establishing and reinforcing special staff units to be in charge of policy knowledge."[111] Both the task forces addressed only that second question, assuming the solution of whatever intellectual problems remained in building a policy science. Thus, they groped with issues of organization and location.

The new organizational principle of super-departments which began to emerge in the Price and Heineman task forces was an expression of reorganization planning's new focus on policy analysis. The Price task force broached a super department format only tentatively, similar to its vague discussion of the proper locus within the Executive Office for an enlarged capacity for policy analysis. Part of the Price task force's appearance of ambivalence on organizational design matters stems from the fact that two different principles of departmental organization undergirded its recommendation. It proposed five new departments to be created out of the existing domestic departments (with Justice and Treasury left untouched). Three of these—Transportation, Education, and Housing and Community Development—were of a contemporary importance such that the relevant federal agencies ought to be built around those purposes and given cabinet status as a matter of policy priority. The two other departments recommended by the task force reflected a different principle. Economic Development and Natural Resources were conglomerate departments, compiling existing departments into large aggregates. Aggregate departments would subsume what had been competing organizations, forcing intradepartmental solutions to competing agency claims.

The Heineman task force embraced the principle of super-departments more thoroughly. It asserted:

> We do not believe that either the Nation or the President can afford, today or in the future, waste the President's major line deputies in the running of interference or errands for narrow groups. We believe that Presidential line subordinates who must reconcile

[111] Y. Dror, *Public Policymaking Reexamined*, p. 266.

competing special program interests will be far more useful and much more responsive to, and representative of, Presidential perspectives and objectives than the scores of parochial department and agency heads who now share the line responsibilities of the executive branch, short of the President.[112]

But the task force believed another condition in addition to aggregation was necessary for the super-departments to fulfill these expectations. They must have adequate staff, and they must have capacities within their departments for the development and assessment of policy. Through new staff means and through systems analysis Robert McNamara appeared to achieve great central control over the separate services at Defense. Thus capable departmental management is not so much related to variables such as size, client, or mission as it is to what might be thought of as managerial leverage based on analytic tools.

Although the Heineman task force's early work on the OEO was influential on the Johnson administration's reform of it, none of its later, more ambitious, recommendations were implemented by the administration. The evidence is that the President favored the task force's central recommendations and planned to implement some of them after his reelection in 1968.[113] But of course there was no reelection; on March 31, 1968 Lyndon Johnson withdrew from the presidential race. His presidency was in tatters, and the rational executive order that administrative reform sought was asymmetrical to the political chaos of 1968.

But the idea of reorganization planning was not yet dead within the Johnson administration. In a new form, it reoccurred in the administration's last months, suggesting the degree to which President Johnson viewed reorganization planning as a presidential tool. In the euphoric period after his March 31st announcement, the President planned to initiate grand enterprises evoking the public interest rather than electoral partisanship. One of those enterprises was to be a broad-gauged

---

[112] "A Recommendation for the Future Organization of the Executive Branch," pp. 5-6.

[113] After all the Heineman task forces reports had been submitted to the White House, Joseph Califano told Ben Heineman that President Johnson had read them all, with great interest. Moreover, he told Heineman that the President intended to act on the reports' recommendations in his second term. Ben Heineman, interviewed by author. In a confidential memorandum written in late spring of 1968. Joseph Califano described to Lyndon Johnson the Heineman task force recommendations as "never used because they are so controversial." Memorandum, Califano to the President, May 16, 1968. Container 1, Study of the Presidency, Johnson Library.

study of the presidency that he would guide during his immediate post-presidential years. The President announced his intention to launch such a study in a May 6th talk to a group of new White House fellows. As he conceived it, the study would be conducted by a committee made up of those who has served in his cabinet and those of Presidents Kennedy, Truman, and Roosevelt. Presumably the study would take its guide from President Johnson's remarks during the May 6th talk about the presidency's needs: "In the years to come we need to improve it, strengthen it, and do whatever we can to make it stronger."[114]

Johnson's idea of a study of the presidency aimed at strengthening the office he was surrendering seems obviously connected to his personal dilemma, as if having given up the campaign for reelection he would begin a campaign to vindicate his vision for and use of the presidency. Through his study, and through the Lyndon Johnson School of Public Affairs, which he began planning for at the same time as he conceived of the study of the presidency, he would campaign for a vindication in the historical record that he might not have won from the electorate. But whatever its fundamental motivations, Johnson's idea for a study of the presidency was flawed in a way that was characteristic of initiatives within the Johnson administration. As of the time of its announcement by the President, the study was little more than an ambition in Lyndon Johnson's mind. As of May 6th there was no fixed format or plan for the study.

In late April Joseph Califano began consulting some key experienced people such as Richard Neustadt and Cyrus Vance to collect ideas about what form the study could take. On May 3rd Califano circulated a memorandum to White House staff members, asking for their suggestions for the proposed study. From late May through July, Califano and several of his subordinates in the White House domestic policy staff searched for a vehicle and agenda for Johnson's proposed study. At the same time, Califano's assignment was twofold because he was also to collect advice for the organization of the soon-to-be-established Johnson School of Public Affairs at the University of Texas. Califano and his associates crisscrossed the country, conducting seminars with academicians as well as some businessmen and public officials.

From the two hundred or more individuals consulted, Califano received a cacophony of advice, much of it suggesting directions that appeared at variance with the President's intentions. For example, Ben Heineman thought that it would be a grave error to have the study

[114] Memorandum and attachment, Joseph Califano to Thomas Gates, May 7, 1968. Container 1, Study of the Presidency, Johnson Library.

commission composed of cabinet members. Heineman observed that his task force had found cabinet members to be "opposed to a strong and effective Presidency that can control and guide them."[115] James David Barber, a Yale political scientist, while proposing that Lyndon Johnson should himself direct the study, suggested that its focus should be "how the President directs the allocation of national attention . . . and how he mobilizes talent for decision making, and how he builds channels for information flows."[116] On the other hand again, the economist Arthur Okun proposed the importance of a study that would examine "the way problems and ideas get channeled to the President's attention" and how advisers shape that flow.[117]

In late June, Joseph Califano winnowed out from the recommendations regarding a study of the presidency those that seemed to best represent a mainstream view of those consulted. Califano told Johnson that it was recommended that the study be thoroughly bipartisan and sponsored by all the living former presidents and vice-presidents. The study should be conducted by a commission composed of respected persons of broad accomplishment and public sector experience at levels close to the presidency. Finally, the study should have a research director who was a distinguished social scientist and who led a strong team of researchers. Califano went on to observe that it was the general feeling that ultimately the focus of the study had to be left to the commission and its research director. This was not the stuff of a study which would allow Lyndon Johnson the opportunity to reshape the presidency or assure his historical reputation.

Consequently, the idea for the study of the presidency fell from favor. If reform planning could not serve Johnson's own interests, why should he bother to push for it? The context in which the idea for the study of the presidency faded with a larger one in which the initial sweetness following Johnson's renunciation of reelection turned bitter. As the summer progressed, Johnson's mood changed. As Doris Kearns reports: ". . . he became withdrawn, [and he] canceled previous plans for new, bold domestic proposals."[118] As the Democratic convention approached, Johnson's party remained torn apart, and it appeared likely that he would be replaced in the presidency by a Republican.

Thus comprehensive reorganization planning never fit well within the Johnson administration; during peacetime the administration's frenetic pace and hunger for innovation were out of step with the

[115] Letter, Ben Heineman to Califano, May 9, 1968, *ibid.*
[116] Letter, James D. Barber to Califano, July 17, 1968, *ibid.*
[117] Memorandum, Arthur Okun to Califano, June 7, 1968, *ibid.*
[118] Doris Kearns, *Lyndon Johnson*, p. 350.

systematic commitment necessary for planning and implementing reorganization. Later, the administration's political problems stemmed from a source that reorganization could not possibly address and were of a magnitude to overwhelm virtually any other consideration. Finally, Johnson's last hopes for reorganization planning concerned his own reputation, misjudging reform's uses and possibilities. But reorganization planning is part of a continuity of ideas and goals. What had become irrelevant to the fate of the Johnson presidency held promise for Lyndon Johnson's successor. Richard Nixon turned to reorganization planning, seeking tools to gain leverage over the executive branch—the same kinds of tools that the Johnson task forces on reorganization had tried to fashion.

Chapter Nine

POWER AND VIRTUE I: RICHARD NIXON AND THE CRISIS OF THE MANAGERIAL PRESIDENCY

At this time what the country needs is . . .
constructive leadership by a real Executive . . . ;
leadership which will demand for itself a
competent staff . . . ; leadership which is based in
a knowledge of existing conditions; leadership
which is not afraid to assume responsibility for
going before the people; leadership which will
utilize the superior powers of the Presidency to
formulate issues . . . ; leadership which stands for
efficiency in the conduct of . . . Government.[1]
Frederick Cleveland (1913)

By the 1970's reorganization planning had become nearly routine
within the staff constellation of the presidency. Both elected presidents
of the 1970's sponsored exceedingly ambitious yet very different reorganization efforts. The routine dimension of reorganization planning
brought presidents under obligation for administrative improvement.
The non-routine dimension of reorganization planning emerged as
each president sought through it ends that were as related to his own
ambitions.

REORGANIZATION IN THE 1970'S

At the outset of his presidency, Richard Nixon created the Ash Council
to make the executive branch manageable from the top. The Ash
Council was related to those other reorganization planning endeavors
since 1952 which operated within the presidency's penumbra. But
more than those predecessors, the Ash Council and its patron were
attuned to administrative reform's implications for power. Just as

[1] Frederick Cleveland, "What Is Included in the Making of a National Budget," paper
prepared for delivery at the annual meeting of the Efficiency Society, New York City,
January 28, 1913, President's Commission on Economy and Efficiency, 030.2, RG 51,
National Archives.

Frederick Cleveland understood the possibilities for empowering the presidency by depoliticizing management, Richard Nixon seemed to perceive the utility of doctrines of administrative reform in making the executive branch a more controllable political milieu.

As an administrative reformer, Richard Nixon highlighted a paradox of the American system. Centralizing change in a decentralized system is nearly impossible without pre-existing centralization in the system.[2] As Nixon sought to centralize the cabinet system he tripped over the dispersion of authority within the federal government. But not content to back-away from the battle, Nixon went a step farther and sought to centralize the cabinet through unilateral executive decisions. While different in fact and principle from the mass of questionable, covert activities of the Nixon administration, those final, unilateral reorganization efforts of the administration appeared to melt into the mass of suspicious activities conducted by a chief executive who seemed not to recognize the limitations imposed by the regime in which he worked. President Nixon's use of reorganization was consistent with a tradition of administrative reform. But he made it too apparent that reorganization was about power. By association with the political embarrassments of his administration, Nixon had made reorganization planning itself a suspicious enterprise.

Elected within Watergate's penumbra, Jimmy Carter differed radically from Nixon in his use of reorganization. While Nixon understood the political uses of reorganization, Carter appeared to see in reorganization planning only its promise of administrative efficacy. Carter embraced reorganization planning as an instrument for government's purification, not as a tool of executive power.

Through his campaign and early presidency Jimmy Carter promised that he would transform government through executive reorganization, making it more understandable and accessible to the average citizen. Instead, after creating the largest reorganization planning staff established by any president, Carter produced two new departments of questionable necessity, a broad civil service reform, and a shopping bag of unrelated recommendations, most of which failed of implementation. By the end of the Carter administration, reorganization looked like a fruitless enterprise.

The 1970's present a tableau of reorganization planning's failure in the hands of very different presidents. It is useful to think of these

[2] Morton Grodzins, "Centralization and Decentralization in the American Federal System," in Ralph Goldman (ed.), *A Nation of States* (Chicago: Rand McNally, 1963), pp. 1-23.

two cases as connected because together they suggest a failure of the promise of the 20th-century's reorganization movement. Furthermore, they underline the remaining severe limitations of the presidency's capacity to deal with administration, limitations which were to be overcome, according to reorganization's early vision, through successive reforms and the articulation of the managerial presidency. The failure of reorganization planning in the Nixon and Carter administrations calls into question the conception of the presidency that administrative theory helped to articulate and that reorganization attempted to implement. The 1970's opened the question that had seemed closed since the Brownlow *Report*; can the presidency be empowered to govern the state by managing it?

RICHARD NIXON AS A MANAGER

In aggravated form, the policy problems Lyndon Johnson addressed with the Heineman task force fueled Richard Nixon's presidential campaign. Reflecting back upon his 1968 victory, he wrote:

> I felt that one of the reasons I had been elected was my promise to break the hammerlock Washington holds over the money and decisions that affect American lives. . . .
> As I saw it, America in the 1960's had undergone a misguided crash program aimed at using the power of the presidency and the federal government to right past wrongs by trying to legislate social progress. . . . The problems were real and the intention worthy, but the method was foredoomed. By the end of the decade its costs had become almost prohibitively high in terms of the way it had undermined fundamental relationships within our federal system. . . .[3]

How were problems in policy implementation to be sorted through and righted? How could policy be designed to reduce the mess of unintended consequences that accompanied the Great Society's programs? How could existing programs be subjected to guidance that ensured their ongoing conformity to overall presidential goals? For all their differences in style and rhetoric, Johnson and Nixon confronted the same general problems in domestic policy implementation.

But the differences in style between Johnson and Nixon would have an impact on their approaches to these problems. Their essential interests lay in opposite dimensions of the presidency's policy role. Nixon was preeminently concerned with foreign policy, while Johnson had

[3] Richard M. Nixon, *Memoirs* (New York: Grosset & Dunlop, 1978), p. 352.

wanted to be a great domestic president. Nixon's greater concern with foreign policy naturally translated into a priority for that policy area in his organization of the presidency. As Rowland Evans and Robert Novak described Nixon's view: "The President must run foreign affairs and let his Cabinet handle the humdrum of domestic affairs."[4] Nixon set out to create a system in domestic government wherein the cabinet would play the primary role.[5]

Another difference between Nixon and his immediate predecessor was their varying interest in organization. Rather than operating in terms of structures and processes, Johnson focused most intently on people as his instruments. Nixon, on the other hand, assumed systems could be structured to achieve his intent. In the administration's early months, John Osborne wrote:

> President Nixon devoted more time and energy to the organization of his staff, and to making sure that the principal members of it understood exactly what they were and were not expected to do for him, than to any other subject or problem. Disciplined order and precision within his immediate establishment, he seemed to realize, was prerequisite to the promise and appearance of orderly administration that he succeeded from the start in conveying to the country.[6]

During the transition period, President-elect Nixon created ten advisory task forces, one of which was to suggest reforms in Executive Office organization.[7] Chaired by Frank Lindsay, president of the ITEK Corporation, it recommended that "the President-elect give first priority to organizing more effectively the White House-Executive Office as the best way to improve the operation of the entire Executive Branch."[8] To provide a continuing source of advice on organizational

---

[4] Rowland Evans and Robert Novak, *Nixon in the White House* (New York: Random House, 1971), p. 11. Describing Nixon's implementation of this view, Stephen Hess writes: "Nixon laid out his plans for a cabinet-centered government in domestic affairs and a White House-centered government in foreign affairs." Stephen Hess, *Organizing the Presidency* (Washington: Brookings Institution, 1976), p. 112.

[5] William Safire, *Before the Fall* (Garden City, New York: Doubleday, 1975), p. 111. In a post-election story on Nixon's plans for the cabinet, the *New York Times* stated that he planned "that his Cabinet officers . . . have the major responsibility for policy making under the President and should be guaranteed regular access to the White House." *New York Times*, November 14, 1968.

[6] John Osborne, *The Nixon Watch* (New York: Liveright, 1970), p. 28.

[7] *New York Times*, November 22, 1968.

[8] Quoted in Larry Berman, *The Office of Management and Budget* (Princeton: Princeton University Press, 1979), p. 105.

matters, Nixon appointed Roy Ash, the president of Litton Industries, as his consultant "on matters of management and efficiency."[9] Among Ash's early suggestions were reforms in the Bureau of the Budget and the use of cabinet-level "councils" to focus in priority policy areas.[10]

Richard Nixon's selection of advisers on management signaled a consistent approach. Aside from their obvious success as private sector managers, men like Lindsay and Ash were untarnished by Washington and permanent government. From the point of view of a Republican president-elect, the national bureaucracy was the enemy's camp.[11] Nixon's promise: "From the first days of my administration I wanted to get rid of the costly failures of the Great Society—and I wanted to do it immediately. I wanted the people who elected me to see that I was going to follow through on my campaign promises."[12] If this was his intention, it would make no sense for Nixon to call upon those who might be captives of the permanent government and its ways.

Another characteristic shared by Lindsay and Ash that might have appealed to Nixon was that as private sector managers they had the intellectual compass of a modern managerial science.[13] The cool calculations of modern private sector managers might cut through the sloppy accumulation of policies, spending, and organization created by undisciplined politics. Exemplifying this approach, one private sector manager who held high positions in the Nixon administration questioned if anyone in government ever thought about whether pro-

[9] *New York Times*, December 5, 1968.

[10] Larry Berman, pp. 105-6. Only one of these councils was created, the Urban Affairs Council, on which sat several department secretaries, Romney of HUD chairing the group, Evans and Novak, *Nixon in the White House*, p. 17. The model evidently in mind behind the creation of the council was the role played in foreign policy by the National Security Council (or at least the role it is supposed to play), *Congressional Quarterly Weekly Report 5* (January 31, 1969), 187.

[11] The perception (fear?) that the permanent government was dominated by liberal Democrats was accurate in the simplest descriptive sense. Whether the fact that civil servants hold liberal attitudes colors their obedience to duty is another question, however. The liberal bias in civil servants' attitudes is shown by Joel D. Aberbach and Bert A. Rockman, "Clashing Beliefs Within the Executive Branch," *American Political Science Review* LXX, 2 (July 1976), 456-468.

[12] Richard Nixon, *Memoirs*, p. 424.

[13] Andrew Rouse (the Ash Council's assistant director and later executive director) described Roy Ash as disdainful of the approach to administrative reform characteristic of the "solons" of public administration such as Don K. Price, Marshall Dimock, Harold Seidman, and Dwight Ink. Ash, he relates, wanted to apply what he viewed as the business firm's principles of good management to the executive branch, assuming that his business management experience was transferable to government. Andrew Rouse, interviewed by author, August 26, 1981.

grams were worthwhile. In making program decisions, he wrote: "The question was really one of how best to allocate . . . resources; it should have been a management decision, but instead it was predicated on politics."[14]

CREATING THE ASH COUNCIL

President Nixon welded his private sector preference to his commitment to reform in creating reorganization planning for his administration. In April 1969 he announced the members of his Advisory Council on Government Organization. Roy Ash was made chairman and four others were appointed to it: George Baker, dean of the Harvard School of Business; John Connolly, former governor of Texas and Secretary of the Navy in the Kennedy administration and currently a partner in a major Houston law firm; Frederick R. Kappel, chairman of A.T. & T.'s executive committee; and Richard M. Paget, partner in the management consulting firm of Cresap, McCormick, and Paget. The President directed his council to focus on three problems. First, it should examine "the executive branch as a whole in light of "changing demands upon government. Second, he directed it to give attention to "organizational problems which arise among the 150 plus departments, offices, agencies, and other separate executive units." Presumably Nixon meant that the council should diagnose and offer remedies of agency-specific problems as well as for those that pertained to the executive branch in an overall sense. Last, the President directed the council to assess the "organizational aspect of intergovernmental relations. . . ."[15]

The Ash Council, as the group was called, combined small-size, prestigious membership, and strong private sector managerial experience. The announcement of the council's creation stated that it would "have direct access to the President."[16] Interestingly, President Nixon adopted Johnson's use of task forces to bring private sector expertise to bear on particular problem areas. But for reorganization he chose a different organizational format, indicating its higher status and direct connection to himself.[17] In particular, given that the council's chairman had already been named as Nixon's consultant on managerial reform,

[14] Frederick Malek, *Washington's Hidden Tragedy* (New York: Free Press, 1978), p. 15.

[15] Announcement of Appointments, April 5, 1969, *Weekly Compilation of Presidential Documents*, Vol. 5, no. 15 (April 14, 1969), 530.

[16] *Ibid.*

[17] Murray Comarow, interviewed by author, April 24, 1981.

the council itself was an extension of an already established advising relationship.

In addition to the Ash Council's creation, President Nixon gave substantial attention to administration in his early days in office. His first message to Congress asked that the reorganization authority, which had lapsed on December 31, 1968, be renewed for a two-year period.[18] Congress complied, and Nixon signed the extension into law on March 27. Nixon also achieved several significant reorganizations, either directly or through legislation. The largest of these was the change in the Post Office Department to the non-cabinet status of a government corporation, following the recommendations of a task force on postal reform headed by Frederick Kappel during the Johnson administration.[19] Also, Nixon established common regional boundaries for several major domestic social service agencies.[20]

The Ash Council's startup was slow, due to Roy Ash's business obligations. Consequently, in early June, to get the council going, Nixon appointed Walter Thayer, president of Whitney Communications, as a sixth member; he was also designated a special consultant to the President, with responsibility for organizing the council's staff and appointing its executive director.[21] Under Thayer's direction a small staff was hired. The most important staff decision was the appointment of an executive director. The council had only an acting director as of mid-summer; Thayer sought a person of long experience in government to serve as director.[22] He found that person in Murray

[18] *Public Papers of the Presidents, Richard M. Nixon, 1969*, "Special Message to the Congress Requesting New Authority to Reorganize the Executive Branch," January 20, 1969, pp. 32-33.

[19] *Ibid.* "Special Message to the Congress on Reform of the Postal Service," February 25, 1969, pp. 147-149.

[20] *Ibid.*, "Statement on Establishing Common Regional Boundaries for Agencies Providing Social and Economic Services," March 27, 1969, pp. 255-258.

[21] *New York Times*, June 3, 1969; and Murray Comarow, interviewed by author.

[22] The acting executive director was Andrew Rouse, who had been appointed as one of Roy Ash's first decisions. He had previously worked for the management consulting firm of Arthur D. Little and had been, by his own description, one of the few Republicans at the Bureau of the Budget during the Johnson years, serving as an assistent director. Rouse had met Roy Ash in early April 1969 and had then been drafted by Ash for the council; Rouse shared with Ash a strong view of the applicability to government of private sector approaches to management. But Walter Thayer had a view of the executive branch as distinctive from the firm, and he pursued a more traditional public administration approach in setting up the council's staff. This led him to prefer a person like Comarow for the council's directorship rather than Rouse, the former being an old Washington hand while the latter was essentially a business management type. Andrew Rouse, interviewed by author; and Murray Comarow interviewed by author.

Comarow, who had left a public service career at the Post Office Department and Federal Power Commission to become a vice-president at the management consulting firm of Booz, Allen, Hamilton. Comarow joined the council in July 1969.[23]

Until the beginning of fiscal year 1970, on July 1, the council subsisted on an allotment of $35,000 from an emergency fund. This minimal funding explains some of the lag in the council's startup. With the beginning of fiscal year 1970, the council received an appropriation of a million dollars and raised its staff size to around twenty-five by early fall and thirty-five by the end of 1969. At its peak, in mid-1970, the staff numbered forty-seven full-time employees. That level was only briefly maintained and by fall 1970 the total number of staff was again under forty.[24]

The staff was hired with little if any regard to partisanship. Until July 1979 Walter Thayer was responsible for hiring, and after that date Murray Comarow took over.[25] The staff assembled by these two was politically liberal.[26] Early members included Josiah Lee Auspitz, the liberal Ripon Society's president in 1970, and Thomas Petri, a former Ripon executive director. While they thought of themselves as managers, it should be added that both Thayer and Comarow were also liberals, the former from the Javits-Rockefeller wing of his party and the latter a self-described "Stevenson Democrat."[27] The council's membership itself was more conservative than its staff. The median partisan identification among the six members was relatively conservative Republicanism. That the ideological differences between the council and staff did not cause conflict is a testimony to the quality of the Ash council as well as to the ability of managerial doctrines to submerge partisan differences. Whatever initial distrust existed was dissipated by the staff's demonstration that it could perform at a high professional level and by the council's willingness to give close attention to the staff's recommendations. Recalling the year that he served as executive director, Murray Comarow cannot remember a major recommendation by the staff that was rejected by the council.[28]

[23] *New York Times*, July 19, 1969.

[24] Data presented to congressional hearing by Roy Ash, U.S. Congress, House, Committee on Government Operations, *Hearings, Reorganization of Executive Departments*, 92nd Cong., 1st Sess., 1971, p. 184.

[25] Neal Gregory, "Washington Pressures/the Ripon Society," *National Journal* (June 6, 1970), 1,209.

[26] Andrew Rouse, interview with author.

[27] Murray Comarow, interview with author.

[28] *Ibid.*

The Ash Council's staff was divided into six working groups and assigned to the problem foci of the Executive Office, social programs, regulatory agencies, foreign trade, the environment, and narcotics control.[29] The last two items were the only ones specifically assigned to the council by the President.[30] The other problem foci were developed through an interactive process between the staff and the council members whereby the staff developed a list of possible topics and the council discussed their relative importance. From the very beginning one topic was understood to be first on the agenda: the organization of the Executive Office for management.[31]

The Ash Council at Work

At its monthly two-day meetings, the Ash Council heard formal presentations from its working groups. The format for those staff presentations was an important factor in dispelling political tension between the council and staff. Staff work was presented to the council along with a detailed reconstruction of the elements, choices, and reasoning which led to the tentative conclusions contained in it.[32] It was the executive director's intention to force the council to share the "pain" of selecting among limited choices and imperfect options.[33]

One element of the Ash Council's operating style which particularly requires notice is its aggressive out-reach to large numbers of individuals in the agencies under study, knowledgeable about them or politically salient to the fate of a recommendation.[34] On the first of its

[29] For a list of assignments and staff personnel as of early 1970 see Dom Bonafede and Jonathan Cottin, "Nixon, in Reorganization Plan, Seeks, Tighter Rein on Bureaucracy," *National Journal* (March 21, 1970), 625.

[30] Murray Comarow, interview with author. Roy Ash's congressional testimony, U.S. Congress, House, Committee on Government Operations, *Hearings, Reorganization Plan No. 3 of 1970*, 91st Cong., 2nd Sess., 1970, p. 42.

[31] Andrew Rouse, interviewed by author; Ash testimony, U.S. Congress, House, Committee on Government Operations, *Hearings, Reorganization Plan No. 2 of 1970*, 91st Cong., 2nd Sess., 1970, p. 15.

[32] Andrew Rouse describes early staff work as deficient, forcing the council itself to do much of the development of the recommendations for reorganization of the Executive Office that became Reorganization Plan No. 2 of 1970. Andrew Rouse, interview with author.

[33] Murray Comarow, interview with author.

[34] Roy Ash described the council's staff as having interviewed 180 people in conjunction with the preparation of the recommendations for environmental organization. U.S. Congress, House, Committee on Government Organization, *Hearings, Reorganization Plan No. 3 of 1970*, 91st Cong., 2nd Sess., 1970, p. 45. Another example of the council's reliance on extensive interviewing can be seen in the council's regulatory

recommendations, concerning the Executive Office, the council and staff spoke with former President Johnson, ex-White House aides, several former budget directors, and a number of academicians. Following the President's adoption of the recommendations, and while the council was sharpening them, its members, the executive director, and several senior staff members visited relevant committee chairmen at Congress and cabinet members to prepare the political ground for the President's action upon the recommendations. Such conversations also provided early warning for any political problems.

Illustrative of this early warning system is the change of the council's name for the reorganized Bureau of the Budget from the Office of Management to the Office of Management and Budget. Before the President sent that reform to Congress in Reorganization Plan no. 2, John Connally and Murray Comarow visited Representative George Mahon (Dem., Tex), chairman of the House Committee on Appropriations. Mahon generally favored the plan, but he expressed affection for the "budget" in the Bureau of the Budget's title. He offered the thought that it could be called Office of Budget and Management. Comarow suggested that the principle of management's priority could be retained by calling it the Office of Management and Budget. Mahon was satisfied and went on to support Reorganization Plan no. 2 in a very close legislative fight.[35]

The council's relations with the President gave it particular strength. Its members met several times with the President, in meetings lasting an hour or more.[36] Personality factors may play an important role here. The council was chaired by a trusted friend of the President. More like PACGO than the Johnson task forces, the Ash Council had access to the President and the capability of passing initial ideas to the Oval Office for a sign of presidential interest before embarking on full-blown projects.[37] The council's ease of access to President Nixon is interesting, and surprising, given the reputation of the Nixon White House for building a "Berlin Wall" around the Oval Office, guarded

---

report, in which it is stated: "Our study consisted largely of indepth interviews with over 200 participants in and observers of the regulatory process." President's Advisory Council on Executive Organization, *A New Regulatory Framework* (Washington: Government Printing Office, 1971), p. 125.

[35] Murray Comarow, interview with author.

[36] Frederick Kappel recalled several hour-long meetings with the President during the preparation of Reorganization Plan No. 2 alone, U.S. Congress, House, Committee on Government Organization, *Hearings, Reorganization Plan No. 2 of 1970*, 91st Cong., 2nd Sess., 1970, p. 22.

[37] Murray Comarow, interview with author.

by H. R. Haldeman.[38] Nixon's closest aides viewed the Ash Council's work on the Executive Office as a threat to their turf; different sources testify to Haldeman's and John Erlichman's attempts to keep the council away from Nixon until they could examine and revise its recommendations for the Executive Office.[39] But Roy Ash and his associates had enough status with Nixon to break through the "Berlin Wall."

THE ASH COUNCIL'S RECOMMENDATIONS

Between August 1969 and early 1971 the Ash Council sent the President a total of nine memoranda. They are part of the still-closed Nixon papers. However, their substance and character is obtainable from public record sources. In adopting the recommendations for Executive Office reform, change in the organization of environment regulation, and the reorganization of the domestic departments, the President made public extensive parts of the council's reasoning. In the cases of the large reports on departmental reorganization and the regulatory reform report, the President made public the complete documents.

Reorganization of the Executive Office

The first set of memoranda the council sent to President Nixon dealt with reorganization of the Executive Office. The Executive Office study was the responsibility of Roy Ash, George Baker, Murray Comarow, and Andrew Rouse.[40] Initially council staff produced a conceptual paper which was given to President Nixon at an August 20th meeting at San Clemente. He approved its general directions, and it became the basis for the council's detailed report on the Executive Office presented to him in October 1969.[41] On March 12, 1970, President Nixon sent Congress Reorganization Plan no. 2 of 1970, implementing the council's recommendations. It contained two organizational changes of great importance: the reconstitution of the Bureau of the

[38] On Haldeman's place in Nixon's White House see William Safire's account of that administration's inner circle in, *Before the Fall*, pp. 278-293. Also see Stephen Hess, *Organizing the Presidency*, pp. 126-127.

[39] James Finch (senior staff member of council), interview with author, July 23, 1981; Rowland Evans and Robert Novak, *Nixon in the White House*, pp. 239-240.

[40] Dom Bonafede and Jonathan Cottin, "Nixon, in Reorganization Plan, Seeks Tighter Rein on Bureaucracy," *National Journal* (March 21, 1970), 621.

[41] Larry Berman, *The Office of Management and Budget*, p. 106.

Budget into the Office of Management and Budget and the creation of a separate Domestic Policy Council.[42]

In his reorganization plan, President Nixon combined the themes of managerial centralism and administrative decentralization:

> A President whose programs are carefully coordinated, whose information system keeps him adequately informed, and whose organizational assignments are plainly set out, can delegate authority with security and confidence. A President whose office is deficient in these respects will be inclined, instead, to retain close control of operating responsibilities which he cannot and should not handle.[43]

The reforms Nixon sought through the reorganization plan were distinctly centralizing in that they aimed at establishing greater capacity for policy formation, assessment and surveillance of administrative implementation. However, his justification for the changes was consistent with his stated intention to delegate authority to his cabinet secretaries and away from the presidential center. In retrospect, there is also some irony in Nixon's message accompanying the reorganization plan. This president, who had built the largest White House staff ever assembled, suggested that his Executive Office reorganization would remove the major impetus for the expansion of the personal staff.[44]

Reorganization Plan no. 2 imposed crucial changes on the Bureau of the Budget. First, the plan made the heads of the operating divisions of the OMB subject to presidential appointment, reversing the long-standing practice of career officers' serving as assistant directors. Second, the managerial, policy coordinating, and program information functions of the agency were targeted for expansion. Third, an office for executive development was to be added to the agency for the purpose of designing policy for the enhancement of the quality of the upper levels of the career public service. Fourth, these new and expanded activities involving managerial support, program coordination, information on program implementation and executive development would be organized into a new division of the agency.

The second council recommendation for the Executive Office was

[42] Murray Comarow, interview with author; also, see Roy Ash's testimony, U.S. Congress, Hearings, Committee on Government Organization, *Hearings, Reorganization Plan No. 2 of 1970*, 91st Cong., 2nd Sess., 1970, pp. 7-31.

[43] *Public Papers of the Presidents, Richard Nixon, 1970*, "Message . . . Transmitting Reorganization Plan No. 2 of 1970," March 12, 1970, p. 258.

[44] *Ibid*. For figures on the growth of White House staff under Nixon see, Hugh Heclo, *Studying the Presidency* (New York: Ford Foundation, 1977), pp. 36-37.

a Domestic Council. Its immediate antecedent was the Urban Affairs Council that Nixon had created shortly after the inauguration, following a suggestion by Roy Ash. The purpose of such a council was to bring together and re-focus the viewpoints of those cabinet members who had a substantial interest in a policy area. The Domestic Council was an idea for throwing together domestic policy operations of the administration into a council format, with an eye on the National Security Council, of which the Domestic Council was to be a fraternal twin.

The Domestic Council would be composed of the president, vice-president, attorney general, and the secretaries of the Treasury, Interior, Agriculture, Commerce, Labor, Health, Education and Welfare, Housing and Urban Development, and Transportation. Under the provisions of the reorganization plan, the president would also have the authority to designate any other members he wished from among the officers of the executive branch. As in the National Security Council, the president would be council chairman. Its staff would be headed by an executive director who was an assistant to the president. The staff of the Domestic Council formalized the development over the last decade of a substantial domestic policy group in the White House.[45]

The Domestic Council would combine two virtues, according to President Nixon. First, it would obviously place those responsible for administration into the cockpit of domestic policy making, fulfilling Nixon's promises of delegated authority to the cabinet. But, in fact, it is another virtue which the President stressed and to which he devoted most of his attention. His message stated

> The Council will be supported by a staff. . . . Like the National Security Council staff, this staff will work in close coordination with the President's personal staff but will have its own institutional identity. By being established on a permanent, institutional basis, it will be designed to develop and employ the "institutional memory" so essential if continuity is to be maintained, and if experience is to play its proper role in the policy-making process.[46]

[45] See the reorganization plan and the administration's testimony in its favor in U.S. Congress, House, Committee on Government Organization, *Hearings, Reorganization Plan No. 2 of 1970*, 91st Cong., 2nd Sess., 1970, esp. pp. 11-14.

[46] *Public Papers of the Presidents*, Richard Nixon, 1970, "Message . . . Transmitting Reorganization Plan No. 2 of 1970," March 12, 1970, p. 259. It should be noted that the idea of a domestic policy council as a means for strengthening presidential capacities for formulating policy arose as early as 1964 in the Johnson White House. A White House Staffer, Richard Goodwin, wrote to Johnson: "I suggest the establishment of a

The Domestic Council staff would greatly increase the president's support system for developing policy proposals at the same time that it removed that system from the White House, thus appearing to fulfill the Nixon pledge for a lean White House. The placement of the Domestic Council in the Executive Office, combined with Nixon's use of the phrase "institutional memory," requires explanation. In congressional hearings, Representative Chet Holifield (D., Calif.), among others, was particularly troubled by the proposed Domestic Council, and he probed at the meaning of "institutionalized memory" as he questioned Roy Ash and Dwight Ink, assistant director for executive management of the Bureau of the Budget. Holifield said that the staff of the Domestic Council would be "a political organization headed by a political appointee, none of whom have civil service tenure, and the director, of course, not being confirmed by the Senate." Dwight Ink admitted the truth of that description, adding that the staff would be heterogenous, coming from different career backgrounds. Also, he said ". . . it is not expected that they have tenure," nor did the administration intend "institutional memory" to be "interpreted as necessarily going from administration to administration." As Holifield responded, it must be "a four-year institutional memory."[47]

The major conundrum of Reorganization Plan no. 2 was the relationship between the Domestic Council and the Office of Management and Budget.[48] The Ash Council had structured the Domestic Council to be distinct from and perhaps distant from the Office of Management and Budget. The Domestic Council was charged with developing domestic policy, but the director of the Office of Management and Budget was not designated as a statutory member of the council. Moreover, the staff strength and capacity of the OMB would perhaps not weigh much in the balance because the Domestic Council was projected as having a large, expert staff. Reorganization Plan no. 2 seemed to signal the possibility that the Office of Management and Budget was being demoted, removed one step from the president. This appearance was reinforced by the fact that through the 1960's the budget directors

---

Domestic Policy Planning. There is such a staff on foreign policy. . . . Yet the need is far more obvious in the field of domestic policy. . . . This would be a full-time council of experienced people—scholars, government people, etc. Its director would be on your staff. It could be attached to the Bureau of the Budget or operate independently and report directly to you." Memorandum, Goodwin to Johnson, November 22, 1964, container 429, FG 999, White House Central File, Exec., Johnson Library.

[47] U.S. Congress, House, Committee on Government Organization, *Hearings, Reorganization Plan No. 2 of 1970,* 91st Cong., 2nd Sess., 1970, pp. 55-56.

[48] For an examination of the Domestic Council's operation, see John Kessel, *The Domestic Presidency* (North Scituate, Mass.: Duxbury, 1975).

had been among the presidents' closest domestic policy advisers. Now, the whole realm of domestic policy formulation was being taken away from the bureau. Administration witnesses attempted to assure the House Subcommittee on Executive and Legislative Reorganization that this was untrue. But Budget Director Mayo's own public statement in this regard served to further confuse the matter:

> The Budget Bureau makes policy recommendations to the President. ... This will continue as far as I know ... except you will have a more formal formalization of what you might call the immediate advice to the President through the Domestic Council in assembling the recommendations, not only as the Budget Bureau, which in turn will glean them from other agencies, but from other agencies, but from individual sources outside the Government.[49]

The issue of the relationship between the Office of Management and Budget and the Domestic Council threatened congressional acceptance of Reorganization Plan no. 2. An equally important threat to adoption would also arise from a small as yet unmentioned provision. The plan's first section (section 101) stated: "There are hereby transferred to the President of the United States all functions vested by law (including reorganization plan) in the Bureau of the Budget or the Director of the Budget."[50] Thus the heretofore statutory functions of the Bureau of the Budget could be placed elsewhere at presidential discretion—in the new Domestic Council, for example. In light of the long-time relationship between senior bureau professionals and the congressional committee staffs and chairman, this provision appeared to threaten a trusted agency just as other provisions of the same plan also could be interpreted as means for undercutting the bureau and politicizing it.

Reorganizing Environmental Organization

Early in the Ash Council's life, President Nixon asked it to undertake a survey of the government's environmental agencies; and he also asked it to review reports prepared by President Johnson's Commission on Marine Science and his own task force on oceanography. The council recommended that the Environmental Protection Agency bring together existing statutory authority over the environment held by several different agencies. But the council recommended against the

---

[49] U.S. Congress, House, Committee on Government Organization, *Hearings, Reorganization Plan No. 2 of 1970*, 91st Cong., 2nd Sess., 1970, p. 23.

[50] Reorganization Plan No. 2 of 1970, in *ibid.*, p. 6.

establishment of an independent oceanographic agency. Its preferred option was that the President hold off the question of what to do with the organization of oceanographic policies until it concluded its work on the possible reorganization of the Department of the Interior. The memorandum added, should the President wish to consolidate ocean-ographic programs at present, he bring these together in the Depart-ment of the Interior.[51] The President, through Reorganization Plan no. 4, chose against an independent agency, instead recommending the creation of the National Oceanographic and Atmospheric Agency within Commerce. Commerce had the advantage of already containing the agency that would be NOAA's major component, the Environ-mental Science Administration with 10,000 employees. In addition, Secretary of Interior Walter Hickle was not Richard Nixon's favorite cabinet member.

The Ash council recommended that those agencies that had stand-ard-setting and enforcement authority in regard to environmental pol-lution, no matter what medium within the environment—air, soil, water—be brought together "cheek to jowl." Recalling that labels such as "function" or "purpose" about administrative activities have a mercurial quality, one might speak of the recommendation as both a reorganization by function and a reorganization by purpose. To wit, the standard setting authority of the Atomic Energy Commission's Federal Radiation Council and the Department of Agriculture's pes-ticide program shared similar functions applied to different environ-mental pollutants. But, at the same time, both operations aimed at similar ends: the control of environmental pollution from whatever source.

The justification of the Environmental Protection Agency's unifi-cation of these similar functions rested on the newly fashionable eco-logical perspective, adding a sophisticated wrinkle to the Ash Council's reading of the hoary principle of organization by like function. In congressional testimony, Roy Ash said that the presence of these ac-tivities in several bureaus spread over different departments was "char-acteristic of organizational responses to problems that were first per-ceived independently." However, he added: "Such piecemeal . . . structure becomes inadequate when the interrelation of the problem or the solution becomes the dominant factor."[52]

[51] Richard Corrigan, "Environmental Report," *National Journal* (July 25, 1970), 1,581-1,582.
[52] U.S. Congress, House, Committee on Government Organization, *Hearings, Re-organization Plan No. 2 of 1970*, 91st Cong., 2nd Sess., p. 45.

The Regulatory Report

In January 1971, after months of press speculation and intensifying interest by regulated industries, President Nixon released for public comment the Ash Council's report on the independent regulatory commissions.[53] The regulatory report stood solidly in a reform planning tradition critical of the independent commissions—a "headless fourth branch," as the Brownlow Committee had dubbed them. The Ash Council leveled four charges at the commissions. One, they "are not sufficiently accountable" to either Congress or the president. Two, they are unresponsive to changes in industry structure, technology, economic trends, and public needs. Three, they cannot attract consistently high-quality commissioners or retain able staff people. Four, they are over-judicialized and habituated to formal as against less formal procedures, isolating their decision processes from economic and financial contexts.[54]

To root out these failings, the council recommended a radical restructuring of regulatory organization. It proposed four new regulatory agencies which would incorporate the existing independent regulatory commissions, with the exception of the Federal Communications Commission and the anti-trust authority of the Federal Trade Commission. The four single-headed agencies would be the Transportation Regulatory Agency, Federal Power Agency, the Securities and Exchange Agency, and the Federal Trade Practices Agency.

The council proposed major procedural reforms as well. To streamline procedure it suggested that in-agency review of decisions by hearing officers be limited to selected cases, a sampling of the whole, and that the chief administrator's authority to reverse a hearing officer be limited to thirty days after the decision. Also, the council advised that review should be conducted to ascertain whether the decisions rendered were consistent with agency policy. Furthermore, review on substantive grounds normally undertaken within the commissions and the procedural review conventionally undertaken by the federal courts

[53] In September 1970 a short report prepared by Professor Marshall Dimock was presented to the President. It was more of an outline for a full report than a full report itself. There was little analysis within it, it being a brisk statement of conclusions. Later in that year, the White House requested a fuller report. This later version was prepared by Roy Ash, Andrew Rouse, and Jim Finch during a ten-day period. Jim Finch, interview with author.

[54] President's Advisory Council on Executive Organization, *A New Regulatory Framework* (Washington: Government Printing Office, 1971), pp. 4 and 5. For a critical analysis of the report see Roger Noll, *Reforming Regulation* (Washington: Brookings Institution, 1971).

would be combined in a new mechanism, an administrative court. This court would be constituted of a panel of as many as fifteen judges. Each case in review would be heard by a panel of three judges, and they would consider the full aspect of the cases before them, substantive as well as procedural.

While one cannot see clearly the internal dynamics of the Ash Council, due to the lack of availability of its records, it appears that the council found this study more troublesome than its other investigations.[55] The disadvantage of appointing businessmen to a study group that will examine regulation is the fair probability that each of them has had business with regulatory agencies. The specter of conflicting interest led every member of the council except Richard Paget and John Connally to stand aside on at least one commission. Roy Ash did not participate in the discussions bearing on the Federal Trade Commission. Frederick Kappel did the same in regard to the Federal Communications Commission, and Walter Thayer chose not to participate in regard to either the Federal Communications Commission or the Federal Trade Commission. George Baker did not participate at all in the regulatory commission study. It was also the only report to which there was a strong dissent. Frederick Kappel filed a protest to the effect that the council had not adequately assessed the viewpoint of regulated industries in designing its recommendations.

Reorganizing the Cabinet Departments

In his 1971 State of the Union message, President Nixon promised major reorganization of the domestic departments:

> I shall ask not simply for more new programs in the old framework. I shall ask to change the framework of government itself—to reform the entire structure of American government so we can make it again fully responsive to the needs and wishes of the American people.[56]

The following March 25th, Nixon sent four bills to Congress; these would create new departments of Natural Resources, Economic Affairs, Human Resources, and Community Development. In his accompanying message, the President spoke of his proposal as "comprehensive," reflecting an understanding of what the national government "*ought* to look like in the last third of the twentieth century."[57] Un-

[55] Andrew Rouse, interview with author.
[56] *Public Papers of the Presidents, Richard Nixon, 1971*, p. 51.
[57] *Ibid.*, p. 474.

dergirding the President's recommendation were Ash Council memoranda on a Department of Natural Resources (May 1970) and several departments in the areas of economic and social policy (November 1970). Fortunately, the President chose to release these reports to accompany the reorganization bills of March 1971. Through them one can see into the council's logic in formulating the proposals for the super-departments.

The spirit of the Ash Council's recommendations was identical with that of the Heineman task force in its report on the future organization of the executive branch. In this shared view, super-departments were enlarged organizational arenas for rationalizing vast areas of national policy. The Ash Council saw three powerful benefits in super-department organization. Assuming that departments should be purpose-oriented, the council proposed that: (1) departments should be "broad enough to foster a large measure of conflict resolution and policy discretion," with minimum need for inter-department coordination; (2) the total number of departments should be reduced, reducing the president's span of control; (3) departmental purposes should be broad enough so that there would be little pressure to represent particular interests or policy positions. These characteristics, the council predicted, would make departments eminently more responsive than at present to presidential direction.[58]

Consistent with these propositions, the new departments were conceived expansively. The May 1970 proposal for a Department of Natural Resources spanned the policy areas of land, recreation, water, energy and mineral resources, and geophysical science activities. Only pollution control was excluded from the proposed department, having already been lodged in the Environmental Protection Agency at the council's recommendation. The new department would include all of Interior and parts of Agriculture, Defense, and Commerce, along with the Atomic Energy Commission's civil responsibilities.[59] Such mergers would subsume within departments agencies with strong constituencies and overlapping jurisdictions, for example, the Army Corps of Engineers and the Bureau of Reclamation. However, it was exactly

[58] President's Advisory Council on Executive Organization, *Establishment of a Department of Natural Resources—Organization for Social and Economic Progress* (Washington: Executive Office of the President, 1972), pp. 6, 43, 50-51.

[59] The memorandum on natural resources organization was prepared prior to the President's decision to submit Reorganization Plan No. 4 of 1971, which created the National Oceanic and Atmospheric Administration within the Department of Commerce. The council's report envisioned a major division of a new Departent of Natural Resources constituting what essentially became NOAA.

those characteristics of such agencies as the Corps of Engineers and the Bureau of Reclamation that made it so desirable to place them within one department that made the move politically unlikely.[60] The council's logic was similar to the proposition that a defanged snake is preferable to one with fangs, but who will defang it and how?

In its November 1970 memorandum, the Ash Council admitted to seriously considering a comprehensive department that would include all the social and economic policy departments, with subdivisions along functional lines.[61] But the council concluded: "Although in many respects the comprehensive department represents an ideal in developing a Federal resource delivery system for socio-economic needs, we rejected the notion."[62] The "most feasible option" was "to move toward comprehensive social and economic program planning and operation by creating a departmental structure which focuses operations on the primary purposes of the government's social and economic programs."[63]

The council decided that social and economic policies could be categorized as aiding individual development and community development or spurring economic growth. Each category became the focus of a new department, HEW becoming the center of the proposed Department of Human Resources,[64] HUD the center of the proposed Department of Community Development,[65] and the combined Commerce and Labor Departments the center of a Department of Economic Growth and Productivity.[66] The pieces of the Department of Agriculture left over after the establishment of natural resources would be divided between community development and economic growth. Major independent agencies in social and economic development policy

[60] A classic account of the tendency of water resource policy battles to rise to presidential level can be had in Arthur Maass, *Muddy Water* (Cambridge, Mass.: Harvard University Press, 1951).

[61] President's Advisory Council on Executive Organization, *Establishment of a Department of Natural Resources—Organization for Social and Economic Progress*, pp. 82-83.

[62] *Ibid.*, p. 84.

[63] *Ibid.*

[64] Human Resources would also include manpower programs from Labor and OEO, food and nutrition programs from Agriculture and OEO, and drug rehabilitation and abuse programs from Justice as well as the Railroad Retirement Board and the Civil Service Retirement and Disability Fund.

[65] Community Development would also include construction programs such as Hill-Burton from HEW as well as community action and VISTA from OEO.

[66] Economic Growth and Productivity would also include enforcement of anti-dumping regulations from Treasury, the commercial attaché system from State, the U.S. Tariff Commission, and the Appalachian Regional Commission.

would also be merged, the Office of Economic Opportunity divided into all three and the Small Business Administration going into economic development.

The council also proposed reforms in the inter-governmental system. Its key recommendation in this regard was that regional staffs of the departments be given increased authority over programs and grants. By and large, such staffs served routine service and monitoring roles, with decision authority lodged in Washington. The Ash Council recommended that the regional departmental staffs be upgraded in terms of both civil service rank and personnel quality to make them capable of performing with new authority. A corollary of this recommendation was a restructuring of departmental authority relations. The council recommended giving a department's regional director sole line authority over the department's personnel within his region: "The line of delegation should be from the Secretary to the Regional director who may then delegate to appropriate regional officals."[67]

The council's discussion of the inter-governmental system superficially appears to be concerned with greater discretion to local governments. The political context within which the Ash Council formulated its views favored devolution. As Richard Nathan, a major author of the New Federalism doctrine of the Nixon administration, described that concept, it involved greater political leeway for the non-federal levels of government. Nathan said:

> The critical difference between the New Federalism and its immediate precursors is that under the New Federalism much more emphasis is given to decentralization policy objectives. This means that under these new policies the influence of central government policy and decision-making is reduced. In turn, policy instruments are devised to enhance the role of state and local community problem-solving.[68]

However, the thrust of the Ash Council's inter-governmental recommendations cut in the opposite direction of this understanding of "New Federalism." The council's recommendations were local—regarding in that they sought to simplify the jobs of local and state officials by

[67] President's Advisory Council on Executive Organization, *Establishment of a Department of Natural Resources—Organization for Social and Economic Progress*, pp. 62-64.

[68] From the published transcript, Woodrow Wilson International Center for Scholars, *The New Federalism* (Washington: Wilson Center, 1973), p. 38. Also see Nathan's discussion of the New Federalism as part of Nixon's approach to the presidency in *The Plot That Failed*, Chap. 2.

making federal practices uniform and simpler. But the clearly higher objective for the council was to make federal activities at local and regional levels conform to national (read "presidential") priorities. Thus decentralization was not meant to bring with it a devolution of power.

THE ASH COUNCIL'S CONCEPTUAL PREMISES

The Ash Council's recommendations are a summary of more than a half century of presidentially centered reorganization planning; they are modern variations on a classic theme. This classic theme within the council's theoretic suppositions is most visible in its choices for the objects of its attentions. The council's highest priority problems were the organization of the Executive Office and the architectonics of the cabinet departments. On the one hand, it addressed the issue of managerial capacity in the presidential office. On the other hand, it addressed the issue of the manageability of the major line organizations of the executive branch. The Ash Council, like its predecessors, saw these two matters as interacting, the president's managerial capacity being not only a function of his tools but a product of the manageability of the cabinet departments.

It must be noticed that it was not a foregone conclusion that the Ash Council would adopt the classic perspective of the reorganization tradition. This group of experienced private sector managers might have imposed another model upon the problem of upper-level federal management. It is not difficult to imagine that Roy Ash's experience as a conglomerate builder or Frederick Kappel's work with the decentralized organization of the Bell System might have produced powerful alternatives to the classical public administration perspective. To grasp that possibility is to sense the pursuasiveness of the normative vision of federal organization within the reorganization tradition, even to those who began their work as private sector devotees.

In contrast to its reliance on the reorganization tradition for its focus, the Ash Council turned to a "policy science" approach to management for solutions. The council's recommendations on policy analysis were variations of the Heineman task force's views. The task force had called for an increase in the policy evaluation capacities of the Bureau of the Budget and the establishment of a coordinating staff in the Executive Office. The council recommended the remaking of the bureau to establish new priorities in its work for presidents. Like the task force, the council also chose to stress the need for both enlarged policy formulation and coordinating capacities in the Executive Office.

But, the Ash Council's solution placed all substantive policy considerations outside the Office of Management and Budget. The Domestic Council was its center for policy considerations and formulation. In turn, the Office of Management and Budget was to be responsible for policy coordination.

The Ash Council's recommendation puts the sensitive question of policy development beyond the reach of the career professionals of the Office of Management and Budget. The Domestic Council was meant to be a presidential staff that was composed of political loyalists. The Domestic Council could call upon the careerists at OMB for technical support, of course, but within a context wherein the president's people and the president's interests would dominate.[69] In distinguishing between the Heineman task force's recommendations in this regard and those of the Ash Council, we should note that they reflect different political perspectives. The task force was composed of Democrats with extensive public service records and a penchant to ignore ideological biases among government career professionals. The council was composed of people who feared that the permanent government was staffed with liberal Democrats. As President Nixon's chief patronage aide described the administrations's situation in regard to the public service:

> After their victory in 1968, Richard Nixon and other prominent members of his team approached Washington with an understandable chariness. . . . a long period of Democratic rule within the executive branch . . . had left a huge reservoir of Democrats in senior positions within the career civil service.[70]

Nixon could well have been in the market for reorganization conceptions that would make policy arenas and departments more easily tamed and more amenable to his direction. After all, the inexorable logic of a president's viewing "the government" as essentially hostile to his programs and intentions is to seek means for taming it.

TRANSFORMING RECOMMENDATIONS INTO ORGANIZATIONS

While the Ash Council worked closely with the President, its reports were evaluated and revised by the ad hoc groups within the admin-

[69] John Kessel's study of the Domestic Council's first two years of operation supports this interpretation. In operation, the council was dominated by presidential priorities to the extent that its ostensible purpose for providing a stable forum for policy development took a distinctly second place to its role as a presidential staff overseeing agency activities. See Kessel, *The Domestic Presidency*.

[70] Frederick Malek, *Washington's Hidden Tragedy*, p. 96.

istration. But the intensity and scope of that review varied significantly from report to report. The council's first set of reports, concerning the Bureau of the Budget and the creation of the Domestic Council, were adopted by the President with a review process confined to his senior White House associates. Because of its clear hostility to the proposal, BOB could not be the review agency.[71] Not even the cabinet was given an effective voice on these recommendations. Nixon had the Ash Council present them to the cabinet in a blunt, set-piece briefing with no opportunity for serious response.

The council's reports getting the most extensive review were those for the domestic super-departments. The Executive Office recommendations were reviewed within the limited sphere of the President's staff because their implementation would benefit from the assumption among Washingtonians that a president ought to have discretion to reshape staff arrangements to suit himself. But, the super-department recommendations had implications throughout the federal bureaucracy and into Congress. These recommendations threatened the organizational routines and political relationships of dozens of interests. To change an agency's organizational locus is to threaten its status, its budget, and its place in its policy arena. Perhaps most fundamentally, to relocate organizations is to tangle the ties that link interests to agencies. Thus the review process for the super-department recommendations had to survey the political environment's capacity to absorb large-scale changes. That process required a more inclusive review group and a more extensive search for the implications of change than did the reforms of the Executive Office.

The super-department reports were sent to the President in May and November of 1970. Once Nixon accepted these recommendations for his 1971 State of the Union, it was crucial that some decisions be made about their details. In short order, Nixon went beyond the council recommendation, adding the Department of Transportation to those that would be folded into the four new super-departments. Because it was only recently established, the Ash Council had left it aside from its recommendations.

Next, the President created a review process to analyze and amend the recommendations, with the object of preparing draft legislation (Nixon also changed the name of the proposed Department of Economic Growth and Productivity to the Economic Development). The organizational focal point for the review was the Domestic Council;

---

[71] BOB fought the reform to the last possible moment. Murray Comarow observed that Budget Director Robert Mayo did not seem to realize the point at which he should stop fighting. Murray Comarow, interview with author. See Larry Berman, *The Office of Management and Budget*, pp. 108-113.

five task forces were formed by it, each composed of department, OMB, and Domestic Council personnel. Each newly proposed department was examined by one task force, and a fifth task force looked at the overall managerial implications of this massive reorganization plan. OMB assistant directors headed each departmental review task force, and the entire review process was under the direction of OMB Associate Director Arnold Weber.[72]

The bills produced by the review process differ in a number of details from the Ash Council's recommendations. Aside from Transportation's inclusion, the most obvious differences between the two plans is in the distribution of existing agencies among the proposed departments. Table 2 shows the number of agency placements on which the Ash Council and administration plan differ.[73]

Another marked difference between the council's recommendation and the administration's plan was the latter's increased attention to top-level management in the proposed super-departments.[74] The Ash Council's focus had been on the federal-state administrative nexus.

Table 2

Differences Between Ash Council and Administration
in Assignment of Existing Bureaus to New Departments

Current Department or Status	Number of Organizational Entities	Number Disagreed Upon
Agriculture	33	10
Commerce	18	4
HEW	11	3
HUD	7	1
Interior	19	1
Labor	11	3
Transportation	11	11
OEO	10	4
Independent Agencies	29	19

[72] "Reorganization Team Organized," *National Journal* (January 30, 1971), 248.

[73] Data drawn from Office of Management and Budget, *Papers Relating to the President's Departmental Reorganization Program* (Washington: Government Printing Office, 1971), pp. 34-38.

[74] The Ash Council's disregard for top-level departmental management and its focus on the inter-governmental aspect of department organization can be seen as an indication of the degree to which this group of private sector men adopted an essentially public sector viewpoint as their work progressed. It would have seemed more natural for such people to give greatest attention to the management of government organization rather than to the interface between governments.

This difference can be seen in the role given to departmental regional directors in each plan. The council wished these administrators to play the key role linking the department's secretary to the field. But in the administration's final plan, the regional director's role varied greatly by department. In the Department of Community Development that role came closest to the Ash Council recommendation, with the regional directors intended to have budgetary and operating authority over subordinates within their region. But, at the other extreme, the planned Department of Economic Affairs would grant no line authority to regional directors, and the draft legislation for a Department of Natural Resources avoided the issue of regionalization.[75]

As the Heineman task force had held, super-departments would relieve presidential burdens and increase control over the direction of departmental missions. Thus to propose a super-department format without addressing top management within these large organizations would seem inconsistent. The Nixon administration's final plan for the super-departments attempted to enhance their manageability by specifying undersecretaries with department-wide, program cross-cutting, analytic responsibilities in areas such as policy, management, research, and planning. These positions would be reinforced by assistant secretaries with functionally narrower department-wide responsibilities. Also, in each department a deputy secretary would back up the secretary, reducing his burden and extending his reach.[76]

Consistent with the reasons for the different intensities of review, the Nixon administration was successful in implementing Ash Council recommendations in proportion to the brevity and narrowness of the administration's review of those recommendations. The recommendations for changes in the Executive Office and in environmental regulation were accepted almost verbatim and implemented shortly afterward through reorganization plans. But the super-department plans simply died without hope of acceptance by Congress, even after having been carefully reworked by the administration's task forces. But the successes and failures of the Ash Council's recommendations have far more to do with President Nixon's ambitions than with the amount of work put into them.

REORGANIZATION AND POWER

Like his predecessors, Richard Nixon sought to increase the presidential influence over the executive branch and consequently over the

[75] Office of Management and Budget, *Papers Relating to the President's Departmental Reorganization Program*, pp. 39, 114-115, 181-182, 251-255.
[76] *Ibid.*

implementation of public policy. At the same time, as many Nixon watchers have noted, President Nixon sought an organizational arrangement in domestic administration that would enhance his power without demanding his time. His political agenda demanded redirection in domestic policy and its management, but his own interests lay in foreign policy. Thus President Nixon sought a domestic organizational system that would locate organizational responsibility such that his staff could act for him, becoming assistant presidents within limited contexts.

To the degree that the Nixon administration's reforms in the Executive Office were aimed at this end, they were failures. OMB and the Domestic Council never quite fulfilled the expectations of the Ash Council. Far from becoming a mechanism for policy formulation, the Domestic Council became a large staff for presidential errands, admittedly increasing presidential reach but providing little analytic or formulative capacity over policy. At the same time, OMB became a center for policy formulation, in large part because Budget Director George Shultze was one of the President's favorites.[77] Thus rather than constituting a mechanism for the regulation of the executive branch, the Executive Office reforms were overwhelmed by the President's short-term demands.

The super-departments were an alternative means for increasing the President's control without increasing his burdens. Of course, the Ash Council saw the OMB and the Domestic Council as prerequisites for the effective guidance of super-departments. But the super-department recommendations were embraced by the administration at a time when it was clear that Reorganization Plan no. 2's promise had faded. In that sense, this more radical reorganization program was an alternative to the earlier Executive Office reform in the search for presidential control of the executive branch. As President Nixon said of this approach in this 1971 State of the Union message:

> Under this plan, rather than dividing up our departments by narrow subjects, we would organize them around the great purposes of government. Rather than scattering responsibility by adding new

[77] Despite the fact that OMB's management oriented staff more than tripled (from 49 to 157) by late 1971, and despite the fact that by late 1971 it had launched ambitious programs for monitoring and improving administrative performance, the assessment of its accomplishments by professionals in and out of the agency was generally negative. See Thomas Mullaney, "OMB Pushes Plan to Improve Federal Management," *National Journal* (December 4, 1971), 2,378-2,388.

levels of bureaucracy, we would focus and concentrate the responsibility for getting problems solved.[78]

These super-departments would create centers of decision free of constituency pressure and attentive to presidential expectations. All the while, the problems of departmental administration and medium-range policy would be dealt with at department level.

The super-department scheme did not have a chance to fulfill that promise seen in it by the President because none of the bills to create the four departments ever left congressional committee. By November 1971 President Nixon himself was undercutting that reorganization program by reversing his position on the Department of Agriculture. When he appointed Earl Butz as secretary of that department, he publicly promised that it would remain in existence, even if some of its peripheral functions were removed.[79] Fourteen months later, and several weeks into his new term, President Nixon attempted to institute through administrative arrangements what he earlier sought in the super-department legislation, declaring that the cabinet would no longer be composed of equals but designating several members who would also be responsible for larger segments of domestic policy and administration. Earl Butz was named, for instance, counsellor to the president and cabinet overseer for the whole of the natural resources activities of government.[80] Thus by administrative action Nixon attempted to achieve what he had failed to do through legislation. But this reform also proved inadequate as more threatening enemies than the permanent government attacked the President, and Nixon's attention shifted from his search for a strategy for domestic governance to a search for a strategy for survival in office. As Richard Nathan observed about the last stage of the Nixon presidency: "The White House hold over the domestic agencies . . . was all but nonexistent."[81]

President Nixon's success in implementing the Ash Council recommendations was itself inversely related to his search for an overall solution to the bureaucracy problem. He was quite successful in achieving implementation of those recommendations that could be instituted through reorganization plans or administrative action. The lesson of these successes seems to be that the ease of implementation of reorganization or related reforms is related to the degree to which the proposed changes are generally seen by other political actors as legit-

[78] *Public Papers of the Presidents, Richard Nixon, 1971*, p. 56.
[79] *New York Times*, November 12, 1971.
[80] *Ibid.*, January 6, 1973.
[81] Richard Nathan, *The Plot That Failed* (New York: Wiley, 1975), p. 76.

imately within the presidential domain. The mechanism chosen for use by a president to implement such a reform is of importance. To submit reforms to Congress through the reorganization authority provides the president with the advantage of presumptive authority to effect the change in question. However, the kind of reorganization proposals that would be submitted through this mechanism would tend to be narrowly targeted and involve changes at a sub-departmental level, within independent agencies, or the Executive Office.

Richard Nixon's attempts to extend presidential influence over the executive branch had some idiosyncratic qualities, but he was engaged in a struggle that has enlisted most of his modern predecessors. Nixon's ultimate failure in this struggle bespeaks some of his personal flaws, but it also attests to the degree to which the struggle for administrative influence remains germane to modern expectations of executive governance. As Nixon's tenure in office lengthened, Congress became more attuned to him as a protaganist. Yet even early in his first term, Congress looked upon the President's reforms in the Executive Office with fear as to the consequences of that reorganization. Coming before Congress after a negative vote in a subcommittee of the House Government Operations Committee and at the same time that an uproar over President Nixon's Cambodia intrusion was peaking, Reorganization Plan no. 2 of 1970 seemed a lightning rod for those members of Congress fearful of presidential power. However, with the help of lobbying by the Ash Council and its staff, the plan squeezed through Congress, relying heavily on a prime doctrine of the managerial presidency: a president must have the ability to arrange and order his organizational household.[82]

During 1971 and 1972, no such presumption of presidential initiative underlay congressional consideration of the plans for departmental reorganization. These bills appeared to be a grand thrust against Congress' intentions in creating federal agencies, against the historic pattern of constituency relations within the executive branch, and against the stable relationships of congressional committees and executive branch organization. Yet during 1971, as the bills went to Congress, the Nixon administration acted as if none of these considerations was relevant to the projected reorganization. Early in 1971 the Ash Council had closed down, removing from the fray the lobbying skills it showed in the congressional acceptance of Executive Office reorganization and the EPA. Even late in 1971, as the first of the super-department bills met intense opposition during committee consider-

---

[82] Jim Finch, interview with author.

ation, the administration acted as if its strongest weapon was the good sense of the proposal. In fact, hearings on the reorganization plan during mid-summer 1971 had won over Representative Chet Holifield, chairman of the House Government Operation Committee, and Senator Abraham Ribicoff, an influential member of the parallel committee in the Senate. The administration acted as if a majority of Congress could be won over as had Holifield and Ribicoff. Dwight Ink, assistant director of OMB, and a central figure in the preparation of the administration's reorganization plan as well as one of its major spokesmen on the bills, reflected that perspective in talking about his estimation of their chances for passage:

> The reason I was not so pessimistic on community development and the entire reorganization plan is that the public and the congressional moods are not hostile to change. Neither the public nor the Congress feels that the bureaucracy is sacrosanct.
>
> What we have to do is exploit that predisposition to change by showing that in government it is the impact of policies on people and communities that count, not the impact on the bureaucracy and Washington-based interest groups.
>
> We believe that the more opposition we get, the more the plan will be talked about and the more that people will see that it is people-oriented and community oriented. Thus we think that time and controversy and exposure are on our side.[83]

But the reorganization bills' failed because they were too large a challenge to the centrifugal forces within the national government. Nixon failed in further centralizing executive branch organization because government was not centralized enough to give him adequate political leverage to accomplish that end.

In the reorganization activities of the Nixon administration, and most clearly in the plans for reorganizing the executive departments, prescriptions for good administration finally appeared to be little more than prescriptions for presidential power. Yet this "plot that failed" was not peculiar to this President and his administration. In reorganization planning Richard Nixon followed the path of his predecessors in the presidency; he understood reform in power terms, seeing that values of good government and ambitions for increased presidential control over government were intermixed within American government.

[83] Quoted in William Lilley, "Hostile Committee Chairman, Lobbies, Pledge Fight Against Reorganization Plan," *National Journal* (October 16, 1971), 2,080.

The Nixon administration's informality about the niceties of the law, for example its plumbers, its covet politicization of super-grade civil service positions, and its misuse of the Internal Revenue Service, obscures a lesson about the uses and limits of comprehensive reorganization planning. The appearance is that President Nixon's ambitions for reorganization were part and parcel of the same personal flaws that led to his misuse of power. However this appearance is false, and it may even put things backwards. Nixon's ambitions for reorganization were not idiosyncratic; they were characteristic of the modern presidency. His misuse of office should not obscure this fact. The failure of reorganization's ambitions for control in the Nixon administration was not caused by the character flaws of the President; it was a failure of reorganization's ambitions *per se*. Reorganization's ideals as they had evolved by the early 1970's were unimplementable within the American system. It may even be this failure that must be understood as the beginning of the Nixon administration's misuse of authority. The imperative of the managerial presidency was that presidents must control. If reorganization could not arrange government to make it controllable, then perhaps other means to that goal are justifiable.

Chapter Ten

POWER AND VIRTUE II: THE 1970'S AND THE END OF THE MANAGERIAL PRESIDENCY

... the bedrock of principle from which all else
derives in American politics is seen to be popular
opinion and scientific management. The
articulation of these principles and their relation
to one another is the whole substance of
American politics.[1]

Herbert Storing

Jimmy Carter offered his good character as a main qualification for the presidency. His self-presentation was in terms of his vision of virtue. And he suggested that his candidacy tapped a moral reservoir in American society. In early 1975 he said to the New Hampshire Senate: "If I can personify in my personal life the aspirations of the American people, I will be elected President."[2]

No candidate before Carter had made executive reorganization a major campaign theme. He promised to transform government, making it "as decent and competent as the American people." To effect this promise Carter called for comprehensive reform. After winning the nomination he told an interviewer:

Incremental efforts to make basic changes are often foredoomed to failure because the special interest groups can benefit from the status quo, can focus their attention on the increments that most affect themselves, and the general public can't be made either interested or aware. . . .

If it's clear, comprehensive and it's presented in such a way as to arouse the support of the people, then the special interests quite often back off because most of them don't want to be exposed to a public altercation against the people of the state or nation. So the

[1] Herbert Storing, "American Statesmanship: Old and New," in Ralph Goldman (ed.), *Bureaucrats, Policy Analysts, Statesmen: Who Leads* (Washington: American Enterprise Inst., 1980), p. 91.

[2] Quoted in Betty Glad, *Jimmy Carter* (New York: Norton, 1980), p. 487.

comprehensive approach is inherently necessary to make controversial decisions.[3]

On November 17, 1976, President-elect Carter identified more specifically the problem that needed addressing through comprehensive reorganization. He said that his goal was to reduce the number of federal agencies from 1,900 to 200. It was assumed that Carter's figure included the approximately 1,400 federal advisory committees.[4]

Carter's promise to reform the federal executive branch owed more to his experience as governor of Georgia than it did to his knowledge of the federal government. Carter had carried out Georgia's most extensive reorganization. It had been his priority program, and it was his greatest accomplishment as governor. During the campaign for the presidency, Jimmy Carter repeatedly cited it to prove his ability to reform federal government. He asked the electorate to believe that his reduction of the number of agencies in Georgia from 300 to 22 was a foretaste of what he could do in Washington.[5]

REORGANIZING GEORGIA

Carter put reorganization at the head of his policy priorities after winning Georgia's governorship in 1970.[6] Carter chose for House Bill no. 1, which traditionally contains the governor's priority legislative request, an enabling act which granted reorganization authority to the governor, subject to legislative veto. After winning executive reorganization authority, Carter sought a comprehensive reorganization program. To prepare it, he created his Reorganization and Management Improvement Study. At its heart was an executive committee, chaired by Carter and including a couple of major state government executives, several influential legislators, and the president of the Georgia Business and Industry Association. Below this committee was the study's director and associate director, who guided task forces assigned to seven different areas of state government.

The personnel for the Reorganization and Management and Improvement Study came from several sources. Arthur Anderson and

[3] "Interview with Jimmy Carter," *National Journal* (July 17, 1976), 999.
[4] Joel Havemann, "Reorganization—How Clean Can Carter's Broom Sweep?" *National Journal* (January 1, 1977), 6.
[5] *Ibid.*
[6] The following discussion of Carter's reorganization efforts in Georgia draws on Gary Fink, *Prelude to the Presidency* (Westport, Conn.: Greenwood, 1980). I also rely on Jimmy Carter, *Why Not the Best?* (Nashville, Tennessee: Boardman, 1975), pp. 105-116.

Company, management consultants, provided technical services. Major corporations in Georgia donated personnel; and appropriate state government employees, including nine faculty members of state universities, were detailed to work on the study teams. Governor Carter took great pride in the high percentage of personnel of the reorganization study who were experienced in business or government. He said: "We had very few professors and young people working on this. We are afraid the professors and young people might come up with a lot of theorized ideas. We wanted practical ideas."[7]

The reorganization plan created during a year of work proposed restructuring state government's numerous independent agencies into one of three large new departments—administrative services, natural resources, and human resources—or into one of several smaller existing departments. Thus Carter's claim on the 1976 presidential campaign trail that as governor he reduced the number of Georgia's state agencies to 22 from 300 was, in a crude way, a reflection of what he had done as a reorganizer.

The reorganization study was continually under Carter's scrutiny. As chairman of the study's executive committee, the governor engaged in its detailed direction, from setting priorities, through overseeing the product of the study teams, to reviewing the detailed draft recommendations. Thus the recommendations of the Reorganization and Management Improvement Study were not literally recommendations to the governor; they were the governor's recommendations by virtue of his participation.

At the opening of its 1972 session, the Georgia legislature took up Governor Carter's reorganization program. The reorganization plan fight in the legislature became Carter's supreme battle as governor. The passage of the reorganization authority in his first months as governor had triggered deep-seated conflicts about executive-legislative relations, and the reorganization plan itself reopened those issues. But now the debate was not simply about the abstract issue of whether or not the governor ought to be granted some authority; the controversy now fixed on the use of authority over real agencies and substantive interests.

The main figures in opposition constituted a coalition of what appeared to be self-interested politicians defending their turf. They were undercut by a massive public relations campaign launched with the aid of the Atlanta advertising firm of Gerald Rafshoon's. The campaign hammered on the governor's reorganization program as tantamount

---

[7] Quoted in Jimmy Carter, *Why Not the Best?* p. 91.

to good government. At the same time, a Citizens' Committee for Reorganization worked at the grass-roots to win support for Governor Carter and his drive to improve Georgia's government. These efforts succeeded, and the reorganization plan survived attempts in both houses to veto its major provisions. While holding fast against opportunities to compromise with some of his strongest legislative opponents, Carter was flexible in negotiating compromises with supporters. For example, he agreed to allow several parts of the plan to be dropped and later introduced as bills requiring affirmative action by the legislature.

Thus Carter won his great struggle against bad government. What did he really achieve in the process? Structurally, the administrative organization of the state was more streamlined, yet it was not smaller nor did it spend less money. Quite the contrary, state government employment continued to rise, and between 1971 and 1974, when Carter left the governorship, the state's budget increased over fifty percent. Yet Carter could argue that government's costs would have increased more without reorganization and that his reforms resulted in declines in the percentage rate of expenditure on the administrative costs of state government.

But the claim for increased efficiency for government was only a part of Carter's state goals for reorganization. In important respects it may have made reorganization attractive for its diverse collection of supporters, including conservative business and financial interests. But there was another goal as well for the reorganization program. As Betty Glad found:

> The original purpose of reorganization as pronounced in the study group's final report . . . was somewhat different from the efficiency claims that Carter would emphasize. The central purpose, as stated there, was the creation of a "structure of the Executive Branch of State Government which is responsive to the needs of the People of this state. . . ."[8]

Carter, in one of his early speeches in his quest for the presidency, adopted this view of reorganization rather than the efficiency language that he had used in selling the idea within Georgia. Speaking in April 1975, he recalled for his audience that when he became governor: "We had three hundred departments and agencies in the Georgia government. We abolished 278 of them, and we established a very fine,

---

[8] Betty Glad, *Jimmy Carter*, p. 178.

simple organization structure with what was left that works. It is open to the Georgia people for their comprehension and control."[9]

As Jimmy Carter went in search of the presidency, executive reorganization became more than a tool for organizational efficiency, however one might define that phrase; it became an instrument for making government more accessible, more comprehensible, and more predictable for its citizenry. Carter's goal seemed to be to make government more virtuous.

PLANNING TO REORGANIZE WASHINGTON

In *Why Not the Best?*, Jimmy Carter said of the national government:

> Drastic changes will be necessary, but such governmental action is not unprecedented. Many state and local governments have devised clear and simple organizational structures, effective and incisive budgeting techniques, comprehensive planning procedures, and ready access to the core of government by its own private citizens. I have personal experience which convinces me that these improvements can be effectuated in Washington.
>
> The mechanism of our government should be understandable, efficient, and economical . . . and it can be.[10]

The electoral politicization of executive reorganization was a natural consequence of the new goal that Carter had attached to the activity, making government understandable—"as good as its people." What did he mean by good government?

> Nowhere in the Constitution . . . or the Declaration of Independence . . . or the Emancipation Proclamation, or the Old Testament or the New Testament do you find the words "economy" or "efficiency." Not that these two words are unimportant. But you do discover other words like *honesty, integrity, fairness, liberty, justice, courage, patriotism, compassion, love*—and many others which describe what a human being ought to be. These are also the same words which describe what a government of human beings ought to be. (emphasis in original)[11]

Carter focused on a relationship between government's structure and its quality. As Aaron Wildavsky and Jack Knott observed about Cart-

---

[9] Jimmy Carter, *A Government as Good as Its People* (New York: Simon and Schuster, 1977), p. 54.

[10] Jimmy Carter, *Why Not the Best?*, p. 147.

[11] *Ibid.*, p. 116.

er's approach to government, he "is skeptical about the contents of public policies but dogmatic about the administrative procedures for arriving at those policies."[12]

The importance of structure over substance can be seen in Carter's campaign organization. During the campaign Carter created a transition group to formulate an approach to running government. While one would not accuse the candidate of lacking confidence, the creation of the transition staff has to be understood as more than presumption. In an interview, Jack Watson, the staff's director, innocently revealed a dichotomy in the Carter view of government that placed administration at a higher priority than policy. Asked about the relationship between his transition staff and the campaign's issues staff headed by Stuart Eizenstat, Watson replied that the issues staff was concerned with the campaign; the transition staff was concerned with government.[13]

A major component of that early transition group was a reorganization planning group. It was headed by Harrison Wellford, an attorney who had worked for Ralph Nader and Senator Philip Hart (Dem., Mich.). Wellford's team included a dozen professional-level people, among them Douglas Costle, who had worked for the Ash Council, and Jules Sugarman, an experienced career official in Atlanta's city government. The reorganization group's first report went to Carter before the November election; it was a recommendation for the creation of a Department of Energy. Carter proudly announced an energy department as one of the major reforms he would institute as President.[14]

Upon winning the presidency, Jimmy Carter set a reorganization strategy built on his Georgia experience. As in Georgia, he chose to win reauthorization of presidential reorganization authority at the earliest possible date, gaining authority for presidential reorganization initiatives prior to raising potentially conflictual recommendations. The Georgia approach was also duplicated in Carter's decision to create a reorganization planning vehicle that would work within a comprehensive framework. However, his strategy veered away from the Georgia experience in three regards. First, instead of an ad hoc, independent reorganization planning operation, President Carter created a new, large reorganization planning staff within the Office of Management and Budget. Second, instead of business and government people, the Presidential Reorganization Project within OMB was

[12] Aaron Wildavsky, *Speaking Truth to Power* (Boston: Little, Brown, 1979), p. 238.

[13] Dom Bonafede, "Carter Staff is Getting Itch . . . ," *National Journal* (October 30, 1976), 1,547.

[14] *National Journal* (September 25, 1976), 1,361.

staffed by young professionals and political activists. Third, instead of the preparation of a plan that would be presented at one time to Congress, Carter decided to adopt "a step-by-step incremental approach" through his first term.

On February 5, 1977 President Carter submitted to the Congress legislation for restoring Presidential reorganization authority (it had lapsed in 1973). Carter proposed a reorganization authority that was different from that held by his recent predecessors in several important respects. First, he proposed that a reorganization plan be subject to amendment by the president (not Congress) within thirty days after it has been sent to Congress (Congress having sixty days within which to veto the plan). This provision, it was thought, would give the president the flexibility to respond to criticism. Second, Carter asked that the limitation of one plan per thirty days be dropped. Third, he asked that the requirement that each plan cover only one subject also be dropped. Fourth, instead of the old statutory requirement, largely honored in its avoidance (that reorganization plans specify expected cost savings), Carter suggested that the plans "would provide information on the improvements in management, efficiency, and delivery of Federal services" that they would produce. Fifth, Carter asked that he be granted reorganization authority for a full four-year period, rather than the two-year renewal typical of past administrations.[15]

Just after his election victory, President-elect Carter had discussed the renewal of the reorganization authority with the chairmen of the House and Senate Government Operation Committees, Representative Jack Brooks (Dem., Texas) and Senator Abraham Ribicoff (Dem., Conn.). His proposed legislation reflected that discussion. Ribicoff had assured Carter of his support for renewal of the authority, but Representative Brooks expressed his overall opposition to the legislative veto in general and its application to reorganization in particular.[16] Rather than flatly opposing the President-elect's request for the renewal of the reorganization authority, Brooks, who could not muster majority support for his own position, suggested the idea of the amendment provision in return for his support; Carter accepted the trade despite the fact that it would weaken his hand in congressional bargaining.[17]

[15] *Public Papers of the Presidents, Jimmy Carter, 1977*, Vol. I, "Reorganization Plan Authority," February 4, 1977, pp. 82-84.

[16] Representative Brooks did not oppose presidential initiative in reorganization, but he thought that to meet the test of constitutionality it must be tied to an affirmative vote in Congress.

[17] This negotiation was described to the author by several persons who choose to remain anonymous.

Congress renewed the reorganization authority, granting it for three instead of the requested four years.[18] Consequently, Carter created the organizational mechanism to conduct his promised reorganization planning. At the signing ceremony for the reorganization act he said:

I think of all the campaign speeches that I made throughout the Nation, the most consistent commitment that was made to the American people was that I would move as quickly as possible to improve the efficiency and the effectiveness and the sensitivity of the Federal Government bureaucracy in dealing with the needs of the American people. . . . We'll begin the process as quickly as we can.[19]

In stressing that his federal reorganization activities would be incremental, Carter was doing nothing more than recognizing the constraints on reform in the federal government. Unlike in Georgia, reorganization at this level would not be novel, and the resistance against some of the reforms that might be proposed would be far more difficult to overcome than had such opposition in Georgia. In this light, the reorganization authority, as it had been altered for Carter, seemed an ideal means for seeking small- to medium-scale organizational change. The alterations gave the president more flexibility about what could be included within one plan, more flexibility over the frequency with which plans could be sent to Congress, and more latitude on the justifications contained within those plans.

But behind a facade of incrementalism, Carter created a mechanism for reorganization planning that reflected his Georgia experience. While he planned to feed Congress his reforms in a piecemeal fashion, his means for planning reorganization was distinctly comprehensive. The Reorganization Project was designated as a division within the Office of Management and Budget.[20] Within OMB, it was clustered with existing activities in management improvement and program coordination under the direction of Harrison Wellford, who was made executive associate director of OMB for reorganization and management. Under Wellford was an associate director for organization stud-

---

[18] Public Law 95-17, approved April 6, 1977. As a consequence of the Supreme Court's sweeping decision in Immigration and Naturalization Service v. Chadha, 103 S. Ct. 2764 (1983), the legislative veto is no longer operative in any subject area.

[19] Public Papers of the Presidents, Jimmy Carter, 1977, Vol. I, "Reorganization Act of 1977," p. 572.

[20] The following is drawn from President's Reorganization Project, "Plan for Conducting Federal Government Reorganization and Management Improvement Programs: Discussion Outline," March 1977.

ies, a post filled by Peter Szanton, a past official of the Bureau of the Budget and formerly a consultant to the Heineman task force.

The Reorganization Project was conducted by study teams addressing energy and natural resources, economic development, human resources, national security and international affairs, general government, and regulation reform. Separately, teams worked on personnel and paperwork reduction under an associate director of OMB for administrative management. The Reorganization Project included support staffs assigned to the task of ensuring reorganization's political success, including a congressional liaison staff, a legislative drafting and legal advisory group, and an office for "public awareness" concerning reorganization. Above the Reorganization Project, President Carter had intended to create an advisory group of ten to fifteen members drawn from professional and government elites—another adaptation of Carter's Georgia experience to the national scene. In fact, this group was never established. But, in June 1977 the President did create an executive committee on reorganization, meant to be "the top-level working group on executive branch reorganization."[21] Aside from the President, the committee included the vice-president, Walter Mondale; the budget director, Bert Lance; the Civil Service Commission chairman, Alan Campbell; the Council of Economic Adviser's chairman, Charles Schultze; and the presidential assistant for reorganization, Richard A. Pettigrew.

The Reorganization Project's creation required an immediate supplemental appropriation for OMB of $2,172,000; included within this figure were salaries for thirty-two personnel added to OMB for the project.[22] A number of persons were detailed to the project from other agencies, and their salaries are not reflected in that appropriation. Describing the origins and growth of the project's staff, a Congressional Research Service report stated: "The permanent staff, as planned, remained relatively small, although the number of 'voluntary outsiders' and detailees from various departments and agencies swelled the total personnel on the Project to nearly 300."[23]

In congressional testimony on the supplemental appropriation request, Harrison Wellford explained the Reorganization Project's substantive goals and the way in which these differed from past reorgan-

[21] *Public Papers of the Presidents, Jimmy Carter, 1977,* Vol. I, "Executive Committee on Reorganization," p. 1,052.

[22] Statement of Harrison Wellford before House Committee on Appropriations, press release of OMB, February 24, 1977.

[23] Ronald C. Moe, "The Carter Reorganization Effort," Congressional Research Service, Report No. 80-172 GOV, September 16, 1980.

ization planning efforts. First, past "reorganization plans were developed in a political vacuum," whereas the Reorganization Project was designed to maintain liaison with Congress and interested groups. Second, prior reorganization efforts did not deal with problems in their real locus, "at the program level where government meets the people." Wellford charged that reorganization had been box shuffling, disregarding the policy decisions happening "within those boxes" and without attention to the improvement of management and inter-governmental relations. Contrary to this, the project's study teams would be problem- and program-oriented. Finally, Wellford stated that prior reorganization planning had been without an institutional base; thus there had "been little connection between the formulators of reorganization policy and those who must implement it. . . ." The grafting of reorganization planning to OMB was meant to provide that base.[24] Wellford failed to mention yet another difference between the Reorganization Project and most modern reorganization planning.

Reorganization planning typically left some distance between reorganizers and presidents. Being outsiders, even when intimate with a president, most reorganizers are distanced from him. This distance allowed the president flexibility while it left the reorganization planners with the capacity to broker reform ideas that would be too controversial for the president to raise directly. The organizational location of the Reorganization Project reduced the distance between President Carter and the planning process, OMB being the main institutionalized staff support of the presidency. President Carter was himself the head of his Reorganization Project, with Wellford responsible to him through the budget director. Thus the President was responsible for the recommendations of the project, even prior to his own decisions regarding adoption. While all of this differs rather markedly from prior arrangements for reorganization planning, it duplicates Governor Carter's domination of reorganization planning in Georgia.

Focusing on Structure

Although there was more public talk about reorganization in the early months of the Carter administration than one finds in preceding administrations, there was still little indication about the President's aims in this regard. Surprisingly, the ideas that began to emerge from the Reorganization Project were far more structural than one might

[24] Statement of Harrison Wellford before House Committee on Appropriations, press release of OMB, February 24, 1977.

have expected, given Wellford's stress on problem and program orientation.

The document prepared by the Reorganization Project to guide its early work spoke of its approach in a way that blithely assumed that its structural approach differed from earlier structural approaches (box shuffling, in Wellford's terms) because the focus would be on problems. The memorandum stated:

> Reorganization goals will emphasize program consolidation and realignment. We will follow a bottom-up rather than a top-down approach—analyses will be made of policy failures at the program level. This is in contrast to previous reorganization efforts which have tried to impose structural reorganization from the top, guided by abstract management principles, not by study of programs.[25]

Thus reorganization planning under Carter would be liberated from "abstract" theory and overall ambitions of remodeling the executive branch's organization. It would begin at the bottom—the program level—and plan its structural changes from there.

The "bottom" is where government organization acts upon citizens, or "the people" in the sense of Carter's campaign phrases. The Reorganization Project specified eleven goals. Six of those goals are statements conveying the traditional or orthodox verities of reorganization at a general level—for example, "ensuring maximum efficiency and economy in government operations," increasing the efficacy of government's planning and coordinating activities, "reducing fragmentation, overlap, and unnecessary paperwork," and "giving managers the authority necessary to do the job and then holding them accountable." The other stated goals expressed those values that Carter had stressed during the campaign. Government should be simplified "so people—average citizens—can understand it." Government should be made "more responsive to citizens' needs." "Government's proceedings and documents" should be open, and its actions should be made predictable and consistent.[26] If there was a rationale to the stated approach of the Reorganization Project, starting from "the bottom up," this seemed to be it: government should be as good as its people.

Consistent with the Reorganization Project's close tie to the White House, its overall agenda and a number of its early projects were assigned to it by the President rather than developed by the project

---

[25] The President's Reorganization Project, "Plan for Coordinating Federal Government Planning and Management Improvement Programs: Discussion Outline," March 1977.

[26] *Ibid.*

staff. The project's initial assignment was those ideas for reorganization that Jimmy Carter had identified as desirable during his campaign, some of which had been developed by the pre-election transition staff. Among these were the Department of Energy, reducing the White House staff and simplifying the Executive Office, reducing the number of advisory committees in the federal government, and consolidating civil rights and equal employment opportunity agencies.[27] Several months after the establishment of the Reorganization Project, President Carter identified four more general areas of governmental activity on which he wanted the Reorganization Project to focus. These were law enforcement, local economic development, human services, and administrative services.[28] In a statement to the press, the President stated that there was wasteful duplication and overlap in the federal government that ought to be eliminated.

Deciding that what was needed was an inventory of all federal entities, Harrison Wellford directed his staff to prepare a "Current Inventory of Organizational Units Within the Executive Branch." This inventory was to be the map of the territory upon which the Carter administration would fight the reorganization wars. True to Carter's campaign claim that the federal bureaucracy was a mess, the inventory produced a huge list of organization units. Interviewed after the completion of the inventory, Wellford conveyed its findings as if it were an antique bestiary, containing "all those marvelous shapes that you really didn't imagine existed."[29] The inventory revealed 2,104 organizational units, that number being used to trumpet the federal bureaucracy's incomprehensibility and irrationality. In fact, lumped into that total were 1,179 advisory committees and 239 inter-agency committees, entities with no budgets and low-activity levels. The count of organizational units, aside from these utterly peripheral committees, included subunits of larger organizations. Thus the count included eleven cabinet departments and 335 sub-units within these departments, and it specified 55 non-cabinet agencies, containing 66 sub-units.[30] Belying its own promise to begin administrative reform with problems at the bottom of government, the administration drifted into a simple, structural approach.

In addition to its focus on structural reforms through the President's Reorganization Project, the administration also sought reform in two

[27] *Ibid.*

[28] *New York Times*, June 30, 1977.

[29] *Ibid.*, May 28, 1977.

[30] Figures drawn from *ibid.* and from Ronald Moe, "The Carter Reorganization Effort."

other areas, budgeting and personnel. In budgeting, President Carter directed the executive branch agencies to adopt a zero-base approach to the preparation of appropriation requests. In personnel management the administration sought a more flexible and incentive-based system for the upper- and middle-management levels of the public service. These three kinds of reform—structure, budget, and personnel—while about different subjects, share assumptions about and an approach to government. Each kind of reform entails an overall change which simplifies government and, presumably, leaves government more understandable. It might also be said that such reforms, if accomplished, would leave government more controllable, but this did not seem to be Jimmy Carter's aim. It was the form in which government operated that interested him, not what it was doing. Aaron Wildavsky and Jack Knott said about Carter (and Carter's reform efforts):

> Carter's basic beliefs are about procedures for making policy, about which he speaks with passion, determination, and consistency. He cares less about the goals than the need for goals, less about the content of policies than about their ideal form: simplicity, uniformity, predictability, hierarchy, and comprehensiveness.[31]

Zero-base budgeting was an ideal weapon for Carter. It required that the program elements within agency budgets be broken into "decision packages," each of which would analyze the program element it addressed and specify alternative funding levels. Furthermore, these program packages would be ranked as they moved from the middle to upper levels of agencies, coming in competition with other packages under the critical eyes of upper-level managers. Zero-base budgeting's intent is to start from the beginning in redistributing government's scarce resources in every budget and to do this on the basis of a rational schedule of objectives.[32] Zero-base, Carter promised, would reduce government's "costs and make the federal government more efficient and effective."[33] The Office of Management and Budget instructed its use for the fiscal year 1979 budget through Circular #A-11 of June 29, 1977. Of the resulting budget, Allen Schick said it "hardly terminates or curtails anything of significance, continues most spending

---

[31] Aaron Wildavsky, *Speaking Truth to Power*, p. 239.

[32] The case for zero-sum budgeting can be found in Peter Phyrr, *Zero-Base Budgeting* (New York: Wiley, 1973). For a critical evaluation of this budget reform concept, see Aaron Wildavsky, *The Politics of the Budgetary Process* (3rd ed., Boston: Little, Brown, 1979), pp. 202-221.

[33] Quoted in Wildavsky, *ibid.*, p. 203.

... and offers few program initiatives. . . ."[34] It was, evidently, a weapon that misfired.[35]

Attention must return to the center stage of the administration's reform efforts; structural changes and the work of the Reorganization Project. Structural change lay at the heart of the administration's efforts both in terms of resources expended and the President's logic of reform. If government was to be made better it must be simplified. The Carter administration conducted a quite consistent reorganization program if its aim was to simplify through consolidation. Its record of accomplishment is considerable—two new cabinet departments, ten reorganization plans that withstood veto attempts, and a major civil service reform.

Departmental Reforms

New cabinet-level departments require legislation. Although HEW had been created in 1953 by reorganization plan, since President Kennedy attempted to establish a Department of Housing and Urban Development with a plan, the Congress had routinely added a qualification to its grant of reorganization authority that it could not be used to establish new departments or abolish existing ones. It is generally agreed, however, that this qualification does not prohibit a president from submitting a reorganization plan which shifts agencies among departments *and* renames an existing department.[36]

On March 1, 1977, the President submitted legislation to create a Department of Energy. In his accompanying message, he described the department as imposing "immediate order to this fragmented system" of energy-related agencies.[37] The department merged two independent energy agencies created in the early and mid-1970's, the Energy Research and Development Administration and the Federal Energy Administration; the former was research-oriented and the latter was involved in data collection. The administration also recommended the

[34] Allen Schick, "The Road from ZBB," *Public Administration Review* 38 (March-April 1978), 177.

[35] John Dempsey observed that benefits of zero-base budgeting might show up in improved processes even while there is no perceptible difference in its program expenditures. See his, "Carter Reorganization: A Midterm Appraisal," *Public Administration Review* 39 (Jan.-Feb. 1979), 74-78.

[36] Even while opposing the congressional veto provision of the reorganization act, Representative Jack Brooks interpreted the act to allow a president to rename departments while shifting about their constituent parts.

[37] *Public Papers of the Presidents, Jimmy Carter, 1977*, "Department of Energy," March 1, 1977, p. 258.

transfer to the department of the regulatory authority of the Federal Power Commission. Also included were several energy-related activities of other departments, management of the Navy petroleum reserves and Defense's oil-shale reserves, the development of thermal efficiency standards located in HUD, the fuel-data collection activities of Interior's Bureau of Mines, and the power marketing organizations of Interior, such as the Bonneville Power Administration.

A number of energy-related activities were left outside the new department. Interior retained authority for licensing federal lands for fuel extraction, and energy-related activities in Agriculture and Transportation remained there, with the draft legislation calling for cooperation among the departments on energy matters. Two other regulatory operations with substantial connections with energy policy remained outside the department, the Nuclear Regulatory Commission and the Environmental Protection Agency.

Having chosen to create a new department, the President was caught between the proverbial rock and hard place. Either his proposal would be "incomplete," depending heavily on inter-departmental coordination, or more comprehensive reorganization would face a difficult battle over moving established agencies from settled domains.[38] Having chosen a less ambitious course of action, Carter nevertheless announced a grand goal for the new department: "This Department will make it possible for us to evolve very quickly a comprehensive policy which we've missed."[39] The new administration quite explicitly kept the discussion of the new department separated from policy considerations; it was meant to be a platform for policy. James Schlesinger, the President's chief aid for energy, told reporters that the administration sought to achieve passage of the Department of Energy Organization Act before any energy policy proposals were sent to Congress.[40]

In Senate hearings Schlesinger argued that once a policy is presented by the administration there will be many who will disagree over one

[38] Some influential senators urged a more ambitious Department of Natural Resources. Senator Charles Percy (Rep., Ill.) proposed a bill in 1977 that would have created a department responsible for both energy and land management within the federal government. Senator Henry Jackson (Dem., Wash.) had attempted to convince Carter of the desirability of such a conception of the new department. Senator Percy's bill was sent to the committee for hearings alongside the administration's bill. See U.S. Congress, Senate, Committee on Governmental Affairs, *Hearings, Department of Energy Organization Act*, 95th Cong., 1st Sess., 1977.

[39] *Public Papers of the Presidents, Jimmy Carter, 1977*, "Department of Energy-Remarks," March 1, 1977, p. 257.

[40] *National Journal* (March 3, 1977), 364.

or another aspect. But, according to him, no such disagreement should accompany organizational considerations; he said "I believe there should be no dispute about the need for establishing an organizational base within which these policies can be carried out."[41] This strong separation of organization and policy carried the day in Congress, with few witnesses or members of Congress willing to address the organization-policy linkage issue. One of the very few who did was Senator William Roth (Rep., Del.), who said that "we are asked to structure a new department ... with no real knowledge as to what direction you are going. ... To me it seems only good sense ... that the two move forward simultaneously."[42]

Finding support both from industry, consumer, and, environmental groups, the Department of Energy Organization Act was passed by Congress. However, Congress made one very significant change in the President's original plan. Instead of lodging overall regulatory authority, as transfered from the Federal Power Commission, in the secretary, Congress created an independent five-member Federal Energy Regulatory Commission within the department. On August 4, 1977, President Carter signed the act creating the Department of Energy and, at the same time, nominated James Schlesinger as its secretary. Carter noted that the new department would be a point of leadership for energy policy; the platform was in place. Carter also observed that there had been some difficulty in resolving what to include in it because it brings "together under one roof, about 50 different agencies."[43]

The second department which President Carter created was the Department of Education. This reorganization used an opposite conceptual justification to that of Energy. The administration's hardest selling job with the education proposal was to convince potential critics that the department had no policy relevance aside from ongoing programs, that it would not be a platform for policy.

The main recurring arguments used by the administration favoring a Department of Education were, one, that it would give greater status and access for education and, two, that the reorganization would produce a more efficient federal education bureaucracy. These arguments for status and speed were carefully distinguished from even the hint that greater clout or efficacy might lead to broader and more

---

[41] U.S. Congress, Senate, Committee on Governmental Affairs, *Hearings, Department of Energy Organization Act*, p. 121.

[42] *Ibid.*, p. 140.

[43] *Public Papers of the Presidents, Jimmy Carter, 1977*, "Remarks on Signing S 826," p. 1,411.

intrusive federal educational policy. The irony of the Department of Education was that it entailed the recommendation for a central and coherent federal agency to oversee a patchwork of programs serving a localized education system. However, that irony escaped the administration. In early February 1979, as the administration proposed to Congress the creation of the department, Vice-President Mondale, who was central to the fight for its passage, observed: "This is the only major industrial democracy in the world that does not have a department or a ministry of education." He continued, education in America suffered because its spokesman "is not at that Cabinet table speaking directly to the President."[44]

While campaigning for the presidency, Carter had used that same access to power argument about education. Announcing his support for the department, candidate Carter said that despite his opposition to the proliferation of federal agencies, he supported the idea of that department because it "would consolidate the grant . . . programs . . . and many other functions currently scattered throughout the government. The result would be a stronger voice for education at the federal level."[45] Hearing in this a friend's voice, the National Education Association abandoned its hundred-year-plus history of neutrality in presidential elections and endorsed Carter.

With Carter's inauguration and the establishment of the Reorganization Project, a study team was assigned to develop a proposal for a department of education; Patricia Gwaltney, the project's official in charge of human services organization (and a deputy associate director of OMB), was assigned to manage the study. While that study was developing, however, the politics of education reorganization flared brightly in a way that probably did more harm than good for the administration's prospects for winning approval for the new department.

Carter had not invented the idea of a Department of Education; proposals for it go back to the early years of the century. But no president had embraced that idea. On the other hand, Congress contained a number of members who were passionate about it, none more so than Senator Abraham Ribicoff. In 1977, independently of the administration, Senator Ribicoff introduced a bill to create a Department of Education, S. 991.[46] Ribicoff's bill would lift the education

[44] Quoted in the Washington *Post*, February 9, 1979.

[45] Quoted in Rochelle Stanfield, "Three 'R's' of the Education Debate," *National Journal* (December 4, 1976), 1,746.

[46] S 991 and some material relating to it, including Senate floor debate, can be found in U.S. Congress, Senate, Committee on Governmental Affairs, *Legislative History of*

division out of HEW and make it the heart of the new department, but there were education-related programs spread across the government and not limited to HEW's education division. Ribicoff's bill aimed at bringing a number of these into the new department. The other elements specified for inclusion were the Headstart program from HEW's human services division, civil rights enforcement in education from Justice, the school lunch program in Agriculture, the science education programs of the National Science Foundation, the operation of Indian reservation schools presently under Interior, the administration of the federal credit program for college dormitory construction in HUD, the operation of schools for military dependents in Defense, the National Endowments for the Arts and Humanities, the Department of Agriculture's Graduate School, and the federal responsibilities for Gallaudet College, Howard University, and the American Printing House for the Blind (HEW).[47]

S 991 was a design for a comprehensive department. All the while, the Reorganization Project was at work on a proposal for a narrow department that would involve little more than lifting to cabinet status HEW's education division. While the narrow bill belied the argument for the virtues of consolidation for reorganization, etc., it had the advantage of upsetting as few interest groups as possible.

In mid-April 1978, just as Budget Director James McIntyre was preparing to testify to Ribicoff's Senate Government Affairs Committee, with the assumption that he would present a narrow department as the administration's position, the Reorganization Project's narrow model was rejected by the President. At the end of the first week of April, the Reorganization Project staff presented its recommendations to the two persons who would convey them to Carter with their own added evaluations, Budget Director McIntyre and the director of the White House Domestic Policy Staff, Stuart Eizenstat. McIntyre and Eizenstat approved the narrow-model department, and they forwarded their recommendation on April 11.

Because of the press of business, President Carter did not make his final choice on this recommendation until the evening of April 13, with McIntyre's Senate testimony scheduled for the next morning. His final choice was for a broad department much like Ribicoff's proposal; thus McIntyre presented quite a different plan to the Senate Govern-

---

Public Law 96-88, Department of Education Organization Act, Part I, 96th Cong., 2nd Sess., 1980, pp. 43-63, and 226-385.

[47] *Ibid.*, pp. 46-47.

mental Affairs Committee than he had expected.[48] The breadth of Ribicoff's bill may have forced the President to match it in comprehensiveness, a value which he had frequently praised. The presidentially endorsed Ribicoff bill passed the Senate during 1978, but its parallel House bill, differing more in internal organizational aspects than in its substantive components, received lukewarm treatment in the House Government Organization Committee, and it never reached a floor vote in that session.

As the administration again approached the problem of creating the new department with the beginning of the 96th Congress, it faced strong pockets of outright opposition and a widely held view that the administration's efforts had more to do with electoral politics than with educational policy. A presidential primary season in which Carter could be challenged was around the corner, and the general election was less than two years away. The National Educational Association's support could be welcome comfort for Carter.

There remained problems of political resistance to agency transfers to a new department. Turf battles accompany any large-scale reorganization effort, but this kind of resistance ought not be dismissed out of hand as merely self-interest. On the contrary, because battles over bureaucratic position involve considerations of self-interest, they present the opportunity to assess the balance between those interests and other merits forwarded as the justification for reorganization. The question that could be fairly raised throughout the debate over passage of the Department of Education Organization Act was, why us? The rhetoric of the administration's broad plan for the department suggested inclusion of a multitude of educational activities as opposed to just lifting HEW's education division into the cabinet. Yet the department could not possibly include all those functions, for a variety of different reasons. Thus, when the National Science Foundation was targeted to lose science education programs, it had cause to ask why they were chosen for transfer and not the Veteran's Administration's educational programs or the Department of Labor's activities in vocational education.

Senator Ribicoff identified the principle of inclusion when he answered a question of Senator William Cohen (Rep., Maine) about why Indian education was not included in the administration's 1979 bill. Ribicoff said: "We are a practical Congress. We couldn't pass it in the

[48] Joel Havemann, "Carter's Reorganization Plans—Scrambling for Turf," *National Journal* (May 20, 1978), 791.

Senate of the United States."[49] Cohen's response pushed back to a more telling point of organizational principle, given the administration's rhetoric of reorganization. He observed:

> The problem is that we have several such obstacles. There are many programs not included because of the practical consequences that the Administration couldn't marshal enough support to pass the bill. If you have the argument made that the new Department would mean greater coordination and more efficiency, yet the practical realities dictate the exclusion of certain educational programs, that doesn't lead to more efficiency. . . .[50]

But, of course, the main justification for the new department's proponents in the professional educational community and the administration had nothing to do with efficiency. It was greater visibility that was offered as the new department's real virtue, and visibility did not require organizational comprehensiveness.[51] Therefore, in the end, it was difficult to find some principle of larger interest to countervail the argument of sheer, narrow interest that underlay the politics of turf in education.

A particular case of these organizational politics is worth citing, because it nicely contrasts alternative models of departmentalization. A necessarily low-profile opponent of the administration's crusade to create the new department was HEW secretary Joseph Califano.[52] Throughout the discussion it was assumed that HEW was unmanageable in its breadth and that its secretary could not possibly give education the attention it deserved; Califano's viewpoint was different.

[49] U.S. Congress, Senate, Committee on Governmental Affairs, *Hearings, Department of Education Organization Act of 1979*, 96th Cong., 1st Sess., 1979, pp. 293-294.

[50] *Ibid.*, p. 294.

[51] When justifying his campaign for the new department, President Carter consistently cited visibility and access to the presidency as the major reasons for creating it. Interestingly, he reversed the principle that shaped concepts of departmentalization over the prior fifteen years. Rather than viewing as desirable an organization that could address issues at the highest level of aggregation, Carter as his test for the failure of existing federal educational policy organization felt that it rarely brought educational issues to his attention. Typical of this defense was the President's remarks in a town meeting he held on September 23, 1978 at Aliquippa, Pa. He responded to a question about his hope to create the new department by saying: "After I became President, it was startling to me that in my regular Cabinet Meeting, where all the issues that are important to our country are discussed for a couple of hours on Monday mornings, that we rarely had come to my attention any matter concerning education. . . ." *Public Papers of the Presidents, Jimmy Carter, 1978*, p. 1,611.

[52] Joseph Califano, *Governing America* (New York: Simon and Shuster, 1981), Chap. 7.

He held that large departments were manageable, and he saw narrow, constituency-based departments as destructive of sound policy development and coordination. In writing about the Carter administration's pursuit of the separate department, Califano says:

> After my first year of experience at HEW, I was even more deeply troubled by the idea of a separate department, and I expressed my argument strongly. From the President's point of view, such a constituency-oriented department put yet another special interest directly on his back, and no buffer of a department head with broader responsibilities to deflect some of the issues for him. . . . Without any serious consolidation, the President would be adding yet another person reporting directly to him, further straining his span of control.[53]

Undeterred by the opposition and the failure of the House to act in 1978, in his 1979 State of the Union address President Carter placed the new department at the top of his reorganization agenda. The 1979 bill avoided some of the components that had been politically hot during the 1978 legislative season. Dropped from the administration's bill were Agriculture's school nutrition and lunch program, Indian education in Interior, and HEW's Head Start. The administration was set on using the issue of inclusion or exclusion in the new department as a bargaining chip for support of the overall bill.

The administration's use of inclusion-exclusion as a bargaining chip can be seen in its dealings with one of the House's leading members on educational matters, Representative John Brademas (Dem., Ind.). Brademas, the majority whip, was the only member of the leadership who was strongly connected to education. Thus it was crucial for the administration to win him to its side. Brademas was skeptical about an education department, more or less on the fence. But the department as proposed in 1979 touched several of the congressman's interests. First, he had made it clear that he could not support inclusion of the National Endowments for the Arts and Humanities, and these were dropped from the new bill. Second, Brademas had been specially concerned with vocational rehabilitation programs in HEW. While the administration bill excluded these, the groups supportive of those programs wanted to be part of the new department. At Brademas' suggestion, the administration changed its position on this. Finally, the 1979 bill gave maximum leeway to the secretary to organize the department and to assign statutory authority within it. Brademas

---

[53] *Ibid.*, pp. 277-278.

feared that the secretary's discretion would endanger another program that was scheduled for inclusion, the Institute of Museum Services. Wishing to insure that this small agency would be protected, Brademas demanded a letter from Budget Director McIntyre stating that the Institute's existence was guaranteed into the foreseeable future; McIntyre complied. In turn Representative Brademas supported the Department of Education bill.[54]

After a Senate debate that was tougher and more acrimonious than that in 1979, the 1979 bill passed by a vote of 71-21. In mid-May 1979 the House Government Affairs Committee approved the administration bill (HR 2444) by the slim margin of 20 to 19. That vote foreshadowed the narrow margin by which the bill would eventually pass the House, winning by 210 to 206 on July 11. The importance of the administration's lobbying with fence-sitting Democrats like John Brademas can be seen in the final vote, and on the negative side were a number of liberal and moderate Democrats whom the administration had failed to convince. Among these were Annunzio of Illinois, Conyers of California, Dingell of Michigan, Holtzman of New York, Obey of Wisconsin, and Yates of Illinois.[55]

President Carter had stated a number of reasons for a Department of Education. His first reason was that it would give professional education access to high-level policy discussions. He had also attributed benefits of coordination, ending duplication and overlap, increased accountability, and increased simplicity to his proposed department. It might be that the department would achieve all these virtues, but it was clear that access for professional education was of high priority for the President. The day after Congress passed the conference committee report on the Department of Education, the National Educational Association endorsed Carter for reelection.[56]

The Reorganization Project's cabinet-level plans went beyond Energy and Education. The record of those ambitions is revealing about the Carter administration's approach to reorganization. By the end of 1978, the Reorganization Project's efforts were focused on reports dealing with four areas: natural resources, economic development, trade, and food and nutrition. The study teams working on these were formulating reorganization recommendations which, while they presented options, suggested that the most desirable course of action was a major cabinet reorganization, reconstituting four departments. In

[54] Representative John Brademas (Dem., Ind.), interview with author, June 9, 1980.

[55] U.S. Congress, Senate, Committee on Governmental Affairs, *Legislative History of Public Law 96-88*, pp. 1,550-1,551.

[56] *New York Times*, October 30, 1979.

this change, two departments would become super-departments. A Department of Natural Resources would be built from Interior plus the civil functions of the Army Corps of Engineers, several agencies from Agriculture, including the Forest Service, and the National Oceanic and Atmospheric Administration from Commerce. A Department of Developmental Assistance would be created, using HUD as a platform to pull together developmental credit programs from Agriculture and Commerce. Losing major programs and agencies in this shuffle, Agriculture and Commerce would be restructured and refocused. The former would become a Department of Food and Nutrition and the latter a Department of Trade and Technology.[57]

The general course of the Reorganization Project teams' thinking on these projects became widely known by late 1978, not through leaks but through the project's practice of "touching base" with groups that were party to the activities under study. For example, in a December 1978 briefing of environmental groups, the natural resources study team was specific about what components would be recommended for a Department of Natural Resources, including water resource activities of the Army Corps of Engineers and Agriculture's Forest Service.[58] Consequently, prior to decisions by the President's policy and political advisers, and prior to his own final decision, the makeup of substantive recommendations was telegraphed to the public.

The process of review and consultation for the reports of the Reorganization Project's study teams ran up through Harrison Wellford, James McIntyre, and Stuart Eizenstat to the White House political advisers. It was Eizenstat who brought a predominantly policy-political focus to bear on the recommendations through the small, substantive policy specialized sections of his Domestic Policy Staff.[59] At the end of December 1978, in that review process, the symmetry of the Reorganization Project's four department model was lost, with the rejections of the plans for renaming Agriculture and Commerce. But, as the 1979 State of the Union Message was drafted, it was decided

[57] Rochelle Stanfield, "The Best Laid Reorganization Plans Sometimes Go Astray," *National Journal* (June 20, 1979), 84-91.

[58] *Washington Post*, March 2, 1979.

[59] OMB reorganization proposals were sent to the President through Stuart Eizenstat. Thus a policy-political evaluation was added to OMB's work by the Domestic Policy Staff. This created some tension between the policy staff and the reorganizers in OMB, but it also created a kind of enforced system of compromise in the production of reorganization proposals. Sy Lazarus, telephone interview with author, January 11, 1981. Lazarus was a member of the Domestic Policy Staff.

to commit the administration to major reorganizations in the natural resources and economic development areas. In his address, President Carter told Congress: "This year, we must extend major reorganization efforts to education, economic development, and to the management of our natural resources."[60]

During January and February 1979, the details of those promised reorganizations were subjects of intense negotiation. One cabinet secretary even went public in opposition to any diminution of her department. More boldly than Califano had been in attempting to quash a Department of Education, Juanita Kreps attacked the transfer from Commerce of economic development programs.[61] While the expansion of HUD into a Department of Development Assistance has been the priority recommendation in the economic development area of the Reorganization Project, to President Carter's advisers it became quickly to look like a battle not worth fighting.[62] Thus instead of simply approving the project's recommendation, McIntyre and Eizenstat gave the President options for the developmental assistance field that ranged from the new department at one extreme, through consolidation of existing programs in Commerce in the middle, to doing nothing at the other extreme.[63] In late February, Eizenstat's Domestic Policy Staff recommendation was to drop the idea of major reorganization in the developmental assistance area and focus on the natural resources department, although the staff also had strong doubts about the proposal's viability.[64]

On March 1, President Carter finally announced what was already widely known: he was going to propose a Department of Natural Resources; December's grand scheme of four new departments had shrunk to one.[65] However, in attempting to design the proposed department to make it politically palatable, the administration excised from it one of its vital centers. For almost fifty years, critics have pointed to the irrationality of federal water resource activities, divided as they are between the Army Corps of Engineers and the Bureau of Reclamation. Candidate Jimmy Carter had promised to bring water

---

[60] *Public Papers of the Presidents, Jimmy Carter, 1979*, "State of the Union," January 23, 1979, p. 105.

[61] *Washington Post*, March 2, 1979.

[62] President's Reorganization Project, "Organization for Development" (unpublished report, February 1979), pp. 36-54.

[63] Rochelle Stanfield, "The Best Laid Reorganization Plans Sometimes Go Astray," *National Journal* (January 20, 1979), 84.

[64] Sy Lazarus, interview with author.

[65] *Washington Post*, March 1 and 2, 1979.

resource activities under one roof. Early in 1979, Interior Secretary Cecil Andrus, a strong proponent of his department's expansion, had gone so far as to say that natural resources would not be worth much if it did not bring together the Corps of Engineers civil functions and the Bureau of Reclamation's operations. But in early March, when the administration announced its proposal, the new department failed to include the Corps of Engineers. The administration decided not to fight the battle over inclusion of the Corps against powerful congressional opposition.[66]

Because the Department of Natural Resources would be a renaming of Interior, the administration understood it as fitting the provisions of the reorganization authority. Representative Jack Brooks assured the administration that its interpretation was correct.[67] The attraction of a reorganization plan as the vehicle for creating the department was that it was thought to be more difficult to muster opposition to a plan than to positive legislation. But the reorganization plan strategy for creating the department was not acceptable to the Senate. Senators Abraham Ribicoff and Robert Byrd (Dem., W.Va.) told the President that while they favored the new department they could not accept its creation by plan.[68] Whether or not the Reorganization Act of 1977 intended it or not, such action would create a department without allowing Congress either to amend its details or to attach specifications and provisions on its use of authority. With that, the last remaining element of the Reorganization Project's grand scheme was dead.

Reforming Details: The Reorganization Plans

Carter's promises to conduct reorganization that would be problem-focused were more in tune with the ten reorganization plans he sent to Congress between 1977 and 1980 than the grand attempt at departmental reorganization. Reform by reorganization plan is typically narrow in scope. Even though the Reorganization Act of 1977 dropped the earlier stipulation that a plan could only include changes relating to one subject, political considerations and tradition dictated narrow breadth within these plans, as the protest against reconstituting Interior by Senators Byrd and Ribicoff indicates.[69]

During 1977 the administration submitted two plans. Plan No. 1

---

[66] *Ibid.*, March 2, 1979.

[67] Anonymous congressional staff persons, interview with author.

[68] *New York Times*, March 1, 1979; and *Washington Post*, May 16, 1979.

[69] For his excellent review of Carter's reorganization plans, I am indebted to Ronald Moe, "The Carter Reorganization Effort: A Review and Assessment," pp. 29-51.

of 1977 removed units from and reduced personnel in the Executive Office of the President. The plan eliminated seven units from the EOP, aimed at reducing its staff by 15 percent, from 1,712 to 1,459; reduced the number of White House staff positions from 485 down to 351; created a new policy management system within EOP, replacing the Domestic Council with a leaner Domestic Policy Staff; and consolidated administrative functions of the Executive Office. Plan No. 2 of 1977 created an International Communication Agency, which would consolidate programs then under the auspices of the United States Information Agency and the Bureau of Education and Cultural Affairs in the State Department. The plan also consolidated two advisory boards, one dealing with information dissemination and the other with cultural affairs, into the U.S. Advisory Commission on International Communication, Cultural and Education Affairs.

Plan No. 1 of 1978 joined the federal government's programs aimed at enforcing non-discrimination in employment with the enforcement auspices of the Equal Employment Opportunity Commission. The plan moved programs dealing with enforcement in private-sector employment and wages from the Department of Labor to the Commission, and it shifted enforcement of fair employment in the federal government from the Civil Service Commission to the EEOC. Plan No. 2 of 1978 abolished the Civil Service Commission, splitting its functions into two separate agencies, the Office of Personnel Management and the Merit System Protection Board. This plan was the organization adjunct to the administration's major civil service reform bill. Plan No. 3 of 1978 was one of a long line of reorganizations in federal emergency mobilization and disaster-preparedness programs. It centralized a number of such programs into a new Federal Emergency Management Agency. Reorganization Plan No. 4 of 1978 untangled dual responsibilities in federal pension regulation placed in both the Departments of Labor and Treasury by the Employment Retirement Income Security Act of 1974.

Reorganization Plan No. 1 of 1979 established an Office of Federal Inspector for the Alaska Natural Gas Transportation System. This plan focused into one new entity the diverse regulatory and oversight authority created in the Alaska Natural Gas Transportation Act of 1976. The act provided for a role by a number of federal agencies in regulating the building and operation of an Alaska natural-gas pipeline, and the new office was meant to incorporate and focus those diverse agencies' roles into one for the purpose of improved coordination and more effective relationships with firms working on and operating the pipeline. Reorganization Plan No. 2 of 1979 created an

International Development Cooperation Agency to coordinate federal aid activities towards the developing world. The IDCA would provide an umbrella organization for the Agency for International Development, the Overseas Private Investment Corporation, and the Institute for Technical Cooperation, which was at that time proposed but not yet created by Congress. Reorganization Plan No. 3 of 1979 consolidated international trade functions, assuming that a rationalized administration of these programs would improve American export performance. The plan converted the existing Office of Special Representative for Trade Negotiations located in the Executive Office into the Office of U.S. Trade Representative. It also located all non-agricultural export trade operating responsibilities in the Department of Commerce, a move which simply reinforced the historical dominance of that department over non-agricultural export trade.[70]

Reorganization Plan No. 1 of 1980 increased the authority of the chairman of the Nuclear Regulatory Commission, lessening some ambiguities in the law concerning the chairman's executive authority. The plan strengthened the executive role of the chairman, gave him primary responsibility for emergency response in crisis situations, and made him responsible for overseeing the agency's planning process.

In the end, what was most characteristic of President Carter's reorganization plans was that they were non-controversial. All ten survived veto attempts in Congress, even though the Reorganization Act of 1977 made it easier to bring a resolution of disapproval to a floor vote. Only one of the plans received less than an overwhelming approval. That exception was Plan No. 2 of 1979, creating the International Development Cooperation Agency. Critics had argued that this plan diminished the importance of the Agency for International Development. They had enough strength in the Senate to marshall 45 votes in favor of disapproval, with 51 votes against vetoing the plan.

The administration's success with reorganization plans can be attributed to two causes. First, the administration was conservative in its judgment of Congress' tolerance. In 1980 hearings considering a one-year renewal of the reorganization authority, Representative Eliott Levitas (Dem., Ga.) said, ". . . there has been a reluctance to submit the really significant, broad, sweeping reorganizations that should have been sent up and let Congress make a judgment."[71] Harrison Wellford responded that in instances like natural resources the administration

[70] See Joseph Brandes, *Herbert Hoover and Economic Diplomacy* (Pittsburgh: University of Pittsburgh Press, 1962).

[71] U.S. Congress, House, Committee on Government Operations, *Hearings, Extend Reorganization Authority to the President*, 96th Cong., 2nd Sess., 1980, p. 13.

decided that there was insufficient support. Levitas' point can be read as suggesting that policy decisions are best made within a conflict system between the executive and the legislature. In short, Levitas favored policy making within a political arena, and Wellford was defending policy making within a planning context.

A second cause for the success of the administration's reorganization plans was the provision of the Reorganization Act of 1977 which allowed the president to amend a plan once submitted. Thus the president can lessen opposition, should it develop, after a plan is revealed. Using the amending authority, President Carter effected changes in four of his ten plans, Nos. 1 and 2 of 1977, No. 2 of 1978, and No. 1 of 1980. But, while this provision gave the President increased flexibility, it also allowed Congress to hold his plans hostage.

The overall appearance of these reorganization plans is that of multiple minor organizational changes, none of which matched Carter's promises for reorganization. Along with the ad hoc character of the administration's cabinet-level reorganizations already discussed, there is little that seems "comprehensive" or fundamental about the program, although President Carter had promised both. In fact, his chief reorganization planner, Harrison Wellford, forthrightly denied that any overall principle, theory, or view of organization, administration, or the governmental system guided the planning operation.[72] This frame of mind suggests an extreme empiricism. It would have it that "problems" are there; they are real and not matters of perspective. Furthermore, remedies are not the function of a perspective on administration; they are self-evident, given the problem.

Reforming the Civil Service

The occasional doubts within the administration about the President's reorganization program only reflected a growing sense on the outside that it was a mundane exercise elevated beyond its proper station. In Carter's third year it was common knowledge that Energy was in disarray, lacking direction and internal coherence—a platform without policy. A report on the department prepared in mid-1979 within OMB found the Department of Energy to be error-prone in its work, given to developing poorly analyzed regulations, and without effective in-

[72] Harrison Wellford, speaking at a panel discussion on Carter's reorganization program at the 1978 meeting of the American Political Science Association; and Harrison Wellford, interview with author, June 10, 1980.

ternal authority.[73] Looking at the administration's overall reorganization activities in the early weeks of 1979, Senator Adlai Stevenson III (Dem., Ill.) thought that reorganization as practiced by Carter was a symptom of a deeper malaise—government that was irrelevant to the challenges at hand. Stevenson said: "We are dominated by cheap and easy answers, and reorganization plans that tinker with the mechanism of government."[74]

In self-defense, the administration's reorganizers said that it was the structural as opposed to procedural reform efforts that their critics attacked. There had been a procedural element within the President's Reorganization Project from the beginning, and it grew in importance in late 1978 and 1979. An overview of some of that activity might hint at whether there is merit in the hypothesis of some in the administration that greater effort on procedural reforms would have been preferable to structural efforts.

The most ambitious of the administration's procedural reforms concerned civil service. The impetus for civil service reform came from the chairman of the Civil Service Commission, Alan K. Campbell.[75] The President was interested in reform in general, but Campbell brought to his job specific ideas and values about the public service which gave direction to civil service reform. He came to government from the deanship of the LBJ School of Public Policy at the University of Texas. Earlier he had served at the Maxwell School of Syracuse University as both faculty member and dean. Campbell joined the Civil Service Commission in early summer 1977, and by August a large-scale study for civil service reform was launched under his direction.

The civil service study, titled the Personnel Management Project, involved about 160 staff members organized into nine task forces, plus a central staff and a management analysis team. Campbell was chairman of the project; Wayne Granquist, an associate director at OMB, was his assistant chairman. The project's executive director was Dwight A. Ink, a retired senior civil servant. Thomas Murphy, head of the Federal Executive Institute, was Ink's deputy. Of the 118 members on the project's nine task forces, only five were not employed within the federal public service. Among the 43 members of the proj-

---

[73] *Chicago Tribune*, September 16, 1979; and Representative Toby Moffet (Dem., Ct.), interview with author, June 17, 1980.

[74] Quoted in *Washington Post*, February 9, 1979.

[75] Sy Lazarus, telephone interview with author.

ect's central staff and its management analysis team, there were no persons who were not career civil servants.[76]

Of all the administration's study groups, the civil service project was the only one wholly composed of experienced federal managers and guided by individuals who were aware of the history of civil service reform efforts. The Management Project contained a memory or inventory of reform ideas as well as an inventory of the problems plaguing the civil service and federal management. The very fact that the project's staff could spin out the reform options for civil service within a couple of months was a testimony to the importance of the memory of reform. As Dwight Ink noted about the project staff's capacity for turning out its final report after only four months of operation:

> In organizing . . . this Project, we drew primarily upon Federal careerists with extensive diversified public experience. . . . This avoided the process of relying solely on outside "experts" who might have had to spend most of the study period learning the problems with little time left for solutions.[77]

The project's final report contained recommendations aimed at easing and decentralizing the hiring and promotion process through assignment of examining responsibilities to agencies, by removing the rule of three (creating a larger pool on eligible persons), and by limiting veterans' preference in hiring. They eased removal of employees for cause by streamlining the appeals system. The report also proposed an Executive Service which would eventually incorporate all the supergrades, making rewards dependent upon performance and freeing its members for reassignment, including the possibility of removal from the Executive Service for inadequate performance of duties. Finally, to improve the organizational system within which these procedural reforms would operate, the project's report recommended the dissolution of the Civil Service Commission and the assignment of its functions to two separate entities. Personnel management responsibilities would be placed within an Office of Personnel Management, headed by a director serving at presidential pleasure, subject to Senate confirmation. The commission's responsibilities for protecting the merit system would be assigned to a Merit Protection Board. The Federal

---

[76] The staff is listed, along with the members' assignments and permanent employers in President's Reorganization Project, Personnel Management Project, "Final Staff Report," Vol. I (unpublished report, December 1977), pp. iii-iv, 251-255.

[77] Letter, Dwight Ink to Alan Campbell and Wayne Granquist, December 28, 1977, in President's Reorganization Project, Personnel Management Project, Vol. I, "Final Staff Report," December 1977.

Labor Relations authority, another entity, would be created to pull together the federal government's growing and complex problems of management relations with multiple employees organizations and unions (over half of all federal employees being members of collective bargaining units).[78]

On March 2, 1979, President Carter sent Congress a bill that incorporated most of the Management Project's recommendations. It created a Senior Executive Service, replaced automatic step increases for managers between GS-13 and GS-15 with incentive pay increases, streamlined the disciplinary and appeals system, created a new Federal Labor Relations Authority (while continuing to rely on President Kennedy's Executive Order 10988 for the basis of federal collective bargaining as opposed to meeting employee union wishes that it be reinforced through statutory recognition), decentralized personnel decision making by decentralizing examination and routine actions, limited veterans' preference to the disabled and to those within ten years of military service, and replaced the "rule of three" with the right of an agency to consider the seven top candidates in choosing a person to fill an opening.[79] Parallel to the legislation which would enact these reform provisions into law, the President submitted reorganization plan, No. 2 of 1978, to abolish the Civil Service Commission and create the Office of Personnel Management and the Merit System Protection Board.

Between early March and mid-September, the administration invested great effort in seeing the civil service reform package through the Congress. President Carter himself busily campaigned for the bill, holding meeting after meeting with members of Congress over aspects of the program, meeting with civil servant's groups to calm their fears about change, and using almost every one of his public appearances to urge his listeners to support civil service reform. The cabinet was also engaged in the lobbying effort, with its members sent over to Congress to visit members of the committees considering the legislation and reorganization plan. For example, when the House Post Office and Civil Service Committee began work on the bill, its most junior Republican, Representative James Leach (Iowa) was visited first by Treasury Secretary W. Michael Blumenthal and then by HUD Secretary Patricia Harris. Representative Edward Derwinski (Ill.), a senior Republican on the committee, received a phone call from Secretary of State Cyrus Vance at about the same time, urging him to support the

[78] The project's executive summary is in *ibid.*, pp. 3-19.
[79] *Ibid.*, "Federal Civil Service Reform," March 2, 1978, pp. 444-449.

bill. Moreover, working both houses on a day-to-day basis was Civil Service Commission Chairman Alan Campbell.[80]

There were two key centers of opposition to civil service reform. Federal public employee unions expressed reservations about the package because it made no advances in legitimating federal employee collective bargaining. Another source of opposition was the very powerful veterans' lobby, which was committed to saving veterans' preference in federal employment and promotion.

The President could grant these concerns and leave the heart of his reform untouched. Carter's recitation of the various purposes of his reform proposal—strengthening employee rights, providing incentives for managers, etc.—left unstated its most crucial goal.[81] It would increase the flexibility of political executives in selecting those high-level career people who fill the positions immediately under their supervision and upon whom they are dependent for policy-related tasks.

The administration struck a bargain with organized labor to support an amendment to its proposed legislation that would write into law the ground-rules for federal employee collective bargaining. Now the law would have to be changed rather than having just an Executive Order revoked to eliminate or weaken collective bargaining.[82] On the even knottier issue of veterans' preference, the administration simply backed off. That provision was eliminated by Congress at the behest of the veterans' groups.

Carter's civil service reform owed a great debt to earlier proposals to reform the civil service. The Brownlow Committee and both Hoover Commissions had called for major changes in that system. Their recommendations considered together highlight the importance of reforming or eliminating the Civil Service Commission so as to create a responsible manager and presidential personnel policy adviser, to separate quasi-judical from the managerial functions within the system of personnel management, and to establish a flexible corp of upper-level civil servants. It was precisely the administration's ability to rely on those predecessors through the memory built into the experienced leadership of the Personnel Management Project that allowed Carter

[80] Harlan Lebo, "The Administration's All-Out Effort on Civil Service Reform," *National Journal* (May 27, 1978), pp. 837-838.

[81] *Public Papers of the Presidents, Jimmy Carter, 1978*, "Federal Civil Service Reform," March 2, 1978, pp. 444-449.

[82] *Washington Post*, October 14, 1978. The Senate's expansion of the place of collective bargaining in the bill can be seen in U.S. Congress, Senate, Committee on Governmental Affairs, Report, Civil Service Reform Act of 1978, 95th Cong., 2nd Sess., 1978, pp. 99-114.

to plan a reform package within four months and then fight it successfully through Congress. It was the plan's virtue that its fundamental recommendations were not novel. Also, by launching civil service reform at a time when the public's evaluation of the federal government and public service was near its nadir, the President enhanced the chances of his legislation's success. The *Washington Post* observed that the bill owed victory "to the apparent public mood in its favor. . . ."[83] The ability of the administration's planners to call upon some familiar solutions to government's personnel problem helped Congress to see the reform plan as a sensible response to that public mood.

Reorganization Without Governance

The civil service reform was the most conspicuous reorganization success of the Carter administration. At first notice that might be taken as support for the proposition favored by some in the administration that reforms of procedure—how government works—have a greater likelihood of tangible success than reforms of structure—how government is organized. But, in fact, the success of the civil service reform had little to do with the degree to which its elements were procedural rather than structural. Rather, that success was due to those who were chosen by the President to plan and win passage for the reform, the tradition of reform conceptions concerning the public service that they could call upon, and the public mood toward government within which the reform plan was offered to Congress.

Thus the case of Carter's civil service reform does not address the central question within the issue of whether that administration should have put more stress on another kind of reform other than structural change at an earlier point in its political life. The question implied herein is: what ought a president seek through executive reorganization? Only upon answering this question can a president properly ask: what ought be his specific targets of reform?

As one member of the Domestic Policy Staff characterized reorganization, it is "a nice second level issue."[84] In expanding on that comment, he observed that reorganization does not normally generate allegiance and votes the way other issues might. Nevertheless, he noted, an administration could achieve some accomplishments in this area,

[83] *Washington Post*, October 14, 1978.
[84] Sy Lazarus, telephone interview with author.

appearing administratively competent. As far as it goes, this is an accurate characterization of reorganization as a political issue.

However, this view of reorganization misses its central character as an element of the modern presidency. It is not primarily an instrument of electoral politics; as presidents since Taft have understood, it is an instrument of governance. Carter sought to use reorganization as a way of attracting voter attention and loyalty, but he gave little evidence of realizing that it might be a means for dealing with government.

In its initial design and intention, Carter's reorganization planning system aimed at a public audience. But the President misjudged the staying power of reorganization's political appeal. In association with a post-Watergate malaise, the promise to clean-up government helped candidate Jimmy Carter in 1976, but reorganization planning in practice cannot provide glue for a winning electoral coalition. It is but a "second level issue." Failing in the political intention of its design, the Reorganization Project failed also to become a governing tool for the President. It lacked coherence and coordination; as its manager proudly claimed, it followed no overall conception of management. It was a collection of young professionals without significant applied or academic experience with administration, working under a president burdened by a rigid and curiously moralistic conception of administration. These reorganizers generated a large bulk of recommendations, but little that they did enhanced the capacity of President Carter to govern effectively.

In the summer before the presidential election of 1980, a distinguished Democratic congressman spoke of his dispair with an administration that seemed obsessively political while lacking interest in the purposes for which politics might be used.[85] Therein is a fitting epitaph for the Carter reorganization program; it was a case of activity without purpose. For Carter, reorganization planning was politics without governance—efficiency in search of popularity.

THE END OF THE REORGANIZATION MOVEMENT

Comprehensive reorganization planning ended badly for presidents in the 1970's. For Richard Nixon, reorganization was subordinated to powerful ambition injudiciously expressed. For Jimmy Carter, reorganization was an expression of a naive understanding of government, beneath which lay a canny sense of naivety's political utility.

After the 1970's, reorganization planning appears less attractive and

[85] Representative Richard Bolling, interview with author, June 9, 1980.

less necessary for a president than it did during the 1950's and 1960's. For all of his criticism of the federal government, Ronald Reagan's strategy for directing government's agencies has relied directly on policy, personnel, and budgets rather than on reshaped organizational structures and reformed processes. In mid-course President Reagan did gesture toward the routine of reorganization planning by creating an unprecedentedly large study group of prominent businessmen, the privately funded President's Private Sector Survey on Cost Control.[86] Yet one cannot imagine that this group was meant as a serious tool of presidential managerial planning.

The failure of reorganization in the 1970's to enhance presidential interests raises fundamental questions about its utility. What ways might reorganization planning serve presidents in contemporary and future circumstances? How has reorganization planning served past presidents? The best evidence that reorganization planning has been understood to accomplish desirable ends for presidents is its recurrence. What about it inspires repetition throughout the twentieth-century presidency?

[86] *New York Times*, September 28, 1982.

Chapter Eleven

ACCOUNTING FOR COMPREHENSIVE REORGANIZATION PLANNING

The quintessential end of theorizing is to arrive at
statements of regularity about the structure,
behavior, and interaction of phenomena."[1]
Harry Eckstein

The preceding chapters associate comprehensive reorganization planning with secular change in the presidency. But that relationship does not explain the recurrence of comprehensive reorganization planning; rather, it illuminates a consequence of it. Comprehensive reorganization planning's recurrence remains a puzzle.

Why do politicians initiate reorganization planning? The simplest reason would be that comprehensive reorganization planning is an effective instrument for increasing efficiency in the executive branch. But reorganization planning's recurrence is a puzzle precisely because that simple explanation is untenable. Judged by its recommendations for improved administration that are adopted within a reasonable length of time (say, within the service in office of a president), reorganization planning has been markedly unsuccessful.

One quite regular feature of the episodes of reorganization planning that have been surveyed above is that their recommendations are fought over and then ignored. Of course, reorganization planning episodes are more successful when examined in terms of the long-run acceptance of their recommendations. An executive budget was established nearly a decade after it was recommended by the Commission on Economy and Efficiency. Presidential reorganization authority was granted by Congress eight years after it was proposed by the Joint Committee. A Senior Executive Service was created more than two decades after the second Hoover Commission's recommendations for a senior civil service. If we look at the longer historical record, it is clear that comprehensive reorganization planning has reshaped the organization of the presidency and the executive branch. But politi-

---

[1] Harry Eckstein, "Case Study and theory in Political Science," in Fred Greenstein and Nelson Polsby (eds.), *Handbook of Political Science*, vol. 7 (Reading, Mass.: Addison-Wesley, 1975), p. 88.

cians do not act with their eyes (and calculations of interest) on the long run. As one wag put it: "In the long run we will be out of office."

So the cause for puzzlement becomes clear. Why have political actors initiated reorganization planning? Unfortunately the scholarly literature on comprehensive reorganization does not go far toward solving this problem.

There is a potpourri of goals attributed to reorganization planning by scholars in political science and public administration. Offering a typology of reorganization's goals with the most inclusive categories, Lester Salamon suggests that three general goals have driven executive reorganization—economy and efficiency, policy effectiveness, and tactical advantage.[2] The scholarly literature on reorganization helps one focus on the aims of reorganizers. But, finally, such typologies exhibit several problems which make them of little use in addressing the puzzle of reorganization's persistence. The first problem is that such attributions of purposes to reorganization planning limits the perspective to the narrowly instrumental. Such a view would have it that reorganization planning is a tool for a specific end: economy, for example. But politicians and reorganizers have diffuse ends as they cooperate to create reorganization planning. Furthermore, reorganization planning may play symbolic as well as instrumental roles. Also, such instrumental views tend to mix apples and oranges in the sense that such "goals" as economy and efficiency, policy effectiveness, and tactical advantage are not incompatible. Finally, such attributions of goals to comprehensive reorganization planning are severely weakened by their ad hoc character. The literature on reorganization characteristically reasons from sweeping generalization. There has been little effort to anchor generalization and interpretation in detailed, comparable cases.

THE PHYSIOLOGY OF REORGANIZATION PLANNING

In the first place, the conundrum of reorganization planning's recurrence will be addressed here through a focus on more fundamental characteristics than its goals. The cases presented heretofore clearly vary in several fundamental respects. First, they are created in different political environments. Second, there is large variation in the organizational mode through which reorganization planning was effected. Third, the different episodes are created by politicians occupying different roles and expressing different political positions. To assess the

---

[2] Lester Salamon, "The Question of Goals," in Peter Szanton (ed.), *Federal Reorganization* (Chatham, N.J.: Chatham House, 1931), pp. 58-84.

variation on these dimensions among cases of reorganization planning is to observe reorganizations physiology, as it were.

Each varying characteristic of reorganization planning identified here can be inverted into a question that probes the recurrence of comprehensive reorganization planning. First, to recognize that reorganization planning episodes have been created in differing political environments is to ask: what events or political conditions stimulate the creation of reorganization planning? Second, to notice the variation in organizational format among the cases is to ask: why are different formats adopted in different cases? Third, to observe that politicians occupying different roles have created reorganization planning episodes is to ask: in search of what benefits do politicians create reorganization planning? To operationalize these questions they must be translated into hypotheticals about what one expects to find in the cases under consideration.

Initiating Reorganization

Why do politicians initiate comprehensive reorganization planning? Politicians tend to justify the initiation of reorganization planning through reference to undesirable events. There are two separate elements wrapped up in a view of reorganization as a response to change. The first element is the objective condition itself to which the political decision maker responds; the second element is the decision maker's *evaluation* of that objective condition.

To examine the role of objective change itself and its relation to the initiation of reorganization planning, it will be useful to focus upon year-to-year change in government's spending. As a measure of objective change in government, change in government spending from year to year is more calculable and traceable than other dimensions of change, such as increasing complexity or changing workload. In particular, the initiation of reorganization planning will be examined in relationship to the year-to-year percentage rate of change in government's spending. Thus, the proposition that will guide examination of the relationship between objective change and the initiation of comprehensive reorganization planning will be the following: *Comprehensive reorganization planning is initiated following large variation in the year-to-year percentage change in government's outlays.*

Degree of change in spending will be assessed by contrasting the mean of year-to-year percentage changes in government's spending levels in the three years prior to the initiation of reorganization planning against those changes for the ten years prior to initiation.[3] Table 3 presents (A) the mean percentage rate of change for the ten years prior to the initiation of nine cases within the universe of comprehensive reorganization planning, and it presents (B) the mean percentage rate of change for the three years prior to initiation.[4] The degree of difference between ten-year and three-year mean percentage rates of change would reflect the degree of change in the level of

Table 3

Mean Rate of Change in Budget Outlays in the Ten Years Prior to Initiation (A) and in the Three Years Prior to Initiation (B): C = A/B.
(The smaller the number in C, the larger is the difference between A and B.)

In Percentage Terms

	A	B	C
Taft Commission	.035	.095	.37
Joint Committee	.09	.338	.27
Brownlow Committee	.137	.235	.59
First Hoover Commission	.354	-.350	-1.0
Second Hoover Commission and PACGO	.005	.298	.02
Price Task Force	.064	.069	.93
Heinemann Task Force	.076	.069	1.10
Ash Council	.076	.152	.54
President's Reorganization Project	.095	.167	.57

[3] The mean percentage rates of change are determined by comparing one budget year's outlays to the next. For example, the mean percentage rate of change for the ten years prior to the initiation of the President's Commission is determined in the following manner. A percentage change is realized for each budget year pairing between 1900 and 1909. The first pair of years for which a percentage change is determined is 1900-1901, and the second pair is 1901-1902. This pairing process is repeated through to 1908-1909. The percentage figure shown in Table 3, column A, is the mean percentage change of these ten pairs. Column B of the same table reports a mean figure for three budget years prior to initiation. For the President's Commission, these years are 1907, 1908, and 1909, comprising the pairs 1907-1908 and 1908-1909. Data on outlays drawn from U.S. Bureau of the Census, *The Statistical History of the United States* (New York: Basic Books, 1976), p. 1,114.

[4] For reasons of their almost identical chronology the second Hoover Commission and PACGO are joined together in Table 3.

government's spending prior to the initiation of reorganization planning. That difference is represented in Table 3 by column C, where C represents the ratio of the mean ten-year change and the mean three-year change. Thus:

$$C = \frac{A}{B}$$

The rank order of reorganization planning episodes in Table 3 is as follows, listing them in increasing magnitude of the ratio expressed in percentage terms in column C, Table 3: first Hoover Commission (C = −1.0); second Hoover Commission and PACGO (C = .02); Joint Committee (C = .27); the Taft Commission (C = .37); Ash Council (C = .54); President's Reorganization Project (C = .57); Brownlow Committee (C = .59); Price Task Force (C = .93); Heineman Task Force (C = 1.10). The four cases with strongest association between their initiation and large changes in government's budget outlays are cases in which the rhetoric surrounding initiation fixed on change as a justification for reorganization planning. Three of these four cases were congressionally initiated, and it was observed in earlier chapters that Congress' continuing stake in reorganization planning has been expressed during this century in the language of economy and retrenchment. Thus the Joint Committee and both Hoover Commissions represent the merger of congressional inclination and objective conditions. One case in the top four was presidentially initiated and controlled, Taft's President's Commission. Of course the fact that the executive budget reform was at the center of the Taft Commission's work is evidence of its response to rapid and apparently uncontrolled growth in federal spending.

Five of the nine cases have less association with changes in government's spending. These five cases are modern and presidential in their origin and orientation. In fact, the case studies above lead one to expect precisely this result; economizing was not the direct purpose of any of these five cases. It is instructive in this regard to consider PACGO for the purpose of disassociating it from the second Hoover Commission. As the reader will remember, never in all of its work during the eight years of the Eisenhower administration did PACGO become concerned with spending in government. The modern presidentially initiated cases of reorganization planning engaged different values from the congressionally initiated cases.

Consider further the break between congressionally and presidentially initiated cases. The former lend support to the hypothesis that change in government spending is a cause of reorganization planning.

But something is still to be learned about the presidentially initiated cases, given the apparent inapplicability of that hypothesis to them. The trend in reorganization planning in the 20th century was for later episodes to be more presidential in their initiation and orientation. The five presidentially oriented cases—make it six with PACGO—all exhibit a concern with planning. In effect, they aim for analytic foresight. Presidentially oriented and dominated reorganization planning was not so much disassociated from changes in government's operations as it was aimed at guiding change.

The measure provided by change of government's spending is aimed at assessing objective change. But how might one assess change in politicians' subjective evaluations of government's activities as it might lead to reorganization planning? Since a politician's evaluations are tied to partisanship, it is useful to inquire into the relationship between change in partisan control of the branches of government and the initiation of reorganization planning. The proposition to guide this inquiry is: *Reorganization planning is initiated after change in the partisan control of at least one of government's elective branches.*

Table 4 shows that six of the ten cases since 1910 were initiated in proximity to changes in party control of Congress and/or the presidency. These six split evenly in terms of initiating institution. Until 1953, initiation of reorganization related to party change was congressional; from 1953 to the present, it was presidential. Five of these six cases were initiated by Republicans after returning to power in one or both branches. It is tempting but uninteresting to proclaim reorganization as a Republican approach to government. In total, reorganization planning cases initiated by Republicans have only a narrow edge over those initiated by Democrats among all ten cases (six to four). Rather the finding that five of the six cases that are initiated in proximity to party change are initiated by Republicans must be taken as a partial substantiation of the hypotheses that parties newly in control have incentive to initiate reorganization. As the out-party of the post-1932 era, they, more than the Democrats, were likely to be swinging back into power for short terms.

What makes reorganization attractive to a party newly in control of a branch of government? A raft of instrumental and symbolic uses of reorganization planning can be offered in answer to this question. As suggested above, the Republicans gaining dominance in Congress might well find reorganization planning a means for attempting concrete changes in government while at the same time conducting a symbolic attack on the policies of the dominant party. However, in light of the details of the cases, such an explanation applies only to

Table 4
Change in Partisan Control and Initiation
of Reorganization Planning
(Salient Years Italicized)

Case and Year Initiated	Initiating Institution	Election Year of Last Change of Partisan Control of Both Houses of Congress	Election Year of Last Change of Partisan Control of Presidency
Taft, 1910	President	1896	1896
Joint Comm., 1920	Congress	*1918*	*1920*
Brownlow, 1936	President	1932	1932
1st Hoover, 1947	Congress	*1946*	1932
2nd Hoover, 1953	Congress	*1952*	1952
PACGO, 1953	President	1952	*1952*
Price TF, 1964	President	"	1960
Heineman TF, 1967	President	"	"
Ash, 1969	President	"	*1968*
Carter PRP, 1977	President	"	*1976*

the Joint Committee and the two Hoover Commissions. But PACGO, the Ash Council, and Carter's Reorganization Project did not originate in such ambitions, nor did they seek such ends, even though they were initiated after change in party control of the presidency.

It is meaningful that the two hypotheses offered to explain the role of governmental change in the creation of reorganization planning do not fully fit the phenomena of the modern, presidentially initiated cases. Those cases are not associated with significant changes in budget outlays, nor do they evidence the kinds of goals that would be expected from reorganization planning that was associated with motivations arising from change in party control of government.

The modern, managerial presidency subsumes comprehensive reorganization planning under the chief executive's administrative instrumentation. Reorganization planning became a confidential element in the institutionalized presidency. Rather than being a reaction to change, either in government's activities or in political control, reorganization planning expressed a continuing managerial agenda even while conforming to the peculiarities of individual administrations. Earlier, reorganization planning had been initiated as an act within the separation-of-power system, publicly addressing purportedly objective problems (and less manifestly expressing partisan interests). But presidentially initiated reorganization planning since the 1930's has expressed a central concern with aspects of top-level management rather than a concern with government's operations or performance in a broader sense. Strengthening this interpretation, the first Hoover Commission, the one congressionally initiated case of the modern era that was heavily influenced by a president, reoriented its perspective to top-level managerial concerns from an overall critique of government as that presidential influence took hold.

Organizing Reorganization Planning

What determines reorganization planning's format? In his notable attempt at comparative analysis of reorganization planning, Harvey Mansfield, Sr., identified three general kinds of organizational formats: congressional initiatives, public commissions, and presidential task forces.[5] One of Mansfield's important contributions is his analysis of the relationship between these formats and what he identifies as distinct periods in the (near) institutionalization of reorganization planning. However, Mansfield fails to inquire further into the functional relationship between the political-institutional interests at stake in reorganization and choice of organizational format. He addresses this issue only once, in his brief comments on what he calls the last (and current) period:

> The relatively unpublicized task force method adopted by four successive Presidents since Truman is a logical outgrowth of the transformation in reorganization objective that had already taken place. The Brownlow report . . . proclaimed that change in doctrine, from economy in operations to the need for strengthening the President's capacity to marshall and wield the far-flung resource of the executive branch. The first Hoover Commission gave this doctrine wider currency. . . . It is a corollary . . . that the President is entitled to avail himself of that method of formulating reorganization proposals which promises him the greatest degree of control over their form, content, and timing, since he has the most at stake.[6]

Mansfield implies a means for extending the comparative work he began. If characteristics of reorganization planning's organizational format have consequences for the interests of the initiating branch (such as secrecy for the presidency), then it seems reasonable to propose

[5] Harvey C. Mansfield, Sr., "Reorganizing the Executive Branch: The Limits of Institutionalization," *Law and Contemporary Problems* 35 (Summer 1970), 461-495.

[6] *Ibid.*, p. 494.

the following: *Choice of organizational format in reorganization planning varies with the branch of government that initiates reorganization planning.*

What qualities might be identified about organizational formats that could aid understanding of their functional relationship to the branch initiating (and designing) reorganization planning? Rather than thinking about organizational formats as characteristic of periods, as does Mansfield, we will find it useful to identify their qualities which can have consequences for the political interests of the branches of governments. The first of these is the degree of public visibility characteristic of an organizational format. High visibility would entail an open, well-reported, working procedure as well as published reports and recommendations. Moderate visibility would describe a less open working procedure producing published reports. Low visibility would describe secret procedure and largely secret recommendations and reports. The second characteristic is the degree of independence given a planning vehicle. "Independence" refers to post-initiation relationship between a reorganization planning vehicle and its initiators. High independence will describe little or no ability for the initiators to direct the planners. Moderate independence would describe a relationship where the possibility of influence exists but the actual conduct of work leaves the planners vehicle substantial independence. Low independence describes a relationship where the planning vehicle is an extension of the initiators, subject to control at any point.

Table 5 classifies cases in terms of their degrees of publicness and independence. The most obvious pattern is the secrecy and dependency characteristic of every case after the second Hoover Commission, all these being initiated by presidents. This supports Mansfield's generalization quoted above, but more on this pattern later. A second obvious pattern is the public visibility of every case prior to and including the second Hoover Commission and the tendency of all of those toward independence. What accounts for the sharp break in the visibility of reorganization planning in the early 1950's? Why are congressionally initiated vehicles far more likely to be independent from the initiating branch's influence than those originating with the presidency?

The public exposure of reorganization planning and its recommendations has the potential of generating wide support for administrative reforms which are likely to be opposed within the relatively narrow arena occupied by agency personnel, interested congressional committees, and agency clients. To broadcast widely the rationale and goals of reorganization planning builds some momentum for reform and places that momentum in the hands of the institution that launched

Table 5
Visibility and Independence in Reorganization Planning

Case	Visibility	Independence
Taft	high	moderate
Joint Comm.	high	low
Brownlow	high	moderate
1st Hoover	high	high
2nd Hoover	high	high
PACGO	low	low
Price	low	low
Heineman	low	low
Ash	low*	low
PRP	low to moderate*	low

*In these instances the president made public some of the studies accomplished by his planners.

reorganization planning and sees some gain to be achieved through it.[7]

Beginning with the Taft Commission and running through the second Hoover Commission, half the planning cases exhibit high public visibility, but the exposition of those cases shows that there are two different, institutionally salient reasons for their publicness. The two presidentially initiated cases of this group exemplify the potential political uses of visible reorganization planning. Both the Taft Commission and the Brownlow Committee were consciously bent on the job of promoting a particular view of the presidency and its necessary place in achieving good administration. The Taft Commission justified an enhanced executive within a theory of efficiency. More directly, the Brownlow Committee argued that "the President needs help." The three other quite visible planning episodes were congressionally initiated. In the first place, their openness was a characteristic of their initiating institution, Congress' investigating activities being routinely open. Beyond this, the openness of congressional reorganization planning had a political end. Each of these endeavors was created by a Congress in which Republicans had recently returned to majority status. Public visibility was a means for broadcasting and justifying an attack on bloated government.

[7] On the relationship between issue visibility and political support or reaction to it, see E. E. Schattschneider, *The Semi-Sovereign People* (Hinsdale, Ill.: Dryden, 1957), Chaps. 1 and 2.

The 1950's saw a break in the organizational format of reorganization planning. What had been a publicly visible process for more than fifty years became secret. Every planning endeavor from PACGO through the Carter administration's efforts were presidentially initiated and largely confidential. As Harvey Mansfield said of these cases: "The post-World War II model of a presidential task force on reorganization was devised in the Eisenhower Administration and has commended itself, with modifications to his successors."[8] From the Eisenhower administration through to that of Carter, reorganization planning was treated as part of the larger, confidential advising system. However, unlike the other operations of that presidential establishment, comprehensive reorganization planning has retained many of its distinctive features while being drawn into the presidential establishment. All five of the relevant cases exhibit both the specialization and eclectic personnel that has always marked reorganization planning.

At first glance, it may be surprising that in a period of obvious presidential domination of this activity, such planning was not institutionalized within the Office of Management and Budget. But the budget agency has been deficient in its managerial attentions and in resources for organizational analysis. At the same time, no other existing staff or agency of the Executive Office presented itself as a logical repository for responsibilities of comprehensive reorganization planning. But that is not to say that a president of this post-1950's era in reorganization planning could not have chosen to commit the resources necessary for the institutionalization of reorganization planning. Thus one has to ask why, given that possibility for institutionalization, four presidents maintained the practiced of ad hoc reorganization planning vehicles?

Each of these reorganization episodes originated in a president's distrust of the permanent government, combined with his assumption that innovative solutions could be supplied only by those who were not wedded to government. Eisenhower and Nixon both brought partisan distrust of the government with them when they took office. For them, reorganization planning through PACGO and the Ash Council, respectively, was a means through which to gain insight into the possibilities for reform from individuals who were not of the government. Lyndon Johnson assumed that innovations of virtually any kind were more likely to originate from outside those agencies occupied with routine practice. Thus he adopted a task-force approach to the whole

---

[8] Harvey C. Mansfield, Sr., "Reorganizing the Executive Branch," p. 489.

range of policy and organizational problems that concerned his administration, comprehensive reorganization prominent among these. Jimmy Carter also distrusted the habits of the permanent government. While his mechanism for reorganization planning appeared superficially to institutionalize that process within the Office of Management and Budget, it was in reality an ad hoc operation that was simply tacked onto OMB.

Independence, the second dimension of organizational format, refers to the relationship between a reorganization planning vehicle and its initiating institution. Having created a reorganization planning vehicle, how much overt control does an institution have over the course of the planning process and its ultimate recommendations? While independence is a characteristic distinct from the public visibility of the ten vehicles examined, Table 3 suggests that it accompanies public visibility.

Independence plays a political function related to that served by public visibility. The latter allows reorganization planning to promote its own cause, drawing support among the public. The former, independence, is a necessary condition for a reorganization planning vehicle that would maximize its capacity to use its public visibility to attract such support. Were a reorganization planning vehicle seen as nothing more than a captive of its initiating institution, its capacity for justifying its recommendations to a disinterested audience would decline.

Only one of the five reorganization episodes between the Taft Commission and the second Hoover Commission was both public and dependent on its initiating institution. This single exception was the Joint Committee on Reorganization, which was simply a committee of the Congress and thus intended to operate within a congressional framework. However, it should be added that with the addition of a non-congressional, presidential representative as chairman (in the person of Walter Brown) the tone of the committee changed greatly, and its deliberations and recommendations were, in fact, quite independent of congressional expectations and interests. The key to this development was the President's assertion through Brown of the right to specify the proper subjects and range of reorganization recommendations.

Beyond this one instance of dependence, two other cases among the five have to be classified as having a qualified independence. Both the Taft Commission and the Brownlow Committee were independent in that some or all their members were from outside government and each had apparently wide latitude within which to identify needed reforms. But both worked very closely with the White House. Frederick Cleveland served as President Taft's assistant regarding matters of organizational and budget reform, and Taft met on several occasions with the commission. The Brownlow Committee's relationship to its initiating president seems more independent; Franklin Roosevelt allowed the committee to operate without any contact with him until its work was completed. But in the end one has to judge its independence as qualified. President Roosevelt was pleased with the committee's preliminary recommendations and requested only a few changes, yet he could have demanded far more.

The key to the fact that Roosevelt did not need to greatly amend the Brownlow Committee's report was the degree to which the members appointed to that committee addressed his interests. Herein is the heart of the matter of independence as seen from the perspective of the initiating branch. A reorganization planning episode is initiated in a specific political context and for particular purposes. Underlying the apparent independence of four of the five episodes of the first half of the century is the fact that their personnel were chosen with expectations about their probable behavior as reorganizers.

The most markedly independent planning vehicles, the first and second Hoover Commissions, exemplify the use of personnel selection as an instrument for controlling the outcome of the planning process while maintaining the literal independence of the planning vehicle. While the legislation creating the first Hoover Commission specified a formula for appointment of its members, the underlying effort was to build a conservative majority into the commission. The second Hoover Commission was almost, but not quite, a carbon copy of the first. The first's failure to achieve its ideological goals led the Republican Congress to drop the requirement for bipartisan membership in creating the second commission. The membership of the second commission was, in fact, more conservative than that of the first, and its reports largely fulfilled the political aims of its initiators. Of course, because of the hands-off policy adopted by the Eisenhower administration, the second commission felt none of the push toward presidential concerns which the Truman administration gave to the first commission.

For Eisenhower, PACGO was the preferable means for exercising his organizational concerns; its membership was of his choosing and comprised people he trusted. Eisenhower shared the field of policy with the second Hoover Commission as the price for preserving the area of organizational reform for himself and PACGO. In Eisenhower's view, the organization of the executive branch was wholly within the domain of a president's authority. From the early years of the century, comprehensive reorganization planning had fashioned a justification for a dominant presidential role over the executive branch out of the fabric of apolitical administrative theory. There is a watershed character to Eisenhower's assumption that this role was implicit within the presidency, needing no public justification. The similarity of every subsequent reorganization planning vehicle to PACGO in their general degree of visibility and independence, along with the fact that these share with PACGO their origin in presidential initiation, suggests the institutionalization of these assumptions about the president's role in administration as well as a routinization of the reorganization planning format which best serves that assumption.

Thus, the case studies support the hypothesized relationship between the organizational format imposed on a reorganization planning vehicle and the institution which initiates that vehicle. If it is seen that the actual organizational details of different planning vehicles are so varied, two underlying organizational characteristics of great political salience were adopted: degree of visibility and degree of independence. The differences found among the cases on the two characteristics can be explained in terms of the basic interests of their initiating institutions.

What Is the Incentive for Initiating Reorganization?

The examination of initiation and organizational format sheds light on the connection between reorganization planning and government's branches. However, branches of government do not initiate reorganization planning; politicians do. Yet, so far, the only explanation evident herein for why politicians initiate reorganization planning is institutional loyalty, a sort of altruism. This seems unlikely. If we assume that the politician can be thought of as a rational actor, he must be seen as calculating the benefits to himself to be gained from involvement in initiating reorganization planning.[9]

This section will examine briefly each of the episodes of comprehensive reorganization planning to identify what, if any, individualizable benefits they exemplify. If we assume that individual politicians are motivated by such benefits, then the following proposition seems

[9] The explanatory power of the assumption of the congressman as a reelection seeker is shown by David Mayhew. He also offers an excellent discussion of this conception of political motivation and behavior. David Mayhew, *Congress: The Electoral Connection* (New Haven: Yale University Press, 1974), esp. Chap. 1.

likely: *Reorganization creates immediate political benefits for its initiators.*

The Commission on Economy and Efficiency. The commission was the only presidentially initiated reorganization planning vehicle created in association with substantial change in the rate of federal expenditure, and it was the means through which President Taft sought budgetary authority. If granted to him, such authority would have benefited him and his successors. Taft used the fiscal problem as a hook upon which to hang an argument for expanded presidential authority. In this the individual's and the institution's interests merged. Of course, Taft had no way to predict that it would take nearly a decade after he began the fight to win presidential budget authority.

Two other individualizable benefits also appear in this episode. The commission gave the President staff services otherwise unobtainable at that time. For example, Taft had his commission collect data on the travel expenditures accumulated by executive branch employees, and with that information Taft composed an administration policy on travel expenses. The President's second benefit was a matter of symbolic politics. The quest for reorganization led by eminent reformers constituted an appeal to the progressive wing of the GOP. It was in this wing of the party that Taft was weakest.

The Joint Committee. Partisan ambitions drove Congress to create the Joint Committee. In 1920 the Republican Party called for a "return to normalcy." Consistent with that theme, the Congress, dominated by the GOP after 1918, struck against expanded executive government through its own reorganization effort, its first since the 1880's.

Partisan interests in this instance overlapped with an institutional interest—a strengthened Congress. But, in turn, that institutional interest was itself individualizable. By 1920, two of the most important features of the modern Congress were in place. One, membership in the Congress had become quite stable, professionalized, as H. Douglas Price put it.[10] The membership of the 66th Congress, which began in 1918, contained almost 80 percent returnees from the membership of the 65th Congress.[11] Two, the Speaker of the House's fall from dominance in 1910 resulted in a greatly strengthened committee system, with more members having a stake in the duties, powers, and interests of the legislature. A professionalized view of congressional service

[10] See H. Douglas Price, "Congress and the Evolution of Legislative 'Professionalism,' " in Norman Ornstein (ed.), *Congress in Change* (New York: Praeger, 1975), pp. 2-23; and Nelson Polsby, "The Institutionalization of the U.S. House of Representatives," *American Political Science Review* 62 (March 1968), 144-168.

[11] Data drawn from Polsby, *ibid.*

means that the incumbent congressman or senator views service as without fixed limit. A member of the legislature, assuming the continued generosity of constituents, could look toward a lifetime career. Consequently, the Congress' action to seek institutional rewards through reorganization also must be understood to encompass the personal interests of the legislators.

With President Harding's representative added to the Joint Committee, that planning vehicle was made over. The benefits for President Harding are clear: he had run hard on a *revanchist* platform, and a strong personal involvement in reorganization planning was a quick way to appear that he was fulfilling campaign promises to recreate normalcy. One also notices that there was a benefit for the institutional interests of the presidency in Harding's cooptation of reorganization planning. But was there a cross-over here between individual and institutional benefits similar to that noted for a professionalized Congress?

Certainly the presidency differs from Congress in that regard because of the chief executive's limited tenure. There appears to be less incentive for the individual to have a stake in long-term institutional interests and benefits. But the presidency stimulates the incumbent to think in terms of institutional prestige and benefit. The office's grandeur is also the incumbent's. Thus it is self-serving for the incumbent to benefit the institution, even if the full fruition of that benefit will fall to a successor.[12]

The Brownlow Committee. Franklin Roosevelt created the Brownlow Committee to address problems plaguing his administration. The committee's charge was to find a means to coordinate the expanding executive branch. To Brownlow and his colleagues, only an institutional solution that reconstituted the president's capacities as a manager would solve Roosevelt's problem. Clearly, the rewards promised by the Brownlow Committee's approach were institutional; it was at the level of the institution of the presidency that the committee recommended changes. However, the committee's recipe for reform, while institutional, addressed problems of coordination, planning, and con-

---

[12] The proponents of the strong executive among the Founders perceived the relationship between duration in office and self-interest of the incumbent to be enormously beneficial in guiding the ambition of presidents to high rather than low ends. See Hamilton, "No. 71," *The Federalist* (New York: Modern Library, 1937), pp. 463-464. Also see Gouverneur Morris's speech to the Federal Convention on July 19, 1787, in Winton Solberg (ed.) *The Federal Convention and the Founding of the Union* (Indianapolis: Bobbs-Merrill, 1958), pp. 231-233.

trol that had plagued Roosevelt's presidency. The cure was institutional, but the problems to be cured were the incumbent's.

The First Hoover Commission. In 1947 the Republican 80th Congress attempted to reverse the trend of big (and Democratic) government through comprehensive reorganization. The political climate following the 1946 election promised a Republican president after 1948 and a changed course for American national government. Consequently, Congress's institutional interests, the Republican Party's partisan interests, and the interests of Republican congressional leaders for enlarged stature and influence, came together to create the first Hoover Commission.

President Truman's interests, on the other hand, necessitated his leading a running battle against the Republicans while attempting to overcome postwar problems that gave his opponents political ammunition. The Hoover Commission became a ripe means for dealing with both problems. Truman coopted the commission and won from it recommendations benefiting the evolving managerial presidency and recommendations pointing to specific possibilities for improved efficiency in government. Thus President Truman gained personally and politically from this array of individual and institutional benefits.

The Second Hoover Commission. The first Hoover commission's accomplishments included few of the rewards expected by its congressional sponsors. The Republican sweep of the White House and Congress in 1952 offered another opportunity to achieve ends sought through the first commission. But, in addition, there is evidence that immediate personal reward plays a more prominent element in the initiation of the second commission. The prominence of the first Hoover Commission made it appear that there were notable political benefits that could accrue to one who was connected with a second commission. Congressman Clarence Brown (Rep., Ohio) and Senator Homer Ferguson (Rep., Mich.) were both vitally interested in the political prestige that might flow from their role. Brown, unlike Ferguson, had sponsored and served on the first commission, and he arranged that he be appointed to the second commission as well. Ferguson was also appointed to it. Between the two, they wrestled over who should be vice-chairman, each pleading with Hoover for that honor. As a consequence of that conflict over precedence, no vice-chairman was designated for the second commission. The importance of Brown's and Ferguson's personal political investment in the idea of a second commission was evident to President-elect Eisenhower. He concluded that for him to oppose the initiation of the second commission would be unwise, in large part because such an action would alienate Brown and Ferguson.

The President's Advisory Committee on Government Organization. With PACGO there is a shift in the apparent benefits expected from reorganization planning. PACGO's array of benefits reversed the traditional tendency for individual benefits to be buried under institutional or systemic justifications. Above all else, PACGO was the President's personal advisory group. Its size and intimacy with Eisenhower underlines the primacy of his own concerns and benefits in creating PACGO. In a 1960 paper Richard Neustadt criticized PACGO's recommendations for restructuring the Executive Office for Eisenhower rather than with an eye to the needs of the presidency.[13] Without intending to, Neustadt's comment glimpsed the way the modern managerial presidency was joining previously separated interests within the presidency—the interests of the role and the interests of the incumbent. The modern president works within organizationally complex roles having large and diverse responsibilities. The central problem for the president is to shape those roles to his capacities and style. PACGO exemplified reorganization planning put to that purpose.

The Price and Heineman Task Forces. The Johnson task forces on administrative reform differed in several respects, but what they shared tells a great deal about the development of reorganization planning after PACGO. Their missions were defined by President Johnson's agenda and the problems of his administration. The task forces reveal that not only are individual incentives given priority in the modern presidential initiation of reorganization planning, but institutional concerns fade into or merge with individual concerns. The particular style, policy concerns, and attendant problems of a president create the incentives for reorganization planning. The Price task force fit neatly into Johnson's early thought that policy innovation might be supported through the redirection of currently committed funds in the budget. The Heineman task force's mission reflected the holdover of some of this concern but was more centrally charged with figuring out a way to bring order to the administrative chaos of the Great Society, a condition that was likely to have political consequences for Lyndon Johnson. Thus the task force's objects of concern were ostensibly those of institutional change, but the agenda and problems underlying it were defined by the President's interests and problems.

---

[13] Richard Neustadt, "Reorganizing the Presidency in 1961: A Review of the Issues," prepared for delivery to the 1960 Annual Meeting of the American Political Science Association, New York, September 8-10.

The Ash Council. Richard Nixon's approach to reorganization planning followed the pattern of PACGO and the Johnson task forces, but it differed in a respect that promised an additional individual benefit. Nixon artfully maintained his reorganization planning vehicle as both visible *and* confidential. Nixon gave full exposure to his creation of the Ash Council. In its respectability and its evocation of private sector values, the Ash Council was a perfect reform gesture by the Nixon administration. To have made its existence confidential would have been to waste its symbolic rewards.

Beyond exposing its creation, Richard Nixon kept a tight lid on the Ash Council's work. Like Lyndon Johnson or Dwight Eisenhower, Nixon protected himself from politically embarrassing or undesirable recommendations by controlling the flow of information about his planning vehicle's work and recommendations. But when he accepted a recommendation from the council, he presented it publicly as the council's work. Thus the recommendation for reform carried the imprimatur of this prestigious council to give it political momentum while it also allowed Nixon to distance himself from it. The utility of the approach can be best seen in the case of Reorganization Plan No. 2 of 1970 concerning the Bureau of the Budget and the Domestic Council. The Ash Council's role in this recommendation naturally defused one possible line of strong criticism that would present the reform as just a presidential power-grab.

Reorganization planning's capacity to displace political-power considerations with organizational-efficiency considerations served President Nixon's general approach to the presidency, just as it served him in the situation of Reorganization Plan No. 2 of 1970. As evidenced by his short-lived super-cabinet, which Nixon had instituted through unilateral executive action, the Ash Council recommendations for the establishment of super-departments appealed to the President's sense of the potential power latent in organizational reforms. Of course, the Ash Council recommendations for super-departments died in Congress, and the President's unilateral response was short-lived. However, it is apparent that within this process of reform planning one sees the President calculating reorganization's potential political benefits for himself.

President's Reorganization Project. At first glance, President Carter's Reorganization Project gives little support to the propositions that reorganization planning is initiated in response to the incentive of personal benefits. Candidate Carter campaigned on a promise of massive reorganization of federal government, using his experience with reorganization in Georgia to legitimize his qualifications for the presidency. It is quite easy to see the benefit of promised reorganization for candidate Carter. It fit into his campaign themes of popular government, moral virtue, and scientific management. But the vigor with which President Carter implemented reorganization planning made it clear that reorganization had not just been a campaign promise. Yet there is little about the President's Reorganization Project which benefited Carter in the way reorganization planning had served earlier presidents. At the most, it would appear that it benefited Carter in symbolic ways, his new departments, for example, testifying to the administration's attention to the country's problems.

There is, however, another way of understanding the Reorganization Project's potential benefits to President Carter. As a presidential candidate, Jimmy Carter had gained advantage from his ability to claim that as Georgia's governor he had reorganized the state, making it simpler and more efficient. So even though Governor Carter had received little if any benefit from reorganization in Georgia in terms of his governing role (as a one-term governor he was not in office long enough to receive any of its benefits), reorganization had paid off quite richly for him. If reorganization for Carter had a strong, continuing potential for campaign appeals, one of Carter's central motivations for pursuing reorganization may have been his estimation of its possibilities for benefiting his 1980 campaign.

Conclusion. The first lesson of this examination of the relationship between individualizable benefits and the initiation of reorganization planning is that a simple dichotomy of individual and institutional benefits does not fit the interplay of incentives and benefits present in reorganization planning. Legislators and presidents associate their own interests with the apparently asymmetric (in terms of both time and scale) interests of their institutions. This is easier to understand in the context of the professionalized Congress, where legislators' timeframes of individual interests expand to approach the time-frame of institutional interests. But despite the comparatively short tenure of presidents, the cases involving presidential initiation or cooptation of reorganization planning reveal the incumbent's interest being shaped by the institutional interests of the presidency.

The discovery that individual and institutional benefits are associated in reorganization planning ought not to be surprising. That politicians defend their roles is consistent with James Madison's prediction of how the Constitution would operate:

> But the great security against a gradual concentration of the several powers in the same department, consists in giving to those who

administer each department the necessary constitutional means and personal motives to resist encroachments of the others. . . . Ambition must be made to counteract ambition. The interest of the man must be connected to the constitutional rights of the place.[14]

The second lesson learned in this examination of the relationship between benefits and the initiation of reorganization planning is that the complex of benefits and incentives observed in cases of reorganization planning changes markedly and permanently with the establishment of PACGO by President Eisenhower. The full-blown managerial presidency was more personalistic than the older, traditional presidency.[15] The greater expanse of its authority, tools, and responsibilities gave each individual who entered the modern presidency the need to carve out a personal approach to its managerial-political tasks. Reorganization planning served that end.

INTERPRETING REORGANIZATION PLANNING'S PERSISTENCE

The preceding reveals that reorganization planning is linked to the continuing interests of the constitutional institutions within the separation of powers regime. Thus reorganization planning is initiated within the push and pull of inter-branch challenges, politicians identifying the interests of their roles as their own interests. But the preceding analysis also shows the limits of this conclusion. Running through that analysis are findings that reflect a developmental movement within the history of reorganization planning. Time itself is a salient dimension in understanding reorganization; the characteristics of planning vehicles change not only in relationship to which branch of government initiated them but also in relationship to when they were initiated. Since the 1950's these vehicles have been less visible and neutral and more a confidential extension of a presidency that had itself changed over time. Thus the preceding analysis has narrowed and sharpened the problem rather than wholly solving it.

Two questions remain. The first, what has linked comprehensive reorganization to the presidency? Second; how has reorganization's aim of managerial strength related to the evolution of the presidency? The first question's answer lies in matters discussed in the first chapter

[14] James Madison, "No. 51," *The Federalist*, p. 337.

[15] The personalistic dimension of the modern presidency is particularly evident in its reliance on rhetoric. See James Ceaser, et al., "The Rise of the Rhetorical Presidency," in Thomas Cronin (ed.) *Rethinking the Presidency* (Boston: Little, Brown, 1982), pp. 233-249.

above and exemplified in the succeeding chapters. A strong, administrative president was a corollary of the theory of administrative organization that sustained the growth of an American discipline of public administration. Through the century, reorganization planners framed the problem of administrative reform through different approaches, centering on organizations and budgets first, then fixing on the possibilities of staff supports for the chief executive, finally seeing promise for a managerial breakthrough in policy analysis. But these foci were just new bottles for reorganization planning's old wine—the managerially competent president seen as a prerequisite for efficient administration.

The second question is more difficult to answer. In effect it asks why has reorganization planning's agenda of presidential managerial strength gained acceptance in American politics? The beginning of an answer to this question lies within the preceding chapters. Recall the role of efficiency values finessing the political conflict inherent in organizational change. Reorganization planning and its guiding administrative theories had a capacity for offsetting power-based considerations of presidential strength. By moving the consideration of presidential strength to grounds of organizational efficiency, reorganization planning went some distance toward defusing the institutional sensitivities of the separation of powers regime.

But how could reorganization planning displace politics to the end of expanding the presidency? Think about reorganization planning's history through the metaphor of a story—a story in which the president is the protagonist and the regime's weakness is the subject. Within this story is a dramatic tension between values of efficiency and dispersed power within the regime. James March and Johan Olson describe the history of reorganization planning as "a history of rhetoric":

> Efforts at reorganization in the United States have produced a litany for conventional discourse. Two orthodox rhetorics infuse the speaking and writing of persons involved in reorganization as well as students of it. The first is that of orthodox administrative theory. ... The second rhetoric of reorganization is the rhetoric of realpolitik. It is equally conventional. It speaks of reorganization, like organization, in terms of political struggle among contending interests.[16]

[16] James G. March and Johan P. Olson, "Organizing Political Life: What Administrative Reorganization Tells Us About Government," *American Political Science Review* 77 (June 1983), 282.

March and Olson contend that these equally conventional and stylized languages within reorganization planning perform the symbolic task of representing a cultural ideal of order while offering an after-the-fact explanation for why order is never really attainable.[17]

The two languages of reorganization fit into our story, and they convey efficiency and disorder, respectively. The language of orthodox administration imposes on the American executive branch a bureaucratic model pertinent to organization within large industrial societies. The *realpolitik* language which accompanies reorganization both in practice and in its academic literature evokes the costs and dangers to administrative order presented by the separation of powers regime and pluralism. So, the story goes, normative modern bureaucratic organization is monocratic and consequently coherent, but the separation of powers regime produces chaos by creating many loci of responsibility for administration. The dramatic tension within the reorganization story is between the opposition of administrative order and political chaos, each with its own language. The managerial presidency resolves that tension, synthesizing the opposition of order and politics. Administrative theory's conception of the president as a manager is the vision of a remade presidency striking a new balance in the separation of powers system. Separation of powers had been created without regard to the needs of modern bureaucratic organization. The presidency, reinvented by comprehensive reorganization, constituted a tacit amendment of that balance; reorganization sought to build an administrative arena within which the presidency would dominate.

Comprehensive executive reorganization is an instrument for reform which carries within itself a normative conception of what reform should entail. In its thematic development in the 20th century it related administrative order (and thus efficiency) to presidential primacy within the governmental system. Reorganization planning as a presidential instrument became a tool for modeling and justifying a strengthened presidency. The ideas about the presidency that develop within comprehensive reorganization are politically ingenious. As earlier chapters have elaborated, reorganization planning episodes consistently attended to the presidency's weaknesses regarding the executive branch, framing one after another recommendation intended to strengthen the chief executive's hand. To see this dimension of executive reorganization is to see the important, supportive role that com-

---

[17] A classic statement of what can be taken for the realpolitik position is Norton Long, "Power and Administration," *Public Administration Review* 9 (Autumn 1949), 257-264.

prehensive reorganization played in building the modern presidency. However, to see only this side of reorganization is to miss the very reason why it could play a role of long-term importance in the evolution of the modern presidency.

What reorganization addressed was the need for building a newly efficient American state; its positive rhetoric was about order and not about power. Reorganization had little if anything to say about the displacement of power that would occur within the separation of powers system should a managerially effective presidency evolve. Executive reorganization proposed a strengthened presidency because that office happened to be the most appropriate means for providing direction to the administrative system. Thus reform in the presidency and resulting changes in presidential power were addressed by reorganization without overt reference to power except in negative terms. Reorganization planning asked that reforms with large implications for the power of the presidency—reforms such as the executive budget, enhanced staff supports, and more direct influence over internal departmental affairs—be addressed in light of the values and language of pure administration. Politically salient changes were dressed in the garb of politically neutral values. Within this reform story, the language of power—the rhetoric labeled *realpolitik* by March and Olson—was used to explain the undesirable consequences of the failure to reform administration. Good government, efficient organization, and orderly procedures were thwarted by power.

The reorganization story created the managerial presidency as a resolution to the seemingly unbridgeable gap between efficiency and power. Rather than trying literally to remove administration from politics, as had their predecessors in municipal reform and public administration, the executive reorganizers aimed at joining efficiency and democratic responsibility together by making the regime's most prominent political leader into a manager.

THE END OF THE MANAGERIAL PRESIDENCY

The reconceptualization of the presidency through reorganization planning was a political project of extraordinary importance in this century. But the importance of that project is not equivalent to its success; reorganization planning (and administrative theory) could justify the managerial transformation of the presidency, but it could not make it work. The plain fact is that no modern president has fully managed the executive branch. The continuing dispersion of power in the executive branch and Congress' remaining authority over administration check presidential power.[18] Additionally, presidents fail as managers because they seem to have little appetite for that task, and their interests lie elsewhere.

It becomes clear that the managerial conception of the presidency is untenable. It places impossible obligations on presidents. It also raises public expectations about presidential performance that cannot be met. The managerial presidency then becomes a trap, offering increased capacity and influence to presidents but creating even greater expectations about presidential performance. But justificatory theories of government do not disappear, discarded when their utility evaporates. Such theories are deep-rooted and guide the evolution of public institutions, provide expectations for incumbents of governmental roles, and offer to the public criteria for the performance of institutions and incumbents. Such theories change slowly. It is beyond the task at hand to propose a full-blown, alternative conception of the president's relationship with the administrative state. But it does relate to the purpose of this book to ask at its end whether a grasp of the evolution of the managerial presidency offers any insight into where the premises of a competing theory might be located.

The conception of the president as manager arose early in the 20th century through the expansion of the expectations of presidential responsibility to include the management of national bureaucracy. To administrative theorists and reformers, it was self-evident that the presidency must perform as the manager of the bureaucratic state. The managerial presidency is the product of that understanding. But a quite different view of the relationship between the president and administration emerges from rejecting the assumption that the president is necessarily a manager and instead formulating a theory of presidential-administrative relations upon the basis of the president's political interests within the administrative process.

So one should not ask: is the president administrative chief, but, rather, why ought the president to be administrative chief? It is the president's functional responsibilities which ought to dictate his relationship to institutions. Presidents may be thought of as having two fundamental interests. First, they must maintain an ability to act within

[18] Testimony to the recognition of the president's failure as a manager is given by the substance and thrust of the recent report by the National Academy of Public Administration, *A Presidency for the 1980's* (Washington: National Academy of Public Administration, 1980). The report states that the challenge to modern American government: ". . . is our capacity to govern ourselves. . . . Effective self-government cannot be manufactured in Washington; much less it is a process that can be run from the Presidency" (p. 1).

government, maintaining what Richard Neustadt calls their reputation. Second, the president must be capable of leading; in Neustadt's terms he must have prestige.[19] Both of these qualities are key to the president's ability to transform ideas and commitments into policies. In turn, to be effective in making and effecting his choices, the president enhances his ability to lead, bargain, and draw upon loyalty. Therein is the link of presidential interests to administration. The president's responsibility as a choice-maker is linked to his capacity to nurture his choices into life; choice and action are linked within the president's interests. The presidency entails sequential choices. A later choice's political viability depends on the fate of earlier choices by that president. If the president's choices are to count, he must have the ability to see them through to action. As Richard Rose observes about the link between choice and action:

> Americans who look to the President to voice objectives that best reflect current political aspirations are interested in results. ... If politics is promises, then government is ceaseless activity. The continuing ability of a President to satisfy rather than frustrate his followers depends upon the translation of his goals and objectives into programs, and the successful implementation of these programs.[20]

Thus the president ought to be concerned with administration, not because he is a manager but because administration is part of the system through which his choices become policy. Therein is the premise for an alternative model of presidential-administrative relations to that of the managerial presidency. The president's political and policy concerns come first and lead him to administration. Policy matters of high priority will define those aspects of administration that the president must engage. In this view the president is not so much a manager of administration; he is a tactician using it.

Although its main story is an elaboration of the managerial presidency, the history of comprehensive reorganization holds numerous examples of the advantages for the president of understanding administration tactically. Within comprehensive reorganization planning, presidents have continuously recognized and used tactical advantages. In these instances, presidential activity has been specific and aimed at achievable, concrete ends. Thus within reorganization planning's stra-

---

[19] Richard Neustadt, *Presidential Power* (New York: John Wiley, 1960), Chaps. 4 and 5.

[20] Richard Rose, *Managing Presidential Objectives* (New York: Free Press, 1976), p. 22.

tegic conception of the presidency there was room for tactical moves whereby presidents could improve their advantage regarding other salient actors in the political system. A few examples will serve as reminders.

The comprehensive planning activities of the Commission on Economy and Efficiency gave William Howard Taft greater leverage in attempting to acquire budgetary authority. Taft also used his efficiency study to address particular problems within the executive branch on which he desired better focus and more control. Franklin Roosevelt achieved tactical gains from the Brownlow Committee's comprehensive recommendations, winning significant increments of staff and organizational support even while the bulk of the committee's recommendations languished. In the first Hoover Commission, Harry Truman found an instrument for gaining new allies for the expansive presidency. Thus, as the commission played out its mandate to comprehensively assess the executive branch, the President and key aides tactically repositioned the commission's link to the White House, affecting the commission's conclusions. Richard Nixon understood that comprehensive reorganization planning might justify unilateral executive actions aimed at expanding his leverage over policy implementation in the executive branch.

A contemporary president would be ill-advised to assume that his proper role regarding the executive branch is managerial. Yet the lesson to be learned from the history of executive reorganization and the evolution of the managerial presidency is that administration is central to the modern presidency, even while it is understood that the claims of the managerial conception of that office are untenable. Additionally, the president who understands that administration must be used tactically within a regime of dispersed authority remains indebted to the long-term project of building a managerial presidency. Even while shrugging off the comprehensive claims of that conception, contemporary and future presidents will find within the armory of tools created for the managerial presidency the necessary instruments of presidential leadership within a bureaucratized state—reorganization planning among them.

INDEX

LIBRARY OF CONGRESS CATALOGING-IN-PUBLICATION DATA

Arnold, Peri E., 1942-
  Making the managerial presidency.

  Bibliography: p.
  Includes index.
  1. Administrative agencies—United States—Reorganization—History—20th century.   2. United States—Executive departments—Reorganization—History—20th century.   3. Presidents—United
States—History—20th century.   4. United States—Politics and government—20th century.   I. Title.
JK411.A76   1986   353'.073   85-43268
ISBN 0-691-07704-5 (alk. paper)